WRITTEN IN THE SKY

Published by Melbourne Books
Level 9, 100 Collins Street,
Melbourne, VIC 3000
Australia
www.melbournebooks.com.au
info@melbournebooks.com.au

Front cover photo by Nick Thorne
Back cover photo by Andy Donaldson

Title: Written in the Sky
Author: Mark Carr
ISBN: 9781925556612

NATIONAL
LIBRARY
OF AUSTRALIA

A catalogue record for this
book is available from the
National Library of Australia

WRITTEN IN THE SKY

MARK CARR

M
MELBOURNE BOOKS

CONTENTS

For I dipt into the future, far as human eye could see,
Saw the Vision of the world, and all the wonder that would be;

Saw the heavens fill with commerce, argosies of magic sails,
Pilots of the purple twilight dropping down with costly bales;

Heard the heavens fill with shouting, and there rain'd a ghastly dew
From the nations' airy navies grappling in the central blue;

Far along the world-wide whisper of the south-wind rushing warm,
With the standards of the peoples plunging thro' the thunder-storm;

Till the war-drum throbb'd no longer, and the battle-flags were furl'd
In the Parliament of man, the Federation of the world.

— From '*Locksley Hall*' by Alfred, Lord Tennyson. He presciently penned these words in 1835, when the only means of human flight was the balloon. The Wright brothers would not fly for another sixty-eight years.

The past is a foreign country; they do things differently there.

— L.P. Hartley

PROLOGUE

Much of this book really *was* written in the sky. I had been in military and airline flying for over forty years, and on commencing the book, I was an airline captain: I flew Airbus A330 and A350 airliners with Hong Kong's Cathay Pacific Airways Limited. The long flights between my home base of Melbourne, Australia, and the airline's Hong Kong hub, by law, required a third pilot to allow each pilot to take a break for a little over two hours in a discrete seat in the passenger cabin. While the captain rested, a specially qualified and experienced first officer was in charge of the flight deck: they would call the captain in the event of a major problem, after carrying out initial emergency actions. Many of these flights droned through the night and, of course, sleep was desirable during a pilot's break. However, during one long daylight flight I fidgeted, wide-awake in the passenger cabin that was darkened to allow people to sleep or watch the in-flight entertainment. I was bored and restless. I could only read or watch movies so much. An idea germinated. I rummaged through my flight bag for my computer and began to type.

I had flown a wide variety of civil and military aircraft, more than many other pilots, and enthusiasts of various backgrounds could find their stories interesting. In parallel, I had travelled a long and tortuous road from relatively humble beginnings to the command of an international airliner. I also desired to give readers of a non-flying background an insight into various aspects of military and civil aviation. I needed to do justice to the wonderful aircraft that I have flown – each a credit to the designer, manufacturer and the people who maintained it. So, at suitable times in an airliner's passenger seat, in hotel rooms 'down route' or at home between flights, I wrote this book.

It can be difficult for pilots to write about their experience. Do they direct their work towards enthusiasts who have knowledge of the technical aspects of aviation, or do they simplify it, translating the language of the air so that a casual reader can appreciate and understand the story? I went 'all in' and included technical descriptions in varying depths of the aircraft that I have flown, aiming to make these intelligible to the non-pilot, but also informative to the enthusiast. Those who, like me, seemingly have hydraulic oil flowing through their veins instead of blood, should find them interesting. However, I have graduated the depth of description so that the non-pilot can sit in the cockpit with me from my early struggles with immaturity and lack of ability through to the twilight of a long and varied flying career. Through this book I hope that any reader can gain an insight into how these amazing machines that we take for granted function, and how the men and women in the cockpits and flight decks operate them safely and efficiently.

I was never formally at war, however, the Cold War between the 'East' and 'West' features prominently in my early life and my years as a military pilot, and naval flying was not without its hazards. The concept of mutual deterrence between NATO and the Eastern Bloc worked because, thankfully, nuclear war did not eventuate. By being in readiness with highly trained and motivated personnel, I like to think that the Royal Australian Navy and the Royal Australian

Air Force played a small part in that deterrence, particularly of the submarine threat.

This book is more about the aircraft than it is about me. It could be regarded as an educational 'techno-biography'. I sincerely hope that the reader, of whatever age or background, finds the work informative, entertaining and, possibly, inspiring.

AUTHOR'S NOTE

To avoid embarrassment to others I have generally used first names or nicknames, and some names have been changed completely. I have given measurements and altitudes in both feet and metres, and aircraft speeds have been presented in both knots (nautical miles per hour) and kilometres per hour (km/hr). I have presented distances in nautical miles (nm) and kilometres.

I have generally avoided making references through the narrative to later events, so that the reader can ride with me to experience the surprises and uncertainties of a journey in aviation. After forty-four years of flight my recall of some facts and events may have gone a little astray, however, I have done my utmost to make this story as accurate as possible.

I have not included photographs or illustrations. This book is thick enough! Imagery that will do justice to the aircraft described in this book can be found on the internet. I have endeavoured to use just words to paint pictures of the aircraft, and the skies in which they flew.

1

DUCK AND COVER

1957 – 1966

O ne of my earliest memories is the Cuban Missile Crisis. It was 1962 and I vaguely remember my father trying to explain something about President Kennedy and Cuba to me, a five-year-old boy. My parents had been listening to the 'wireless' a great deal (as radios were called). I only had a vague idea who President Kennedy was and that missiles were involved.

Kooringal was a dusty new suburb of what was an equally dusty town, Wagga Wagga, in Australia's New South Wales Riverina region. Grove Street, where we lived, edged with growing plane trees, was initially just a gravel road to be later surfaced with sharp brown stones embedded in tar that would cause many a graze after falling off bicycles, scooters or billy-carts (soap box racers). The street was almost without exception populated with young couples producing and bringing up 'baby boom' children.

The houses were recently built, wooden-floored, wooden-framed, clad with fibro (a form of asbestos-cement sheeting) and topped with uninsulated corrugated iron roofs. They were frigid in winter, and stifling in summer under blazing blue skies. However, most of the houses were owned, or at least being paid off, by those who lived in them. A lean-to carport, occasionally a garage, would be adjacent, but the backyards were generous in area.

Our house was painted pale blue and faced west toward Wagga's Willan's Hill. It had a carport to one side, three small bedrooms, a lounge room, kitchen and bathroom; but for many years, there was no inside toilet. Before 'the sewerage' came to Kooringal, the toilets were small fibro-clad backyard sheds with a commode inside that enclosed a can which was changed weekly by the 'sanitary man'. A child's night visit to the unlit toilet in the middle of winter was a dark, freezing experience, and the smell of it during the hot inland summers was powerful.

To the west, Willan's Hill was prominent from the lounge room windows, and at dusk I often gazed out at it and the glowing western sky that beckoned beyond. A few years later, I would tear down its red, stony tracks on a bicycle or billy cart. Oceans of long grass rippled in the vacant lots a few streets away, in the paddocks beyond and out the back of our school, and, according to the season, they were filled with locusts, paddy-melon or yellow daisies. There was also the occasional snake. On hushed windless winter days, crows cawed mournfully from the gum trees under grey skies while the family huddled around the simple gas fire in the lounge. During the ferocious summers, a single electric fan constituted the family's cooling appliances for many years. I would not live in a house that had an air conditioner until 1983.

My parents were hard working and 'correct', as most people were in the 1960s. My father was secretary of the local horse racing club and my mother was house-bound, bringing up my two younger sisters and me. With no television, much less internet, toys and playmates were important, but to me, books were equally as important and reasonably available. I was a voracious reader, and I read, or tried to read, anything I could get my hands on, including my parents' novels that lay around the house, some subsequently confiscated with little explanation as to why. Early evening's entertainment was sitting near the 'wireless' listening to children's 'serials', stories and cartoon soundtracks that had been adapted for radio.

I attended Kooringal Public, a government school. It had the usual standards of the day: a good grounding in spelling, grammar and maths, strait-laced teachers, and lots of reading. There was corporal punishment – 'the cane' – but I recall being taught binary notation, set theory and other concepts, which seemed quite advanced for primary school. I was not good at, or interested in, sport. Clumsy and lacking stamina, I found it boring and pointless, and I attended school and extra-curricular sports training and games under sufferance.

I had experienced television during yearly visits to grandparents' homes in Melbourne. In the evenings, especially at my paternal grandparents' home in West Footscray, the lounge rooms would be darkened and the hushed extended family would gaze at the flickering black and white images. Soon came the long drive back to Wagga and for me it would be back to school, my books, playing outside, my beloved Meccano set and model railway, and the after-school or evening gathering around the wireless. I relished visits to Wagga's new library, and a book as a present was rarely greeted with an inward groan. I had a growing collection of them in the shelf in my bedhead.

Finally, in 1964, television came to Wagga Wagga. After-school life changed. Cricket games were still played in Grove Street (the cars obligingly slowed down while the pitch was cleared), along with the then-normal childhood games of 'cops and robbers' and the politically incorrect 'cowboys and Indians'. Children still pelted down Willan's Hill on bicycles and billy carts, but even with parents and teachers wary of this new medium, most of us became avid watchers of television.

When bored with the other games, we played one that was simply called 'war'. We were products of our time. Many fathers were veterans of World War II, and some families had lost relatives during the global conflict. There was gratitude to our armed services for delivery from the Germans and the brutal Japanese. Not long after World War II came the Korean conflict, and now in the sixties there was a war in Indo-China. I recall a neighbourhood backyard party on a sweltering, still night in Kooringal, a farewell for a group of young men who had been conscripted for army service as part of Australia's involvement in the Vietnam War. Aside from this proxy to the actual Cold War, the arms race between the Soviets and the West was in full swing. Australians were overwhelmingly of British or European descent, conservative in outlook, and stood when the national anthem, 'God Save the Queen,' was played before the start of the films at the 'pictures'. The communist threat was taken very seriously by most.

Then there were the toy manufacturers.

For boys, 'war toys' were readily accepted by society, and lucrative for the producers and the retailers. Plastic weapons were available in all shapes and sizes: pistols, rifles, grenades, daggers, bayonets, machetes, machine guns. Toy shops were full of them. Many looked vicious, and some fired projectiles with varying degrees of potential for injury. We couldn't get enough of them! Wagga was a military town that hosted two military training bases: Kapooka Army Camp lay to the west and later notably for me, not far from Kooringal, was Forest Hill RAAF Base. Military bands featured at many social and civic events, men in uniform were common in the main street and there were open days and air displays at Forest Hill. Another early memory is a visit to a display at the air force base and nervously standing under an immense four-engine aircraft. I later worked out that it was a 'long nose' Avro Lincoln patrol bomber, its extended 'glasshouse' nose towering overhead, angled to the sky. Under-stimulated by the routines of school and household, and with the advent of war movies and a series called 'Combat' shown on television, I became obsessed with war and the military.

The obsession became unhealthy. After school it was straight into my green combat suit, complete with a plastic helmet. On went the belt with a plastic dagger and a pistol, then I grabbed the plastic or wooden rifle and went out to find my playmates, who only to a degree shared my interest. Murderous assaults were launched on the 'Krauts' or the 'Japs', to the backdrop of vocalised gunfire and explosions.

There were other aspects to a childhood in Australia in the 1960s. Radio news was barely understood by a child, but when the family's Pye television showed images of missiles, atomic tests, fuzzy images of goose-stepping Russians in Red Square and talk of 'Civil Defence', a more thoughtful and sensitive boy couldn't help but absorb the general unease and concern about nuclear war. I don't know if the infamous *Duck and Cover* cartoon was shown on Australian television, but it was certainly taken seriously in the United States. This grotesque short film encapsulated the madness and danger of the Cold War. Opening with a cartoon turtle marching along to a corny jingle, it was designed to educate American children and civilians on the importance of recognising, and reacting immediately to, the flash of a nuclear detonation: 'duck and cover'. Then, a sudden bright flash appeared from off screen; children, my age, *ducking* under school desks; pedestrians diving into doorways; a man *covering* himself with a newspaper!

Most nights, there were grainy black-and-white images on the TV news of Australian soldiers and airmen operating in Vietnam. Floppy-hatted troops, laden with gear, leapt out of Iroquois (what the Americans called 'Huey') helicopters and, bent double, ran through overgrown rice or grass that rippled in waves from the rotors' downwash.

But I was still always looking for something to read. There were several novels by Neville Shute on my parents' bookshelf. Desperate for something new, I took his most famous book, *On the Beach*, from the shelf. With the Cold War never far from the news, even in Wagga Wagga, Shute's post-apocalyptic portrayal of radiation from a nuclear war slowly drifting south from the northern hemisphere to Australia, the metamorphosis from normal life to creeping radiation sickness followed by the self-euthanising of the protagonists had me, at eleven years old, turning the pages in fascinated terror. At the time, I thought that the haunting verses from T.S. Eliot's *The Hollow Men* that Shute included as an introduction had been written especially for the book.

A by-product of the Cold War, however, was the exciting 'space race'. I had an understanding of what the American 'Project Gemini' was, and I knew some of the astronauts' names. Eventually, to my parents' (and some teachers') relief, my avid reading and the few television shows relating to soldiering that I was permitted to watch began to portray army life to me as dull, dirty and boring. Children's television dramas were becoming more sophisticated as the decade wore on, and the machines in the famous Gerry and Sylvia Anderson puppet productions *Fireball XL-5*, *Stingray*, *Thunderbirds* and *Captain Scarlet* held me spellbound after school, particularly those that flew. I began to assemble model aeroplanes.

One day, a game of war turned into space commander, and a lifetime obsession with aerospace began.

2

LOCATE AND CEMENT

1966 – 1969

Along with the 'war toys', in every toy shop were racks of 'Airfix' models. These were among the first plastic model aeroplanes, assembled using Airfix's proprietary pungent, corrosive glue, which came in a blue and white tube. 'Are you right for glue?' was on the lips of every shopkeeper when a child or parent appeared at the counter with their latest purchase. A 'Series 1' kit came in a plastic bag stapled to a paper flap which, on the front, showed a thrilling image of the subject aircraft, usually shooting or dropping some form of projectile, and information with facts and figures about the real thing on the back. On the inside were the instructions: the classic 'locate and cement' written directions, in English only, which accompanied the drawings.

There were no pictograms or multiple languages as most model kits provide now. I learned some of the language of aviation – 'nacelle', 'tailplane', 'cowling' and 'aileron' – through the solemnly worded assembly sequence of an Airfix model. My construction of a single seat fighter usually commenced with liberal coatings of glue applied to the backside of the pilot to attach him to the seat.

Eventually the model would be complete, its polystyrene pilot almost indistinguishable through his canopy under smears of hardened glue. The model would be embellished with those decals that had not floated away or became wrapped around my fingers and broken, but oh boy! Another sleek fighter for the collection.

I began to live and breathe aircraft. During meals, the *Observer's Book of Aircraft* was always beside me and, because I was often bored and causing trouble, this was tolerated by my parents; it kept me quiet at the dinner table. I borrowed books on flying from the Wagga library, many of them quaint British hardbacks printed on shiny paper. One urged me to construct a primitive control column and rudder pedals to practise the movements, which I duly did using Meccano. I was given a copy of Paul Brickhill's *The Dam Busters*, which I read and reread. I could quote tracts from it. My bicycle was named after Australian pilot Micky Martin's Lancaster bomber, 'P for Peter' which he had nicknamed 'P for Popsie'. I didn't know what a 'popsie' was until I was much older. I gave 'lectures on flight' to anyone who would listen. Silhouettes in the *Observer's Book* were memorised; any appearance of an aircraft on the television news was accompanied by a shout from me as to what type it was, only to be shushed by my parents who would be concentrating on the television news of the day, after a life of gleaning world events from newspapers, cinema newsreels and the wireless.

Later in the sixties, the new City of Wagga Wagga prospered, as did my father's 'turf club'. Money became available for some basic house improvements, and an annual holiday additional to the visits to the respective grandparents in the Melbourne suburbs of McKinnon and West Footscray. Long drives interstate were made over successive summers in an un-air conditioned car containing three restless and occasionally fighting young children. In the Gold Coast in Queensland, our family visited an attraction called Gilltrap's Auto Museum. Although not particularly interested in cars I enjoyed it, and even more so when I noticed a sleek green and yellow aeroplane suspended from the cavernous roof.

'Look, that's a de Havilland Moth Minor,' I told anybody who would listen.

Hand in hand with my fascination for aircraft was my interest in space exploration. The Gemini program was near its conclusion and the Apollo lunar missions were imminent. I was allowed to stay up once more to watch some of the Saturn launches that lofted the Apollo crews into space, including that of Apollo 11. Many of my contemporaries and I clearly remember where we were when Neil Armstrong stepped onto the moon. Unfortunately our teacher was punctilious enough to keep us at schoolwork rather than watching the black-and-white images on a television set up for the class next door. After school I hared home and caught some of the fuzzy images transmitted from the lunar surface there. I dressed as an astronaut for the end-of-school year play, in borrowed white overalls and *papier-mache* helmet. I tried to replicate the astronauts' lunar gait in full Earth gravity. I had asked my mother to sew the top of my swimming pool snorkel, a ping pong ball trapped in a plastic cage, to the side of the overalls to depict some sort of valve.

I joined the Australian Air League, of which Wagga had a squadron, essentially Boy Scouts with aeronautical education and military-style drill. Younger than most of the boys, my enthusiasm stood me in good stead, but some of the subjects were just too advanced: Mr Adams, who taught navigation, had actually been a navigator in RAAF Lancasters during World War II, and his diagrams of 'heading', 'track' and 'wind' produced on dark sheets by an old spirit duplicator were a bit too much for me. Still, I listened intently while he described missions over Europe, on one occasion being told to leave his curtained navigator's station to 'Come up and have a look at this *flak*!' However, I was also made to attend football training, Police Boys' Club and confirmation classes, all of which were requirements that, particularly the last, distinctly lacked enthusiasm from me. Perhaps, my parents thought that my attending these would make me more 'normal'.

Although a voracious reader, interested in science, with no

problems with English and spelling but only fair with maths, I was 'young' for my age, and I also suffered some physical problems, notably recurring severe headaches and asthma. I may have been on the Asperger's spectrum, and I was timid and easily bullied. I was just hopeless at sport. My immaturity and behaviour lead to the strict but kindly principal of Kooringal School, Mr Potter, determining that I should repeat Sixth Class.

Despite some of the scary stories about high school, I took it for granted that after Kooringal Public I would attend the nearest government secondary school, Mount Austin High. I was in a band that had been organised by a classmate, John, who was old for his years and a musical prodigy. We played jazz and I used a music case as a drum until my maternal grandfather, who was musical, passed a primitive drum kit on to me. But one day in 1969, after arriving home from school and running noisily into the wooden-floored house in Grove Street as usual, my parents were waiting.

'Mark, we've got some news,' my mother said. 'We're moving to Melbourne.'

3

ON THE BEACH

1970 – 1975

I took the news of the impending move hard. I was an odd child with an aircraft obsession, but I had three close friends, and we enjoyed playing in the vast spaces that were still in reach from the expanding new suburbs of Wagga Wagga. There was also the band. However, after understanding that my father's new job was to be the secretary of the Mornington Racing Club, south of Melbourne on Victoria's Mornington Peninsula, my ears pricked when I heard who the president of the club was. It was Sir Reginald Ansett, one of Australia's most prominent airline pioneers and at the time, still head of one of Australia's domestic airlines, Ansett Airlines of Australia.

Our family moved into a house in Amelia Avenue, north-east of Mornington's centre. Unlike our previous house of fibro, wood and galvanised iron, it was of dark brown brick veneer with a tiled roof and a proper garage. It stood in a different world to that of southern, inland New South Wales: greyer skies, a milder climate, and Victorian people even had a discernibly different accent. It was more 'urban', but I liked the ti trees and softer vegetation compared with that of the great New South Wales plains. The smell of coal 'briquettes' hung in the air during winter, not unpleasant to me after happy memories of visits to grandparents in their Melbourne suburbs. There were several airfields in the area, and the then bustling general aviation field of Moorabbin was not far away. Port Phillip Bay sparkled when it was sunny, and scallop boats rubbed against Mornington's pier. Lush green fields and rows of tall she-oak trees lay to the north and east of our suburb.

My first day at the government Mornington High School was a shock. It was *huge*. Accommodating well over 1,000 students, it comprised rows of grey breeze-block classrooms with multiple white wooden window frames, vast areas of asphalt and several massive sports ovals. The sixth-formers looked gigantic and awkward; near-adults in school uniform. There was a different teacher and room for each subject. After each period, hundreds of pairs of shoes pounded along the grey or brown linoleum of the corridors that smelled of stale sandwiches and floor polish. Locker doors slammed, and adding to the din was the traffic on the busy Nepean Highway outside. I knew nobody and found it hard to make friends, my angular skinniness and massive overbite not helping. The buildings were grey, the sky was often grey, the asphalt was grey and the uniforms were grey; but slowly, things got better.

Eventually I found others in the same situation. Tony, an immigrant from Britain, was one. I also began to realise what a mixing bowl a big government high school can be. Many children were bussed in from the hinterland and villages of the Mornington Peninsula, some with backgrounds significantly more humble than my own. One boy, Peter, had a scarred cheek and I do not think his home life was particularly pleasant. He was a tough customer but generally kept to himself, and no one would take him on in a rumble. He once surprised me when he surreptitiously showed me some artwork he had done, worried that the others would laugh at him. He left school early and I do not think that he ever got to make use of his talent. Whenever I was outside, especially at school, I always looked skywards at the Fokker Friendship and Douglas DC-9 airliners when they alternately droned and jetted across the sky, climbing out towards their cruise altitude from Melbourne Airport to destinations in Tasmania. What a life of flying and travel those pilots must be leading!

One day I reread *On the Beach*, which had never been far from my consciousness as an impressionable and sensitive child. Now we lived in the same area where much of the story was set. I became familiar with places from the novel: Frankston and its railway station, the beaches of Port Phillip Bay, and not far away was Berwick, where my parents occasionally visited friends. There were outings to Phillip Island. Much of the book had been set on the shores of the Bay, and family drives to Sorrento and Portsea gave glimpses of the roiling waters of the Rip, through which the fictional submarine USS *Scorpion* passed. It was to be scuttled with the crew outside the Heads, watched from the land by the heroine, Moira Davidson, pale and sick, before she took a suicide pill while sitting behind the wheel of her parked car with the last humans on the planet about to die after the northern hemisphere's nuclear war.

My aviation enthusiasm continued unabated. I did jobs for neighbours in order to put a few cents aside for a model aircraft every few weeks: on those days, school would pass agonisingly until that last bell. Then I would pedal down to the shop on a corner in Main Street where row after row of model kits, most of them unaffordable, waited enticingly. I bought any aviation magazine I could afford and devoured books on flying. I could not see myself as becoming anything other than a pilot.

My parents had tracked down a local boys' group for me, the Peninsula Air Cadets. Once again I found it awkward to start with but apart from the usual bully one may find in any youth group, it was generally well run by the adults. Unlike the Air League, its focus was on civilian aviation rather than the air force. Out-of-date Department of Aviation publications such as the Visual Flight Guide were given to us to study, and one avuncular instructor would read to us excerpts from the 'Crash Comic', the respected and long-gone Aviation Safety Digest. Thanks to this publication, even at the age of thirteen, I was beginning to understand the implications of flying aircraft in cloud or at night without suitable qualifications – it seemed that every second fatal accident in the Crash Comic was summed up as '... the pilot continued flight into weather conditions for which he was not qualified', or words to that effect. There was also talk of actual 'flying days' for the Air Cadets, funds permitting. Despite this, I was still finding it difficult to adjust to my new life but on a visit to my paternal grandparents' new house that lay in bare fields at Melton South on Melbourne's western fringe, I was in for a day I would never forget. After years of reading about, modelling, spotting, sitting in, and talking about aircraft, I had never actually flown in one.

A Fuji FA-200 waited on the grass on a sparkling Easter day at Fogarty's Field, near Melton. My paternal grandparents were with my parents and me at the airfield, and I think they had arranged the flight. I was allocated the front seat next to its pilot, an older white-haired gentleman, maybe one of the Flying Fogartys himself. Two other passengers sat behind. With its little engine roaring and the propeller buzzing, the Fuji accelerated along the grass. The rumble of the undercarriage diminished and this was it – airborne! The ground fell away and I gazed, fascinated – yet nervous – at the dwindling trees, fields, houses and fences as the Fuji, a Japanese low-wing four-seater, climbed.

The air was smooth, but the feeling of being airborne was one of fragility, yet wonder. The greenness of the paddocks, the tiny cars and animals! The lengthening afternoon shadows of the trees on the earth beneath! When the pilot made a few gentle turns, I marvelled at how the horizon ahead tilted but, thanks to his correct flying technique, we still felt normal in our seats, with no tendency to fall sideways. Looking down along the wing during the turns at trees, fields and the occasional house was intoxicating. Too soon the pilot came in to land, easing the Fuji onto the grass with its wheels rumbling once more and the aircraft bucking until it slowed and was taxied in. The propeller stopped and in the silence I climbed out, shaking with excitement, telling anyone who would listen for weeks afterwards, that I had 'been up'.

The Peninsula Air Cadets were coming into their heyday, and funds became sufficient to organise occasional flights for the boys at Moorabbin and Moorooduc. Each flying day was looked forward to with great anticipation and the education provided by the Air Cadets and my own reading made these flights more than joy rides. Instruments started to make sense and the sensation of being suspended by an invisible gas, our atmosphere, never lost its wonder, but became more familiar and predictable with each flight.

I worked diligently at school and still read widely. In my mid-teens my mother began hounding me to get a job, which coincided with my teenager's requirement for cash. A few hundred metres from our home, sitting in the middle of green fields with a treed perimeter, was a large but exclusive restaurant called John Thornton's. Wide full-length windows were framed by arched brickwork. Plush red carpets set off snowy linen tablecloths and red cloth napkins in two separate dining areas. Prints of English hunting scenes adorned the walls.

One day in the early seventies, a sound from the sky reached my ears but it was nothing like the noise of any aircraft that I had ever heard. A tiny dot grew into an oval-shaped bubble that sprouted a slim tail boom, skids and a rotor. It was a Hughes 300 helicopter. Its tiny two-seat cabin with an engine revving furiously behind was attached to an open framework. It was on approach to the restaurant! I pedalled down to John Thornton's to watch it land. It started to operate into the restaurant every few days, and during holidays and weekends, I was like that classic kid with their bike against the airport's fence, but this was at a restaurant's helipad!

The helicopter pilot also owned the restaurant. An imposing

man with many business interests, Richard 'Dick' Thornton patiently answered my many questions about the machine. One wondrous day, he motioned me over to it after landing and with the rotor still turning, I clambered in. He whisked the machine up into a short circuit of the area to another landing. I started reading up on helicopters and how they flew. One day I plucked up the courage to ask him for a holiday job in the restaurant, and in a few months I had progressed from serviette folder, gardener and menial kitchen worker to drinks waiter and single-handedly waiting on diners during weekday lunches. I was now fifteen. Over the next few years the restaurant prospered and much of my non-school time was taken up with working at John Thornton's. It was often hard and constant work, especially during holiday periods, but the overtime payments were put to good use: I could now afford the biggest model aircraft on sale at the Variety Centre. I could also think about learning to fly!

Outside of the village of Moorooduc, then just a 'co-op' store and a few houses in lush fields to the east of Mornington, was its eponymous airfield, a north-south grass strip with towering she-oaks at one end. It was home to 'The Pilotmakers' flying school. Its owner and chief pilot was Jack Ellis, somewhat of an aviation identity in Victoria. He suffered fools lightly, and he was often at odds with 'the Department': the Department of Civil Aviation, now the Civil Aviation Safety Authority (CASA). In determined anticipation, I obtained a Student Pilot's Licence, purchased textbooks and started reading up on the theory required for the inevitable ground exams. The Pilotmakers ran an eclectic mix of aircraft including Cessnas, several old British Austers and other more obscure types. The Air Cadets had previously organised a few flights for us boys in one of the Austers, and the cheapest aircraft available for lessons was the smallest, oldest and tattiest Auster. It bore its registration of VH-BYJ.

BYJ's fading paint scheme was all-over yellow. It sat tail-down on two main wheels and a tail wheel, and pointing skywards was the squared-off 'puppy nose' of a Gipsy-powered Auster. The Gipsy Major engine also powers the famous Tiger Moth biplane. It is an 'inverted four': four in-line cylinders drive a crankshaft in the conventional manner, but the engine is mounted upside down compared to that in a 'straight four' car. Having the crankshaft at the top enables more clearance for the propeller from the ground, improves visibility over the nose for the pilot, and allows efficient lubrication of the cylinders' valve gear, which is permanently bathed in oil contained in the rocker covers under each cylinder. The engine is air-cooled through an asymmetric opening in the cowling, just below the propeller, and a separate oil tank is drained and fed by engine-driven pumps. The Gipsy Major is still a popular and generally reliable engine today.

BYJ's Gipsy turned a wooden two-bladed propeller which dragged its airframe, made from tubular metal covered with fabric tightened drum-taut by liberal applications of a pungent chemical called 'dope', noisily and slowly through the air. BYJ's two occupants sat in a tubular steel cage and looked ahead through an inverted 'W' of tubular struts and a thin Perspex windscreen over the curved upper cowling that covered the engine. This cowling was the only streamlined feature of the Auster. The wings sat high with their 'roots' (the ends that join the fuselage, or body), just above each occupant's head, and they efficiently blocked any view to the side or above. Square windows on each side enabled a tantalising view of the earth below through a 'V' of struts, which braced the mid-wing structure to the fuselage and landing gear mountings. Ironically, BYJ had been built for the Royal Australian Air Force in wartime 1943 as an Auster Mark III, its role observation and army cooperation, with large areas of its cabin clad in clear Perspex. This was done away with, as was then the fashion, when the aircraft was civilianised post-war. Blue-painted plywood panels now lined the interior around the occupants, which grudgingly yielded an additional rounded car-type window behind each seat, and instead of a glorious view behind and upwards through the tubular metal framework, there was only the ghastly reddish-grey of the inside of the fabric covering.

The machine was controlled in pitch (up and down) and roll (banking and turning) by two joysticks, which curved up from under the instrument panel. Two rudder pedals and the Auster's notorious heel-operated brakes were on the floor in front of each occupant, and one throttle lever, that controlled the engine's speed, protruded from the middle of the panel. A larger lever protruded from the cockpit roof. Hauling down on it and releasing its unlocking mechanism at various positions set the flaps, surfaces on the underside 'trailing edge' of the wings which provided extra lift, or on further extension, 'drag' to assist landing. Instrumentation was the minimum required: an air speed indicator, which showed the speed that the machine was travelling through the air in 'knots', or nautical miles per hour; an altimeter that showed height above sea level in thousands and hundreds of feet; a primitive compass, a 'turn indicator' that showed whether the pilot was turning and, if so, whether they were using the rudder pedals to correctly 'balance' the turn; and for the engine, an oil pressure gauge and a revolutions indicator. Two switches similar to those in an antique light switch controlled their respective, redundant magneto systems and associated spark plugs that supplied ignition to the engine, and a fuel shutoff cock completed the equipment required to fly an Auster. VH-BYJ had no starting system; the propeller was 'hand swung' in the manner of decades before. Today, Austers are generally regarded with nostalgia and affection particularly by those who own them, but my main attraction to BYJ in 1974 was that it was eighteen dollars per hour to hire, instructor included. So, at the age of sixteen, my flying lessons began.

However, work at John Thornton's started to peter out. I cannot recollect if it was due to the business environment or if it was sold on by Dick, but coincidentally, I had spent some of my earnings on a better second-hand drum kit, and some school friends and I had formed a garage band. Paul, the bass player, was older for his years, and eventually a new band formed that included acquaintances of Paul's who were grown men in their twenties. We practised and eventually got work. I played the drums by ear – I still do – and our brand of fifties and sixties rock 'n' roll must have been in demand because we had no problem getting regular Saturday night engagements in hotels around the Peninsula and in particular, the Sorrento Hotel. Occasional restaurant work and regular Saturday nights of unsophisticated drumming to progressively inebriated pub patrons while the nights wore on allowed a flying lesson with The Pilotmakers about once every two weeks.

My instructor was Simon. Patiently, he led me through the steps of controlling an aeroplane: 'straight and level' flight, then turns, descents, climbs, and steeply banked turns. I dutifully learned the few checklist items related to starting and flying an Auster. The sensitivity of an aircraft's flight controls can be off-putting to many new pilots and I was no exception, particularly as a sixteen-year-old boy. Simon taught me the basics of flying 'attitude'; that is, using the control column to select a picture of the aircraft's nose with regard to the horizon. Side to side movement of the column banked the aircraft to the right or left. This, along with the application of the appropriate rudder pedal to balance the turn, resulted in a smooth and comfortable change of direction. Back and forward movement raised and lowered the Auster's nose with respect to the horizon to climb and descend. 'Attitude' flying, rather than just chasing the indications on the instruments, was the correct technique. 'Steep turns', which were turns with the Auster's wings at forty-five degrees to the horizon, became easier after I grasped this very basic principle of aircraft control.

Every two weeks, I would be driven out to Moorooduc along Tyabb Road, or occasionally pedal my bicycle, for a precious hour in the Auster. Some ground would have to be re-covered over each session, because fortnightly is not an ideal frequency for flying lessons, but it was all I could afford – often southern Victoria's fickle weather would preclude flying for longer periods.

Occasionally Simon would be away or occupied with another student, and Jack Ellis, the school's owner, took Simon's place. I had graduated to take-offs and landings, and with the patience of Job, the instructors showed me the principles and practice of an approach and landing.

The two basic ingredients of a successful approach and landing are 'glide path' and 'airspeed'. The glide path is the angle of descent and this was set by using the Auster's throttle in my right hand to adjust the engine speed and therefore the rate at which BYJ would descend. Adjusting the aircraft's pitch attitude with my left hand on the stick correctly set the speed, and the aim was to keep the threshold, the start of the runway, in a constant position in the windscreen and at a constant angle. Movement of one control would always result in a correction required by the other. In the meantime, the aircraft had to be kept on the centreline of the approach path using side-to-side movements of the column to turn. There were towering she-oak trees just before the clear space of Moorooduc airfield's grass runway and to safely clear these, yet not be too high for a safe landing, was desirable. With the trees passed, the threshold's position would be kept constant in the windscreen, and then it was time for the 'round out', nowadays generally referred to as the 'flare'. This was the tricky part.

Flare too high, and the little yellow Auster would float along about a metre off the grass, lose speed, then settle down with an uncomfortable lurch and thump. Worse, flare late, and whump! The main wheels would thud onto the ground. In both cases, the aircraft would bounce, its 'tail wheel' configuration ensuring that it would kangaroo hop down the runway, its young pilot trying desperately to smooth the situation out but out of synchronisation with the aircraft's movements. Extreme cases would result in the far safer option of a 'go around' where power was applied, the nose raised to the climb attitude, and the aircraft climbed away for another attempt. The correct point for the flare could only be judged by experience; first of all by watching Simon's landings and then, with him sitting patiently through my attempts, reasonable flare points resulted. Then, it was important to keep raising the aircraft's attitude as the speed bled off, engine ticking over at idle, to play the rate of raising the nose with respect to the horizon against the rate at which the speed reduced, in order for the Auster to settle onto its main wheels which rumbled and rattled on the grass: an acceptable 'arrival'.

However, being a 'tail wheel' aircraft, it was vital to keep the Auster straight once its main wheels were on the ground. 'Tail draggers' have their centre of gravity behind the main wheels, and any inattention to tracking straight down the runway will lead to physics taking over and the tail swinging, with extreme cases resulting in the machine running off the runway. With the aircraft on the ground, moving in two dimensions, directional control was done with the rudder pedals, but even then, one still had to 'fly' the Auster. After landing, its tail would eventually settle gently onto its little wheel at the back making directional control a little easier, but in windy conditions, even taxiing BYJ could be challenging.

An airfield's traffic 'circuit' or 'pattern' has four stages: firstly 'upwind', where the aircraft is climbed out into the wind after take-off; then a 'crosswind' leg to left or right depending on local regulations (usually to the left), still climbing. Then a level turn is made onto 'downwind', parallel to the runway, the strip appearing through the vee of the struts beyond the pilot's shoulder where a memorised 'downwind checklist' is spoken to oneself. On the 'base' leg at ninety degrees to the runway, power is reduced and a stage of flap selected (in the Auster, by hauling down on that flap lever); this starts a gentle descent. Looking for a feature on the extended centreline of the runway, the pilot judges the final turn onto the final 'approach' leg, looking for that correct picture of glide path angle and aiming point. With a final stage of flap, speed dribbling back to the correct 'threshold' or 'over the fence' speed, and a successful judgment of the flare point, the Auster would settle onto the grass, sometimes for a 'full stop' landing but increasingly, during training, the tail would be held up, power applied and the aircraft would be lifted off again for another circuit. This was called a 'touch and go' landing.

Circuit training was interspersed with sessions of stalling the aircraft. It is vital that a pilot can recognise signs of, and can recover from, an aircraft stall. A stall occurs when too much is being asked of the aircraft's wing; usually due to pilot mishandling or lack of awareness, extreme manoeuvring or bad weather.

Drifting high at 4,000 feet over a patchwork of countryside, under Simon's supervision I practised stalls and recoveries from them. With waves of vibration from the idling engine rippling through the structure, the propeller blades almost visible, the yellow nose was lifted higher into blue sky to maintain altitude. The controls became sloppy as the speed of the wind over them reduced. I kept the wings level with the horizon, then at that moment when the wings' clutching hands on 'lift' let go there was a little buffet, a 'break' and a pitch down, stomach slightly noticeable as the natural stability of the aircraft took over. With gentle forward 'stick' to positively reduce the wing's angle of attack then on with the power the Auster would be flying again, although in a slight dive. Unnerving at first, practicing stalls was vital so that I would be able to recognise the onset of one: the high nose attitude (in most cases), the low and decreasing airspeed, controls sloppy, buffet and then the stall itself. At height the stall is a benign manoeuvre and is routinely practised, but near to the ground, especially in a turn, it can be a killer.

Engine failure in a single engine aircraft is a serious matter, and it was vital to cope with loss of power at any stage during flight. With the Gipsy engine at idle BYJ became a virtual glider, and provided that the correct attitude and speed were flown, a gentle descent would result, enabling its pilot to select and head for a landing area, preferably into wind, at forty-five knots, eighty-three kilometres per hour. Most reasonable farmers' fields were usable. These practice forced landings would end in a 'go around', not an actual touchdown unless being practised on the runway. The critical case was failure at, or soon after take-off, where the pilot would either 'abort' the take-off run with the aircraft still on or near to the ground, or smartly lower the nose, maintain the safe gliding speed, select a clear area, turn off the ignition, shut off the fuel and do what else was necessary to ensure survival. Above all, avoid the stall!

On one hot day over brown paddocks, even the Peninsula was dusty under hazy summer skies. Once again, Jack had replaced Simon as my instructor for the day's flight. He gave me a thorough workout in the heat: circuits, simulated engine failures and stalls. There was a passable final landing and the usual weaving and straining to see past the Auster's upthrust nose to clear the way ahead back to its parking spot, but then Jack shouted over the ch-chug ch-hug ch-chug of the Gipsy's idle, 'Don't shut down, I'm getting out. Taxi out, do one circuit and come back in.' I was going solo!

As with most pilots, my first solo was unforgettable. Alone! No instructor to intervene or provide advice. I taxied the yellow Auster, carefully ran up the engine and worked through the simple memorised 'take-off checks'. Now, on to Moorooduc's grass runway, open the throttle, and the aircraft eagerly became airborne without fifty per cent of its human load on board; it seemed a different aircraft without the weight of Simon or Jack. Now the other seat was vacant, its harness secured to avoid fouling the dual controls. A carefully flown circuit and a little 'float' just before touchdown, then the taxi in, shut down and final checks. A handshake from Jack, and there it was. I had lifted a machine into the sky unassisted and returned it and me in it undamaged to earth at sixteen years of age.

Two more years of school remained. As fanatical about aerospace as ever, I devoured any book I could obtain on the subject, but I also read other topics. However, with the throes of adolescence, schoolwork had slipped somewhat and there were often heated clashes with my parents, particularly my mother. I had little in common with my sisters and the rest of my family were sport-mad where I was not, so I spent many hours in my room making models, reading, and dreaming of the day I would be out of that house and flying. I read up on schemes to join the air force, civilian training options and all aspects of aviation including helicopters and gliders.

A few of the mixed bag of Mornington High's students with whom I hung out were rather wild, and the combination of frustration with home life and the inevitable peer group expectations led to typical adolescent behaviour, some arrogance but awkwardness in many other situations. Not good looking, I was still skinny and angular. Acne raged. My overbite had been partly reset by some orthodontic work, but my mouth was, and still is, not pretty! However I still read widely and even though it was a government school, Mornington High had many teachers of a high calibre.

A few teachers were not so respected. A music teacher proudly wore a badge that displayed a Viet Cong flag – only recently had Australian troops been withdrawn from Vietnam, after many of our servicemen died there. One teacher had a penchant for gripping boys by the tie, pulling up on it and cuffing their heads. He was known as 'Boston', after the Boston Strangler. 'Fags' was a heavy smoker. 'The Fuhrer' was a moustachioed disciplinarian, and there was the recently immigrated Business Studies teacher from North Africa: he was absolutely humourless, and his English was almost indecipherable. He was frequently seen using the corridor telephone outside the staff room to call his stockbroker, so he was known as 'Dinger', which was also then a word for condom. 'Grondy', one of the sports teachers, departed the school suddenly after parents became aware of his predilection for lining the boys up after a supposedly poor performance, getting them to bend over, then tapping their backsides with a cricket bat.

We also had nicknames for each other. One boy was albino in appearance, small of frame, very thin and already had a receding hairline. He was affectionately known as 'Healthy'. A huge sixth-form boy was 'Lurch', after the Addams Family butler. To fit in I tried to grow my hair long like the other boys, but it merely stuck out in thick wads like antlers on either side of my narrow head, so to my classmates I was 'Bullwinkle', after the cartoon moose.

However, I realised that good school results would be a ticket out, and I was going to have a career in aviation come what may. I made Mornington High's team for a television school quiz show called 'It's Academic'. We won our first round against two other government schools. In the next round, one question asked was, 'What was the name of the U.S. nuclear submarine that sank in 1963?' I knew it! I pressed the buzzer and immediately blurted out, 'USS *Thresher*', but my impetuosity led to no points for the answer – I had not waited for Mr Webb, the quizmaster, to call my school's name and direct me to answer. We were a state school up against two highly coached teams from private schools on this round and predictably, we lost, but we were proud to have made it to the semi-finals. However, impetuosity and thoughtlessness would cause problems for me in the future.

As the restaurant work petered out, the band became more important. The lead guitarist had to pick me up from my home for practices and 'gigs'; I could not legally drive and even if I could, I was not able to afford to run, let alone buy, any car. Also, in those times, the state of Victoria stipulated a higher minimum driving age. On Saturdays, at least during summer, there would be our regular engagement in the Sorrento Hotel, but other work became patchy, and the reduction of earnings, weather and other factors conspired to reduce the amount of flying at Moorooduc. For the next few years until I finished school, my flying was a desultory mixture of dual lessons, much of it recovering past ground, and the very occasional solo flight, circuits and 'steep turns' in the training area and not much else.

My father arranged work for me at Mornington Racecourse: menial jobs such as picking up empty glasses around the bar areas, working on the track, cleaning and watering. I worked with a gang of labourers and was shown no special treatment as the boss's son. The workers were down to earth fellows, not well-educated, but they accepted me as one of them and I enjoyed their company. I made it known that I was going to become a pilot, and even only with the stated intention, they asked questions about aircraft and air travel, and in return, during our mind-numbing routine of 'treading in' the track (replacing the divots kicked out by the horses' hooves), they spun yarns and told awful jokes. I was taught to drive the tractors, and I was occasionally allowed to drive my mother's old Morris car on the course.

Ansett Airlines was one of two domestic airlines under the highly regulated 'Two Airline Policy' of Australia in the late 1970s. Its chief was still its founding father, Sir Reginald Ansett, one of Australia's most accomplished and respected airline pioneers. My father's secretarial job at Mornington Racecourse was onerous for him in one respect: the hard-working Sir Reginald devoted little time to pleasure but a rare pastime, as president of the Racing Club, was spending Sunday afternoons at the racecourse. On most Sundays, 'Sir Reg' appeared at the track in his big blue Cadillac. In would get my father and the head groundsman, and round and round the track they would drive, talking horses, race meetings and grass. I was introduced to Sir Reginald only once, shortly after we first arrived in Mornington; young and in awe of a knight and my father's boss, I couldn't bring myself to blurt out that I wanted to be a pilot. Therefore, guidance for an aviation career did not come from Sir Reginald Ansett; but he did have his own helicopter pilot.

Sir Reg famously commuted by helicopter most days from his bay side home to Melbourne's heliport on the Yarra River, then to be chauffeured to the Ansett Airlines city office. His Bell JetRanger was also famous – its fuselage, as much as a helicopter's can be, was streamlined, and adorned with the same Ansett livery of the day as its airliners: red, black and white, with a stylised red 'A' in a white circle. My father knew Cal, his helicopter pilot slightly. Cal had also flown fixed wing aircraft with Ansett Airlines. He had previously been a pilot in the Royal Australian Navy and had flown fixed wing aircraft and helicopters from its aircraft carrier, HMAS *Melbourne*. One evening it was arranged for him to visit our home. Cal talked of naval flying, and he awoke in me an appreciation that Fleet Air Arm aviators have something that no other pilots can boast: the ability to take off from, and land on, a ship at sea. He recounted naval life, the flying, the travel, the camaraderie in the tightly-knit Fleet Air Arm, a service far smaller than Australia's air force. Its only land base was just outside the town of Nowra, south of Sydney near the New South Wales coast. I had always liked ships – one of my prized models was a large sailing vessel. I had noted with interest newspaper advertisements for civilian merchant naval cadets, and although flying was my first love, naval aviation might just be a way to enjoy both. With the Cold War in full force, Australia's navy operated Skyhawk attack jets, Grumman Tracker patrol aircraft and various helicopters, and the more I read and heard, the more my excitement mounted about becoming a pilot in the navy. Unlike the air force, you did not need a Sixth Form education to join! Fifth Form was acceptable.

I studied the material that the navy's recruiting office posted out after my enquiries and at the age of seventeen, I excitedly travelled on the electric train from Frankston to Melbourne city to begin the selection process. Frankston Station had achieved mild fame in scenes from the film version of Neville Shute's *On the Beach*. Along with Melbourne's remote southerly location from the northern hemisphere's nuclear war, Shute had chosen the city for his setting because of the massive reserves of coal that lay to its east in Gippsland. With the supply of oil non-existent with the approaching end of civilisation, Victoria's coal continued to produce electricity for homes, industry and transport. This allowed Melbourne's inhabitants to stoically live a 'normal' life to the end.

There were preliminary interviews and medical examinations: IQ tests, time/speed/distance problems, chasing a blob of light around a screen with a joystick, long cold waits in cubicles clad in a paper dressing gown for the medical tests ... it all seemed to go well. I had bought paperback books of IQ tests, studied the Royal Australian Navy's order of battle in ships and aircraft, and Lieutenant Commander Henry, the middle-aged naval officer who ran the recruiting office, was kind and helpful. My feeling about how I had done was correct, and some weeks later I was invited for more tests, with an interview by a Selection Board to follow.

I was elated. I was going to leave school early to become a navy pilot! Flying Skyhawk jets, wearing a crisp white uniform, travel and life at sea on an aircraft carrier – what a life for a teenager! I worked through more books of IQ tests, flew at Moorooduc when I could afford it, played in the band, worked at the racecourse and carried on with the initial term of Sixth Form. Finally, the great day dawned, and there I was again at the navy recruiting office in Flinders Lane for more tests in greater depth this time, and then to face the Selection Board.

I was directed into a room furnished with the classic green baize-covered table, introduced to its occupants and told to sit. Facing me were men in civilian clothes – no brass buttons or gold insignia here. They were all naval officers except for a psychologist, and the questions commenced. Lieutenant Commander Errol Kavanagh, urbane and polite (wow! A Skyhawk pilot!), asked most of the questions. I answered the technical questions well, but I was awkward with those about my personal life, holidays, girlfriend (actually, the lack of one) and relationships. Well, what would they expect from a seventeen-year-old? Also, they alluded to staying at school and passing the Higher School Certificate (HSC). Still, I thought that it hadn't gone too badly, and on the train home I wondered when I would hear the result. I looked forward to leaving home for an exciting life of flying with the navy.

Schoolwork was getting hard. I never possessed a particular mathematical bent and I replaced two advanced mathematics subjects with French, which I had always enjoyed, and 'general' maths. I was coping but not particularly distinguishing myself, distracted by social life and the notion that I was going to become a navy pilot and I wouldn't need to pass the HSC. The weeks dragged agonisingly while I waited to hear from the navy; being away for a school camp near Castlemaine during the green Victorian winter was excruciating. I called home every day from a pay phone to ask my parents – 'No, we haven't heard anything.'

On my return from the camp, I couldn't stand it any longer. I telephoned Lieutenant Commander Henry, who said: 'I've got bad news, I'm afraid, Mark. Your application has been unsuccessful – I was about to ring you. The board indicated that you are a little immature, so I would suggest that you stay at school, get your HSC, and you can try again next year. I'm sorry.'

I was devastated.

On reflection, this was indicative of the navy always having been a 'people' service. A ship runs twenty-four hours a day: its captain, officers and petty officers (who are equivalent to sergeants in the army and air force), apart from their required technical abilities, need to know how to handle people well in a floating community. A naval vessel is cramped, noisy, pitching and rolling, its crew far from family and potentially at war. The Board's response was typical of the calibre of many in the navy, not just a flat 'you have missed out', but one that was also accompanied with advice and encouragement for the future.

Time is a healer – particularly to an adolescent – and the navy dream faded a little. There was always the air force or civilian flying, and I was interested in the workings of the human body, with an ulterior motive of becoming a 'rich doctor' in order to own my own aircraft. With the HSC looming at the end of the year, schoolwork was intensifying, and there were conflicts with my mother about late nights out with the band, so that income was petering out, and the Moorooduc flying became even less regular. It did not help when old BYJ was grounded for refurbishment and the other aircraft were too expensive to hire. Not particularly happy at home, I wanted out, and as the academic year drew towards its climax, I decided that I had better knuckle down and apart from occasional work at the racecourse, I would concentrate on schoolwork.

I have always believed in preparation, removing as much of an unknown as possible before a test, and, as with the IQ test books I worked through for the navy, I started working through past paper after past paper of the Victorian HSC examinations. The real thing would, therefore, not be an unknown. Most of Mornington High's Sixth Form teachers were helpful to those who put the work in, so this, the past papers and, at last, some increasing maturity, provided a basis for tackling the HSC.

It can be funny how things work out sometimes. My parents had decided to heavily renovate our house by adding an upstairs room, during the time of my exam preparation. The place was a shambles; hammering and sawing reverberated through it, so the only alternative for daytime study was in the cubicles of the newly-constructed library building at school. In the library, free of the distractions of home (with or without renovations), I was motivated to work hard. In the meantime, university courses were on 'offer', so, with little thought about how I or my parents would pay for them, I submitted preferences to the various universities for Medicine and Meteorology. However, although I was now hard at work with an eye on the future, I was still thoughtless and impetuous at times. One day the librarian overheard me outside the library 'sounding off' to friends about her, calling her names, regarding some rule she had introduced. She promptly banned me from the library.

After I spent the following day at home with the renovations then the next lying in cold sand at Mills Beach trying to study, the penny dropped: I had been dreadfully rude, and under stress. The next morning, I apologised to her. She told me, 'Thank you, it took a man to do that.' Lesson learned. Welcomed back to the peace of the library, once again I was able to work at past paper after past paper.

I remember well the examination days of late '75. A girl sobbed behind me after she opened the first paper while I began mine, plodding through the questions. Most seemed straightforward after all the preparation, and I made sure to read the questions carefully and to doublecheck the answers. The final exam, English, ended with a 'free essay' requirement. Figuring that not many HSC candidates would be in a position to write a description of their first solo aeroplane flight, I did just that using appropriate amounts of flowery adolescent prose. After handing in the paper, my school days were over.

After that came the long hiatus of the Australian summer. Even on the temperate Mornington Peninsula there were days of relentless blue skies, turquoise sea, brown fields under waves of heat, with the she-oaks and ti trees being the only green in sight. It was an agonising wait for the HSC results: they would determine the offers of placement at the universities.

I now laboured full-time at the racecourse. I could not afford to undergo a structured course toward a Private Pilot's Licence and beyond to Commercial level, so there was little else to do but wait for my results and socialise. One muggy, windless afternoon under grey sky I was shifting hoses at the racecourse when my father's car appeared on the road outside. It stopped, and Dad poked an envelope through the fence. I tore it open to reveal my HSC results, and I had done well. My avid reading through the years had even contributed to a Distinction in English.

Coincidentally, a thunderstorm broke. I stopped work and was driven home. With the storm's passing, the telephone rang with excited calls from friends. My friend Tony would soon pick me up and we would drive to another mate's house towards the other side of the Mornington Peninsula to see how he had fared; Rod lived in humble circumstances and did not have a telephone. Tony and his girlfriend arrived in their old grey Toyota.

I remember a screech of tyres and me calling 'Hang on!' After that, stillness and blackness. I could not see or move, but I could hear. I was aware of a girl moaning and reassuring words from strangers. No visual picture remains in my conscious memory, but I can still recall the sounds. Later came a slow drive in another vehicle (am I in an ambulance?), with continued groans from the girl. The black became grey, and I did not feel much pain. Eventually, I realised that I was in a bed somewhere and I could hear my parents' voices. Still unable able to see, I asked, 'What happened?'

'You've been in a car accident,' my mother replied.

Later I could see again, and I was aware of nurses and a hospital room. I could put my tongue into a hole under my lower lip. Now my shoulder hurt, and an arm was in a sling. I was still in the clothes I was wearing at the racecourse, and, because of a medical reason, my body had not been washed.

Distracted by his girlfriend, Tony had been late braking at an intersection and the old car skidded on the asphalt, still slick from the thunderstorm. We hit a vehicle that was travelling along the intersecting road. A family group at a nearby sports oval had rushed over to the scene; theirs had been the comforting voices. Tony was unhurt but his girlfriend's body had not been treated well by the seatbelt she was wearing and the deceleration severely injured her spine, hence the slow ambulance trip to minimise her distress. I had been in the little car's back seat, but wore no seat belt, because they were not fitted to the rear seats of many vehicles then. I never saw the wreck of the car, but Rod later described the 'V' that my body had made in the front bench seat of the old grey Toyota, which at least had absorbed my momentum and prevented me from being hurled through the windscreen. The occupants of the other vehicle were uninjured, although my mother later said that the other vehicle's driver had been found over the legal blood alcohol limit.

All that work … good exam results … then a thunderstorm to clear the air … but after that, a car crash and injuries … could I become a pilot now?

4

FLY NAVY!

1976

People sleep peacefully in their beds at night only because rough men stand ready to do violence on their behalf.
Attributed to George Orwell

University College, in Melbourne's leafy residential college area, provided accommodation for students, some tutoring and two meals each day. Its inmates included future engineers, lawyers, musicians and artists. There were just two prospective doctors and I was one of them, still eighteen years old.

Several months after the accident my injuries had generally healed, but one shoulder was shorter than the other because the collarbone had not been set properly, so I carried myself at a slight angle. A livid scar underlined one side of my mouth (which I carry to this day) and one of my front teeth was black, but thankfully there were no ongoing symptoms of concussion. My HSC marks had been good enough for admission to Medicine at the University of Melbourne. Plan B, to become that rich doctor and own my own aeroplane, looked like it could come to fruition. Also, injuries from the crash would not jeopardise that path. My parents, particularly my mother, were thrilled. But the subject of how they were to pay for city accommodation, books and various fees lay un-broached.

Mornington was quite a distance from the university – a daily commute to lectures would have been difficult and studying at home virtually impossible. The residential colleges such as University provided the opportunity for 'freshers' from the country to settle into university life and develop a social network in their new world, however, it was expected that after their first or second year, the students would move out into their own accommodation.

At University College I belonged to a small social group, one member of which was a music student, Yvonne. However, the medical faculty at the University of Melbourne was huge. The lecture rooms were vast and packed with young people. However, there seemed to be very few students who had come from government schools. I listened and made notes, but in my college room of cream brick walls and varnished wood, with music floating from the neighbouring boy's room and the dull roar of traffic in the background, study was desultory and I still made model aeroplanes! Posters of aircraft and cockpits adhered to the walls. Aviation works featured among the piles of medical textbooks. Six years of this to go.

I had contributed my meagre savings toward the first term's accommodation and fees, but how were I, or my parents, going to pay for the rest? I found organic chemistry difficult and I had not elected biology as a subject at school. I had a lot of catching up to do. The thought of living in noisy student digs while trying to study medicine was daunting. Above all, I couldn't get the idea of being a navy pilot out of my head.

One morning, I had had enough. Near the end of the first term of Medicine, I strode into the navy's recruiting office in Flinders Lane, this time a little more mature, and with good academic results to show.

Lieutenant Commander Kavanagh once again led the selection board, and he remembered me from my previous attempt. I thrilled at the sight of a navy flying jacket, emblazoned with his nickname of 'Clump' draped over a chair in the interview room – I might wear something like that one day! I answered the board's questions truthfully and confidently, including those about my personal life and relationships, and this time I was not awkward regarding my ongoing lack of a girlfriend. A few weeks later, a telegram arrived at home advising of my acceptance onto the Royal Australian Navy's 'Supplementary List' as a pilot, but subject to further physical checks because of the car accident. I was elated and relieved, but my mother was furious. I would not become a doctor.

However, I was anxious about the injuries sustained from the car crash, although it is wondrous how the young body heals. The navy provided an air ticket to Sydney for a specialist's check, and I will never forget the orthopaedic surgeon's final words to me: 'I see no problem resulting from your injuries; that door is now open for you.'

I was going to be a navy pilot! 'Fly Navy!' was a recruiting slogan of the time – it was not just the air force that operated warplanes. While I waited I would undergo more routine medical checks and reason with my still-frosty mother, who had her heart set on a medical career for her son.

At the end of May, my parents drove me, awkward in my cheap suit, to the main gate of HMAS *Cerberus* that lay outside Hastings on the eastern side of the Mornington Peninsula. There, a life in the sea and sky began.

HMAS *Cerberus* is a land base but regarded as a 'ship' in the tradition of the navies of Britain and Australia. Being a training base, *Cerberus* was very formal, scrupulously maintained and highly disciplined. Much of the establishment was park-like, its buildings were neatly kept, and its wardroom (Officers' Mess) was wood-panelled and smelt of fresh varnish. Two beautiful stone chapels were set in immaculate parkland.

The navy speaks a different language: its recruits become

immersed in a vernacular that in some instances dates back centuries. During our weeks in *Cerberus* (you are always 'in' a naval ship, not 'on' one), we became fluent in the language of Australia's navy: a melange of ancient British words and corruptions of them, and modern Australian coinage, some of it obscene.

The navy itself was often known as 'Pusser's' ('pus' pronounced as per the bodily excretion), an ancient corruption of the word *purser*: those who hold the purse strings, now the modern-day Accounting and Administration Officers. Therefore, everything in the navy was Pusser's, including the people, the ships and the equipment. Naval aircrew were known as 'birdies', while their seaman counterparts were known by the birdies as 'fish heads', or 'dib dabs', from the motion of that universal and omnipresent sailor's tool, the paint brush.

The original *Cerberus* was HMVS (Her Majesty's Victorian Ship) *Cerberus*, the old Colony of Victoria's first warship, advanced for its time, which is now a rusted and stunted wreck that lies off Black Rock. I learned that you still 'went aboard' the current HMAS *Cerberus* over its gangway or brow (actually the main gate), back over which you would go 'ashore'. At the brow was stationed the Officer of the Gangway. The base's hierarchy, also like a ship, included the Captain, the Commander (second in charge) and the Jimmy (First Lieutenant). It had a Gunnery Officer, responsible for drill and ceremonial. *Cerberus* had a quarterdeck, part of the parade ground, with mast and flags flying. 'Colours', the ceremonial hoisting of the naval White Ensign, was held on the quarterdeck every morning, and all officers were expected to attend. The Ensign would be hauled down at sunset, also with ceremony.

Mainstays of the navy were senior non-commissioned ranks, the petty officers (an ancient term derived from the French word for 'small', *petit*), equivalent to sergeants in the other services, and the warrant officers. The NCO's were seasoned navy hands, specialists in their various categories and generally, proven leaders. Below them in rank were the seamen and at this training base, the recruits and apprentices. Female navy members of all ranks were then known as

WRANs (Women's Royal Australian Navy).

Cerberus' buildings included the wardroom, which provided meals and accommodation for the officers. For the lower ranks there was a Petty Officers' Mess and a Junior Sailors' Mess. Buildings had no walls, floors or ceilings, but there were bulkheads, decks and deck-heads, respectively. Individual rooms, for officers and petty officers lucky enough to have them, were always cabins linked by a passageway. At the end of the passageway were the heads, the toilets, named from time immemorial in sail, where the crew relieved themselves from primitive platforms at the bow, or 'head' of their ship. Inspections by senior officers were known as Rounds. All spaces and cabins had to be clean and ship-shape. 'Stand by for Rounds!' the petty officers would shout, and everyone had to be present, standing at the 'ho' (attention) while the Captain or Commander satisfied himself that all was clean and in order, with possibly a polite word or an admonishment to various sailors or midshipmen.

Food served from the galley was known as 'scran', supposedly an acronym for 'Shit Cooked by the Royal Australian Navy'. Breakfast scran could include 'train smash' (tomatoes and onions) with eggs and plenty of 'redders' (tomato sauce). Morning tea could be a 'WRAN's nipple' (coffee scroll) or a 'snot block' (vanilla slice) from the goffa wagon followed by a 'maggot bag' (pie) or 'snorker' (sausage roll) for lunch. A day's work or long night duties were sustained by frequent 'brews': tea or dry, powdery instant coffee, served up from the brew boat: an urn and its accoutrements.

Soft drinks and unaccountably, salutes were goffas; one drank a goffa or 'threw' one to a superior officer. The naval salute is different to that of the army and air force. Reputedly, the hands of the Royal Navy's sailors (the 'tars' of sail days) had perpetually tarry palms from handling and scaling the ship's 'standing' rigging, tarred to protect it from the sea; therefore it was decreed that they would salute with palm inwards to hide the unsightly blackness. The air force, army and most other disciplined services of the Commonwealth countries salute with the palm outwards.

A buzz (rumour) could be discussed with our oppos (friends) over a brew or a goffa. At the end of the day one might do one's dhobi (washing) and if low on soap powder, one might purchase some dhobi dust, perhaps along with a goffa, from the ship's canteen. In the navy, most objects were 'dhobied' including oneself under the shower, clothes, vehicles and aircraft. Slops was clothing and uniform provided by the navy. A complicated knot was a 'bunch of bastards'. An easy task was 'a piece of piss'.

Officers' evening meals in the wardroom were formal. A WRAN or RAN steward would present a card to the diner outlining the joints (main courses), and one would choose, for example, Joint Two. Officers were charged mess bills for food and drinks through their allocated mess number, which the steward would note. Rations and Quarters was a charge deducted from the officer's pay for basic food and accommodation if he lived 'on board' in the wardroom of a land base. Later, he may live 'ashore' in private accommodation. Later still in life, he might live with his young family in the married patch in a house provided by the navy, or privately rent with a small subsidy from the service.

In a naval wardroom, officers were expected to dress for dinner. If you wore civilian dress ('mufti'), you were to approach the senior uniformed officer present (usually at the bar) and ask him to 'excuse your "rig"'. While I was in *Cerberus*, that was invariably an elderly, tipsy Education Officer of Irish descent, perched on a bar stool, who would reply with, 'Oi don't like yer tie, but oi'll let yer go joost this once.'

Operational units and ships would occasionally hold a banyan (barbecue) at some beach, with plenty of beer, and goffas for the very few non-drinkers. For watch keepers at their posts: duty sailors and officers, their scran would be brought to them in a 'fanny' (billy-can or mess tin). 'Fanny' harks back to the gruesome murder of little Fanny Adams in nineteenth century England; cynical English sailors of the day speculated that her butchered remains had found their way into the Royal Navy's victualling system. 'Victuals' (pronounced 'vittles') was food and consumables. 'Sweet Fanny Adams' has generated an abbreviation that is in common use among impolite society today.

A comic book (some of the apprentices were as young as sixteen) was a 'mickey duck', and an improbable yarn, an outright lie, a film or a novel was a 'dit'. If one was on good terms with the 'chippie', the carpenter, his workshop might provide you with a 'rabbit'. Rabbits were anything obtained for free, favours, or presents brought home from some exotic port, often for your 'squarie' (girlfriend).

Sailors were organised into Divisions for administrative and disciplinary purposes. Divisional Officers were responsible for their sailors' wellbeing, discipline, reports and promotion. It was a challenging job and additional to the officer's primary duties. Divisions was also a regular parade held on the ship's quarterdeck, where all turned out in ceremonial dress, whites or 'blues', (the colour actually almost black) according to the season. Naval drill is somewhat different, the term 'attention' is not used, as the command is 'ho'. For example, 'Squad, *ho!*' The air force was known as the 'crabs', because reputedly they could be commanded to march sideways, whereas army personnel were 'pongoes'.

My joining rank in the Royal Australian Navy was 'midshipman', an ancient term. In centuries past, boys as young as eight joined Royal Navy warships as midshipmen, effectively apprenticed officers, to be inculcated in the ways of the sea and naval battle, living with their peers in the ship's gunroom, often located in the 'middle' of the ship. My rank insignia comprised black shoulder boards that carried a white square topped with a brass button. In naval folklore, young midshipmen of the days of sail would often neglect to wipe their noses, so handkerchiefs were buttoned to their uniform reefer jackets, which gave rise to the formalised insignia and the terms 'snotties' or 'reefers' for midshipmen.

A mixed bag of potential naval aviators gathered in *Cerberus'* wardroom on that first afternoon. We had been directed there from the gangway, and met by Lieutenant Jones. Jones sported gold Observer's 'wings' high on the left breast of his dark blue, almost black, winter uniform coat. He was responsible for transforming a group of civilian boys into naval officers, fit for training as aircrew. He would excel at his job, using just the right mix of formality, friendliness and support. Among my group were the long-haired and cheerful Ray from Goondiwindi in Queensland; Tony, an urbane graduate of Italian descent; and other boys from all over Australia with varying degrees of hair-length and age. There were also several older, worldly-looking lads who were obviously more comfortable with their new environment than the rest of us. They were previously enlisted sailors, who had applied for and been accepted for officer and aircrew training. Collectively we were known as Basic Aircrew Training Course Number Four of 1976 (BATC 4/76), and Lieutenant Jones very quickly apprised us of the fact that we had been engaged as naval officers first, and aircrew second.

Not all of us were prospective pilots. Half our group had been recruited as observers. Naval observers were the equivalent of the air force's navigators, sensor operators and air electronics officers, a highly specialised and demanding role. Jones ushered us to our accommodation in the gunroom, basically a dormitory. After organising scran for us in the wardroom, he advised us to get an early night.

The flicker of harsh neon lighting shattered our sleep at 0500 the following morning. So it began: a run in the chill Victorian winter darkness, dhobi (shower), breakfast then haircuts, where Ray's long blond locks fell to the floor. There was a uniform issue at 'slops' then lectures: naval ranks, the ships in the fleet and the structure of the navy's hierarchy.

From the outset, midshipmen were regarded as officers, unlike the air force's aircrew cadets, and incongruously we had to be saluted by passing ratings and petty officers in this training base. However, a drill instructor summed up the general attitude to us by saying, 'I don't mind calling you "sir", because I *know* I'm superior.' The ex-sailors on our course were charged with mentoring, leading by example and occasionally, making known our shortcomings. A young and unsophisticated eighteen, early in the course I was told in no uncertain terms that my table manners left much to be desired. Chastened, I paid particular attention to the 'knife and fork' lecture on wardroom etiquette. Wardrooms were formal and the navy excelled at silver service.

Several times a year, a wardroom would host an even more formal 'Mess Dinner'. After cocktails, the officers in black tie and mess jacket (and their ladies if it was a mixed affair) would file in, waiting for the President of the Mess to take his seat at the head of the vast table. The meal would proceed genteelly with the clink of cutlery and wine glasses, a quiet buzz of conversation, the stewards solemnly waiting on the diners, and perhaps the ship's band in one corner, playing quiet and appropriate music.

After the meal came time to 'pass the port'. A huge decanter of port wine would be slid along the table, always to the left, in accordance with tradition, ensuring that the decanter never left the surface of the table. Legend had it that in the ancient Royal Navy, naval officers loyal to Scotland's 'Bonnie Prince Charlie' would pass the decanter over their glasses of water, an unspoken tribute to the exiled prince, 'over the water'. After the game was up, the navy decreed that the port decanter was always to be in contact with the table. The tradition would also be far more practical in a rough sea.

Eventually, it was 'Mister Vice's' solemn duty to toast the Monarch: 'Mr Vice, the Loyal Toast!' Mr Vice was a junior officer, seated at the opposite end to the President, selected for the role either as a tribute to his wit, as a punishment, or both.

'Gentlemen, the Queen.'

'The Queen.'

A clink of glasses, and the toast was made, but with a difference: the navy toasted the monarch while seated, a throwback to the cramped wardrooms of the wooden ships, their deck-heads too low for officers to stand upright properly. Then followed the traditional naval toast, one for each day of the week. The port would continue on another round of the table, and then another.

From the cumulative effect of pre-dinner drinks, with the toasts and other formalities over, the atmosphere would descend into general disorder and hilarity. Through Mister Vice, an officer could accuse a friend or colleague of a real or imagined transgression, who would then have to supply a suitable excuse. If the riposte was considered lame or un-amusing he would incur a fine from the Mess President, usually in the form of further 'rounds' of premium port, the cost placed on his Mess number by a grinning steward. Bow ties had to be hand-tied; a suspected 'clip-on' could be revealed by a tug on the suspect's tie, leading to a round of port bought by the wearer if found false, but if found correct, the challenger would have to pay. Later the President would stand up, which would signal general adjournment to the wardroom's bar.

The drinking and ribaldry would increase further if the Mess Dinner was not a mixed affair. In the tradition of the military's 'work hard, play hard' way of thinking, an area would be cleared, and the Mess games would begin. One game was called *Moriarty*: two officers would be blindfolded and would lie on the floor gripping a rolled-up newspaper (preferably the Sunday edition) in one hand and the other officer's arm in the other.

'Are you there, Moriarty?' one player would call.

His opponent would reply 'Here' then attempt to manoeuvre out of the way. Then wham! Down would come the first caller's newspaper. Turns were taken until one of them gave up. In the game of *St George and the Dragon*, a ceiling fan would be turned on and the challenging officer would stand underneath it and follow its revolutions with the end of a broomstick until somebody called 'Charge!'. The player then lowered his broomstick in the manner of a jousting knight's lance and charged a target set up at the end of a line of chairs and spectators. However, the dizzying effect of following the fan blades would result in the player careering off to one side and ending up in a pile of furniture and people, to the multitude's entertainment. *Carrier landings*, a game also played by the air force, involved the lining up of several tables, lubricating their surfaces with beer, and candidates launching themselves upon it to slide to the other end. 'Night qualifications' could be attained by candlelight.

The Mess Dinner would eventually end after childish games and excessive drinking in formal uniform, an outlet for young men who worked hard for long hours. But, in strict naval tradition, it was still expected for all officers to attend Colours the next morning at 0800.

For us midshipmen, Mess Dinners lay well into the future. On the BATC, every day commenced with the flicker of the dormitory's neon lights at 0500. We immediately changed into sports gear and made the group run through the cold early dawn with masses of starlings twittering from the ancient palm trees lining the roads of the base. After dhobi and breakfast, we started the day's program of lectures, drill, physical training and more lectures. Then, an early dinner in the wardroom, ravenous, but ever so careful to follow the required etiquette. After that, study, assignment work and then sleep. The BATC was a six-week mix of physical, academic and practical training. Practical training included drill, survival at sea, rifle and pistol firing, boat work and emergency training as applicable to ships.

Drill featured but not excessively so, nor to the detriment of other subjects. The course marched to each lecture or training event. The petty officer drill instructors bawled their commands and criticisms at us with the same fervour as they did at the junior sailor trainees: 'Squad, *ho!* That was bloody woeful! No wonder we'll have the bloody Russians loose in the Indian Ocean with you lot out there to defend it … sirs.'

'You there! Midshipman! Where's your fucking cap … sir?'

Fire fighting was realistic: at the training ground, metal structures were fed with fuel to replicate violent fuel fires, to be extinguished by the trainees. A low, rectangular steel building nearby represented the interior of a warship. The multiple compartments inside were accessed by 'knee knocker' hatchways through the bulkheads, and the whole structure was pumped full of real smoke. Torches, masks and air cylinders were issued, and we were directed to enter this structure and make our way to the other end and exit. A fellow mid, his exercise complete, handed me his mask and cylinder, and into the building I went, and the door was shut behind me with a clang.

I proceeded in total blackness. Air flowed through the valve in my mask and I felt along with the back of my hand. Over a 'knee knocker' ... the next compartment ... another breath, then, the mask sucked against my face – the air had run out! No problem, there was a reserve, so I activated its switch.

Nothing.

Fighting panic, I shouted through the rubber of the mask. There was no air left. I stumbled forward, scrabbling for the exit. I heard noises behind me and, fortunately, a course-mate had heard my muffled calls. Grabbing his belt, I could only try to hold my breath while he led me through the steel maze and finally out into open air. It was a revelation of how dangerous the environment inside a ship could be under emergency or combat conditions and it was also one of the very few occasions where equipment let me down: the breathing device had not been refilled properly. It was also an important lesson in thoroughly checking survival gear.

After the final examinations and assessments, BATC was complete. However, over several days during the course, a sobering sight in the wardroom at mealtimes had been a solitary midshipman. He had failed the pilot's course at Point Cook. Marking time back in *Cerberus*, he was waiting for allocation to an alternate naval career path, most likely that of Observer or Air Traffic Controller. For young Midshipman Carr, this was the first inkling that successful completion of the pilot's course was not by any means guaranteed, and that an intense and difficult road lay ahead.

5

COURSE OF THE CENTURY

1976 – 1977

'**S**ANGaaarzz!'

The cry was taken up through the antique wooden building – the Course Orderly had brought the evening tray of sangers (sandwiches) from the Cadets' Mess. Doors banged and running feet reverberated on grey linoleum floors, vibrating the wood of the old structure. Block 46 was an ancient two-storey building at the Royal Australian Air Force's basic flying training base, Point Cook. The base sat to the west of Melbourne on Port Phillip Bay, where the air alternately carried the tang of salt and seaweed, industrial smells from Melbourne's factories, and the occasional whiff of a huge sewage farm. Skies were often grey and overcast, and produced a stiff cold breeze blowing off the bay.

My fellow midshipmen and I had just arrived at Point Cook in mid-1976 to join our air force counterparts on Number 100 Pilot's Course. Like my navy group, the air force 'Cadets Aircrew' were a mixed bunch: boys just out of school, an ex-Queensland policeman, an older fellow who described his occupation as an 'inseminator' (his previous job had been at an animal breeding research station), and a lawyer. There were also several counterparts of our ex-enlisted navy sailors, 'airmen' (as air force enlisted personnel as opposed to officers were described) and one officer, a flight lieutenant, who sported the half-wing of an Air Electronics Officer. They had been successful with applications to retrain as pilots. Phil, like me, was essentially straight out of school, but dry of wit and approachable.

Several older cadets had a good amount of flying experience with the civilian world. Some of the 'crabs' were brash and worldly, and what I would come to know as the usual jokes about the navy flew our way; there was cause for much hilarity in the showers that first night. The ex-sailors on our course had spent time at sea, and due to the hazard of scalding water and doubtful water pressure in the ships' showers, it was *de rigeur* for them to call, 'Watch your backs!' when the taps were turned on or off. It was from that a natural progression for the air force to joke about 'dropping the soap'. Many of them were just, as were we, little more than schoolboys.

In all, there were some forty of us. We were attached to Number One Flying Training School (1 FTS). The RAAF cadets had just completed their introductory officer training and, like us, were about to commence proper flight training. But there were shadowy references to names of others who were not now present, and we midshipmen learned that there had already been some dropouts, and a failure or two. The aim was to successfully complete some sixty hours of basic flying training at Point Cook. Those who made the standard would then proceed to advanced training on the Macchi jet trainer at Number Two Flying Training School (2 FTS) at RAAF Base Pearce, Western Australia.

Next morning, the air over the base was filled with two distinct sounds. A throaty roar from big, stocky Winjeel trainers, and a higher pitched snarl and buzz from other more streamlined but smaller machines – these were CT-4's. The Winjeel was singing its swansong as a tool for training military pilots. Australian-designed, powered by an American 'radial' engine, the Winjeel dated back to the late 1950s, but as we were to later find, spoken of fondly by the instructors. Its engine had nine cylinders radiating from a central crankshaft and produced 450 horsepower. It stood imposingly on tail wheel-type undercarriage, its blunt nose upthrust. A man's aeroplane! However, 100 Course was to fly the CT-4.

I caught glimpses of the CT-4s during the days of the initial ground lectures. Derived from an Australian design, these New Zealand-built machines sat on springy 'tricycle' landing gear, level on a nose wheel, which made for easy handling on the ground. I savoured the sight of a CT-4 taxiing, two white-helmeted figures under a glistening 'bubble' canopy which promised a great view of the earth and sky. A red beacon pulsed purposefully behind the cockpit. Unlike the gaudy silver and 'DayGlo orange' Winjeel, the CT-4 was mustard yellow on top with dark green lower surfaces, punctuated by the air force's 'kangaroo' roundels and large 'side numbers'. The wings were square and stubby. The engine's horizontally-opposed six cylinders, three on each side, snarled through whiskery exhaust stacks. It would be thrilling to fly one of these machines: so modern in comparison with the old Auster, with me kitted out like a fighter pilot under a white helmet and spooky opaque black visor, encased in a fire-resistant green Nomex flying suit, gloves and a yellow 'Mae West' life jacket. But, before that would be 'ground school'.

Air force cadets and by association, we naval midshipmen, were not treated with the grudging respect as trainee officers that we had been in *Cerberus*. 1 FTS students messed (ate) with several hundred Air Force Academy students, who were working towards degrees in Engineering or Science, in a huge dining hall which was at least of a modern construction, unlike our accommodation. I felt insignificant among the forty odd members of 100 Pilots' Course, the two senior courses and the masses of Academy cadets. There was, however, a Senior Naval Officer (SNO) assigned to 1 FTS who was also a working flying instructor, one or two other navy instructors, and a petty officer who attended to the administration of the midshipmen on the pilots' courses. The navy instructors mixed and matched with those of the air force in exactly the same role, and trained air force students as well as the navy midshipmen. The SNO and the other navy instructors were reasonably approachable, but I was to find out that some of their air force counterparts would not be so easy to deal with.

It was initially a matter of doing what I had done in my last year of high school: study diligently, summarise, and prepare, prepare, prepare. The routine was: awake early after a fitful sleep on an ancient, sagging sprung-wire bedstead, downstairs to the communal shower and toilet, dress, cold eggs and greasy bacon cafeteria-style in the Cadets' Mess, form up outside the accommodation block complete with bulging brief case of manuals and notes, then march off to lectures. One cadet or midshipman would be nominated as the Course Orderly ('Course Horse') for the week, responsible for punctual attendance at all lectures, and other menial responsibilities, including fetching the evening sangers from the mess. Aircraft Operations (engine and airframe construction), Airmanship (rules and regulations, air traffic control), Aerodynamics, Navigation, Flight Instruments, Radio ... each alone not a difficult subject for a motivated trainee military pilot, but the sheer volume of information was a challenge, along with the short time allocated to absorb it all and then to regurgitate it on an examination paper.

After a hurried lunch there would be afternoon lectures and possibly a physical training session or drill. We then marched back to Block 46 to study or chat with course-mates. We might have a few drinks before dinner in that vast mess with the food slopped out of tureens that we would take back to bare wooden tables topped with blue plastic table mats. After dinner would be evening study in earnest. There was always an exam to prepare for and I was now well aware of the situation: a failure would result in just one re-test and if still unsatisfactory, the candidate would be 'scrubbed' even before flying training commenced. Later, the shout of 'sangers!' would result in the noisy stampede down the wooden stairs, the sandwiches devoured in an instant. Then more study for me until lights out with the clatters, door slams and bangs in the old wooden building slowly diminishing as my course-mates turned in.

Scrubbed. One can scrub a floor, dirty clothing, or scrub a sporting match or other event due to bad weather or change of plans. Since World War II, the word has been brutally applied to the removal of a pilot from his course after failure at RAAF flying training units. Course photographs displayed in various locations of the 1 FTS administration and operational areas baldly bore crosses through the faces of those students who had been scrubbed. Some faces were just white silhouettes after liberal use of correction fluid. Failed students would be offered the choice of other military career paths, or a return to civilian life. One or two of the students on 100 Course were already starting to struggle, and the day came when a further one or two were scrubbed before they got near an aircraft. I recall despondent yet relieved faces that it was all over. It was usually the younger ones, like myself, and most would be off the base in a day or two. The training of a military pilot was expensive, and, while an individual student may have been intelligent and motivated, he had to come up to standard within the required time: the air force and navy had neither the budget nor the manpower for much remedial training. Failure of an air test would be followed by a session of remedial instruction, then one more, and only one, retest, known as a 'scrub ride'. For the ground school, my previous avid reading, aviation background, motivation and diligent study habits kept my head above water, and my academic training results were good.

Interspersed with the aviation theory was drill (air force style) and occasional weapons training. We were issued with Self Loading Rifles (SLRs), 7.62 calibre weapons that were to be kept clean, used for drill and very occasionally, live firing. These were kept in racks in our rooms and subject to inspection. My room (there were no cabins in the air force) in the old block was a wooden world. Green-painted planks lined the walls down to a blue linoleum floor laid on second-floor boards that supported a small mat, an old wooden wardrobe, a tiny wooden desk and the ancient iron bedstead. It was of course kept in military neatness, but a few photographs and cuttings of military aircraft and one or two familiar books added a homely touch. Rooms and personal kit were inspected on Tuesday evenings, the air force colloquialism being 'panic night', and in fact 'panic' was also a verb in the air force: one 'panicked' one's room before inspection by the Warrant Officer Disciplinary, or WOD. The WOD shadowed the courses like a predator, eying dress and drill standards, punctuality and discipline, ready to pounce on transgressors.

As with most high-pressure courses comprising young men, the ethos was 'work hard, play hard'. After a late afternoon trip to the canteen or private study in the classrooms, I often approached Block 46 to the increasing sounds of running water, shouts then a splash, swearing and laughter from the downstairs ablutions area, where semi-naked figures were chased by others wielding towels or metal waste paper bins full of water – it was horseplay at its finest.

One evening, when I was working upstairs in my wooden room, I heard the sounds of high-jinks downstairs that developed into a commotion. The noise brought me and others to the ground floor. There was blood and glass everywhere on the veranda outside. A naked ashen-faced cadet was being held with a reddening towel around an arm that was gashed from wrist to shoulder. While being chased he had accidentally thrust his arm through the glass door at the end of the passageway. At that moment, Schmitty, the laconic ex-lawyer, emerged from his room. He eyed the mess of water, blood and shards of glass for a moment and, referring to preparations for the forthcoming 'panic night', remarked, 'Christ, who's on verandas this week?'

Soon, actual flying training would begin. Now interspersed with the theory classes were 'Mass Briefs': lectures from the flying instructors on pure flying technique, stick and rudder, effects of controls, use of checklists and emergencies. Prior to the first Mass Brief and outfitting for flying equipment, we were marched to the Flight Operations area, directed into a classroom and told to sit. An imposing squadron leader strode in, and patches on his green flying jacket denoted that he had flown the American Phantom fighter bomber, a legendary brute of an aircraft that had up until recently been operated by the RAAF. He was one of the senior instructors, and his nickname was already known to us: 'Scrubber'.

'Stand fast!' called the course orderly, and we sprang up to attention. Scrubber motioned for us to sit. An incongruously high-pitched voice emanated from the big man: 'You'll soon be coming down to "flights", alrighty? You had better start putting the work in, get into those books. You've got to come up to standard in the required time, and if you don't, you'll be on your way out, alrighty?'

'Point Tower, Dual Three Seven, taxi one, P.O.B. two for area famil, clockwise from above,' Squadron Leader Heyfield radioed to Point Cook's control tower. He had started the CT-4's engine and remained in control of the aircraft, and I sat passively, trying to take it all in. The CT-4 did not smell of the Auster's dope, leather and oil: a more sickening aroma of plastic and fuel permeated the cockpit. Even on a winter's day it was hot under the Perspex canopy while clad in flying suit, gloves, life jacket (Mae West) stuffed with survival gear, and a helmet that seemed a size too large on my narrow head, but at least the helmet somewhat attenuated the rattle of the engine. The cockpit comprised metal panels with no soundproofing, in military grey. The pilots looked forward over a black painted nose and the view to the side was remarkable: the wings were tiny! I tried to follow the drills as Heyfield taxied, ran up the engine and carried out the before take-off checks. Then, after a brisk acceleration down the runway, for the first time I was airborne in a military aircraft.

Even this first flight was to be productive, because it was the Area Familiarisation. Several designated training areas had various boundaries, mainly roads, towns and coastlines of Port Phillip Bay, all of which, along with the altitude limits, were to be memorised. And this aircraft was no Auster. The CT-4 flew some fifty knots – or 92 km/hr – faster and Heyfield, a fighter pilot, purposefully manoeuvred it around the training areas, pointing out the boundaries and questioning me as to whether I was absorbing it all. He then started manoeuvring more violently, saying, 'We'll do a few aero's before we go back', and he commenced some aerobatics.

It is hard to describe 'g-force' (or just plain g to pilots) to someone who has not experienced it. As an aircraft moving rapidly through the atmosphere changes direction, the laws of physics dictate that it and its occupants will want to maintain their previous state of motion; that is, to continue in a straight line. As a turn steepens, or the nose of the aircraft is raised abruptly, one's apparent weight will increase, as at the bottom of a high-speed elevator ride. But, unlike the elevator, a high-performance aircraft can maintain this change of direction, and the sensation is increased and prolonged. It is as if one is lying under a leaden quilt, with the force of the direction change pressing on every cell of one's body, arms and legs. In extreme cases, 'tunnelling' of vision occurs as blood is momentarily drained from the visual centre of the brain. This is painless, and vision 'opens out' when the g is removed.

G came on as Heyfield pulled back on the control stick and pulled the nose to the sky to start a 'wing over', where he over-banked the wings to nearly vertical to the horizon. Off came the g and the nose 'fell through' in an arc downwards past the horizon, then more g came as he pulled up to regain level flight. The view of fields and houses when I looked outwards through the canopy and then filling the windscreen was unforgettable. Then we did a loop, with four g showing on the cockpit 'g meter'. I felt a momentary violent weight of four times my normal: the nose sliced up into a clear blue winter sky and I felt a floating sensation over the top of the loop with my head back while I looked for the horizon to reappear, until the nose once again pointed down vertically at fields and rows of trees. The g came on again as Heyfield pulled the nose upward towards the horizon to complete the loop. The world then spun ahead of us in a roll. Nauseated by the manoeuvring and the smells of plastic and sloshing fuel yet exhilarated, I was given control of the aircraft for a short time, its controls highly responsive. I still could not get over how stubby those little wings looked. But the noise, the smell, the brusque, no-nonsense instructor, the equipment I was wearing, the g, and the academics that had to be applied to this … adequate performance in the class room was one thing. Now, Scrubber's words: "You've got to come up to standard in the required time, and if you don't, you'll be on your way out, alrighty?" appeared ominous indeed.

Flying training began in earnest. Up at – oh – six-thirty, with breakfast, ground school, then flight – or flight, then ground school – before completing the day with evening study. It became obvious that this was a 'pressure' course. The aim was to weed out the academically weak, the airsick, the unassertive, the argumentative; that was, seemingly, almost everyone. Unlike Jack and Simon at Pilotmakers, these instructors were not teaching paying customers in a benign civilian environment. These men had all served on operational squadrons, and some had flown in the Vietnam war as helicopter, transport and bomber pilots. It became apparent – even now to a nineteen-year-old recent civilian – that many of them did not want to be at Point Cook. Some derided the comparatively dainty CT-4, calling it 'The Plastic Parrot', after having flown its predecessor that was still being used to train the senior course, the manly Winjeel with its bellowing engine of over twice the CT-4's power. The Point Cook sky would still reverberate with the Winjeels' rumble for a few months yet.

There were usually some three pilot's courses at any one time at Point Cook, and at morning briefing, all students gathered in the briefing room, where a weather report was given and operational and administrative announcements made. The quiz officer would then rise and commence questioning, and on the cadet or midshipman being called, he was required to stand, snap to attention and answer the question, which usually regarded a procedure, an aircraft limitation, or an emergency drill. An incorrect answer would be responded to by a contemptuous, 'Remain standing', and further victims were selected until the question was answered correctly. All instructors were 'Sir' on the ground and in the air. At any time a 'squawk box' in the students' crew hut could rasp, 'Spare student to Ops', requiring one of us for a menial task such as making the instructors cups of the ubiquitous powdery Service instant coffee, or running an errand.

My flying training started reasonably well. Heyfield was generally patient, but would become short with me when I muddled or forgot checklist items or procedures. I made progress with Turning, Climbing, Descending and Effects of Controls.

The instructor emphasised that each aircraft flight control does not just cover one axis of manoeuvring the machine. For example, pressing a rudder pedal induces its 'primary' effect of yawing the nose left and right in a flat plane, but it also induces banking, as each wing will move at a different air speed that has to be compensated for. There can also be 'tertiary' effects. 'Trimming' – almost never an issue when flying the slow old Auster – was essential. A change in airspeed or power results in different pressures on the flight controls, and it is essential that these are 'trimmed out' by switches, levers or wheels to reduce pilot workload and increase flying accuracy. The Point Cook instructors were red-hot on trimming from the first flight. They freely bandied about the slogan 'Trim or fail', and they were not joking. The CT-4's engine did not have a straightforward throttle that controlled RPM like the Auster. The RPM of the propeller, and, therefore, the engine, was controlled by a separate propeller lever, and the actual engine power was 'manifold pressure', set by the throttle lever. Selecting an optimum RPM for a given manifold pressure is like gears on a bicycle or car, which greatly contributes to efficiency and fuel economy. There was also a 'mixture' control. Combinations of manifold pressure and RPM for the various phases like climb, cruise or aerobatics had to be memorised along with maximum and minimum acceptable readings on the engine instruments.

The old Auster had not been fitted with a radio. One was not required when flying in the uncontrolled air space around Moorooduc: pilots 'saw and were seen'. But, at Point Cook, as the air space was controlled and densely trafficked, radio calls had to be learned and made at the correct time using the exact phraseology.

There was an introduction to military aerodrome traffic 'circuit' procedures. I was mistaken if I thought I was familiar with circuits from my Auster flying. Military circuits were flown as tight ovals. The 'crosswind' leg turned into a continuous short downwind, followed by a curving base turn to line up on final approach with the nose facing the runway to land, 500 feet, 150 metres above ground. The result was almost constant manoeuvring, configuring and trimming of the aircraft with two military circuits flown in the time that would be taken to fly one civilian 'square' pattern.

Heyfield kept on at me about spacing, height control, where to turn 'base' and of course trimming the aircraft, and under his guidance I attained a reasonable standard but increasingly came frustrating instances of inconsistency, silly mistakes and 'bad days'.

'Have you heard the rumour? The CT-4s have been grounded!'

In-service failures had contributed to a decision to stop operating the CT-4s until these problems were rectified. There would be a hiatus for several weeks. It was decided that for our edification our course group would be deployed to operational bases for exposure: the air force cadets went to the various front-line airfields, but the navy students had only one: HMAS *Albatross*.

The town of Nowra, just inland from New South Wales' south coast and south of Wollongong, is surrounded with remarkable lushness. To the east lies the green flood plain of the Shoalhaven River. Westward there are rolling hills, also verdant, dominated by conical 'Nowra Hill'. Tucked next to this hill is HMAS *Albatross*, also known as Naval Air Station (NAS) Nowra. Further west lies deceptively-flat drab green eucalypt country on ground that inexorably rises towards the Great Dividing Range, riven by occasional great gorges. With ears ringing from the bellow of two massive radial engines, the midshipmen of 100 Pilots' Course alighted from the air force's dumpy green Caribou tactical transport, for an early visit to what would become the centre of our world – should we graduate. And what a world! As we walked away from the Caribou, Skyhawk tactical jets shrieked overhead while RAN Macchi jet trainers flew circuits in their smart blue and white livery. A Grumman Tracker snarled at full power for take-off, and there was the constant *wup-wup-wup* of the Fleet Air Arm's four different types of helicopters. A miniature air force! The air hummed.

The tools used by this small air arm were potent and flexible. Australia was embroiled in the Cold War, its military geared to face the perceived threat from the Soviet Union and its client states. The Russians had no practical sea based naval aircraft, apart from a few helicopters, and the vast military-industrial complex of the United States ensured that America would project superior power at sea through the medium of mighty aircraft carriers, conventional and nuclear-powered. Having participated in the proxy cold wars that became very hot in Korea and Vietnam, Australia also knew the value of sea-based air power and, using the resources this small, young nation had, it did its best to contribute with one modest aircraft carrier: HMAS *Melbourne* and her air wing.

HMAS *Melbourne* was old, even then. Her construction began for Britain's wartime Royal Navy as HMS *Majestic* in 1943. With the end of World War II, she remained in limbo until 1955 when she was commissioned into the RAN as HMAS *Melbourne*, her angled flight deck one of the first. Until then, carrier aircraft landed directly behind the ship, parallel with its axis. However, missing the ship's arresting system or a late 'wave off' could be disastrous if aircraft, men or machinery were ranged near the bow in readiness for launching other aeroplanes or helicopters. The angled deck alleviated this problem and enabled almost simultaneous launching and recovery of naval aircraft by canting the rectangular landing area about five degrees to port (left), leaving the forward part of the ship clear for launching and ranging (parking) more aircraft. This design is still evident in the American 'super carriers' today, and *Melbourne* was among the first!

HMAS *Melbourne* was no super carrier. Her engines were entirely conventional, of the technology in use to power any British cruiser of the 1950s. Fuel oil and air were mixed in boilers, which produced steam to drive two Parsons turbines and, consequently, two propellers. This technology had changed little since the days of the *Titanic*. Designed to operate British piston-engine fighter and attack aircraft, Australia was very much stretching *Melbourne's* capabilities by operating Skyhawk jet fighters, big Tracker anti-submarine aircraft and heavy Sea King and Wessex helicopters. Although the ship was made in Britain and was operated by a navy that still followed the traditions of 'the mother country', the frontline aircraft and the way they were flown and fought were overwhelmingly American.

The Douglas A-4G Skyhawk was as tiny as an attack aircraft could be. Despite this, the little jet packed powerful capability for aerial warfare both against other aircraft, and against sea and land targets. It could carry a special fuel tank under its wing that was equipped with a reel-out hose to enable buddy refuelling of other Skyhawks in the air. That was a capability that Australia's air force did not have. All that, with the capability of going to sea, made it Australia's most potent way of projecting power. However, operating the Skyhawk jets was not *Melbourne's* main role. She was an 'anti-submarine' carrier.

The Soviet Union did not have any viable aircraft carriers, but they did have nuclear submarines aplenty. These steel sharks, along with their U.S. counterparts, prowled the oceans in two main guises: 'hunter killers' that attacked surface ships and other submarines, and huge missile carriers, 'boomers', that could mete out nuclear destruction from their missile silos. Anti-submarine warfare, ASW, was the most expensive form of warfare in the late twentieth century. The machinery involved in it tested the limits of man's ingenuity and was extremely manpower intensive. Today, submarines are almost undetectable. An air arm can spend thousands of hours trying to detect one and still fail. Nuclear war aside, in a conventional war of the twentieth century, a submarine had to get reasonably close to its target and then, somehow, acquire it and come up with a firing solution. It would, just slightly, have to expose itself. And that's where the aircraft came in.

By simply being there, at sea with the surface ships, anti-submarine and patrol aircraft made the submariner's job difficult. Limiting the opportunities for submarines to raise a periscope, charge batteries (if the submarine was conventional) or surface to launch missiles, the Trackers of the Royal Australian Navy, ready to drop a depth charge or homing torpedo, played an important role in deterring, detecting, and, if necessary, attacking hostile submarines.

The Tracker's powerful piston engines propelled a stubby airframe. Its pilots looked out through goggling windows to the side and through arched eyebrow-like windscreens ahead. Two sensor operators were crammed into spaces behind racks of electronics and instrument panels. Under the floor hung two homing torpedoes, and the wings could carry depth charges and rocket pods. A searchlight, radar and a magnetic detector helped the specialist observers in the hunt for their quarry. Like the Skyhawk, the Tracker was built to be tough and was jam-packed with equipment. It had minimal comforts for its crew. It could fly for over six hours, ranging far from the fleet, an eye in the sky for the Admiral and his staff, and a deterrent to the prowling submariner.

The Sea King helicopter was massive. Twin turbine engines powered a huge rotor atop its boat-like hull. Designed to operate closer-in to the ships that it was to protect, the Sea King carried a powerful sonar. This unit was lowered on a cable directly into the water from the hover, where it could passively listen for a submarine or, alternatively, ping sound waves off its hull. The big helicopter also had a radar and carried torpedoes.

The Skyhawks, Trackers and Sea Kings were the frontline aircraft of the Royal Australian Navy. In secondary roles were the old British Westland Wessex helicopters used for utility purposes and, most importantly, rescue operations. Wessex crews and maintainers distinguished themselves after Darwin was destroyed by Cyclone Tracy in 1974. The helicopters operated from HMAS *Melbourne* to ferry people and supplies. Dainty little Kiowa training helicopters built up pilots' skills, while the bigger Iroquois that were used in the Vietnam war provided army cooperation and support. RAN Iroquois pilots had operated in Vietnam as part of a detachment during that war alongside the Americans, to whom the Iroquois was known as the 'Huey'. There were fixed-wing support aircraft as well. One type was the Macchi MB-326 jet trainer.

Macchis were operated in numbers by Australia's navy and air force. Advanced training where we would fly the air force Macchis was, for us, the glittering prize for successfully completing our training at Point Cook. Unlike the orange and white training 'Fanta cans' of the air force, the navy's Macchis were blue and white with yellow flashes on the tail that proclaimed they belonged to VC 724 Squadron. These Macchis were used for advanced training in fighter tactics and weapons. They could carry rocket pods, practice bombs and machine guns beneath their wings.

There were other noteworthy aircraft at NAS Nowra. Belonging to VC 851 Squadron were two airliners. These were British Hawker Siddeley HS 748s, powered by two 'turboprop' engines (a turboprop is a jet engine which drives a propeller). The original civilian airliner design carried some forty passengers. Also operated by the air force for VIP carriage and navigator training, the HS 748s were used by the navy as general transports, navigation trainers and, importantly, to accustom new naval pilots to flying multi-engine aircraft, because the Tracker was considered challenging to control with one engine failed.

There was no midshipmen's gunroom in HMAS *Albatross*. Accommodated in the officers' wardroom and on our best behaviour, we rapidly unlearned the air force patois, hearkening back to our six weeks in HMAS *Cerberus*. We found that Fleet Air Arm squadrons, six in all, were smaller than their air force counterparts. Three were regarded as 'frontline', routinely embarked in Australia's only aircraft carrier, *Melbourne*, with the three second-line squadrons ashore devoted to training and fleet support. Although they carried traditional ex-British squadron numbers, the exigencies of the Cold War dictated that Australia's military be more aligned with the United States. The traditional squadron numbers were prefixed with letters that denoted the squadron's role. For example, frontline VS 816 was 'fixed wing, anti-submarine'.

At this shore base, the naval aircraft were kept clean. The front-line Trackers and Skyhawks gleamed in glossy paint and were crammed in hangars to replicate the below-deck environment of the aircraft carrier for effective training. The Trackers' 22-metre wingspan required that the wing panels, outboard of each engine, be folded overhead, Then the aircraft looked like honeybees, with the pilots' side windows reminiscent of compound eyes. The curved delta wings of the Skyhawks were tiny, and did not need to fold. The hangar lights were reflected in the grey and white gloss of the Trackers and Skyhawks. They were resplendent, in colourful squadron crests and markings. **NAVY** was printed in prominent black letters on the fuselages. Sailors ('maintainers') in grey-blue denims tended their charges under the watchful eyes of the petty officers.

Hosted by various squadrons, our group was shown around the station. We looked over the various aircraft, sat in the cockpits and listened attentively to 'old and bold' carrier pilots in the squadron crew rooms and in the wardroom bar. Many of them sported beards. The air force began as a branch of the army, so it restricts facial hair options to a neatly-trimmed moustache. Cultivating a beard is the prerogative of the navy, the 'Senior Service'. However, there is a protocol to be followed. The prospective beard grower must approach his commanding officer who then assesses the candidate for facial hair-growing potential and if considered suitable, grants Permission to Cease Shaving. Reassessed after a suitable period, if the beard is not of sufficient fullness or just wispy bum fluff, the order is to 'shave off'. 'Shave off!' was also used as a derisive, dismissive term in various circumstances.

A ride in a Sea King helicopter, the pilots almost unintelligible through the intercom because of their throat-mounted microphones, was the introduction to naval flight for most of us. Having had a taste for what was to come should we successfully complete the pilot's course, it was time to get back to work. At Point Cook, after one refresher training flight after the forced hiatus, I had to start showing that all-important trend of improvement at the required rate. And now I had a new instructor.

A tall, gingery ex-helicopter pilot with an outgoing personality, Flight Lieutenant Clough was a contrast to the stolid Squadron Leader Heyfield. I commenced training in aerobatics, forced landing practice and spinning. An aircraft can be spun deliberately, or when it is mishandled. The indications of a spin and the recovery procedure were drilled into us and often asked for at the morning quiz. A spin at low altitude can be catastrophic. Then there were the various types of circuits: after achieving a satisfactory standard with normal circuit patterns to 'Sir's' satisfaction, we started on flapless, glide and low level circuits, each with its own considerations and visual picture. Flapless circuits simulated a failure of the electrically-driven wing flaps on the CT-4, leading to challenging speed control on a flatter approach, a higher nose attitude and a faster speed for landing. Glide circuits simulated the last part of a forced landing from what was called 'low key', which, at 1,500 feet – or 460 metres high – was adjacent to the touchdown point of a runway or selected field. Low-level circuits were for bad weather or the instructor's enjoyment.

Despite the workload, the pressure, and the military discipline, there were a few opportunities for relaxation. During the seventies and eighties, Australia's military services worked hard and played hard. The vast majority of officers and men were well below the age of forty. There was a culture of letting off steam at Mess Dinners, on Friday afternoons and Saturdays. The ex-airmen on our course organised get-togethers with groups of trainee 'WAAFs', as female members of the air force were called then. It was the 'disco' era, and at various pubs and nightspots we looked incongruous in the flared trousers and colourful shirts of the day but with short, military haircuts. I had no driver's licence – much less a car – but many of my course-mates did. 100 Pilot's Course was, with one or two exceptions, slowly becoming closer-knit and more supportive of each other.

I managed to travel home to Mornington by train a few times for weekends to catch up with friends and family, but already I was being absorbed by military life. Life 'in civvies' had little interest for me. But would I pass the training? Younger than most on my course, I was immature for my age and unworldly. My performance in the aircraft was becoming more and more inconsistent. However, Clough sent me solo. Flying the CT-4 without the weight of the instructor and feeling it leap into the air was very memorable for me, even though I had soloed the Auster on a few occasions. Now I was alone in a military aircraft, with the roundel – the red kangaroo in his blue circle- painted on each wing. But, on subsequent flights as more sequences and requirements were introduced, I began to slip further.

I had always been a little tense and nervous in the air, despite the magic of it all. My immaturity, combined with Clough's outgoing and matter-of-fact manner and the workload of ground training, led to the deterioration of my performance. A forgotten checklist item, a missed radio call, incorrect speed or a wrong aircraft configuration could lead to a thump on the arm or helmet from Clough. On the downwind leg of one circuit, he began calling me names over the intercom in a calculated tirade. As I approached the base turn for final approach, my lips tightened under the boom microphone. I concentrated on flying accurately and tried to focus on the rest of the flight. It was an attempt to break me. An outburst or emotional collapse would have resulted in immediate course failure. I had been marked as too young, under-confident, and probably not suitable for further training as a military pilot. It would be up to me to prove them wrong.

Other course-mates were struggling too. As spinning and aerobatics were introduced, some were chronically airsick, and had to be contemptuously flown home by their instructors while they clutched full paper bags. Most pilots – myself included – gradually became desensitised to motion sickness, except for an unlucky few. There was an establishment at Point Cook called the School of Aviation Medicine. The chronically sick students were grounded and sent to AvMed for a desensitisation program. This involved four sessions a day in the 'Vertigon', an enclosed box that rotated on a pivot with a simulated cockpit inside. The students sat in the box, its lid was closed, and various head movements had to be carried out while the Vertigon was rotated round and round, the occupant's head moving up and down, to bring them to the point of vomiting. One or two fell by the wayside, while other determined students returned after a thoroughly unpleasant few days.

Most of us underwent 'sight board runs' at various stages of our training at Point Cook. A forgotten checklist or action, a whiff of overconfidence, a poor landing, and it was off to the sight board. One of the Point Cook runways was a sealed asphalt strip, but the rest were grass marked by white gable markers, and at the end of one of the runways was the infamous 'sight board'. Steering the CT-4 straight down the centreline of the runway was important, and the large red and white checkerboard was set up at the strip's far end as an aim point for the pilot nearly a kilometre away. A miscreant would have to run to the sight board, breeding magpies swooping, usually wearing a helmet, a parachute pack and a life jacket, very hot under all of the equipment. There could be no cheating by turning back early; he would have to sign and date his name on the board. The signature would be checked by the instructor later.

Another punishment was being ordered to get out of the aircraft immediately after landing and while the instructor taxied in, the student had to grip the aircraft's wing tip and run to keep up, for onlookers to watch and to point at. Poor drill from the course when marching to lectures once resulted in Scrubber following our squad close behind in a van while we ran 'at the double', briefcases bouncing, to lectures.

Life at Point Cook was not always grim. At one of the discos I had met a trainee WAAF with whom I spent occasional weekend afternoons. A small group of army officers had joined our course, in training as army pilots, and were mature and pleasant. Those of them who graduated from Point Cook would not proceed to the Macchi jets; they would go to their base at Oakey, Queensland, for specialist training on army aircraft. They lived in the Officers' Mess, not our ancient cadets' accommodation.

A separate course of students from Papua New Guinea (PNG) arrived. Good humoured members of the PNG Defence Force, the 'PNGs' were accommodated in a nearby block. Few could drive a motor vehicle, and they (and their flying instructors) had a hard road ahead. One of the first evenings after they arrived was Panic Night, where rooms had to be cleaned and polished for inspection by the WOD. This involved use of the 1960s vintage floor polishers that had huge single rotating bristle brushes that spun and throbbed while the operator clung to the handgrips. The PNGs had not experienced any form of floor-cleaning appliance before, and there was much hilarity and mock fear as the things came alive, with some of them jumping up onto their beds. Later, a group of PNG students purchased an old car that had been sitting up on blocks for months in the Cadets' Mess car park. The fact that none of them could drive was not a problem for them: Friday afternoon's entertainment was to sit in it while they worked through the contents of several cartons of beer. Many of these men passed their training at Point Cook and went on to successful careers in the PNG Defence Forces and later, with international airlines.

My battle with the CT-4 began to ease a little thanks to one bright spot: I was reasonably competent at 'instrument flying'. It was becoming apparent that my feel for the aircraft was not great: my circuits were average, and I was not good at aerobatics (even the basic loops and rolls). We had begun navigation training, and my calculations and map reading were often muddled. Instrument flying was somewhat of a relief, because I did not have worry about what was going on outside! Most of the other students hated flying on instruments.

Simon at Pilotmakers had stressed the importance of looking at the aircraft's 'attitude'. It was vital to focus on the picture of the horizon, the attitude, in relation to the windscreen rather than chasing the needles on the instrument panel. But the air force made an art form of 'attitude flying' using the 'selective radial scan', like the spokes of a wheel: look at the horizon, then inside to one instrument, maybe the altimeter, back outside to the horizon, in to another instrument, say the air speed indicator, back out to the horizon, and so forth. Staring at one instrument for too long, or looking inside at other instruments, would inevitably lead to the aircraft's attitude with respect to the horizon (and the surrounding airflow) changing, especially if the pilot had committed the cardinal sin of not trimming the aircraft properly. 'Attitude plus power equals performance!' This mantra joined 'trim or fail' from the instructors. 'Select the correct attitude, set the required [engine] power, and you will get the [aircraft] performance you want,' they stressed. Instrument flying merely meant replacing the sometimes-vague horizon of earth and sky ahead through the windscreen with a small artificial one in the cockpit. And this instrument had numbers on it.

A diligent studier, all I had to do was to memorise the various attitudes (expressed in degrees), the power settings and the 'by numbers' instrument flying procedures, and the CT-4 would do my bidding. No need to look outside: in fact, we had hoods placed over our helmets to restrict vision. No need to look for, avoid and report to 'Sir' any other aircraft spotted in the vicinity. No harsh manoeuvring or aerobatics. The military were insistent on good instrument flying skills, because its pilots were required to not just fly but to 'fight' their aircraft in all weather conditions, day and night, in cloud or rain. Regardless of how good a student's aerobatics or visual flying skills were, if his instrument work was not up to standard, he was finished. Most of 100 Course scraped through the rudimentary instrument flying at Point Cook: the basic manoeuvres, 'homings' and 'let downs' through 'cloud' directed by radio to overhead the fields at Point Cook and Laverton. But apart from the occasional silly procedural error,

I did reasonably well at instrument flying. Then things looked up further: I had a new instructor.

'Hawkeye', another air force flight lieutenant, was as urbane as a Point Cook instructor could be, and less aggressive about mistakes. I had scraped through the early progress tests in circuits, aerobatics and practice forced landings, and did reasonably well in the flight devoted to assessing the candidate's instrument flying. A junior course, Number 101, had arrived at Point Cook, and those who remained of the senior course, 99, were about to move on to the coveted jets at Pearce. There were more solo consolidation flights, the manoeuvres and requirements strictly laid out and monitored by a Duty Instructor in the control tower, and I experienced the joy of solo circuits, navigation and aerobatics. But I was still having good days and bad days. The academic workload eased gradually as the exams were cleared, and the syllabus flights were counted down until the final one: the Basic Handling Test, or BHT. Pass this, and it was off to the golden west where the Macchi jets waited for us: advanced aerobatics and instrument flying, low level navigation, even formation flying!

An instructor known as Rocky was held in awe at Point Cook. A balding, shortish squadron leader with a round red face, he was older than most, possibly in his final years as an active air force officer. But he was an outstanding aerobatic pilot. Loops and rolls and so forth, by their nature require lots of vertical airspace. The general rule was that aerobatics had to be performed not below a height of 4,000 feet, or 1,200 metres above the ground. This allowed for errors such as 'falling out' of a manoeuvre or flicking into an unintentional spin. Exceptionally qualified and talented pilots are approved to do aerobatics closer to the ground, at 'low level', which leaves little room for error. Since man first flew, many pilots have been killed while performing low-level aerobatics. Rocky was qualified for, and very good at, low-level aerobatics in the CT-4 and Winjeel. Furthermore, he was not put off by 'negative g'. Negative g is the force of hanging upside-down on trapeze rings or in the seat belts of an inverted aircraft. Unlike the crushing weight of 'positive' g, negative g forces blood to one's brain. Your eyeballs feel as if they are about to pop. As negative g builds up through manoeuvring it becomes painful, it starts to feel like your head is bursting and your vision starts to 'red out'. Through a painful red haze, the pilot eases off the negative g that he feels after the aircraft's nose has been pushed rather than pulled, generally with relief, and even a large amount of subsequent 'positive' g can be a welcome change.

Rocky's low-level aerobatic displays on most Friday afternoons were eagerly anticipated. Usually in a Winjeel, he would dive at high speed toward the tarmac then pull up into a huge loop, a barrel roll, and then vertically upwards, the aircraft gyrating until it would flop back down, its centre of gravity taking over to pivot the engine to point towards the earth. Then down into a half loop but holding the machine inverted, another half-roll and skywards again. The silver and orange Winjeel would flash past in another low pass with an immediate half roll. Inverted but pointing towards the sky, Rocky would be hanging in his straps, then a rapid push up to half an outside loop, several negative g's forcing the blood to his upper body. Some of us would involuntarily groan in vicarious discomfort. More manoeuvres, then a final inverted pass. Hanging in his harness, he would kick the rudder pedals, yawing the upside-down Winjeel from side-to-side as if to wave goodbye, while working the control column to keep the wings level. Legend had it that the ground crews often found fluid leaking from the Winjeel's battery due to Rocky's unnatural and violent manoeuvres. Soon, he would land and in military aviation tradition, head straight to the officers' mess bar. And every Friday afternoon, students were invited – in fact, expected – to attend the same.

Pilots learned much of their trade through the camaraderie of sharing alcohol. Tongues loosened by the cheap beer, with the usually free weekend of a training base in the offing, some of the instructors would show a slightly more human aspect. Many of these men had seen active service in Vietnam, and the occasional story or anecdote would have their students hanging on to every word. Flying wisdom and even the occasional hint or tip would be imparted. The students would begin to get a vision of an operational squadron and possibly what type of aircraft they would like to fly operationally … if they passed the course. The navy instructors talked of carrier landings and engaged in friendly banter with their air force counterparts. No. 100 was now the senior course at 1 FTS. Most of us were almost salivating at the prospect of flying the Macchi, with the erroneous notion that passing Point Cook would be the biggest hurdle. Once we got to 2 FTS, it would all be easy! I was still a very low-average student, but I was saved by my instrument flying ability. Hawkeye had put me up for the final assessment: the Basic Handling Test. This had to be successfully completed in order to go on to Pearce. And the instructor who would test me on the final scheduled flying day of the course at Point Cook would be Rocky.

'Taking over,' called Rocky through the intercom.

It was the Basic Handling Test, and the CT-4 had been pointing earthwards in one of the training areas, accelerating downwards after a vicious flip backwards after hanging in the sky. I had been demonstrating my ability to recover from an 'Unusual Attitude' (UA), another vital aspect of military flight training. A UA can develop through disorientation, error or a botched aerobatic manoeuvre. This can occur when the nose is pointing skywards with no airspeed to give control or, conversely, by accelerating earthwards in a spiral dive or in a spin. High above the earth, Rocky had set me up in the standard manner, taking control, making sure my eyes were closed. His call 'recover now' was the prompt to open my eyes, take control of the aircraft, and return it to normal flight. Nose-high, with nothing but blue in the windscreen and the aircraft slowing against gravity's pull, I had closed the engine's throttle, centralised the flight controls and firmly held them as the aircraft fell backwards, the reversal of air over its elevators and rudder at the tail producing unnatural forces on the stick and pedals. I knew that the CT-4's natural stability would prevail, and accordingly its nose flopped down, speed built up over its wings, and again I was in control, easing out of the dive.

'Taking over,' Rocky called.

In his opinion, I had applied the wrong recovery technique. He had expected me to increase the engine to full power and *push* the nose back down to the horizon, and he then proceeded to demonstrate what I should have done.

'Handing over! Take me to Laverton for some circuits!' he said.

'Yes, sir,' I replied.

Dutifully, I flew towards the satellite base of RAAF Laverton, with its crossed, sealed runways. Trying to focus on the remainder of the test, I set up for a standard 'rejoin' of Laverton's traffic circuit, recited the appropriate checklist, radioed my intentions to Laverton Tower, and then concentrated on the required joining procedure.

'Practice!' Rocky called.

Rocky's hand went to the engine's throttle lever, simulating an engine failure. This was nothing new: it was almost expected, especially on this test. Practice Force Landings, PFLs, had been drilled into us from before 'solo'. The instructors would, without warning, simulate an engine failure by throttling back the engine and call 'Practice!' over the intercom. The student was then expected to enter a gentle glide to earth, carry out the memorised troubleshooting and safety checks, select a landing area (a field, or an airstrip if close), and exercise his judgement to place the aircraft in a position from which it could land without engine power. Approaching the landing field, the instructor would command 'Go round' and with the engine power restored, the aircraft would be climbed away. If near a runway, the student would successfully complete the last stage of the 'glide' type of circuit and land the aircraft.

Laverton's runway was not too far away, and I manoeuvred the little trainer towards an actual landing. Although I was a bit low, the aircraft passed over trees by the road that lay before the runway's threshold. They were close, but a safe touchdown eventuated. I applied power for the usual rolling 'touch and go' procedure, lifted the aircraft back into the sky and waited for Rocky's next instruction.

'Taking over,' he shouted. He wrenched the aircraft around in a tight turn. 'I'm going to show you just how low over those bloody trees you were!'

He flew a low circuit, clearing the trees as I had done. Then, without a word, he pulled the aircraft around, hard, into another turn and flew it low and at high speed back to Point Cook. We roared low along the flight line, and then we fanned up into a climbing turn to join the circuit and land. Through all this, with the g periodically tugging at my body, I stared ahead, dejected.

Time had been of the essence because of the delays to our course's training after the grounding of the CT-4s. Procedures for posting out of Point Cook for Western Australia had to be completed before the entire base shut down for Christmas. Even at 1 FTS, failure of the final flight test was relatively rare. This same day there was just enough time for one remedial flight, of which I remember little. Another flying instructor went over my weakest areas and I plodded through the exercises, aerobatics, circuits and another PFL. UA recoveries would have been practiced again to ensure that I would apply the correct technique. After landing, I found that I was to be given my one chance: a 'scrub ride' with Flight Lieutenant Edwards. It was to be on the following day, Friday, the last flying day of the working week at this training base before the Christmas stand-down commenced.

After my remedial flight that afternoon, there was an end-of-course bar session with the instructors, and I dutifully showed up. All my course-mates had completed their BHTs and were in various degrees of elation and relief, now focused on the final administrative procedures involved with clearing Point Cook and taking leave over Christmas before starting advanced training on the Macchi in Western Australia. I was *still* not through, and this time inconsistent performance had reared its head on a test. Rocky approached me in the bar, a little softer in demeanour. He would have spoken to the instructor who had carried out my remedial flight. Almost apologetically, Rocky again ran through the points that he hadn't liked, which was almost too much for me. I fought tears of frustration and self-pity as he spoke, and, at least believing my own words, could barely blurt out, 'Thank you, sir, I'll do my best tomorrow,' and I retreated to the block.

The following day dawned gorgeous: a deep, cloudless blue sky, the air cool for December and not a breath of wind, which was unusual for the area. Port Phillip Bay glinted beyond Point Cook's runways. The flight line was quiet except for one other CT-4 starting up. In grim determination after a fitful sleep and desultory breakfast, I changed into my flying clothing and presented at Edwards' briefing cubicle. Soon we were airborne, the flight lieutenant in the CT-4's right seat.

After some general handling, Edwards said, 'All right, Mark, show me your aero's.'

In preparation, I cleared the area, diligently looking for other aircraft, and there was that other CT-4, also airborne, less than a kilometre to our left, its wings flashing yellow as it manoeuvred. I was rattled. Should I start aerobatics with that aircraft in sight? Was he too close? I waffled on with more 'clearing turns' and wingovers until Edwards, in frustration called, 'Come on, get on with it.' After the conclusion of some very average aerobatics, I took us back for some circuit work, flying the various types of pattern. Now we were climbing out after a touch and go on the grass runway.

'OK, just fly one more "normal" and make it a "full stop",' Edwards directed.

I didn't know what to think. No gross mistakes, but an uninspiring flight. Edwards hadn't said much. Was that it? I supposed I would go for Observer training, or maybe Air Traffic Control. Maybe Seaman Officer – I liked ships. How would I tell my parents after throwing up Medicine for this? What would I tell my prospective girlfriend?

It was now time to complete the crosswind turn for that last circuit. Edwards called, 'Practice!' and cut the power, simulating an engine failure at a very awkward point that was past the far end of the runway. What would I do? There was no wind. My brain worked seemingly on a separate channel as I recited the simulated emergency checks. Nil wind! With no wind, it would not matter which way I landed the aircraft. If I could manoeuvre it to any runway, not just the 'duty' runway designated for operations by the control tower, I *could* land.

'If I turn now, I'm in a position to land on the other runway, sir,' I said.

This would give me the full length of the longer runway to use – if I could pull it off successfully. Edwards just sat there, blank under his black helmet visor. I spiralled down tightly, careful not to let the speed decrease in the simulated glide. With no wind, and the only other aircraft flying on this exceptionally quiet Friday morning still out in the training area, the airfield was mine. With those circumstances, application of training and by blind luck, I flew a safe approach and the wheels kissed the asphalt.

My successful practice forced landing had salvaged the 'scrub ride'. Of the entire flight, it was the only exercise that had impressed Edwards. After his debrief, there was an interview with Scrubber. My ground school results, fortunately, were solid and I showed promise with the all-important instrument flying. But, Scrubber told me, 'You had better get comfortable in the air, it's not that strange an environment, alrighty? You need to show some confidence and ability.' To him, I was immature and not military pilot material. But, against his better judgement, he had advised the Senior Naval Officer that I was suitable for further training.

Nearly half of my course-mates had already been failed on this brutal course. However, notwithstanding reservations from the navy and the air force about my ability and just three months into my nineteenth year, I was off to the jets with the other boys.

6

THE BLACK SWAN

1977

We couldn't help ourselves. Although we had only just arrived at RAAF Pearce, with our gear still unpacked we strode straight down to the flight line of Number 2 Flying Training School, known as 2 FTS, in the northern outskirts of Perth. On this training base weekend, the Macchi jets sat quiet under massive white open-sided 'car ports' that fended off the Western Australian sun. The jets' undersides were silver and the topsides of the wings, tails and fuselages were painted in panels of alternating white and orange. Prominent 'tip tanks' full of fuel were bolted to the wingtips, orange outside but the sides facing the pilots dull black, as were the tops of the noses ahead of the curved windscreens. The rounded noses were tipped with small panels of shining polished metal, with a little round ventilation hole at the very front. Emblazoned on each tail fin, behind vertical stripes of the standard RAAF red, white and blue 'cockade', was the badge of 2 FTS, a large white circle with a grey torch aflame, superimposed over that unmistakable symbol of the city of Perth: the black swan.

During the early sixties I had gazed out from the front windows of our house towards Willan's Hill and the glowing west at sunset:

it always seemed to hold promise of an exciting future. Now it was January 1977, and I was in that golden west. If I could just apply myself and not foul it up … I shared a car from Melbourne with course-mates. I was still not licenced to drive, but the other boys were happy to let me have a go at times, not that there was much steering to do on the interminable straight stretches of road that ran tangential to the abrupt limestone cliffs of the Great Australian Bight. Near the long journey's end, our car coasted down the hills east of Perth toward the city, clean and shimmering in heat haze, with the sparkling Indian Ocean beyond. Then we turned north to Pearce, which sat on flat terrain to the west of the line of hills. We were in a new world after grey Victoria: tawny brown grass, small eucalypts and sandy soil. We passed low scrub and dull green pine plantations with the hills always prominent to the east. The land baked in dry heat. We came to the village of Bullsbrook which sat outside Pearce's main gate on the Great Northern Highway. It included some ancient wooden air force houses, a few of which were still being used as married quarters for base personnel.

The students' accommodation comprised relatively modern brick buildings of three storeys, constructed during the Vietnam War to fulfil the requirement for large numbers of air force and navy pilots. Now half lay empty with the Cold War still rumbling on but Vietnam's 'hot' war over. A modern brick mess building catered for the students of, as at Point Cook, the three pilots' courses that were resident.

The Western Australian base was dedicated to just one task: the advanced training of air force and navy pilots; namely, to transform them from cadets and midshipmen who could just barely operate a basic training aircraft, to budding operational military jet aviators proficient in advanced aerobatics, high- and low-altitude navigation, advanced instrument flying, and formation flight. Students graduating from 2 FTS were considered suitable to transition to fighters, bombers, transports and helicopters. The instructors were still 'Sir' in the air, on the ground and in the bar, but there was some inkling that they would deal with us on more equal terms, and that there seemed a reasonable chance that many of us here would make the grade. Most instructors were content to be at Pearce: it was a stable posting with little time away that enabled them to bring up young families in generally good accommodation in a clean, warm city. Many enjoyed hurtling around in jet trainers with students who had survived the weeding out process at 1 FTS. Night flying was only one or two nights a week, and most weekends were free.

Macchi pilots sat in tandem on ejection seats under a long, boat-shaped canopy. The canopy was hinged at one side like a coffin lid. Except for instrument training flights the instructor sat in the rear, and his words over the intercom were the prime method of instruction; there could be no thumping the student on the arm or helmet here! The cockpit was air-conditioned, however the Macchi was of an Italian design, built for European conditions, and we would find that at low altitudes, the system was next to useless in the hot Western Australian skies.

Behind the cockpits was a fuel tank and behind that, the Rolls Royce Viper jet engine. The Viper sucked air through a small intake in the root of each wing, and compressed it into combustion chambers where it was mixed with fuel and ignited. The hot expanding gas then blasted out through a turbine and out a long jet pipe that comprised the interior of the rear fuselage. The turbine drove a shaft, which in turn powered the compressor, electrical generator and fuel, hydraulic and oil pumps.

An orange 'spine' on top of the white upper fuselage gracefully faired-in the canopy and ran down the fuselage's length before curving up to join with the vertical tail fin. Raked tailplanes with square rear corners and sharp trailing edges sat at the base of the fin, with the jet's exhaust below.

The Macchi's wings were slab-like, their leading edges very

slightly swept back, but the 'trailing edges' were straight, at right angles to the fuselage. The Macchi was not supersonic, but in a high-speed dive it could approach eighty percent of the speed of sound, where some 'local' airflows over parts of the aircraft would become supersonic, causing changes in handling and some vibration. Special flights in the training syllabus would be dedicated to exploring this regime. Those large wing-tip tanks, like elongated teardrops, provided extra fuel for the ravenous little jet engine. For us, the landing gear on the Macchi was special, because it was retractable; the consequences of forgetting this fact before landing was never far from most students' thoughts.

There would be comprehensive ground training before we would be allowed to fly a Macchi, but the classrooms were modern and airy, reflecting the fresh feel of the base. The syllabus included the expected aircraft operation, jet engine theory, aerodynamics, air traffic control procedures, but there were extra dimensions: high-speed flight, the effects of high altitude on the human body and importantly, the understanding and use of the Macchi's ejection seat.

We had worn parachutes in the CT-4. They were lugged out to the aircraft and strapped onto our backs prior to clambering into the cockpit. The aircraft's canopy could be jettisoned should the machine become out of control or unable to be force-landed, and then a pilot would heave himself out of the cockpit and dive over the trailing edge of the wing, to manually pull the parachute's ripcord and float to earth. However, in a jet, which could be conceivably doing 360 knots – or 660 km/hr – at over ten kilometres above the earth, bailing out in the air blast in a similar fashion would be a risky proposition. Force-landing even a small jet like the Macchi into a field would be almost suicidal; its approach speed and momentum would rip it apart on impact. A Macchi's crew needed a safe and rapid means of escape from an aircraft that was, unless near an airfield, not capable of being force-landed safely. Especially at low altitudes, a fire or sudden control problem could be catastrophic and, likewise, a manual bail out would not be an option. At high altitude windblast, cold and the sudden lack of oxygen could render a pilot unconscious before he got to pull any ripcord. In any case, the high-speed airflow could tear his opening parachute to shreds. Therefore, the Macchi was fitted with the Martin Baker Mark 4 ejection seat.

The ejection seat can be likened to both an aircraft in its own right, and a loaded gun. Today most seats are rocket-propelled, however, this relic from the sixties used explosive charges to blast the seat up 'rails' and out into the airstream. A metal pan formed the base of the seat, which contained an inflatable dinghy and small survival pack beneath a thin, hard cushion, and this was what the pilot sat on. It had to be hard, because under the vertical acceleration of an ejection, any soft cushion could increase the potential for spinal injuries. A 'gun' attached to the seat structure fired it and its occupant upwards to clear the aircraft's tail surfaces, which at high speed, could slice a pilot in half if he hit them.

The pilot's back rested against another hard cushion behind which, level with his upper torso and head, was an inverted horseshoe-shaped brown canvas package crossed with a vee of white straps. This contained the main parachute. Two separate shoulder harnesses, straps of brown and blue, emerged from the centre of the horseshoe: one set for the seat, and the other to hold the parachute to his back. Another set of double harnesses formed the 'lap straps', of the seat and leg straps which looped around his upper thighs to support him under an opened parachute. A heavy round knob was the central point to which the complicated harness assembly was attached. Turning and giving it a sharp slap with the palm of the hand enabled the pilot to detach himself from aircraft harness and parachute.

Ejections, we found in the lectures, were basically of two kinds: the 'pre-meditated' ejection occurred in relatively slow time, perhaps after an engine failure at high altitude, the aircraft gliding, plenty of time to gather ones thoughts, adopt the correct posture (back erect against the rear cushion, head and legs back, elbows in) and to operate the 'face blind' handles. These handles, actually two yellow and black striped rubber loops, protruded forward from the top of the seat over the pilot's helmet. After pulling a prominent T-shaped handle on the instrument panel to jettison the canopy, a vigorous tug downwards with both hands on the loops pulled an attached canvas 'face blind' over the pilot's helmet and face, forcing his head back into the correct posture and providing a modicum of protection from the windblast to come. The last part of the movement would fire the explosives in the gun, propelling the seat up the rails and out of the aircraft.

However, loss of control, fire or engine failure at low altitude was another matter. With only a second or two to react in an 'un-premeditated' ejection, the pilot needed a quicker means to fire the seat: this was done with the 'seat pan' handle that could be pulled in a split second. This was a metal stirrup, again black- and yellow-striped, accessible in a hollow between the pilot's thigh supports, not far from his hand that would still be gripping the Macchi's control column. When used, there would be no protective face blind or optimum posture, but he would be almost instantly clear of an out-of-control aircraft, probably injured but at least alive. And the canopy? Two 'canopy breakers' protruded up like ears at the top of the seat. These would splinter the canopy and save valuable seconds in not having to blow it off beforehand; the pilot would just blast up through shattered Plexiglas, his helmet, its lowered face visor and his oxygen mask protecting him.

As the activated seat moved up the rails, straps called 'bowyangs', that were clipped around the pilot's calves when strapping in to the Macchi, tightened and pulled his lower legs back against the base of the seat. These kept his kneecaps clear of the metal rim of the windscreen. They also stopped the pilot's legs flailing in the blast of air.

Now the pilot, still strapped to his ejection seat, was out of the aircraft. What now? We learned that as the seat was fired up the rails, mechanical linkages on various devices 'armed' them to do their work. First, slowing and stabilising the seat was vital; too fast and the parachute would tear to shreds as it opened, the pilot plummeting to his death. Also, spinning and tumbling end over end could injure the pilot or foul the parachute. So a small 'drogue gun' would fire, extracting a little 'drogue' parachute to slow and stabilise the seat, readying it for the automatic deployment of the main 'chute'. With the pilot torn from the aircraft's oxygen system, a small bottle attached to the seat forced oxygen at high pressure into his mask. At high altitude, opening the main parachute could be catastrophic; the higher speed of fall in the thin air could shred it, or if it did open, the pilot could freeze to death, swinging under a slowly descending parachute kilometres above the earth, the temperature as low as minus sixty degrees Celsius. So from high altitude, the pilot still in his seat, stabilised by the drogue, would fall to a reasonable and comfortable level for opening of the main parachute, around 10,000 feet – about 3,000 metres – above sea level. To achieve this, a 'barostat' device caused the small drogue parachute to yank the main 'chute out from its pack.

After suffering an aircraft emergency and the violence of an ejection, the wind blast and the fall, the pilot then had to withstand the reverse shock of the parachute opening. Correctly fastening those thigh loops (clear of the 'family jewels') when strapping into the Macchi was desirable! The seat would drop away from under the pilot. who then be swinging beneath the parachute, shocked and sore, but marvelling at being alive and that all this had happened automatically, courtesy of a purely mechanical device, intricate and meticulously designed and maintained, no electronic or manual input required, most of its operation completed in the blink of an eye. As a child, I had read the story of the invention of the ejection seat. The inventors had used Meccano to work out some of the mechanics of the device!

The Martin Baker seat was rarely known to malfunction; however in the unlikely event of the parachute not opening automatically the pilot could pull up on the 'guillotine', another yellow and black metal handle under his left arm, to release the seat straps then he could push away the seat. Tumbling through the sky, he would pull a D-ring (rip cord) handle to deploy the main 'chute'. The seat's emergency oxygen supply could also be activated manually, even while still in the aircraft should its main supply fail, by pulling a small green knob.

Over water, the pilot released the dinghy and survival pack, now loosely dangling in the straps under his bottom, which fell to the end of a lanyard, its impact with the surface a useful cue for the pilot himself to get ready to plunge in himself and immediately release his parachute to avoid entanglement and drowning. He could then inflate his Mae West life jacket, pull in and inflate his little dinghy, and activate an emergency survival radio, fitted in a pocket of his life jacket. The survival pack contained water, flares, signalling mirror and a dye marker. All this equipment in one seat! And so many explosives to fire the seat itself and actuate its peripheral devices!

Because of these explosives, the ejection seat was always treated with the utmost respect. Seven safety pins with little red labelled discs were fitted to the various devices on the seat when unoccupied. These prevented the 'sears' from being pulled from the miniature guns and firing them, which would be catastrophic during maintenance, pre-flight inspection, strap-in or taxi, after an accidental snagging or movement of a handle or cable. I tried to think of the ejection seat as a small but dangerous 'aircraft' in its own right, with its own documentation, procedures, maintenance regime and specially qualified personnel to tend it. The cartridges had 'bang by' dates, after which they had to be changed … parachutes had to be periodically inspected and repacked …

Strapping into a Macchi was a lengthy and exacting business, and especially difficult alone; so airmen, 'strappers', were delegated to assist the pilot to strap in and then hand him four of the safety pins that were difficult for him to reach. The pilot placed these pins in a little rack on the Macchi's side panel, each in its own hole. The other pins, those which locked the face blind, seat pan and guillotine handles, were left to the pilot to remove and place in the rack just prior to take off, the total of seven checked and now the seat ready to function. Conversely, after landing, one of the pilot's first actions was to 'safety' the seat by inserting the three critical pins into the handles; the others would be fitted to their respective points on the seat by the ground crew.

Modern rocket-powered ejection seats are extremely capable. They can extract the pilot from his cockpit and propel him up to a safe height for parachute deployment, even with the aircraft on the ground and stationary. However, the sixties-vintage Martin Baker Mark 4 was a 'zero-ninety' seat. This meant that the lower limit of its 'envelope' for safe operation was ground level (and vitally, not descending, if near the ground), and the aircraft would have to be doing at least ninety knots – or 167 km/hr – in order for the seat to work properly and the parachute to open in time. If the Macchi was descending (having a 'downward vector') near the ground, the chances of a successful ejection would be significantly reduced. So apart from learning the seat's mechanics and procedures, knowing its limitations was vital, as were the procedures for setting the aircraft up for a successful ejection, landing in the parachute on ground, in trees or in water, and then survival and location. All this was taught and examined on, as was the myriad of other subjects associated with advanced jet training.

As at 1 FTS and still somewhat of a loner, I studied diligently and passed the initial exams. Soon the time came for the fitting of 'safety equipment', which comprised a helmet, oxygen mask, Mae West and that trademark of the military jet pilot, the 'anti-g' suit. The oxygen mask was a vital life support device. The little CT-4, as with most light piston engined aircraft, was never operated above 10,000 feet – or 3,000 metres – which is the maximum height at which pilots can safely function without masks in the increasingly thinning air of altitude. However, the Macchi was capable of operating well over 30,000', nine kilometres above the earth. Its cockpit was pressurised by air from the engine's compressor, inflated like a metal tank, in routine operations to equal the environment on an 8,000', a 2,400 metre-high mountain. However, any malfunction of the pressurisation system, loss of the canopy, damage to the aircraft, an ejection, or smoke or fumes in the cockpit made it vital that the pilots had a clean and plentiful supply of oxygen. The gas was delivered from tanks in the aircraft through hoses to their rubber masks, tightly clipped to their faces. The masks incorporated microphones that enabled the pilots to communicate with each other over the Macchi's intercom, and with air traffic control and other aircraft over the radio.

We had been given a good grounding in the effects of low oxygen and low pressure on the human body at Point Cook. Not only was Point Cook's School of Aviation Medicine the custodian of the infamous Vertigon, the bane of those of us who were persistently airsick, it also housed a decompression chamber.

At Point Cook, a 'chamber run' had been included in the aviation medicine syllabus that was part of the pilot's course. We sat on bench seats along each side of the interior of a heavy metal cylinder, which was padded on the inside. Its thick walls, were pierced by a few small round windows of thick glass, through which an occasional face would peer in from the room outside. A heavy door had been slammed closed at the end and secured by multiple latches. Each of us wore our flight suits with our ubiquitous shiny green Nomex jackets, and a cloth 'Snoopy' style helmet with an attached oxygen mask, which fed us pure oxygen. We communicated with microphones in the mask and headphones in the Snoopy hats connected to an intercom system. We had already spent half an hour breathing this pure oxygen to purge our bloodstreams of nitrogen, which in a sudden low-pressure environment, could bubble in our joints and cause the painful symptoms of what divers call 'the bends'. An RAAF doctor was inside the chamber with us. He sat at a control panel, also wearing the same equipment.

The decompression chamber created the same environment for its occupants as at high altitude. Our atmosphere thins as one climbs up, which creates several problems, including lack of oxygen, lack of air pressure, and cold temperatures that would freeze a human. The chamber replicated high altitudes by having the air sucked out of it by pumps. Controlling these pumps and various valves could 'climb' and 'descend' the chamber at various rates as required by the doctors and technicians for research, testing and training.

'Right, the first thing we will do is a decompression.' The doctor's voice came through my helmet. 'You will feel an outrush of pressure, there will be mist and it will suddenly get cold. Ensure your masks are correctly fitted. Three, two, one ...'

Whooosh! Air rushed out of the chamber, as it would from a pressurised aircraft after a malfunction or breach of the pressure cabin. My ears popped and air rushed out of my lungs, which was a strange feeling. At the same instant, white mist filled the chamber as moisture in the air condensed with the sudden pressure drop. The mist dissipated, and then we were breathing oxygen, the regulators on the hoses feeding it to our masks at the correct pressure. The doctor's commentary through our headphones was punctuated by an alternate wheeze and suck of the valves in his mask as he breathed, all picked up by the mask's microphone. This was to become a constant sound in our ears from the instructors in the Macchi and would eventually be filtered out by our brains while we flew.

'Now, we will gradually climb to high altitude,' the doctor said. 'Remember what I told you about pressure breathing technique. If you have to let out a good fart, don't worry about your mates, they'll be doing the same thing.'

It is one thing for a human to have pure oxygen available at high altitudes. However, above some thirty thousand feet, nine thousand metres up, the extremely low pressure causes a further problem:

there is just not enough pressure to force even pure oxygen through the walls of our lungs' alveoli, the multiple tiny air sacs that allow oxygen to transfer to our bloodstream. So, above these altitudes we have to 'pressure-breathe'. While the chamber was 'climbed', the regulators automatically forced oxygen into our masks at higher and higher pressure, to force the vital gas into our lungs and thence to our bloodstreams. At the same time, air trapped in our bodies' cavities started to expand. Uncomfortably, our guts became bloated; abdomens bulged noticeably. The air pressure in my mask increased and breathing out became an effort. Just relaxing my diaphragm forced pressurised oxygen to forcibly inflate my lungs and opposite to the normal breathing reflex, an effort had to be made to *exhale*. It became hard work as the chamber climbed and climbed. Hold … a burst of oxygen in … two, three, force the air out … two three … hold … and so it went on for a few minutes at the equivalent of thirty eight thousand feet, eleven and a half kilometres above the earth. It took almost all of my concentration just to breathe (and live). Talking was difficult, and after a few gasped comments by the doctor, the chamber was brought down to twenty five thousand feet, about eight kilometres, which was far more comfortable. In fact, some climbers in the Himalaya, after careful acclimatisation, can survive without oxygen at this altitude. However, an un-acclimatised young trainee pilot was about to learn a lesson.

'OK, remember the symptoms of hypoxia, which means low blood oxygen levels. You will, in turn, take off your mask and, as briefed, start counting aloud up in multiples of threes until you feel that you are hypoxic, then put your mask on.'

One by one, we did as ordered. Some of us were occasionally smirking or laughing outright into our masks when the victim showed the symptoms. One lad got stuck on one number: 'twenty-four … twenty-four … twenty-four …' The symptoms of hypoxia are insidious and dramatic. All panted in the thin air, many developed a bluish tinge in their lips and fingernails, some started giggling or slurring their speech, but they would eventually clip their masks back in place. All they needed was a few breaths of oxygen and they were back to their normal selves. Some realised themselves that they were hypoxic, others were told by the doctor to put the mask back on. Then it was my turn. I was 'Number Eight'.

'Eighteen, twenty-one, twenty-four …' I counted, gasping a little from the thin air. But this didn't seem too hard! I kept counting up – I was doing well.

But then I heard the doctor interrupt, 'Number Eight, put your mask on.'

No problem. With my oxygen mask on, the exercise was over.

'So, Number Eight, what do you think? What were your hypoxia symptoms?'

'I was gasping a little, but otherwise no problem, Sir. I counted OK and then put my mask on.'

'It wasn't you who put your mask on,' the doctor said. 'You lost consciousness and I did it for you.'

I had not responded to the first call to put my mask on. The doctor gruffly told me that there were several commands, and that I had started to slump over on the bench seat of the chamber, the doctor clasping the mask to my face. I remember nothing of it to this day. Hypoxia is an insidious killer. There have been instances of military and civilian 'ghost aircraft' winging along on automatic pilot, the occupants unconscious or dead at the controls, with the aircraft doomed to run out of fuel or begin a pre-programmed descent to crash.

A notorious and distressing accident of hypoxia involved a Helios Airlines Boeing with 121 people on board in 2005. A combination of mechanical failure and crew error led to the airliner depressurising slowly after it left Cyprus for Athens, its captain and first officer unconscious or dead. As I had done, they failed to recognise the symptoms of hypoxia. Greek Air Force jets intercepted and flew formation on the Boeing. Helpless, the fighter pilots could see a flight steward moving about in the airliner's flight deck, alternatively attempting to revive his pilots and to control the aircraft. But the Boeing followed its pre-programmed course to Athens airport and then entered a preset holding pattern. It wandered zombie-like for a while until it ran out of fuel and spiralled down to impact a hillside. There were no survivors.

The 'Anti-g suit', normally referred to as just the 'g-suit', is an important piece of equipment to a military jet pilot. Propeller-driven aircraft like the CT-4 do not have sufficient performance to 'sustain' g; it eases off rapidly when the aircraft slows, unable to overcome the increased aerodynamic drag that g causes. However, military jets can 'pull' more g and pull it for longer. The Macchi could pull 4 g in tight manoeuvres and sustain it for minutes. It could produce a crushing 6 g for short periods. Prolonged g drains the blood away from the brain and eyes. Initially, this causes tunnel vision and breathing becomes difficult. For a while, the pilot can still hear and work his muscles, but as g increases in amount or time, complete G-induced Loss Of Consciousness (G-LOC) occurs. This is normally self-restoring because, provided that the aircraft is at sufficiently high altitude, the pilot's hand applying back-pressure on the control column that maintains the g will relax and the aircraft's natural stability will ease off the g. But, at low altitudes, or in aerial combat, G-LOC can lead to death. Therefore, we wore g-suits.

The g-suit was essentially a pair of inflatable pants! I laughed when I heard a British jet pilot refer to his 'turning trousers'. Another pilot called the g-suit his 'speed jeans'. Worn over the flight suit and with holes cut out at the knees and crotch, each g-suit was laced up by the safety equipment specialists to fit the individual pilot tightly around the legs, lower abdomen and lower back. Metal zips were tugged up the tight abdominal band and the side of each leg to don the suit. One of the many considerations when strapping into the Macchi was to plug in the g-suit. A hose dangled from the side of the suit, which was snapped into a fitting in the aircraft. When the pilot began pulling g, a valve in the aircraft forced compressed air bled from the jet engine into the g-suit, its bladders squeezing the pilot's calves, thighs and lower abdomen. This forced the blood back up toward the upper body, and therefore delayed the onset of tunnel vision or G-LOC. We were also taught to tense our legs and diaphragms, and to audibly groan, pant and strain against the pressure of the g-suit during manoeuvres – 'hmmmnngg, hmmmnngg' – to force blood back up to where it should be. It was physical work while manipulating an aircraft, fighting the g and pushing back against the suit, keeping one's vision and mind clear for as long as possible. One instructor described the technique as 'speaking Japanese while straining on the toilet at the same time'. Now, with all this safety and survival equipment learned and fitted, it was time to fly the Macchi.

I had never been so intimately connected with an aircraft. The ejection seat and parachute straps were done up tight across my torso and hips. The leg restraint 'bowyangs' were tight around my calves. The g-suit's hose was plugged in on my left. A lanyard attaching the dinghy pack to my parachute harness was attached to my right. Helmet on and plugged in to the intercom and radio. A large ribbed rubber hose stretched from my oxygen mask to the aircraft's supply, the mask tightly clamped against my face. The emergency oxygen hose was attached as well. This was the familiarisation flight, and I was flying with another navy pilot, the 'SNO' (Senior Naval Officer) at Pearce.

We were on the runway and he advanced the jet's throttle to take-off power. Early jets had the peculiarity of taking a period of time to accelerate and the Macchi was no exception. The whine of the engine behind us increased to a subdued roar. Plumes of mist from the air conditioning cascaded from various vents around the cockpit and canopy. The jet rolled slowly at first but as the engine's compressor and turbine RPM built, the Viper swallowed more air and its increased thrust accelerated us faster, with a noticeable push in the back. At 100 knots – or 180 km/hr – the SNO lifted off the nose wheel with a positive movement back on the control column. The Macchi reared up on its landing gear, still accelerating but on the ground, and then the runway fell away. He held the jet at a shallow angle, still accelerating while the wheels were retracted, and then up came the nose and we were climbing, the scrubby eucalypts below falling away fast. Wow! No vibration of a propeller or throbbing piston engine, just the hum of the Viper engine behind us, and a 'husshhh' of air over the canopy punctuated by the suck-blow of our breathing through the masks over the intercom, which was normally set to 'hot mike' – always on – for 'dual' flights. The black faces of the wing-tip fuel tanks loomed either side like wingmen. On came the bank angle to turn toward the training area, and, oh, the rate of climb! It seemed no time at all when we were at fifteen thousand feet, four and a half kilometres above the earth. In a repeat of the Point Cook 'famil' flight, the instructor started manoeuvring And now, the g! The g-suit inflated and I felt uncanny squeezing on my legs and abdomen. I could hear the SNO in the front seat grunting through the intercom, and with vision starting to fade, it prompted me to strain against the g myself, which seemed to last forever thanks to the jet's performance and available thrust. Now, a loop: four g came on, the suit squeezing tighter, and the nose arced up into the dazzling West Australian sky, but far slower than the CT-4 because jet loops are huge. At last, the g came off while we floated over the top of the loop, the earth even further below, then the sandy fields and blotches of eucalypt and pine forest slowly started to loom and then the g again, the suit obediently constricting and becoming familiar already.

'Handing over,' the instructor called, and I had control. So much better than the CT-4! With no propeller causing whorls of air around the tail surfaces, power changes in the jet did not affect rudder or trim settings: the Macchi just went where it was pointed. The control stick felt solid but responsive, promising precise and accurate control of the jet's flight path. The SNO allowed me to manoeuvre it for a while, then took over for the return to base. Unlike at Point Cook, all returns for visual flying for both instructors and students flew through an initial point, some eight kilometres, five miles from the runway, the aircraft doing 250 knots – or 460 km/hr – until level with the landing point, at circuit altitude. Then, there would come a hard turn onto downwind called the 'pitch', with the jet's throttle snapped closed and the speed brake deployed by the pilot to slow down for landing.

The Macchi's design was so clean that a hinged panel was forced out from its belly by a hydraulic ram: an air or 'speed' brake, to rapidly slow the jet. We passed through the initial point, bouncing through heat-induced turbulence but strapped solid in our seats, and when abeam the runway the instructor yanked the wings into a hard bank, simultaneously smartly closing the throttle lever and flicking a little switch on top of it that extended the speed brake. Whiirrr – thunk! The brake deployed and we were thrown forward against our straps with the deceleration, simultaneously g pushing us into our seats in the hard turn until we were on 'downwind'. Speed now below 150 knots – or 280 km/hr – and there was another schloop-thunk as the speed brake came in: the instructor throttled up the engine but now at this much lower speed the Macchi was a different machine, its nose uptilted higher into the sky to maintain height and, as I would find out, its controls noticeably sloppier.

The landing gear was put down with a rumble and vibration and further deceleration as the extending legs and covering doors fought the airstream, then 'thunk-thunk-thunk' as the three landing gear legs locked into position. In no time at all, we were on final approach, the engine behind now warbling near idle. With the large wing flaps deployed, the nose pitched down and all the instructor had to do was to point the jet at the white runway numbers on the threshold, the near end of the runway, controlling speed with movements of the throttle until at last the concrete loomed, and he 'flared' the little jet for landing. A squeak-squeak as the main tyres touched the runway but the nose stayed high in the air, the pilot 'holding off' the nose wheel, the attitude of the Macchi now creating aerodynamic drag and helping it slow. Then the nose came down to rest on its wheel and while taxiing in I realised how hot I was under all that equipment, the huge canopy and that cloudless summer sky.

Marshalled by the ground crew, we parked under the car port, and after double checking that I had correctly inserted the ejection seat pins, we lifted the canopy, which then locked vertically on its hinge like an open coffin lid, and my first military jet flight was over. What a machine! It had seemed to go just where I pointed it in almost vibration-free flight, the rudder pedals just footrests, the physical control of the aircraft so much easier than that of the CT-4. However, I already knew that the headwork required to operate the Macchi, as opposed to just controlling it would be significantly more important.

The first phase of the course at 2 FTS was essentially a 'conversion' onto the Macchi in order to achieve an equivalent point in competency for successful testing at its end in manoeuvres and standards to that of the end of the Point Cook training. We would have to 'come up to speed' with the various circuit types, basic aerobatics, navigation and instrument flying. There was also a lot of night flying. I applied myself diligently, the 'visual' flying and aerobatics mediocre but in what seemed to me at least, a much more straightforward aeroplane to control, and a basic handling test at the end of this phase went reasonably well. 'Medium level' navigation was not too threatening, because the huge dry lakes of south west Western Australia were visible for miles, making the task fairly easy.

Importantly, my diligence and, dare I say, my unusual enjoyment at the time, of instrument flying became a saving grace, which made up for the razor's edge of low-to-mediocre standard in the other areas. Night flying also went well: it is a combination of instrument flying and looking out for other aircraft (easy to see with their lights and flashing beacons), and keeping track of the lights of Pearce's runway to make sense of where I was. Even in the accommodation blocks, the roar of the jets was magnified at night. The Viper engines crackled on take-off into the cool, velvet night sky, fading into a dull, slowly reverberating roar until the next aircraft in the sequence, its beacons flashing, launched into the blackness.

My first instructor, 'Nobby', was an outgoing and even personable RAAF flight lieutenant, but after successfully completing the battery of ground exams and flight tests in visual and instrument flying, it was time to move on to the next phase. And, a new instructor.

I had been considered safe enough for solo flight in the Macchi, the first flight alone in the jet being a circuit at a 'satellite' runway called Gingin, set in a rectangle cut from low olive green scrub to the north of Pearce. Keyed up, I taxied out, my helmet's earphones quiet as there was no need for intercom, so there was no continuous schloop-puff of two pilots breathing through rubber masks; just the occasional radio traffic. Onto the runway, push the throttle forward; the familiar muffled roar from behind, checking engine RPM and exhaust gas temperature within the memorised limits, condensation mist spewing from the vents around the canopy and that push in the back ... rotate the nose to the lift off attitude, now climbing at 120 knots – or 220 km/hr – forty-five degrees of bank onto downwind, speed now about 140 knots with the nose cocked up above the horizon to maintain height, the controls at their accustomed 'sloppiness' at this low speed. Check spacing ... Gingin's runway centreline tracking between the 'roundel' on the wing and the black face of the tip tank ... now for the downwind checks, 'Speed below 150, speed brake in, landing gear down, three wheels, 'flasher' out, fuel quantity noted, threshold speed will be 105 ...' In no time, came the 'base' turn point: power back, select 'take off' flap, re-trim ... judging the turn onto final approach then pointing at the looming 'numbers' on Gingin's runway threshold, speed about 120, now to select 'land flap'; this would bring the speed back to the sacred 105 knots – or 195 km/hr – at the runway, once again re-trimming to neutralise the force on the control column ... the flare point ... gently raise the nose, power off, hold the attitude, 'squeak-squeak' and the main wheels were on, hold the nose up for aerodynamic braking, but lower it gently before the nose wheel 'falls' onto the runway ... there it was, now I was down. First jet solo!

In the meantime, a few more of 100 Pilot's Course had failed; various combinations of ground school problems, insufficient preparation, and failure to mentally keep up with the jet had ended it all for them. But our remaining band was becoming tighter-knit. As numbers fell there was more opportunity for getting to know our course-mates a little better. Some of the 'oddballs' were gone, and the few of us in our late teens were inexorably growing up. Pearce was isolated to the north of Perth but most of the course had cars except me and one or two others, and on a Friday or Saturday night there was usually a 'push' into the huge pubs of Perth's northern suburbs or occasionally into the city itself. During Easter leave, I found Victoria cold, old-feeling and grey with autumn after the brightness of Western Australia. I used Melbourne public transport to visit family, friends and new girlfriend, who was also on leave and staying with a distant relative; it felt incongruous as a trainee jet pilot using buses and trains to get about. Then the break was over, and this course that I would never forget was on again. How could I return east a failure now?

A few drinks on a Friday or Saturday – OK. But the work went on; I had no car anyway, and as a naïve nineteen-year-old with little stamina for weekend parties and late nights, I was sometimes almost alone in the accommodation block. This was a benefit, because there was little excuse not to keep on with the work except for the occasional letters to home and friends. How incongruous that is now in the age of email and mobile phones.

The second of the three 'phases' would introduce us to formation flying, 'low level' and 'high level' navigation, along with advanced aerobatics and high speed, high altitude flight. Instrument flying was becoming more advanced: not just controlling the Macchi but there was headwork to be done with procedures, orientation and instrument approaches. We were now just not expected to 'fly' the Macchi; we had to 'operate' it.

I found formation flying hard work. Thoroughly briefed then demonstrated by the instructors, there came a time when 'Sir' had to relinquish the controls to his student, just a few metres to the side and slightly aft of the leader's tip tank, the new pilot looking for certain reference points on 'lead'; there were three of them. To obtain the correct 'three dimensional' location relative to the lead aircraft, the 'wingman' had to line up the three points on the leader's aircraft. No matter what the leader's aircraft was doing, you 'flew' those points. This sounded reasonably simple in theory, but, in practice ...

Yes, it was hot, physical work. In flight suit, Mae West, g-suit, trussed up under the inverted boat-like canopy in dazzling sunshine, the controls were never still: stick forward or back to maintain the vertical line, banking left and right to maintain the correct distance out, and then the throttle, up and down, ever adjusting, the moan of the engine rising and falling; power off to move back to the correct spot, then power on to stop the rate of movement, then power off again, not so much, to maintain position, then uh-oh, lead's turning away from us, I have to 'ride up' on his extended wing as it rises, lots of power as now I'm falling behind ... adjust ... now I'm in the right spot, the beautiful shape of lead's orange, white and silver Macchi back-dropped against the blue Indian Ocean kilometres below while we turn as one ... but now he's turning the other way, towards me. Off with the power as I am now on the 'inside' of the turn, I'll race ahead if I'm not quick with that, trying to ride down with his wingtip as it banks, as if a rigid, invisible rod is joining us ... the concentration is intense, nothing else matters except to line up those points. I now understood how entire display teams had crashed as a group, the wingmen still locked on to their leader in the final seconds of their lives. I bore the dazzle of the sun as, looking up into it on the 'inside' of the turn, lead turned into a silhouette, the instructor behind exhorting, 'Come on, get back in there'.

Leadership. As the feeling of flying formation on another's wing became a little more 'instinctive', though never really easy for me, being the leader of a formation threw up its own challenges. My course-mate would relinquish the 'lead' over the radio, now he who had been leading me was now trying to 'hang in' off my wing, and I was now thinking for two aircraft, keeping the turns gentle, at a constant 'rate' of bank so that the wingman could follow my tip tank, but there was more to it than merely being smooth. The wingman would not be looking at anywhere else in the sky, just focusing on those points on my aircraft. He would now be burning fuel at a greater rate than me with all his power changes. He could not look out for other aircraft; check that he was staying correctly in the training area; talk to air traffic control. Those were my responsibilities as leader, remembering that with a fellow 'rookie' off my wing, manoeuvrability would be reduced. Thinking ahead was essential. The wingman would then commence 'station changes' directed by his instructor in the back seat as I had done, sliding aft and across into 'line astern', sitting directly behind my Macchi, sitting slightly low to avoid the buffeting jet blast from my exhaust. Line astern was slightly easier to fly than 'echelon', so I could turn a little more tightly … 'Need to manoeuvre? Put your mate into line astern', the instructors would advise, the leader having the prerogative to 'call' the wingman into the various positions. Then 'echelon' on the other side, now I am giving him a few turns for practice, he's settled down quite nicely, just bobbing up and down with the occasional ripple in the air, the helmeted, masked head in the front seat with its anonymous black visor fixated on my jet, the instructor in the back also staring, never relaxing.

It would now be time to lead the formation back to Pearce, judging my run in to the 'initial' point, so the turns would be gentle, calling the radio frequency changes, checking our fuel states and now, making sure he is in the correct 'echelon' position, as I will fly the standard 'initial and pitch', the run parallel to the runway at 1,000', 300 metres, followed by hard individual breakaways onto 'downwind'.

The wingman must be placed on the other side to the direction of the pitch into the circuit. Runway now below, lined up nicely, checking for no other traffic in the circuit (I am responsible for two aircraft!), a little 'waggle' of my wings to indicate to the wingman, still totally focussed on my aircraft, that we are about to 'pitch' (he may not even know that we are abeam the runway), and then that hard bank and 'pull' onto downwind, throttle idle, speed brake out … now the wingman is on his own, my aircraft has abruptly whipped away to his right, he now maintains level, counts three 'bananas' or 'elephants' according to taste, and now he follows suit, pitching out to follow me in trail onto downwind. We are still a formation however, so I am responsible for clearance to land and the wingman takes 'interval' on me, just touching down as I vacate the runway. We taxi in to the carports as a 'pair'. It is only after the canopy is opened and the cooling 'tick tick' of the engines' metal is heard and harness buckles clink as we unstrap, that my course-mate and I realise how hot we are, our suits drenched with sweat. A joint debrief, the instructors picking and critiquing, notes taken, but thankfully the 'ride', while not brilliant, is a 'pass' and another flight in the syllabus is over.

The instrument flying became very involved. Instrument flying, that is in cloud or at night, was simulated in the CT-4 by a rudimentary visor worn over the helmet that gave its wearer enough of a field of view ahead to see the instrument panel, not much out of the windscreen, but there was always some peripheral vision. Several of our course were now having serious problems with their instrument flying, and inevitably suffered that cruel 'X' through the course photograph on the walls of the Operations Room and the various offices. On one occasion, through a distressing oversight one course-mate would spot the X through his face on a photograph before he was informed of his failure.

In the Macchi, instrument flying sorties were flown with the instructor in the front seat and the student occupying the rear. The instructor had to be able to see straight ahead out of the aircraft for landing and importantly, the student in the rear could be fully enclosed by the instrument flying 'hood'. It was, in fact, a tent. Not a skerrick of a view outside remained. The student's world was dirty white canvas, the grey metal of the cockpit interior and the instrument panel. There could be no cheating. 'Under the hood' in the Macchi was serious instrument flying. Conflicting senses from one's inner ear could not be resolved by a quick, sneaky peek out. Ninety per cent of the pilot's attention was locked on to the Macchi's big attitude indicator, the 'A.I', a mechanical gyro-stabilised world, with its numbered graduations that showed bank and pitch. And now there were more than rudimentary manoeuvres required; there were 'unusual attitude' recoveries, advanced instrument approaches and exercises and even take-offs conducted by the student blind 'under the hood', carefully referring to the equally large horizontal situation indicator (HSI), directly under the AI, which showed quite an accurate compass heading.

TACAN was a system widely used in the western military air forces. It was a ground radio 'beacon', usually located on a military base, that radiated coded signals that enabled a special system in the aircraft to calculate its 'bearing' (compass direction) and distance in nautical miles, from that beacon. This was displayed to Macchi pilots on the HSI, a 'bar' indicating the selected 'radial' (bearing) from the beacon, superimposed on the compass, and a little counter that showed the distance away. We were taught to fly TACAN approaches, 'homing' onto the beacon and descending to certain altitudes as directed by the special approach chart to a minimum altitude, at which the instructor would do one of two things: call 'taking over' and landing the aircraft, usually for a 'touch and go' and further approach, or he would say nothing. O.K., I'm not 'visual' with the runway ... 'Going round, Sir', I would call: on with the power, locked onto the AI for that vital climb attitude (we are very close to the ground), gear (wheels) up, flaps up, full power makes the nose want to pitch up, so trim ... fly the required 'missed approach' course on the compass, quick, start levelling off, we're nearly at the stipulated altitude, re-trim, 'Call Pearce Approach on Stud 3' would come from the air traffic controller through my earphones, acknowledge ... change frequency ... call 'Approach' ... then, more often as not, 'OK, another approach' from the instructor, perhaps another TACAN, a more rudimentary teardrop-shaped 'NDB' approach or a precision 'GCA' until the Macchi's fuel would be getting low and it was time to land.

The Non Directional Beacon (NDB) was a primitive 'homing' device. The pilot tuned the beacon's frequency and then a needle superimposed on a compass card on his instrument panel pointed to it; the needle often quivered and wandered as the NDB's radio frequency, essentially the same as medium-wave public radio, was subject to various forms of interferences and inaccuracies. The NDB provided no distance information, however the pilot could tell if he was directly overhead the beacon. The instrument's needle would swing and circle drunkenly as the aircraft passed through the 'cone of confusion' above the NDB antenna. It would then wobble and eventually stabilise to show the direction back to the aid. It was vital to recognise the 'overhead', then to position the Macchi correctly 'outbound' from the beacon on the correct course, commencing a descent to an intermediate altitude, then after minute or two, turn 'inbound' to intercept the correct bearing toward the beacon, descending to the published Minimum Descent Altitude, carefully maintaining height and bearing. Most NDB approaches, and some TACAN approaches, were teardrop shaped and the NDB approach enabled the pilot, homing to the simple and inexpensive Non Directional Beacon, to penetrate a cloud layer to fly directly in to land or to 'circle' a few hundred metres above the ground, to line up with the correct landing direction.

GCA stood for 'Ground Controlled Approach', and I relished these. All I had to do was follow instructions and fly accurately. A specially qualified military air traffic controller would peer at two extremely accurate radar screens that presented the Macchi's 'blip' in both bearing and height down a three-degree 'glide slope' down to the runway's threshold. Giving tiny corrections over the radio to the pilot, it was the classic 'talk down', a constant voice in the earphones: 'Viper 36 turn left 185, commence rate of descent, coming onto centreline, heading 182, slightly increase that rate of descent, on glide path, heading 185, slightly reduce that rate of descent ...' The corrections became smaller and smaller as we flew down an imaginary 'funnel' to the runway, then, 'Approaching decision height, look ahead and land visually'. If you had flown accurately the jet would end up some 200 feet, sixty metres, above the ground with the runway directly ahead. Once again, there would be either, 'taking over' from the instructor, or that silence, meaning 'Make a missed approach'. A GCA was always a welcome relief from the other approaches with their mental gymnastics of bearings, radials and distances.

The navigation exercises were becoming more than just visually flying triangular routes at some 8,000 feet – or 2,400 metres – above Western Australia's 'wheat belt', tracking from dry lake to town to dry lake then back to Pearce. There were high and low 'navexes' to be planned, flown and assessed, the high ones flown at, some 9,000 metres, up in airliner territory. There was no airliner's autopilot for us, and accurate flying was more demanding in the thin air with less engine power while we homed to radio beacons dotted around the Western Australian countryside. There could later be a 'visual' segment to a huge dry lake, sometimes obscured by a cloud deck far below, so an accurate heading and airspeed had to be flown until the next position 'fix'. The Macchi used slightly less fuel at high altitude, but the quantity gauge still had to be watched carefully and the feed from the tip tanks monitored, with the fuel amount remaining plotted carefully on a small paper graph. Then perhaps an instrument approach through the clouds back at Pearce: this time it's 'for real' from the front cockpit, breaking out of the cloud to find Pearce's runway, fortunately for me, generally where it was supposed to be: ahead in the windscreen. Various aspects of the course that were previously separated were coalescing into one picture: a navigation exercise becoming an instrument flying routine at the end; 'operating' the aircraft. Ability at this was, as ever, closely followed by the instructors, debriefed, and later written up in the 'hate sheets' (reports on the students).

In the same vein, formation flying was becoming more advanced, especially when leading one's wingman back to base through cloud for an instrument approach as a 'pair', or as the wingman, absolutely focused on the leader's jet with ragged grey wisps of cloud flitting by, feeling weird and contradictory sensations through my inner ear. Lose sight of him for an instant and it would be a rapid 'break away' from his last known position – two aircraft in close proximity in cloud is a hazardous situation.

'Low level' navexes were flown over the countryside just 200 feet, 60 metres, off the ground with a carefully prepared and folded large scale map in one gloved hand held up high, tick marks along the marked course indicating time markers, and a stopwatch running on the gun sight platform right there in the windscreen. It was hot at low level in the Macchi, the sweat ignored while I tried to stay 'on track and on time', craning for landmarks, but still marvelling at the speed, 240 knots, four nautical miles or seven kilometres per minute, while farms, cattle, dry lakes and scrub slid underneath, the Macchi bumping and wallowing and fishtailing in sharp-edged turbulence. Later the instructors would command 'diversions' where mental arithmetic had to be used to correct times and speeds, because the low level navexes terminated with a 'target' which was to be overflown exactly and at a nominated time. Phew! Made it this time, but the timing not great. Barely a 'pass'.

My overall performance was still a poor average. Silly mistakes and poor aerobatics often prompted gruff and sarcastic responses from the instructors. I was not a great navigator – I fixated on inappropriate priorities and found it difficult to read features at low level over the vast West Australian wheat belt, with the tiny towns hard to spot and all looking the same. As at Point Cook, my saving grace was my instrument flying and good ground school results, but I barely scraped through each progress test flight. However, like the others, I was entrusted with more solo flights including navexes and night flights.

Still nineteen, I was slowly maturing, and 100 Course had bonded further, whittled down to a little over twenty students from the original forty. I became accepted into the fold of the 'drinking buddies' as the study eased a little, and I was usually invited along for Friday night outings to the pubs and clubs. We had a course song, and roared lewd ditties and chants, most of them picked up from the beer-swilling instructors on Friday afternoons while we let off steam in the Students' Mess and the noisy pubs:

'Who's the man with the big red nose?'
Hoo, ha, hoo ha ha
The more he drinks, the more he knows!
Hoo ha, hoo ha ha
Where are we from?
PEARCE!
And what do we eat?
FISH!
And how do we eat it?
RAW!
And when we win,
WE SHIT IT IN!
So up the old red rooster, and drink *MORE PISS!'*

The 'Neptune Song' was an ode to the old Lockheed Neptune maritime patrol aircraft, often bawled out during Friday afternoon hilarity in the Students' Mess by instructors who were ex-maritime patrol pilots, sung loosely to the tune of 'Bless 'em All':

'Neptunes they don't bother me,
Neptunes they don't bother me.
Clapped-out abortions with holes in their wings,
Poofter co-pilots and engines that "ping".

So if you've got a MiG on your tail,
Don't let your Aussie blood boil.
Don't hesitate, slam it right through the gate,
And cover the bastard in oil!'

They go up,
They go down.
The engines, they go round and round.
If you've got three burning, and only one turning, you'd best get
*   your arse on the ground!'*

After each song glasses were refilled from the jugs of frothing brown liquid. Not a big drinker, I did my best to fit in and joined the ribald songs with growing enthusiasm. Some of the fellows had local girlfriends who joined in the merriment. The course would run from January to September so there was almost a settled feeling at 2 FTS for many of us.

I managed time for driving lessons: a course-mate, Gerry, let me attach 'L' plates to his old Volkswagen and gave me some road experience. After a few lessons to polish up, I presented for a driving test in Perth, where a gentleman in a suit and tie introduced himself as the tester and asked me what I did. I told him I was a trainee navy pilot, qualified to fly a single engine jet solo, day and night, but I was not legal to drive a car. At last, I had a driver's licence, but still no car.

There were two forms of motivation to remain focussed on the course and to keep putting the work in and not get distracted by girlfriends and social life. First were the sobering 'scrubs' that occurred late in the course. One farewell was particularly sad. Nicknamed Luigi from his Mediterranean appearance, his eyes filled as we farewelled him noisily in a bar at Perth Airport. Luigi had often been the life of the party. Gerry had gone and another student, worldly and older than most of us, had been caught carrying out solo aerobatics low over a girlfriend's house, spotted by an instructor in another Macchi. Schmitty, also older but intelligent and dry of wit, had not adjusted well to military life and had also gone. He would return to the legal profession.

The more positive motivation was the 'Postings Dining-in Nights' and graduation parades, of which there were three each year. The air force's Dining-in Night was equivalent to the navy's Mess Dinner, but with variations. Full formal Mess Dress, solemn ritual and formality would likewise descend into happy chaos after the Loyal Toast, where the 'crabs' toasted the Queen standing up. At each course's Postings Dining-in Night, the students' fates would be read out one by one: 'Smith, Thirty-Four Squadron' (VIP transport), 'Jones, Thirty-Eight' (transports), with elated yells from those earmarked to fly fighters or F-111 bombers. Then, the navy postings: they would be to fly Skyhawks, Trackers, or helicopters. Next morning, more sober heads would realise that the course was not yet over, and any posting to an operational squadron would evaporate should the pilot's training not be completed successfully. It would be back to work for the final phase and the final tests: formation, navigation, instrument flying and lastly, the 'Wings' test.

100 Course marched in support of two graduation parades, impressive affairs with families, friends and senior officers looking on. The air force cadets would become commissioned as pilot officers and depart on their postings to operational squadrons. The navy graduates, however, would remain as midshipmen and would cross the continent to Nowra for further training. I hoped fervently that I would be doing the same.

Phase Three, the final phase, was that coming together of the separate aspects of the advanced training syllabus, and the final test flights. For the Formation Test, my friend Phil was the candidate in the other aircraft. I 'hung in' on his wing as best I could, completed the 'rejoins' and station changes and then slipped back to a few hundred metres astern of his Macchi in a 'tail chase'. I manoeuvred in an imaginary cone as Phil threw his aircraft around aggressively while I moved in or out of the cone's edge to try and maintain a constant distance and to follow him.

High in the sky, Phil pulls over me in a huge loop. I follow him over and I pick up the orange and white of his Macchi, smaller now, arrowing down thousands of metres below us towards the dry lakes and scrub, two white helmets visible in the darkness of its cockpit … Then the g comes on as I cut to the inside to catch him … now he's pulled up into dazzling blue, gravity takes over and his Macchi slows, so I had better get to the outside of the cone otherwise I will get too close …

A few minutes later, the tail chase was over. Now it was my turn to take the 'lead' with Phil flying on my wing, to repeat the entire exercise. In the debrief, my flying on Phil's wing was considered satisfactory and despite comments on my mediocre leadership, Phil and I were told that we had both passed the test.

The Navigation Test was a struggle: a 'high-low' profile where I was to fly the first leg of a triangular course at high altitude, descend, and then complete the 'mission' at low level using the technique of stopwatch and large-scale map. A silly mistake at the first turning point almost did for me, but I managed to identify and correct it, which probably gave the testing officer an inkling that, with experience, I might eventually become a competent military pilot. After that the dreaded 'FIHT' loomed. A few candidates, especially those who were uncomfortable with instrument flying, would fail to make the grade, even at this point.

The Final Instrument Handling Test was, in some ways, more important than the 'Wings' test. Accurate instrument flying was a must for military pilots who were expected not just to fly, but to 'fight' their aircraft in all weather conditions, day and night. I worked and worked for it. I thought through every possible scenario: fuel shortage, diversion to an obscure alternate airport, instrument failures. All these things could be thrown at me, either actually flown or questioned as a scenario, and the Macchi's high rate of fuel usage was always in the back of my mind.

The instructors were of various backgrounds and of various temperaments: from the serious fighter pilots, full of ego and elitism, to those from transport, bomber and helicopter backgrounds. One of them held a senior position and was known as 'Five Balls' by virtue of his deep, dry, gravelly voice. Unlike the rest of the instructors, Five Balls' office was bare of any photographs or badges, with his green flying jacket equally unadorned with any unit patches or flags. I occasionally flew with him when my regular instructors were unavailable, and I experienced his unique instructional style.

Unlike the other instructors, he sat through his students' flights with his intercom system turned off. He would click down his button, say what he had to say, then it would be back to silence. The student would feel like it was a solo flight: no suck/blow of the instructor breathing through his mask, no grunting from him under the g-forces, no casual observations or very occasional banter. But almost always, Five Balls would 'ghost' the controls: you could feel his hands and feet through the 'stick' and rudder pedals when you were supposed to be in control of the aircraft. Perhaps he had had a few scares during his previous exchange duty with an Asian air force. A course-mate swore that when he was flying with Five Balls, he had completely removed his hands from the controls and the aircraft flew a perfect circuit, the student debriefed on minor points later.

While flying a circuit with Five Balls in the rear cockpit to a 'touch and go', and with full power on and climbing back up from Pearce's runway, all I would hear through my earphones was, 'Click ssshhh' (the usual background hash of the intercom system), then the gravelly voice: 'Surprise me, Mr Carr, and land on the bloody centreline next time … ssshhh click.' Typical of Five Balls, as was his debrief. As with all his students, he directed me to make him a strong black instant coffee, then, occasionally lifting his huge mug to his lips from the bare desk, he faced the window in his ever-present opaque black sunglasses, five o'clock shadow and short-cropped black hair, and made slow, laconic, dry statements in his bass voice: 'The normal circuit was reasonable but your flapless ones tended to turn into a can of worms …' and more in similar vein. His knowledge of the pubs around south-western Australia was encyclopaedic: he rattled off their names and details as we flashed over them on the low-level navexes. From his capacity for alcohol he was also known as 'The Bionic Liver', and regardless of how much beer he consumed his demeanour never changed. Legend had it among the students that he was never seen to eat.

My Phase One instructor, 'Nobby', had relinquished me to Flight Lieutenant Tony who was personable but exacting, of 'maritime' background like Nobby, with most of his operational experience gained on Lockheed Orion patrol aircraft. Tony had coached me through the second phase, patiently teaching the rudiments of formation, low and high level navigation, and advanced instrument flying. Perceived as a weak student, for the final phase of the pilot's course I had been passed on to Flight Lieutenant 'Johnno'.

Johnno was a solid, impressive chap, and colourful medal ribbons attested to his having flown helicopters in a combat environment as part of the RAAF's involvement in the Vietnam War. Many of these veterans were given a 'first choice' of postings subsequent to their war service, and Johnno had gone on to fly Mirage fighters. Fighter pilots were sardonically referred to in the air force as 'knuckleheads' or 'knucks', single-minded pilots of supersonic jets, around which the whole service seemed to revolve. Many fighter pilots considered themselves of the elite and itched to get back to their operational squadrons. Johnno was an exception. He took a genuine interest in his students, and the taking over of a very young navy midshipman of marginal ability would have been regarded as a challenge for him.

'That's a pass.' I still remember those words over the Macchi's intercom today. I was still strapped in under the instrument flying 'tent'. The testing officer was taxiing us in, having completed my Final Instrument Handling Test. They were the only words he spoke until I reported to his cubicle for debriefing. He was known by us as 'The

Cucumber': a fighter pilot's fighter pilot, cool and laconic behind dark glasses under blond hair. I emerged from his briefing room feeling that for once I had flown a reasonable test, the reward of hard work and thankfully, good instrument flying. Later, Johnno accosted me in a corridor. Beaming, he held up four fingers. 'Mark, you got a 'four'! Shit hot!' The 'Cuke' had graded my performance as a 'four'. 'Fives' were assigned only to students of exceptional ability. I had not let Johnno down and maybe, just maybe, I would graduate from 2 FTS.

We had been asked for our preferences for aircraft types early in Phase Three. The choices for the navy midshipmen were the Skyhawk fighters, Grumman Tracker anti-submarine aircraft, and helicopters. I expected to be assigned to helicopters. In our youth and inexperience, helicopters were perceived as slow and boring, a different form of aviation, noisy and vibrating. How wrong we were, as later I would have much to do with the helicopter crew and occasionally have the chance to take the controls of one. However, the weaker students were often sent to them, because the helicopter's slower speed would give them more time to think and 'stay ahead' of the aircraft. I was convinced that helicopters would be my posting, assuming that I actually passed the course at Pearce. But I had always liked the look of the Grumman Tracker.

The Tracker was a blunt brute of an aircraft with its two powerful piston engines. It bristled with sensors and had those deep side windows for the pilots to observe the earth and sea below. Like the Skyhawk, it would be flung off the carrier, HMAS *Melbourne*, by a catapult, to be caught back on board by its arresting hook engaging the ship's wires. Unlike in the U.S. Navy that used two pilots, Australia's Trackers were flown 'single pilot': the occupant of the right hand seat of the cockpit a specially trained observer called the Tactical Coordinator, or 'TACCO'. But the Tracker didn't have the speed of the jets and, with my own realistic appraisal of my flying ability, it could be an operational aircraft that I just might be able to handle. So on the appropriately named 'dream sheet', I had written Trackers as first choice. At the Postings Dining-in Night for 100 Course, instructors and students at the long tables, the port decanter circulating, the list was called out, which included: '... Midshipman Carr: VC 851 Squadron, Grumman Trackers.' I was very happy with that.

Most of the remaining navy students had Skyhawks as first choice. However, a mediocre student who had reasonable instrument flying skills and who actually wanted to fly the Tracker was a rarity so by default, I was to train on the powerful Grumman. Ray, who was doing well on the course, ever cheerful and confident, was to fly the Skyhawk. The few remaining navy students on 100 Course would fly helicopters.

'As for your "aero's" ...' The wing commander then laughed at the aerobatic sequence I had demonstrated to him during our flight. We were debriefing, and I had flown a very marginal Wings Test with the Commanding Officer of 2 FTS. I had been 'saved' by circumstances; strong academics and good instrument flying, the political messiness of a failure at this stage of the course, and the fact that I was navy: I would not be the air force's problem any more and it would be up to the navy to further train and assess me. I left his office emotionally drained, but now I would march with my course-mates on the Graduation Parade.

Later I was debriefed by the Senior Naval Officer, with whom I had experienced my first Macchi flight seemingly a lifetime ago. He pulled no punches, stating that the navy had reservations about my ability and officer qualities. He alluded to marginal performance in the air, immaturity (I would turn twenty the following day) and instances of sloppy uniform. I was still thin and angular, my uniforms never seemed to fit properly, and I still carried myself at a discernable angle from the poorly healed collarbone. The front tooth was still black from effects of the car crash. I had not done well in practical exercises during a leadership evaluation in bushland south of Perth. 'We're sending you to Trackers because you were the only one who asked for 'em', he said. 'Your report states that you prepared for your flights well, but your performance was inconsistent. You lack common sense and have little potential for development as an officer.' The report concluded with the words, 'Midshipman Carr has a difficult task ahead.'

'One Hundred Course! By the left! Quick ... march!' RAAF Pearce's band struck up a stirring tune as we stepped off from the flight line area, heading toward the parade ground. While we marched with band playing, a lone Macchi plunged up and down ahead of us in a joyous display of low-level aerobatics, the whistle of its engine modulating as it dived then swooped skywards again, now into a 'hammerhead' as it reached the top of its arc. It hung nose-high, between momentum and gravity in deep blue sky, its throttled-back engine warbling, then it fell backwards until its natural stability flipped it nose down. It wobbled then stabilised as its speed built up again, then another swoop and pull up into a roll ... we had marched as support squads at two graduation parades previously, and now this one was *ours*.

We made a ceremonial march-past for the distinguished guests and the senior officers. My mother and my paternal grandmother were in the audience, my father unable to attend because there was the all-important race meeting at Mornington. He would join us on the following day for the Graduation Ball. My 'wings' were pinned on by the 'Father of the Air Force', Air Vice Marshal Sir Richard Williams. He had been among the first to train as a pilot at Point Cook in 1914. Frail but erect, he pinned the 'wings' to my uniform jacket with the help of his aide-de-camp. Then the prizes were announced: a surprise 'dux' to a course-mate that we had not expected, various other prizes then, 'Most Improved Student: Midshipman Carr.' A hissed 'Well done, Carcus' from Phil just behind, and it was forward to receive a tangible reward for unrelenting hard work, determination and luck. Then we made a second march-past and as the last of us passed in front of Sir Richard while he took the salute on the dais, there was a rumble in the sky from the west.

Five dots in the sky became Macchi jets headed directly toward the parade ground at low level. They were spread in 'echelon' formation. The building roar of the engines at full power was impressive. While I marched carefully, I could see out of the corner of my eye the formation split in a 'bomb burst' just in front of the audience at the parade ground; the wingmen simultaneously broke up and away at each side and the leader pulled vertically up until he was inverted, then into a half roll. Then, the individual jets streaked off to rejoin in formation out in the area, to later belt low over the base in echelon then fan up and away, one by one, for landing. Meanwhile, Sir Richard had been chauffeured away, and the parade was over.

Eighteen students of the forty who had started on our course so long ago at Point Cook now wore 'wings'. Those of the air force were heavy pewter affairs, and the cadets had simultaneously become qualified air force pilots and commissioned pilot officers. But the navy was different. Firstly, naval 'wings' are traditionally gold in colour. Secondly, we were still midshipmen. Thirdly, and significantly, naval 'wings' were not confirmed until the wearer had passed an OFS: an Operational Flying School on a front line naval aircraft: for me, the Tracker. Fail that, and off those wings would come. I had barely scraped through the Pilots' Course with marginal officer qualities, and now the OFS was the next hurdle.

However, I would have some time to wait for that. The Tracker OFS had been delayed, and it had been decided that I would continue to fly Macchis for a while: but not those with orange tails emblazoned with the black swan. The jets that I would fly were the blue, white and silver Macchis that belonged to VC 724 Squadron at Nowra.

7

A PRELUDE TO SEA

1978

One evening in December 1976, a mentally unstable sailor set fire to a hangar at HMAS *Albatross*, the Naval Air Station (NAS) at Nowra. The building housed the navy's fleet of Grumman Trackers, packed together with folded wings, their tanks full of high-octane aviation fuel. Keeping the tanks full was standard practice to avoid water condensation during prolonged inactivity. Nowra's personnel, most of them off-duty, mobilised to try to save the aircraft inside, some risking their lives to move burning aircraft clear. Officers rushed from a function in the wardroom in formal dress; one pilot managed to start a nearby airliner-sized HS 748 and taxi it clear. Twelve Trackers were incinerated, and the Fleet Air Arm's anti-submarine and patrol capability was devastated through this insane act. Replacement Trackers from the United States were hurriedly arranged which arrived in Australia in April 1977. These machines had been declared surplus by the U.S. Navy and, although flyable, work was required to restore them to full combat capability.

With no Trackers to fly, my initial posting was to VC 724 Squadron to fly its Macchis. This would keep me flying prior to the Operational Flying School and would allow the navy to further assess my potential to become a frontline naval aviator and competent officer. Ray, destined to fly Skyhawks, was initially to learn elementary weapons training in 724's Macchis and although I had been earmarked to fly Trackers, I was to join him in undergoing the same preliminary training. After leaving Pearce, it was a given that we could fly and 'operate' the Macchi, but now it was time to learn to 'fight' it.

At Pearce, the air force's Macchis were well-kept training jets, but their navy counterparts were worked hard in this small service, the Fleet Air Arm. That showed in dulled paint and worn cockpits, sooty jet pipes and stained undersides. However, where the air force jets had been painted in the lurid 'Fanta can' scheme, the navy had replaced the orange panels with an elegant dark blue. The VC 724 Squadron Macchis proudly sported their large yellow arrow motif on their tails, and NAVY in large white letters adorned the outsides of the blue tip tanks. The 724 Squadron naval crest was emblazoned on each forward fuselage along with a white serial number. There was further difference: unlike the Macchis at 2 FTS: these aircraft could carry weapons. There was an armament control panel in the front cockpit and a complicated weapons sight protruded up from the coaming below the windscreen, which blocked much of the forward view. Some of the jets were fitted with underwing racks that could be loaded with practice bombs, rockets or 'Minigun' machine gun pods.

It was the spring of 1977, and after leaving Pearce, I spent some leave back in Victoria, drifting between relatives and girlfriend. Then I proudly drove my newly-acquired car to Nowra in sultry weather after staying overnight at Wagga in Grove Street with old family friends. It had been an interesting ride from my childhood in this town to operational training as a navy pilot.

I lived 'on-board' HMAS *Albatross* in a modern block of cabins. A steward would bang on my door every morning and leave a tepid cup of tea or the typical service instant coffee. Back then, it was the system! The wardroom itself was a wooden ramshackle building that had open rafters inside. For decades, naval aviators were occasionally dared to hang upside-down from these rafters and down glasses of beer during alcohol-fuelled hilarity, but a new, rafter-less wardroom was soon to be built nearby. The park-like surroundings were reminiscent of a country club. After fifteen months with the air force, it was back to 'excusing your rig', cloth napkins in silver holders bearing your mess number, and the unique and ancient vernacular of the navy. The base was overseen by a commodore in rank. Under him was Commander 'Air' and then the individual Commanding Officers: the COs, of the three frontline and the three support squadrons. It was the ambition of most naval aviators to become the Commanding Officer of a squadron at sea. Each unit had its Senior Pilot and, on the Tracker and helicopter squadrons, a Senior Observer. 724 Squadron had an affable but capable Senior Pilot who, like all the staff pilots, flew both the Macchi and the Skyhawk. To maintain standards, a Qualified Flying Instructor (QFI) was on all squadrons' staff, and the jet squadrons also had Air Warfare Instructors (AWIs).

I flew several area familiarisation and 'check' flights with the QFI and the Senior Pilot, which went well. The navy treated instrument flying skills with as much importance as the air force, but there was little requirement to produce intricate and exact aerobatic sequences; there was work to do! Formation flying was important, and mine was still mediocre, especially compared with Ray's: he was a natural. NAS Nowra's aircraft could range freely in huge areas that were restricted from civilian traffic: far out over the Tasman Sea, and to one hundred miles south along the New South Wales coast. Air traffic control procedures were similar to those at Pearce, and Ground-Controlled Approaches and a TACAN beacon were available to guide aircraft down through the decks of ragged grey cloud that drifted in from the ocean. There was a firing range at Beecroft Head at Jervis Bay, and a small runway sat near the same area for launching Jindivik target drones. These machines, designed and built in Australia, incorporated the Macchi's Viper jet engine into their orange, missile-like shape, and could tow various targets for ships and aircraft to fire at. The Jindiviks were controlled by radio links by operators on the ground and were sometimes lost due to technical problems or hits from gunfire. In fact, the little Viper jet engine had been especially designed as a 'throw away' power unit for the Jindivik but had proved such a successful design that it had been uprated and improved to power many jet aircraft, including the Macchi MB 326.

Ships of the Royal Australian Navy were almost always exercising in these restricted areas seawards of Nowra, and one of VC 724 Squadron's roles was to provide 'fleet support' by operating aircraft to provide training for the ships' crews. This training ranged from relatively routine 'tracking' exercises to exciting mock attacks on the vessels and occasionally, the simulation of a ship's missile. Over several 'back seat' flights I was familiarised with the fleet support duties, procedures, flight profiles and radio work until I was considered competent to operate these flights on my own.

I found the special radio procedures interesting and at times, humorous. The language was an informal code to make it difficult for listening snoopers to decipher. My Macchi would accelerate down Nowra's runway, lift, build speed, then almost immediately make a climbing hard turn seawards. I would soon transmit to Nowra's air traffic controller: '867 feet wet, switching tactical.' My Macchi, its number 867, was now over the water and I was changing to the assigned frequency for communication with the warship. A special call sign would have been assigned for both my aircraft and the ship: 'Mike four-two, this is Tango three-six at angels ten inbound.'

'Angels' was a time-honoured code word dating from the Battle of Britain, which meant height in thousands of feet. But now, I was not talking to an air traffic controller or even another pilot. It would be a young sailor or officer on board the warship, being trained in the radar detection and controlling of aircraft. These air controllers were known as 'Freddies'.

'Tango three-six, this is Mike four-two. I am your Freddie. Confirm your parrot is squawking?'

He was asking if the jet's transponder, a device that amplified radar signals for a ground operator, was operating.

'Affirmative.'

'Roger, I've got you on my gadget bearing two seven eight, three six miles.'

The 'gadget' was the ship's radar, meaning that my Macchi was producing a blip on the operator's screen, amplified by the 'squawking' transponder.

'Fly heading zero nine eight and report Mother in sight.'

I would scan the horizon, and eventually I would spot a greenish-grey sliver, the warship. It would usually be pitching and rolling among whitecaps in the Tasman Sea. Sometimes, I thought of the possibility that the engine humming behind me could fail. If it did, I myself would be tossing in that roiling sea, miles from shore, in a tiny dinghy and life jacket, shivering cold. But the satisfaction of being on my own in a navy jet, exercising with a warship, eclipsed this foreboding thought. Almost as serious was the thought of making a mistake during the exercise; there was rivalry between the 'birdies' of the navy's air arm and the 'fish heads' of the ships.

Exercises would commence, and generally the Freddie would pass various heading and altitude requirements: 'Vector zero one five and descend to angels one point five.' He wanted me to steer 015 degrees and descend to 1,500 feet – or 450 metres – above the sea. It was a new experience for the seagoing naval operator, controlling a small jet moving at 220 knots – 400 km/hr – from a moving ship. The aircraft would be just a blip on his radar screen that took several kilometres to turn, was subject to wind, and flown by a raw twenty-year-old pilot. With the primary exercises complete, the ship sometimes asked for mock attacks.

When the controller said, 'Tango three six, strangle your parrot, make your bearing two five five, descend to cherubs three, and buster,' he really meant turn off the transponder and come in from the south west at 300 feet – or ninety metres above the water – at maximum speed. This gave the trainee Freddie experience in picking up the aircraft's radar return or 'skin paint': just raw radio energy from the ship being reflected off the Macchi's aluminium skin, out of the sea's 'clutter' on his scope. I would run in toward the destroyer, swells and whitecaps sliding under the Macchi's nose, the air usually smooth this far from land. The ship would bloom, looking toy-like on the sea, greenish-grey, topped with a tracery of black masts, antennas and a black topped funnel. There would be time to watch its sharp bow rise and crash once into a swell but then I would be overhead, just a bare hundred feet clear of the masts, before a hard 'pull up' and turn. Then more random attacks with the ship's crew not knowing from which direction I would appear, but only a few runs: the Viper gulped fuel at a prodigious rate at low level and high speed, and I was miles offshore. Finally, I would report 'bingo' to the ship, meaning my fuel state was such that it was time to fly back to base.

'Tango three six, confirm you have father-lock?' asked the Freddie. He was asking if the Macchi's TACAN set was picking up 'father', Nowra's beacon. That would give me a direction to fly and distance to run for home.

'Negative,' I said.

'Roger, your pigeons are two eight zero at four six.'

'Pigeons' was the direction to fly and the distance to go for 'homing' to Nowra.

'Tango three six, roger. Departing for home plate.'

Climbing now to conserve fuel, I would head for the coast, the massive vertical headlands of Jervis Bay visible with the high ground of the Divide in blue haze beyond. Somewhere there lay the Naval Air Station, west of Nowra town, and as I climbed the TACAN needle would quiver, then point to home. Numbers tumbled in the distance readout window then settled to give a distance to the beacon. Soon I would call air traffic control with my position and height. But sometimes, before leaving the ship's radio frequency, a different voice, usually more authoritative, would call. It would be that of the ship's Principal Warfare Officer, the PWO or 'Peewo': 'Tango three six, this is Mike four two. Thank you for your assistance'. Occasionally after that, he would pass me a 'Dolphin' code word.

The Dolphin Code, also known as the Falcon Code, was a number transmitted to another aircraft or ship that denoted a humorous, sarcastic or ribald remark from a 'code' sheet. These remarks related to the unit's performance, and often contained an obscenity. Today's Dolphin Code number was relatively benign: 'You have met the abysmally low standard that you have set yourself.' Other Dolphin code numbers decoded as: 'After working with you, I understand why some animals eat their young', the rare complimentary 'Shit hot', but then there was the derisive 'Fuck you and the horse you rode in on.' Seagoing naval officers had much time to dream up these diversions.

On occasion, I was tasked to simulate an Ikara missile. Ikara was a rocket launched from a destroyer that carried a torpedo out from the ship, to be dropped on a bearing and range to where a submarine was suspected to be. The Ikara needed to be tracked by equipment and operators on the vessel, and a far cheaper alternative to firing multiple Ikaras for training was to simulate one. This job fell to VC 724 Squadron. The maintainers removed the rear ejection seat from a Macchi and in its place they secured the fin of an Ikara rocket, which contained the tracking devices and antennas for the ship to track. The tasked profile was to run in at high speed and extremely low level over the ship on a designated bearing (direction), and then simulate launch of the missile by a sudden pull up, with no time to groan under the five g, because then there was a 'push' back to level flight at just a few hundred feet, blood flow reversing up to the head, uncomfortable but now, vision clearing, rushing out on the bearing at 300 knots – or 550 km/hr – rippled sea flicking by underneath, for the required distance then, to pull up again to position for another run from overhead the warship on a different bearing to simulate the next launch.

'There's only enough fuel for a few of these runs, so don't screw up!' I would tell myself.

In March 1978, a destroyer had just come out of refit at Williamstown Naval Dockyard near Melbourne, on the shores of Port Phillip Bay. Lieutenant Jerry was to lead a detachment of Macchis from 724

Squadron to the air force's Laverton base which lay just to the north of Point Cook, to work with the ship. I was excited to be selected to be part of this detachment: I was flying a navy jet not that far from my home town! There, I often stared out over Port Phillip Bay from the end of Mornington's main street, the nearby beaches or the crumbling red cliffs. The Bay displayed many moods that varied from sullen grey skies with wind and whitecaps, to thousands of glittering blue prisms on blazing sunny days, but my favourite was the pale grey sheet of water under off-white thin overcast on a windless afternoon, with occasional shafts of sunlight breaking through as the sun lowered toward a western horizon which was as straight and defined as a knife edge. And now I was to fly in that very sky.

Our Macchis were to operate with the destroyer in a special restricted area over Port Phillip Bay, 'working up' its radar operators and equipment in tracking exercises. One of us would take off from Laverton, work with the warship, recover back to Laverton, then off would go one of the other pilots to continue operations with the ship, daily for a week. Here, we had to pay particular attention to our jet's position in the designated area over the bay: there was much 'controlled' airspace nearby, including that for busy Melbourne International and Essendon airports, and Point Cook's training areas.

'Mike six four, do you have fatherlock?' radioed the destroyer.

'Affirmative,' I replied.

I had just pulled up in a joyous zoom over the destroyer, my task complete, with fuel remaining in the Macchi's tank approaching the minimum prudent for a standard 'recovery' along with a small safety margin. The TACAN indicator showed the direction and distance to Laverton's beacon, and I continued my climb through a low layer of 'scud', parades of low clouds over the water, and I radioed Laverton Approach for clearance to proceed to the air force base. The cloud deck below thickened as I commenced a descent for a TACAN approach. The aim was to 'break out' of the overcast with Laverton's runway directly ahead.

With the aircraft stable and descending on the final course, the clouds that loomed engulfed us as I continued the descent to the Minimum Descent Altitude (MDA) depicted on the approach chart strapped to my knee. I could not fly lower than this altitude, just a few hundred feet above the ground, if I was not 'visual' with the runway. And at MDA, this time, I was not. There was still only grey. Locked on to the instruments, I raised the Macchi's nose to the climb attitude on the Attitude Indicator, and pushed the Viper's throttle all the way up. Raising the landing gear and flaps, I climbed away in the specified 'missed approach' that was published on the chart.

Meanwhile, the cloud had thickened and lowered even more, but now I was on top of the layer again. What now? I could not land at any of Melbourne's civilian airports. The Macchi did not have the civilian Instrument Landing System (ILS) that was specifically designed for very low cloud or poor visibility, and nearby Point Cook did not have any instrument approach facilities. So, levelling off a few thousand feet above Melbourne's western suburbs, I tried another TACAN approach into Laverton. Into the cloud and again at MDA there was nothing but grey. My scan began flicking more often to the fuel gauge. These approaches were consuming fuel at a heavy rate. One more instrument approach. Not 'visual'. This was getting serious. My mind was racing. I recalled small 'holes' that I had seen in the overcast below – I had had fleeting glimpses of fields and occasional houses below through these gaps on the approaches – but there were no gaps near the runway. Once more I set the aircraft up on the inbound bearing towards Laverton's beacon. I glimpsed a few gaps in the low scud beneath the aircraft. That one! I smartly closed the throttle and dived for the rent in the clouds, dropped through it to just a few hundred feet above the houses and then on with the power. I could now see ahead but I was very low. I 'dragged' the Macchi, its frame rumbling with the air resistance of the extended wheels and flaps, Laverton's runway was ahead, but low and flat in the middle distance. Clouds and vapour flickered just overhead the canopy. Finally, I attained the correct approach angle, throttled back and … phew! It was nice to hear the chirp from the Macchi's wheels as they touched the runway. There was not much fuel left.

Jerry and another pilot met me, remarking on the unforeseen deterioration in the weather. After my first missed approach they had rushed up to Laverton's control tower, anxiously following the radio calls of a young, inexperienced midshipman trying to land. They told me that they had worked on an *in extremis* plan to divert me to the air force base at East Sale, 210 kilometres to the east that had better weather. They had calculated that the fuel required would have been about the same amount that was in my tanks, with no margin: the tanks would have been dry near landing at East Sale. A lucky break in the cloud, a 'dirty dart' through it and for once, I had thought outside the square under a little pressure, alone in an aircraft. But I should have considered diverting to East Sale myself after the first attempt to land. I had had no plan. And dealing with bad weather in a single-engine jet would soon again provide a challenge.

A few days later, three blue, white and silver Macchis taxied noisily out to Laverton's runway, nose to tail, the shrill sound of each engine rising and falling as they manoeuvred. They lined up in an arrowhead pattern at the take off point, with Jerry's in front, and the engines' whine became a roar. Our three jets lifted off as one and turned smartly to the north east. Jerry was leading us in a formation transit back to Nowra; the Laverton detachment was over. It was the peacetime military, and I had enjoyed two weekends free with friends and family, We climbed to 31,000 feet, loosening our formation in order to 'relax' a bit, with Jerry as the leader navigating and making the occasional radio call to Melbourne Control. Being the least experienced, I sat a comfortable distance from Jerry's right wing in the easiest position. This far out I could occasionally flick my eyes into the cockpit, monitoring fuel and the Macchi's basic navigation aids. All I had to do was follow Jerry's jet, a blue and white rounded bullet against a darker blue sky with a dazzling white cloud

A PRELUDE TO SEA   133

deck below us, and soon I would be drinking a brew in 724's crew room and perhaps munching on a snorker bought from the goffa wagon. However, the cloud deck gradually rose beneath us. Jerry's voice came through asking Melbourne Control for a higher cruising altitude. His Macchi nosed up … quick, put the power on and stay with him, I told myself. The undercast rose further. Now, wisps of cloud licked at our aircraft, so I moved right in close, and now it was even harder to monitor instruments. I had to stay close to Jerry and now we were completely enveloped in grey nothingness. The other Macchi on Jerry's left was also sliding in towards him. The horizon disappeared and our world became grey mist and our aircraft. There was no 'up' or 'down'. The flickering of our rotating beacons became distracting, so we followed suit after Jerry turned his off. The little green navigation light on his tip tank became prominent. I *had* to keep Jerry in sight. I had not flown formation in cloud much before and if I lost him, I would have to make a rapid 'break away' a 'lost contact' call and then, in cloud, where was I? Had Nowra's TACAN beacon locked on? What about the weather? The Macchi had no radar to detect hazardous storm clouds, nor had it any equipment for preventing engine or airframe icing. Worse, there would be merciless ribbing later in the crew room if I broke formation.

I could hear myself breathing hard even with the intercom off. As my gloved hand clenched the control column, I told myself to try to relax. I had never flown close formation in the thin air above thirty thousand feet, where the aircraft is less stable and its engine delivers less power. Whether Jerry was turning, climbing or descending, I could not know in the grey void that surrounded us; I was focussed on maintaining the correct reference points on his Macchi: if I lost him, I could be in trouble. Senses in the inner ear sent strange messages – is that a turn? Or are we straightening out of a turn? I stuck to my formation and instrument training and tried to ignore the conflicting signals. When Jerry called us across to Nowra's approach control radio frequency I relaxed a little. But come on, stay with him! My Macchi had started to ease forward as Jerry reduced power for descent, but I was late catching it, and I fought to get back to the correct position. His extended gloved hand and a nod of his helmet gave the signal for 'speed brakes', and I quickly thumbed the speed brake switch on top of the throttle. Down through cloud we sped with the speed brakes hanging like open trap doors beneath the Macchis' bellies, the cloud not homogenous now, wisps of darker and lighter grey blinked past. Suddenly, we were in a blinding new world, three jets in formation bursting out of the cloud, and in glances I could see a horizon and the familiar coast ahead, and now there was Nowra Hill and our base. Jerry arranged us into an extended echelon formation and with the familiar 'run and break', the equivalent of the air force initial and pitch, we entered Nowra's traffic circuit, and then we were home.

Jerry had led us over the top of a developing line of thunderstorms above the Great Dividing Range. With the Macchis not fitted with any weather-detecting radar, we had no idea of what was brewing below. Not long after our debrief, a greenish-grey roll cloud approached from the west, a gust front whipping dust and leaves ahead of it. Then large hailstones pelted, and lightning cracked through driving rain. This had been the developing storm that we had 'topped', enveloped in upper reaches of relatively stable cloud. Gone were the training days of formation flying in fine skies and instrument flying in benign conditions under hood or screen, flying approach after approach in canned exercises. Now I understood why formation and instrument flying skills were vital along with planning for unforeseen weather, along with the leadership qualities that Jerry had displayed as the formation leader. I had watched, listened and learned.

Apart from the flying, there were also ground duties. Being assigned as the 'Duty Officer' for the squadron came about regularly: days where I coordinated flying tasks, passed messages and liaised with the aircraft maintainers and the Engineering Officer. All pilots had to attend 'Divisions', which were the regular parades, and carried out other 'secondary duties'. Still immature, I was remiss with my uniform at times, and I remained angular and skinny, still carrying myself asymmetrically with the poorly healed collarbone. The scar under my mouth was still livid and I did not present myself as an authoritative naval officer. Until now, for quite some time most midshipmen joining the squadron had been older than us, and I recall one of the squadron pilots shaking his head on the day that Ray and I reported for duty: 'They're so young! They're just kids!' But between the ground duties and fleet support flights, there was also training in aerial warfare. And I was to find out that that was mostly about *turning*, and *seeing*.

I sweated, despite the several kilometres high we were in the upper atmosphere. Two of us grunted under the g as I pulled the Macchi out from a plunge toward the blue sea. The g suit squeezed legs and stomach and I fought against it to clear my vision. Now the jet's nose was arcing up and its speed began to wash off. I kept back pressure on the control column until I began to feel a 'buzz' through it, then the vibration and shuddering of the whole aircraft as the wings approached their stalling angle. But now, contrary to my previous training, I deliberately maintained the buffet at the lower speeds as I had been taught by the Air Warfare Instructor. He was sitting through all this in the rear cockpit. Buffet meant that the Macchi's wing was at its maximum lift-producing potential, which would enable the pilot to out-turn an opposing jet and bring his weapons to bear. The g had eased and I was gasping through my oxygen mask, over the top of the huge loop, and once again the speed and the g built up, the buffet disappearing with the building speed, because now I had to flick my eyes to the g meter on the panel to ensure that I did not overstress the aircraft near its g limit. I also had to crane my neck up and back to look through the canopy, which was an effort, because my head and helmet now felt four times their normal weight. There was another blue and white Macchi with two red and white helmets visible in the darkness of its cockpit, in plan view opposite, plummeting down while I was now zooming up again, and I *had* to keep it in sight.

We were locked in a simulated aerial combat. I was trying to bring my nose to bear towards Ray's Macchi and he was trying to do the same to mine. Winning the 'fight' was about getting 'angles' on the opponent: to turn or pitch the nose at a greater rate than him, to be able to bring my simulated guns to bear and in turn prevent Ray from doing the same to me. All this was to the subdued roar of the engine at 'maximum continuous' power, the periodic rattle and shake of the pre-stall buffet and the rasp of myself and the AWI panting over the intercom, with occasional grunts and groans when the g built. In this fight, instead of continuous level turns our aircraft were locked in a vertical 'yo-yo' manoeuvre: continuous back-to-back loops requiring constant and correct movements of the 'stick' to in turn respect the g limitation at the bottom of each manoeuvre and then to 'pull to the buffet' near the top as the speed bled off under gravity. Should one pilot break out of the yo-yo, the other would be on his tail in an instant. It was a simulated 'dance of death', which would only finish with one pilot running low on fuel, gaining 'angles' on the other, or conversely, having 'angles' gained on himself. With the two aircraft of the same type, the only variable was the ability of each pilot.

As the fight wore on, I was getting the idea but had been heavy-handed with the buffet, which had lost us some performance. I knew I had lost this fight, as I had with most of the other ones. Ray had worked his way around, his jet sliding more and more astern of me with each yo-yo.

'OK, knock it off,' came over the radio from the AWI in Ray's Macchi. The exercise was over. Soaked with sweat under my g-suit and Mae West, still breathing heavily and having been 'shot down' several times, I led the other aircraft back to Nowra. Later we would be debriefed in our sweat-stained flight suits. Ray and I had had a taste of aerial combat. The exercise had stirred up some surprisingly aggressive emotions and motivations, along with the soreness of muscles in our necks that we never knew we had from all the craning around while pulling g.

We learned that apart from well-developed neck muscles, above-average visual acuity was an asset for pilots being trained for aerial warfare. Aloft in the designated training area, our Macchis would split: break formation left and right, and after a pre-briefed interval, turn back in towards each other like jousting knights, each pilot desperately trying to spot the other. The first pilot to get visual always had the edge. Also, combat formations were not flown close, wing to wing. We were taught to fly well-spaced and abeam each other, in order to look behind the opposite aircraft and to clear his tail. Our eyes constantly searched the sky, looking for that tiny dot.

Several times we trained with gun cameras attached to the bulky weapons sight mounted on the coaming in front of us, and in a formation pair we took turns to individually climb up to a perch position above and behind the other aircraft. We would then 'roll in' down towards it, then reverse the turn to track the illuminated central 'pipper' surrounded by a circle of dots that was beamed onto the glass of the sight, in a simulated attack on the other jet. Although I had been showing some promise with the 'turning' fights, I was having difficulty grasping the concept of these tracking exercises. I just did not have the eye or spatial awareness to position my aircraft correctly and produce a textbook film of the 'bogey' being tracked in my gun sight. Also, my vision, although not requiring correcting glasses, was not acute enough. I won only a few turning fights, and there was just one proud occasion where I 'shot down' a staff pilot.

Once, I was entrusted to fly a Macchi back to Nowra that had had heavy maintenance carried out on it by Qantas, Australia's overseas airline, at Sydney International Airport. As a child, me flying out of Sydney as a grizzled Qantas captain was a frequent daydream and now I really was at Sydney Kingsford Smith International Airport but flying a single engine jet. A Boeing 747 'Jumbo' loomed behind my aircraft as I waited for my turn to take off. It filled the sky behind the tiny Macchi. Airborne, I carefully followed directions from Air Traffic Control and eventually set course past the sandy crescent of Cronulla Beach and south for Nowra with the beautiful green coast of New South Wales beneath and glittering blue sea to my left.

Flying to elsewhere from Nowra was always interesting. I diligently prepared for these flights, and I usually managed to avoid fouling up air traffic control procedures, navigation or fuel planning. There were even hints that I might remain on VC 724 Squadron to convert to the Skyhawk along with Ray. But I had produced mediocre results on some navigation exercises and instrument flying tests, some of which were flown 'under the hood' in the back seat with my test nerves jangling.

On one navigation exercise to be flown with an instructor, weapons racks fitted under our Macchi's wings had increased its drag and therefore its fuel consumption, which added to the amount of fuel that we would need to complete the rather complicated route that I was to fly among the mountains and dams of the Great Dividing Range. I did not think to question the instructor about the reduced range of the aircraft. I should have suggested modifying the plan before we launched. He suddenly noticed our lower-than-planned fuel state, and he hurriedly ordered the exercise to be abandoned. I had given the impression of being thoughtless and 'behind the eight ball'. This, and my poor gun camera results reinforced to both myself, and the instructors of 724 Squadron, that I just was not fighter pilot material. I would go to fly the Grumman Tracker, as had been originally planned.

Despite the Macchi flying and one exhilarating flight in a two-seat Skyhawk trainer, the brutish Tracker still had a pull. Many of the observers on the Tracker squadrons had become friends. The Tracker routinely rumbled along at 130 knots – or 240 km/hr – which gave a pilot more time to think. Although the RAN operated the Tracker 'single pilot', the Observer Tactical Coordinator (TACCO) in the co-pilot's seat navigated the aircraft and was there to read checklists and make radio calls in addition to his important role as Mission Commander. I found this reassuring, yet I would still be the only qualified pilot on-board, and was therefore the aircraft captain – not bad for a twenty year old! However, before I would fly the 'Grey Grumblie', there were two more obstacles I had to overcome.

Ray remained on 724 Squadron to fly the Skyhawk but we were not to go on our separate paths just yet. We were required to complete a Combat Survival Course. After that, I had to master the Hawker Siddeley HS 748.

We were told to get out of the enclosed back of the truck, unload our limited amount of equipment and to move off. As a mixed group of navy, army and air force pilots, we had completed a week of lectures at Amberley RAAF Base, on Brisbane's fringe. We were now in the practical phase of the course and our task was to fix our position on a map and then get to a designated set of coordinates, set up camp and 'survive' for a few days. Many challenges lay ahead, the main one being that we were initially in an 'evasion' phase.

The scenario was that we had bailed out from an aircraft over rain forest in enemy territory. We only had the equipment that would normally be in our aircraft survival packs. We would be hunted day and night by army units, which acted as enemy forces trying to capture us. I had already undergone training in survival at sea and I had dangled under the blast of a helicopter's rotor in 'wet winching' exercises, sodden flight suit flapping under an inflated Mae West, to be unceremoniously dragged into the helicopter by the aircrewman at its door. But this was to be a new experience.

The army pilots were in their element. They fixed our position on the topographic map, and we moved quickly into the rain forest. We had each been issued with a parachute, a machete, combat rations and a water bottle: reasonable equipment to assume that we would be carrying when operating over tropical areas in wartime. But that was all. We had been told to keep away from roads and settlements of any form. We waded up and down through dense, steep rain forest in mountainous terrain inland from the Gold Coast. Our parachutes were our saviours because the canopies formed a primitive tent at night, and their cords were invaluable. For a few days we stumbled, footsore, through bush and forest, hungry and sleep deprived. Under no circumstances were we to light fires. The area had been used by many courses before us and there was little to catch or eat. An old macadamia nut plantation and mushrooms in the wet earth provided little food. Any live animal that was captured was to be handed in and exchanged for food when the instructors later visited the fixed campsite. Once, we risked moving along near a ridge-top road, but after nightfall, we huddled and shivered in silence under rain-soaked parachutes in the undergrowth of the ridge-top just below the road. We heard the tramp of boots just above: the army 'enemy' were out looking for us.

The next day, deep in a rainforest gully and pushing through dense bush, suddenly the world exploded in blank weapon rounds: the enemy had found us and, crestfallen, we continued on to the specified location for the 'survival' phase. Luckily, we had not decided to emulate Ray's group, which had decided to break the exercise rules: cosily ensconced in a local community hall for the night, they were reported to the army by locals then 'captured'. These hapless pilots would be made to undergo the entire course again. I was very pleased that I wasn't assigned to that group.

At the fixed camp, the combat survival instructors visited the groups, and we were thankful to learn that we had passed muster by staying inside the boundaries and delivering a reasonable performance, despite our capture. Even more gaunt than usual, I arrived back at Nowra to start yet another course: conversion to the Hawker Siddeley HS 748. Successfully flying this machine was a prerequisite to commencing the Operational Flying School on the Grumman Tracker.

Compared with the Macchi, the '748' was a monster. It had been designed by the British Avro company as an airliner. Its cabin could seat forty passengers and included a galley and a toilet. The Royal Australian Navy used two of these aircraft for several roles: general transport and support, carriage of senior officers and VIP's and interestingly, the teaching of raw pilots, just out of basic training, to fly multi-engine aircraft. Years later, the navy 748s would be fitted with sophisticated electronic warfare equipment and they would bristle with antennas in an additional role of training ships' crews in electronic warfare and jamming.

The aircraft required two pilots to fly it and RAN pilots wore normal naval uniform, not the usual baggy green flight suits. In summer, 748 pilots wore regulation white shorts and long socks with hairy legs and knobbly knees projecting around the control 'yokes'. The air force also used HS 748s, but primarily as a navigation trainer based at East Sale, Victoria, and they called the HS 748 the 'Draggie', while the navy called its aircraft the 'Speedbird'. The navy's 748s, belonging to VC 851 Squadron, were even painted much like the airliners of the day, with glossy grey lower fuselage and wings. The fuselage had a smart blue 'cheat line' running along the line of cabin windows, and its upper surfaces and tailfin were white.

Sitting in a fold-out jump seat behind the two pilots, I could see that learning to fly this thing was going to be interesting. Being in essence an airliner, it was easy to jump on board to watch a flight, when other squadron duties and ground school permitted. The aircraft captain in the left seat manipulated a large handlebar-like yoke in front of him, but the machine did not seem to be doing much. It was as if he sat in an armchair flying a small room. Occasionally, he wrestled with the yoke to turn the aircraft, and the horizon would grudgingly tilt in the flat windscreens ahead. Almost unintelligible patter passed over the headphones between the two pilots: lengthy 'challenge and response' checklists were constantly in use, the co-pilot reading the required action and the captain responding with a set reply or confirmation. There was an overhead panel with a multitude of dials and clunky switches. Starting the engines and taxiing for take-off seemed to involve much reaching up and flicking and snapping of switches on this panel. Vast black panels of fuses were located on bulkheads behind each pilot's seat. Another console sat between the pilots. Prominent were the two engine power levers in their quadrants, big round Bakelite trim wheels with knurled edges, the lever that controlled the flaps and behind all that, then row after row of controls for the radio and navigation equipment, grey rectangles with white numbers on counters that corresponded to radio frequencies, controlled by knobs. In a compartment behind the 'flight deck' was a desk and instruments for the navigator (in this case a navy observer), who was part of the crew on most military HS 748s.

The 748's two Rolls Royce Dart turboprop engines, putting out over 2,000 horsepower, produced a combination of a constant shriek (the aircraft was sometimes known as 'The Twenty Ton Dog Whistle'), counterpointed with a buzzing whirr from the propellers. Rolls Royce have a tradition of naming their turbine aircraft engines after British rivers, in this case the River Dart. Coincidentally, the engines were dart-like in their appearance, reminiscent of traditional fountain pens, with futuristic-looking grilles on their sides and then the big four-bladed Rotol propellers with bullet like 'spinners' over their hubs. The spinners covered intricate mechanical controls that set the angle of each propeller blade while it revolved. A turboprop engine is essentially a jet engine that drives a propeller. While the 748 cruised at 220 knots – or 400 km/hr – at altitudes around 15,000 feet – or four and a half kilometres – above the earth, moaning waves of vibration buzzed through the airframe that regularly rose and fell in 'harmonics' as the propellers, synchronised by a mechanical device, beat waves of air and sound onto the fuselage

Engine power was set by a lever for each engine. These were linked to complicated mechanical components that regulated fuel supply to the Darts while a governor mechanism maintained the propellers within a certain RPM range. There were, however, other secondary engine controls, especially 'pitch stops' and 'fuel trimmers', the operation of which I was to find would be important.

The HS 748 was, as I would also find out, full of British character. Most aircraft have clearly-labelled circuit breakers, little buttons that that pop out if an electrical circuit overheats or shorts out, because an electrical fire in an aircraft is a dire situation. However, the 748 mostly had 'fuses'. A 748 pilot had to look up a book to ascertain what fuse corresponded to the piece of equipment that it protected. Then he would use a 'tester' at the end of a spiral cord that would only light up when inserted in a serviceable fuse.

Another piece of rudimentary British engineering was the electrical fire detection system. The bulkhead behind each pilot's seat was the front face of a cabinet containing the radio and navigation equipment, manfully referred to in the 748's flight manual as the radio 'crate'. A thin metal pipe led from each crate, passed under the floor and up onto the left hand window sill, its outlet beside the aircraft captain. Any electrical smoke or fumes in the radio crate would emanate from this tube, convenient to the captain's nostrils. Having detected the fumes by the olfactory method, he would direct the co-pilot to isolate the equipment by turning it off and locating its fuse by referring to the book. If this course of action was unsuccessful, there could be problems if smoke continued to emanate from the tube. However, Avro's designers had planned for that very contingency. A little cork dangled on a chain under each outlet, which the captain could insert to stop the smoke.

The 748's other systems were conventional for larger aircraft of the day but for me, far more complicated than those of any aircraft I had flown. Each turbine not only powered a propeller but also energised an electrical generator and a hydraulic pump, which lowered and extended the landing gear, actuated the brakes, steered the nose wheel (by means of a little 'tiller' near each pilot) and operated the wing flaps. A separate 'blower' driven by each engine pressurised the aircraft's cabin for flight at altitude.

After the Macchi, operating this relative giant would be serious business, especially getting on top of the two-pilot operation, the navigation and communication electronics, and the aircraft's systems. There was another important skill I would have to attain: this was a twin-engine airliner: I would need to be competent to fly it safely and accurately from just before lift-off all the way back to touchdown with one engine failed, or more likely, simulated failed in exercises. I had been told that the Grumman Tracker, also a 'twin', was a handful with one engine out of action, and the inference was that a satisfactory standard of single engine handling had to be achieved on the 748 before I would be allowed anywhere near the smaller but pugnacious Grumman.

'Rowwrrrrr ...'

Over the scream of the turbines, the 748's buzzing propellers came 'off the bite' as I gingerly taxied the aircraft towards Nowra's runway. The intricate mechanisms in the propellers' hubs automatically controlled the angle at which the blades bit the air, commanded by the pilot's power levers. Spinning at high revolutions per minute, on the ground the blades could 'fine off' when the throttles were retarded, turning the propellers' discs into virtual flat plates, with other devices in the engines adjusting fuel as required to the combustion chambers to maintain a relatively constant RPM. This 'flat disc' effect was very effective in slowing the aircraft down after landing and making taxiing easier.

Ground school for the HS 748 had been intense: thick manuals, lectures, then cockpit drills and emergency checklists to memorise. However, there were only two of us students: my 'oppo' was 'Ras', a lieutenant who had been one of the navy instructors at Point Cook while I struggled with the CT-4. He was to become one of the navy's specialist 748 pilots, in preparation for when the two aircraft would take up their intended role as Electronic Warfare trainers. Apart from the technical details of the aircraft and its operation, I had to learn how to operate in all types of airspace from remote outback fields to intensely controlled airspace at major airports, military and civil. The training was also an introduction to the effects of weight, altitude and temperature. Higher altitude and hotter temperature both mean 'thinner' air, which reduces performance and safety margins and, therefore, the weight that an aircraft can safely lift. The Hawker Siddeley manuals were thick binders from the 1960s full of type-faced descriptions, procedures and intricate diagrams. One volume also contained graph after graph. Before starting, the pilots entered one of these graphs by inserting the wind, temperature and airport height above sea level. They could then extract from the graph the safe maximum load that the 748 could lift, along with 'Vee' speeds for the actual aircraft weight. Gradually, my knowledge of transport aircraft performance became slightly clearer than mud.

Most larger multi-engine aircraft are required to be able to safely operate with one engine failed from any time before take off, right up to landing. 'V1', known as 'Vee one', is a speed called out by the non-flying pilot during the take off roll which is the maximum speed at which the aircraft can be stopped safely on the runway: 'aborting' or 'rejecting' the take off. This would typically happen after an engine failure or indeed, any other major malfunction. After V1, the pilot is committed to take-off come what may because there is now insufficient runway available in which to stop. He takes his problem into the air, to sort it out when safely clear of the ground. The take-off continues to 'Vr' where the aircraft is 'rotated', – nose lifted – for take-off and at V2 speed, the aircraft can safely climb away. If an engine fails either on the runway or in the air, it is vital that the pilot keeps the aircraft straight. With the rudder hard over, the wings have to be kept level and the correct, lower nose attitude has to be maintained to keep that all-important V2 speed straight after lift-off. Any slower or any faster, and the aircraft may not climb.

At a safe height above the ground, the aircraft can be accelerated. By now, the pilot would have 'trimmed out' the massive forces on the rudder pedal using the 'trim' knob. But with an engine failed, for every change of power or speed, the rudder will have to be re-trimmed as the forces on the aircraft change. In the meantime, the landing gear has to be raised to reduced drag and the correct drill called-for and carried out by memory until the engine is safely shut down.

The complicated equipment in the propellers' hubs enabled the blades to be 'feathered' against the airflow: the leading edges of the blades set end-on to the rushing air stream to reduce drag. The oars of racing skiffs are feathered as they come out of the water, the blades turned end-on to reduce air resistance. A 748's feathered propeller would sometimes slowly rotate like a windmill in a light breeze. The aircraft could be cruised on one engine and then landed at an airport. Pilots were busy with extra drills and checklists on top of what was required for normal operation, and the handling pilot was constantly adjusting the rudder trim knob with every change of power and speed. An instrument approach would often be required: it was one thing to have good instrument flying skills but, in this aircraft, I was required to be able to fly an approach to a landing or missed approach with one engine failed (or simulated failed). But, as this was my first training flight in the beast, it would take a series of flights, familiarity and study to become proficient.

851 Squadron's instructors were generally patient and supportive of an immature twenty-year-old coming to terms with a large multi-engine aircraft. Once again, diligent bookwork and preparation helped. There was little call for visual navigation (in any case, there was usually an observer navigator onboard), and there were no aerobatics or formation flying to worry about. Therefore, the 748 was a natural fit for my reasonable instrument flying ability and weaknesses in the other areas. It had an autopilot – the use of which I embraced enthusiastically. At the 748's usual cruising height the autopilot flew the aircraft accurately. However, I quickly absorbed the importance of not blindly trusting it and monitoring its operation carefully. To this day, many dreadful aircraft accidents are the result

of pilots blindly following automation. Also, the autopilot could not control the aircraft with one engine shut down.

Now we were cruising at altitude, and this was the training flight to introduce me to 'asymmetric flight': flying with an engine shut down. With the routine call of 'Practice' the instructor pulled back one of the power levers. Immediately, the aircraft's nose smartly yawed left, towards the 'failing' engine and the wings started to roll left. My scan went to the 'skid ball' on the instrument panel, the slip indicator that the Point Cook instructors incessantly hounded their students about. The port engine had been reduced to idle, simulated 'failed'. The skid ball was hard over to the right in its liquid-filled tube and, as briefed, I pushed hard on the right hand rudder pedal to centre it again and therefore keep the aircraft straight and true. I concentrated on levelling the wings with the yoke and my leg strained on that right pedal. It was hard work.

'OK, trim it out now,' said the instructor.

My hand flew to the knob on the console between us, with relief as the little tab on the rudder took the strain. But every time we changed airspeed or power on the working engine, I had to adjust the rudder with my leg and re-trim it. After I got the hang of that, we would shut the idling engine down completely.

The instructor started reading from a checklist, and one-by-one he carried out its requirements on the various switches on the panels.

Dzzzzzh!

The tone of the whirring propeller beside the left window rapidly diminished and the engine stopped. I stole glances at the near-stationary propeller to my left, its four silver blades and bullet-shaped hub very slowly rotating against the blue of the Tasman Sea, between scans of the horizon and the instruments to maintain an accurate speed, heading and altitude. We flew like that for a while, twenty tons of aircraft on one engine, then we began the checklist for restarting the one that we had shut down. Its propeller began to revolve as its twisting blades caught the air's blast, its drag shimmying the aircraft toward it even more, then fuel and ignition was introduced. Now at idle, the turboprop's electrical generator was brought back online, and then I brought the power lever up and re-trimmed the controls.

The exercise had gone well, but it was made clear that I would have to control the HS 748 accurately and safely after an engine failure at take-off. Then I would have to fly it, completely on instruments, to an instrument approach and landing. At the end of the course, I would undergo an instrument rating test: a long navigation exercise to various airfields and military bases around New South Wales, making instrument approaches to the various runways, landings, missed approaches and handling simulated emergencies that would include engine failures and fires.

Descending the HS 748 from altitude was not just a matter of pulling the power back to idle and maintaining the correct descent airspeed as one did with the Macchi. The complicated gearbox that connected the Rolls Royce Dart's jet engine to the propeller had lay shafts in it that could not tolerate negative torque. Torque is a raw description of the turning power of an engine. As the Dart powered the aircraft through the air, its torque was 'positive', turning the propeller against the air resistance. However, reducing its power too much at high speeds resulted in the propeller acting like a windmill: 'driving' the engine instead of being driven by it. Therefore, the 748 had to be descended with power on its engines, which resulted in a flat descent gradient with the aircraft near its maximum allowable speed. On this flat, fast descent profile, the machine was like a toboggan sliding downhill. Therefore, careful planning of the descent point was required. To further complicate matters, the fuel going into the engines had to be trimmed by the co-pilot, who referred to a circular scale that took into account height and temperature. Little switches had to be blipped to fine-tune the fuel mixture going into the Dart's combustion chambers by referring to small dials under them. This, in turn, also increased the engines' power, which flattened the aircraft's descent gradient even more.

The complicated propeller system required special actions after landing. 'Pitch stops' in the propeller's hub prevented the blades from becoming too 'fine' (low angles relative to the hubs tending to increase propeller RPM). In the air, these pitch stops prevented the blades from twisting too far back, a vital function, for if the blades 'fined off' completely, the propeller disc would be like a huge flat plate facing the blast of air, the drag disastrous to the aircraft and its occupants. But on the ground the high RPM of the Dart's propeller would cause too much thrust, making stopping after landing and taxiing difficult, so immediately after landing, the co-pilot had to 'withdraw' the stops so that the propeller would become more like that flat plate which would help to slow the machine down and make taxiing easier. This also prevented the engine from catastrophic heat damage. Therefore, the co-pilot's withdrawal of the pitch stops immediately after touchdown, using two little levers with serrated knobs that sat near the throttles on their quadrant, was important. All this on top of the checklists, radio calls, tuning the various radio navigation aids, controlling the pressurisation, monitoring fuel, hydraulics and electrics ... always being prepared for an engine failure ... whether in control of the HS 748 or acting as its co-pilot, I considered the man-machine interface of this aircraft 'intense'.

Flight after flight, we practised circuits, aborts on the runway before V1, simulated engine failures after, engine shutdowns, re-starts and, then, the same exercises using instrument flying, with screens placed over the flight deck windows. No longer were we always returning to Nowra: we flew to other airports in eastern Australia. I took turns with Ras to occupy the left seat – the seat for the captain – under instruction, learning to navigate primarily using radio aids, the TACAN and ADF as fitted to the Macchi. Like those of airline pilots, our charts were just lines on a basic map with annotated directions and distances. The various ground radio beacons all over Australia looked like the nodes of a colossal nervous system. If a pilot could interpret the chart properly and tune the correct radio navigation aids (navaids) in a logical, disciplined manner, they could fly anywhere, day and night, in any weather conditions.

Approaching the destination pilots still referred to the charts, carefully tracking the navaids and aware of any terrain beneath ('Minimum Safe Altitudes' were also printed on these charts). The aircraft would then normally be picked up by ground radar and assigned headings to fly or directed to fly a TACAN approach, its civilian near-equivalent, the VHF Omnidirectional Radio Range (VOR) approach, or the primitive 'non directional beacon' (NDB) approach. At a military base, a GCA approach could be offered, just as I had flown in the Macchi but in this aircraft often with a simulated engine failure and, in any case, all those checklists! But there was also a new sort of instrument approach I had to master: the ILS.

The Instrument Landing System (ILS), even at the time of writing, is the primary method for landing large aircraft at airports in poor weather conditions. Two transmitters near the runway provide very accurate beams for the pilot (or autopilot) to follow. One beam provides steering information to fly down the runway's extended centreline (the 'localiser') and the other provides an accurate 'glide slope', showing where to fly to maintain a constant three-degree approach angle to a safe touchdown. At the relatively low height of around two hundred feet – or sixty metres – the pilot needs to be able to see the runway and, if not, commence a 'missed approach' to try again, enter a holding pattern, or divert to another airport.

Initially, I just 'chased the needles' on the ILS indicator in front of me, but I was told to treat them as an imaginary Ground-Controlled Approach controller, to smoothly make corrections towards the centreline and glide path with gentle changes of heading and rate of descent. The instrument became more sensitive as the aircraft got lower as we flew down an invisible cone towards the runway threshold, and accurate flying was essential. A timely reaction to not seeing the runway ahead was important. Barely two hundred feet from the ground, the aircraft had to be climbed away immediately, sometimes with a leg shuddering against a rudder pedal after a simulated engine failure, the working engine at full power but the 748 sluggish and climbing slowly while I wound the rudder trim knob to relieve the strain.

My standard was satisfactory, and the day came when Ras and I would take turns to fly the 748 as the aircraft captain, a 'first solo' for us on the big machine and for me, my only one. He flew first while I acted as his co-pilot, carrying out my duties correctly and in a timely manner to help my oppo, who was busy manipulating the heavy controls. South of the base we went through a shutdown and restart of one of the Darts, taking care not to miss any of the checklist items, and then Ras bought our 748, its side number and callsign '709', back to Nowra.

With the engines still running, we swapped seats, and it was my turn as the Captain. Once more we carried out a shutdown drill and then conducted a restart. With everything back to normal, I called for yet another checklist to set the aircraft up for its shallow descent back towards Nowra, Ras backing me up as I wrestled the machine into the circuit pattern, doing my best to fly accurate heights and speeds. Then we performed *another* checklist.

We made a long final approach until the numbers and 'piano key' markings of Nowra's runway loomed in the windscreen … now! I gently 'flared' the machine to almost level flight just off the runway and my right hand flew down to the elevator trim wheel to give it a quick twist back as we had been taught. I closed the power levers, applied more back pressure on the yoke to hold that landing attitude in the windscreen, and then, 'chirp-chirp … chirp.' The 748's double mainwheels and then the nose gear were on the runway. Ras withdrew the 'flight fine' propeller pitch stops, to make the big propellers act like flat plates, making use of the wheel brakes almost unnecessary. Using the nose wheel steering tiller on the console with my left hand, I steered the 748 along Nowra's taxiways to 851 Squadron's tarmac. Marshalled to the parking position by the duty sailor, I set the park brake, and we shut down the Darts. Ras and I shook hands. There would be a few celebratory beers in the wardroom that evening. However, a few days later we would fly '709' on a long journey. As co-pilots, we would form part of a crew to take personnel and stores to the navy's detachment of Grumman Trackers, which flew from the RAAF Base near Darwin, in Australia's Northern Territory.

Vietnam was still in chaos. With its long war over, thousands of Vietnamese, most from the capitalist south, were fleeing the recently unified country. Many were getting on shaky boats to try to reach Australia in order to claim refugee status. Also, Australia had expanded her economic claims further from her coastline and fishing vessels from Asia were encroaching into these areas. Darwin-based Trackers were tasked with flying daily patrols to search for refugee and illegal fishing vessels in Australian waters. When found, they were reported and photographed. Navy patrol boats would then intercept them. This surveillance effort was called Operation Seawatch. Most of the personnel of VS 816 'DET DAR' (DETachment DARwin) were rotated through every few months. The detachment was generally supported by routine air force Hercules transport flights, but occasionally the smaller HS 748s of the navy were used. Along with the transport of personnel and equipment, the long flight north west to Darwin and back would be good experience for student pilots and observers.

Two crews shared the flying to Darwin that required two refuelling stops. The 748's cabin was full of personnel, the off duty crew, equipment and even some navy wives. At the two outback airports the heat became a significant issue with the performance of the HS 748 and I craned over the shoulders of the two experienced captains as they pored over graphs and tables to determine take off speeds and maximum allowable weights. I had never flown in the tropics, and I marvelled at the heaped cumulus and cumulonimbus storm clouds as we weaved to avoid them. At Darwin we checked into one of the air force's wooden accommodation blocks that sat high on stilts with the ubiquitous louvred glass windows. It was a fitful night's sleep under a ceiling fan (there was no air-conditioning), but an interesting day lay ahead for tomorrow: I would finally fly in a Grumman Tracker.

There was no window in front of me – just a vast black panel festooned with dials, knobs and even a pen trace on rolling graph paper. There was a little table that held something that looked like a typewriter keyboard. The panel extended to the ceiling of padded grey soundproofing. Once again, I wore a 'bone dome' style helmet, but it had a boom microphone. There were no oxygen masks here: crews in this aircraft would never fly high enough to need them. In an olive-green flight suit and yellow lifejacket, I was strapped into one of the two rear sensor operator positions of a Grumman Tracker, 'along for the ride' on one of VS 816 Det Dar's routine surveillance flights for Operation Seawatch. A parachute pack was my backrest on the steel bucket-like seat. Although Darwin's wet season was petering out, a grey overcast arched above us with occasional moody cumulus clouds beneath it. The air was almost as humid as it had been on the ground in Darwin. The Tracker had no air-conditioning. There was a small square window at my right elbow, but most of the view from it was just the inboard face of the Tracker's big engine nacelle, its black paint adding to the gloom. Grey water with occasional whitecaps was some 1,500 feet – or 450 metres – below. The engines were throttled back for cruise, their rumble partly muffled by the helmet. Desultory conversation crackled over the intercom between the pilot in the front left seat, his observer 'TACCO' (Tactical Coordinator) in the front right seat, and the radar operator immediately to my left. The radar man (who I had learned whose position was 'Sensor Three'), was detecting surface vessels on his radar scope then giving steering commands to the pilot toward the 'contact'. If the contact was visually identified as one of interest: a suspected refugee boat or illegal Asian fishing vessel, it was photographed by the TACCO, and its position plotted and passed by radio to higher command who would, if necessary, despatch a navy patrol boat to investigate further. Today was quiet: only one or two rusty ramshackle fishing vessels had been detected. In the 'Sensor Four' position, I was given the task of passing the routine position reports to Air Force Darwin over the HF radio. HF is typically crackly, inconsistent and occasionally unreliable, and in the days before routine satellite communications, it was the only option for long-distance messages from low altitude while the Tracker ranged hundreds of miles from Darwin in its search. Studying the vast panels in the back of the aircraft and passing the reports kept me occupied and, after several hours, on our way back to Darwin the pilot invited me to switch positions with the TACCO: at last, I could be in the co-pilot's seat!

The TACCO and I squeezed past each other in the little passageway that connected the cockpit and the sensor operators' stations. To enter the cockpit I bent over and pushed through a tiny arched doorway of riveted metal. I floundered into the co-pilot's seat. Wow! What a view, after being cooped up for hours in the cramped interior. The visibility through the small eyebrow-shaped windscreen over the Tracker's blunt nose was good, and I could lean into the side 'bubble' window that bulged outwards. Under the windscreen was another vast instrument panel, but this one included instruments that were familiar. The panel was raked, and shaded by huge coamings like bat wings. A vast array of switches, dials and levers projected from the ceiling panel overhead, and there was yet another console between the pilot and me, which had to be swung upwards on a hinge to allow the TACCO and me to change seats.

'Handing over,' said the pilot. 'Just keep her on this heading and at fifteen hundred feet.'

I grasped the control wheel, which was even heftier than that of the HS 748, but the Tracker seemed much more manoeuvrable and its controls felt lighter. The wheel had an electric trim switch for the elevators on it, no big (folklore had it, World War II surplus) HS 748 trim wheel here. The pilot's hand occasionally came up to adjust the throttles and propeller levers of the engines. Unlike in most aircraft, many of the Tracker's controls projected down from the panel in the ceiling between the pilot and the TACCO. A Tracker pilot set the twin throttles with his gloved hand curled around their two grips, his arm hanging off them, with the propeller RPM levers and mixture controls adjacent. The landing gear and flaps were also controlled by levers that projected down from the overhead panel, I flew the aircraft for a half-hour while we rumbled along at 130 knots – or 240 km/hr – with the overcast lowering in front of us and darker shafts of grey studding the horizon when rain showers fell from the sullen puffs of cumulus.

The Tracker was jam-packed with panels, instruments, knobs, switches and equipment. I was fascinated by it all, but there was so much to learn, and … I would have to operate it from Nowra to a satisfactory standard and, after that, safely and consistently land this thing on an aircraft carrier.

Home at Nowra, it was back to training in the HS 748, especially in emergency and instrument flying procedures, followed by the Instrument Rating Test in the aircraft. The test went surprisingly well and resulted in a good report from the laconic testing officer and kind words from the Senior Pilot, who granted me an early departure on a few weeks' leave.

It had been an intense two years. I had scraped through the air force pilot's course. I had flown the navy's Macchis in fleet support and air combat manoeuvres. I was now qualified to fly a small airliner. But, until I successfully completed Operational Flying School on the Grumman Tracker, my 'wings of gold' were still only provisional.

8

THE HEAVING STEEL

1978

I n order to become familiar with the carrier, the other trainees and I had visited HMAS *Melbourne* on several occasions when she was alongside in Sydney. It was important that we became familiar with her decks: how the compartments were numbered, the bridge, Flying Control or 'Flyco', and the aircrew briefing room. The ship was sparsely occupied – the rattle of paint chipping and the hammering of machinery echoed through the vast, empty hangars below *Melbourne*'s flight deck.

However, on the previous night of this particular visit, I had spent the night in an outer cabin while the carrier was at sea. On the previous afternoon, a group of us had been flown out to the ship by helicopter for further familiarisation. Water swished past outside the thin steel cabin door, and the space was alive with the throb of the propellers and the muffled roar of fans outside. It rolled and pitched, with no window to provide a stomach-steadying horizon. I had got to know some of the ship's officers, who were 'working up' the ship in preparation for the arrival of the pilots, observers, their aircraft and support crews. Despite the jokes and banter about 'birdies', HMAS *Melbourne* would be just another ship until her air group came aboard.

The keel of a new aircraft carrier for the Royal Navy of wartime Britain was 'laid down' in England in 1943. She would be named HMS *Majestic*; however, with the end of World War II imminent, the construction of the vessel was halted until it was decided that she would be delivered to the Royal Australian Navy for post-war service. She was renamed HMAS *Melbourne*. Australia's new aircraft carrier had a displacement of 20,000 tonnes, measured 214 metres in length and her beam (width) was just over twenty-four metres.

From the waterline down to her keel, *Melbourne* was similar to most of the Royal Navy's larger warships. In the engine room, three oil-fed boilers fed steam to two Parsons turbines, each of which drove a propeller. *Melbourne* could move through the water at over twenty knots – or 37 km/hr. The lower decks contained the accommodation areas, Messes, offices, sick bay and other facilities vital to some 1,300 men embarked in any warship. But above the lower decks, she was different to any cruiser or battleship. Slab-like steel sides enclosed cavernous aircraft hangars that ran almost the full length of the ship. The tops of the hangars were essentially the ship's flight deck. Compact Skyhawk jets fitted into the hangars easily, so their small rounded 'delta' wings were not designed to fold. But the ponderous Grumman Trackers and helicopters had wings and rotors folded against their bodies in the manner of giant insects, not to be unfolded until just before launch. Two massive square elevators (lifts) were inset into the flight deck to move aircraft to and from the hangars. Along the sides of each hangar, between their walls and the ship's side, were workshops, storerooms and offices.

Melbourne's flight deck had been built 'angled' – an innovation at the time. Before her completion, most aircraft carriers had a 'straight' flight deck, where aircraft were 'landed on' directly from astern. During launches, a landing aircraft would have to wait, because in the event of a 'bolter', (where the aircraft missed the arresting wires that would bring it to a halt), or a 'wave off' (the aircraft suddenly aborting an attempt to land and climbing away), there was danger of colliding with aircraft being launched from the forward end. Some carriers rigged 'barriers' to prevent overshooting aircraft impacting those about to be launched from the bows, but this was a hazardous and inefficient arrangement. HMAS *Melbourne* was one of the first aircraft carriers fitted with an angled deck. The landing area, approximately the aft two thirds of the carrier's flat top, was angled to port (left) by about five degrees. This allowed any overshooting or 'boltering' aircraft to safely fly away to one side, clear of the launching area, and enabled simultaneous aircraft landings and launches. The angle improved clearance between a landing aircraft's wingtip and the large 'island' that towered on the starboard side of the deck, and the design also increased the area of the deck where aircraft could be safely 'ranged', or parked, clear of flying operations. *Melbourne's* flight deck was of dark grey steel, with hundreds of painted markings on it.

The 'island' – the towering structure on starboard (right) side of the flight deck – supported the funnel, masts, a forest of antennae, lookout positions and a huge black radar dish that rotated like the wind-up key of a giant clockwork toy. The island also contained the bridge, from where *Melbourne's* captain and his seaman officers and crew navigated the vessel. A double row of windows looked forward from the rounded front face of the island: one row for the bridge, with its external 'wings', and the other for the admiral's area. The carrier was not just a platform for operating aircraft: she was also the Flag Ship of the Royal Australian Navy, which embarked an admiral in charge of the fleet or task force, along with his staff and communications equipment. Not only an aircraft carrier, *Melbourne* was a command and control ship, a stores ship, a hospital ship and she could also refuel other vessels.

Melbourne's boilers not only fed the voracious propulsion turbines, but they also provided steam to power the carrier's catapult that flung the Skyhawks and Trackers from the ships bow into the sky. Two massive pistons ran in parallel cylinders just below the forward flight deck, yoked together to drive the catapult's 'shuttle'. The shuttle protruded from a slot in the deck and would, when the catapult was fired, tear straight ahead along the slot for 111 feet – or thirty-four metres – in seconds. A looped wire 'strop' connected the shuttle to the catapult hook of a Skyhawk or Tracker, to launch it as would the rubber band of a child's toy glider. The pistons impacted a mechanism at the end of their stroke that would absorb the momentum of tonnes of steel thudding into it at up to one hundred knots – or 185 km/hr. A catapult firing could be felt throughout the vessel. Later, I would be invited to the Petty Officers' Mess, in the forward part of the ship, while flying was in progress. We would hear the bellow of a Tracker's engines at full power somewhere above the deckhead, then a bang, a squealing shriek that increased in intensity and pitch with waves of vibration, faster and faster, and then an almighty thump that would reverberate through the compartment: the catapult pistons had reached the end of their stroke. There would be loud grinding and squealing as the catapult was retracted back for the next launch. Again, a roar from above, this time a jet, and again, an ear-splitting squeal would follow. Astonishingly, men had their berths in this area and slept attuned to the indescribable racket of sometimes round-the-clock flight operations.

The catapult was controlled from a little room embedded in the flight deck, and small windows of armoured glass gave its operators a view from just above deck level and importantly, the signals from the Catapult Officer. Appropriately named the 'howdah' – after the box-like seating platform on the back of an elephant – it was manned by ship's stokers who controlled the catapult, a piece of equipment intimately connected with the operation of aircraft, but operated by seamen.

Having been flung from the bow of the ship by the catapult, *Melbourne*'s fixed-wing aircraft had to be 'landed on' or 'recovered' on completion of their missions. The landing area, which was the aft two-thirds of the carrier's flight deck, was marked with white and yellow lines that formed a rectangle slightly angled to port, to conform to the angled-deck configuration. A prominent centreline marking of thick broken lines was painted in yellow, which later in *Melbourne*'s life would be repainted in a fiery DayGlo red. At the beginning of the landing area, just forward of the rear of the flight deck or 'round down', the arresting cables or 'wires' stretched across the deck, supported a few centimetres above the steel. There were several wires, and any one of these could be snagged by the landing aircraft's arrester hook that hung from the tail like a long, grasping claw. A wire would have to absorb the momentum of a Skyhawk or Tracker's landing in order to bring it to a halt from flying speed in less than one hundred metres. The ends of each cable were attached to a hydraulic mechanism below the flight deck to. absorb the kinetic energy of the landing aircraft. Like the catapult, the arresting system was manned by ship's sailors who tended its mechanisms and made sure that its settings were correct for the aircraft type that was recovering. *Melbourne*'s complement would become used to the sudden 'bang, thump' of an arriving aircraft, then the shrill 'whee' of the arrester system doing its work. The noise would reverberate throughout the rear part of the ship including the sleeping accommodation, and the wardroom.

On the port side of the landing area, a small platform projected over the sea, grudgingly protected from the windblast by a screen on its forward side. A safety net stretched out over the water around its perimeter. The platform was for the Landing Signals Officer (LSO), responsible for guiding aircraft to a safe landing and arrest. The LSO was the man with the oversized 'bats' in the old films of carrier landings, but after World War II the bats had gone, his tools now special light signals and radio. However, he was still known as 'Paddles', and an LSO still 'waved' an aircraft aboard. An unsafe approach, a lurching deck or a blocked landing area would result in a 'wave off': frantic waves of the 'bats' in olden times but now bright flashing red lights controlled by the LSO's 'pickle switch'. With him stood his 'writer', who was often another LSO or a squadron pilot. Every landing attempt, or 'pass', was assessed and dictated to the writer in arcane language, to be entered in a special shorthand notation on his pad for de-brief of the pilot later. Also on the platform stood the 'talker', a sailor who coordinated with the deck crew and advised the LSO of the state of the landing area. The LSO was in radio contact with the aircraft in the 'pattern', and 'Flying Control' high in the carrier's island. However, the LSO was not the primary means of getting aircraft safely to the deck. Except in the roughest of seas, where an LSO would 'talk' an aircraft down, the primary landing aid was the ship's mirror system. I had flown in formation on other aircraft. Soon, I would find that I would be 'formating' on something else: the 'meatball', usually just called the 'ball'.

Naval aircraft had become too fast and heavy to be safely guided on to a carrier's deck by a chap waving a pair of over-sized ping-pong bats. The 'mirror' system provided a navy pilot with a precise indication of whether he was too high, too low, or just right on his approach to land on a small, moving deck, in daylight or on the blackest of nights. A bright orange light shone from a position at the left stern (rear) of the ship. Its beam pointed forward at a parabolic mirror located further forward, which also projected from the port side of the landing deck. The mirror faced astern and upwards toward the pilot on his landing approach. A horizontal row of green lights was fixed to each side of the mirror. A light beam's 'angle of incidence', the angle at which it hits a mirror, is equal to its angle of reflection away from it. At the beginning of his approach to land on, a pilot would see an orange 'ball', the reflection of the powerful light, and the bars of bright green fixed lights on either side of the ball. If he flew to keep the meatball centred between the green lights, he would be approaching at the correct angle. If the ball was high, he was high. A ball sinking below the datum lights meant the aircraft was going low. It sounded so easy … but as the pilot approached the carrier the ball became more and more sensitive, because he would be flying down a narrowing 'glide slope' that would be barely half a metre wide at his impact point with the deck. What if the deck was heaving, pitching or rolling? There was a stabilising system for

Melbourne's mirror, but I would learn that this was rudimentary at best and in rough seas, almost useless. Learning to 'fly the ball' on the 'dummy deck', a square painted on the runway at Nowra using a replica of the mirror landing aid, would be one thing; but flying it onto a lurching carrier would require a melange of formation skill, attention to the LSO's radio commands, the judgement to even out the oscillations of the ball as it moved up and down with the deck, 'feel', experience, and discipline.

Flying operations were managed by Flying Control, or 'Flyco'. Its windows on the rear corner of the island provided a view for the senior officers in charge of the flying. These officers ensured that the deck would be ready for launches and recoveries. They were in constant communication with the aircraft, the LSO, the ship's Air Traffic Controllers, the catapult officer, the arresting space, the deck lift operators, the bridge, and the Aircraft Control Room, the ACR. The ACR was a cramped space at the base of the island where in this pre-computer age, scale wooden shapes of *Melbourne*'s aircraft were shuffled around on table tops that represented *Melbourne*'s flight deck and hangars. Directing the movement of the aircraft around the ship for flying, maintenance and storage was a specialisation in itself. Sailors pushed the models about like croupiers in accordance with reports and the ACR Officer's orders.

The flight deck of an aircraft carrier is one of the most hazardous working environments. *Melbourne*'s flight deck was under the iron control of the Flight Deck Officer and his warrant and petty officers. It was not unknown for physical violence to be visited on any sailor or officer, irrespective of rank, who acted negligently there: dropping equipment, walking onto the landing area during flight operations, moving in front of running aircraft … One learned never to walk backwards, because in many areas there were no safety nets or catwalks beneath to arrest a fall from the open deck. The cacophony from propellers, jet engines, rotors and engines required the wearing of hearing protection, so robbed of one sense, heads on the flight deck were always swivelling, looking … scanning … ever aware.

The deck was a doubly hazardous area in the black of night, with the ship's lights turned down to a minimum and occasionally, completely off during an exercise. One wrong step; a blast from an unseen jet, propeller or rotor; a slip while inspecting or working on the upper surfaces of an aircraft that projected over the water … you would drop thirteen metres to the black sea below, unheard in the racket of the flight deck, unseen in a black oceanic night unless you could get to your tiny light and the flare in your life vest: assuming that you were wearing it in preparation to fly, and that somebody was looking in your direction. Off-duty personnel wanting a vantage point to watch the spectacular launches and landings climbed to a far safer place: the 'goofers' platform', a small balcony high on the island just beneath the island's forest of black masts. antennae and the huge rotating radar dish.

Melbourne's flight deck crew were of many different specialisations, and the colour of their vests and cloth helmets with their 'Mickey Mouse' ears, hard plastic cups that contained hearing protection and sometimes radio headphones, indicated these skills. Electrical technicians' gear was green; so these specialists were called 'greenies'. That of weapons crew was, appropriately, red. The muscle on the flight deck was provided by the 'aircraft handlers'. Their jackets and helmets were a greased-stained white or yellow. The handlers pushed, pulled, towed and marshalled aircraft into and out of tight areas on an often lurching flight or hangar deck. They manoeuvred aircraft onto and off the massive lifts. When not being moved, the aircraft were always tightly chained down, each chain hooked onto one of the ring bolts that lay in the thousands of little recesses that spotted *Melbourne*'s flight and hangar decks. Seemingly always shambling along dragging chains, the handlers were known as 'bears'. A yellow articulated mobile crane known as 'the Beast' sat immediately behind the island. Among its other roles, the bears would use it to drop a crashed, immobilised aircraft over the side so that others still airborne would have room to land on. Multitudes of carts, small tugs, chains and trolleys were corralled in areas behind it.

The main domain of the pilots and observers was the briefing room. A few square windows gave a grudging view of the sea to starboard and theatre-like, rows of high-backed grey vinyl seats faced a multitude of black and white boards attached to the bulkhead on a small stage. To one side was the 'greenie board.' Every landing on the carrier by every pilot was assessed and debriefed by an LSO. The grades of every landing were displayed on the board next to each pilot's name for all the ship's aviators and crew to see, and remained there for the entire 'cruise'. There were four grades of landings: the 'OK', the mediocre 'fair', the barely safe 'no grade' and, in the case of dangerous or poor flying, the 'cut pass.'

In the bowels of the island lay the carrier's Air Traffic Control section, a dark windowless space where radar scopes and consoles dominated, as they would in a land-based centre. The Air Traffic Control Officers could talk a pilot down a 'Carrier Controlled Approach', the CCA, just as in the Ground Controlled Approaches that I had flown previously; except of course, the carrier was moving. When the approaching aircraft appeared from the murk and was visible to the LSO on his platform, he would call 'Paddles, contact', and take over from the CCA controller to 'talk' the aircraft down until the pilot 'called the ball'. At the base of the island near the Aircraft Control Room was a Safety Equipment section where, after briefing for their mission, pilots and observers would collect their helmets and Mae Wests, then carrying flight bags and other equipment would waddle out onto the noisy, windy flight deck, heads scanning for hazards, to their allocated aircraft for its pre-flight inspection and boarding.

The ship's decks and its innumerable compartments were designated by numbers and letters. Most floor surfaces were merely plain unpainted steel. White painted bulkheads were everywhere with their hatches and 'knee knockers', high thresholds that I eventually got used to stepping over. The bulkheads and deck-heads (ceilings) were a maze of wires, colour-coded pipes, speakers, painted signs, letters, numbers and light fittings. To me, the interior of the

Melbourne was reminiscent of that of the *Nostromo*, the space ship of the famous science fiction film *Alien*.

A little nauseous, I left the tiny cabin to explore the ship, making my way along the windowless decks and up and down the ladder ways through seemingly static rooms of steel but where strange forces pushed at my body from side to side, up and down, while *Melbourne* rolled and pitched. Several decks were below the waterline, and included the ship's laundry that smelt of stale bilge water, the chapel and various storerooms and offices. The ship exuded obsolete gentility; even then, she was getting on for forty years old. The numerous coats of paint on the bulkheads and deck-heads were makeup on an ageing actress. Her hull and outer decks were constantly being 'chipped' and repainted by the sailors. Also, she was working at the limit of her capability: the ship's designers had envisaged her operating relatively small World War II-vintage propeller aircraft. Today, Australia's navy was operating fast Skyhawk jets, heavy Grumman Trackers and big Sea King helicopters from the old girl.

Throughout, the ship hummed with the noise of fans, the metallic banging of hatchways and doors being slammed, the hollow thump of heavy boots on steel and the frequent 'pipes': loud announcements that issued from the ship's PA system, amplified into every part of the ship, including the sleeping quarters. They started with 'Do you hear there, do you hear there?' and then, 'Able Seaman Smith to the Regulating Room' or 'Tonight's movie in the Petty Officers' Mess is ...' The ship's announcements were still called 'pipes' even with the days of sail long past, where various modulations of the shrill whistles of the 'pipes', or 'bos'un's calls' – used today for ceremonial purposes – directed the actions of sailors on deck. Where olden-time armies used specific bugle calls for reveille, charging into battle and 'lights out', the navy used pipes. When *Melbourne*'s Air Group was on board, the pipes were incessant: three double clangs of a bell was followed by

'No smoking, no naked lights … AVGAS refuelling in B Hangar'. Or, 'Gash may not be ditched, gash may not be ditched, flying operations now in progress.' At sea, *Melbourne's* 'gash' (rubbish) was merely thrown overboard in punctured plastic bags: a still-floating black bag of garbage could attract seabirds, hazardous to aircraft engines, propellers and rotor blades. One could also be mistaken for a man in the water, so as soon as flying operations were complete, a cavalcade of slowly sinking bags of garbage strung behind the carrier as the Messmen disposed of the detritus of over one thousand seamen and Air Group personnel. Unlike modern ships, there was no garbage-processing facility in HMAS *Melbourne*.

I had visited *Melbourne's* engine room when she was alongside, but nothing prepared me for the experience of it at sea. Escorted by an engineering officer and with the ship rolling gently, I squeezed into a square hatchway to a narrow, laddered shaft, clambered down and emerged into another world. Even while wearing the regulation ear defenders, the shriek of huge fans, the hissing and clanking, and the amplified broadcast of the pipes and engineering officers' orders were almost overwhelming. Then there was the heat. It was a cold, wintry day in the Tasman Sea but in the heat of the boiler room, sweat already dripped inside my borrowed off-white overalls. Engineering personnel – still known as 'stokers' even though the days of shovelling coal into boilers were over – shouted to one another, while my escorting officer bellowed a running commentary at me on how the engine room operated.

He pointed out one of the boilers, fed by fuel oil to generate steam for the two turbines that drove the propellers. On a grating stood two stokers who stared at huge gauges as, arms outstretched, they manipulated wheels on either side of them that controlled the flow of fuel oil and air to the boilers. They stood under trunking that blasted cold air over their bodies in the boiler room heat, but they were still sweating. This was a stoker's life at sea, serving the furnaces in mind-numbing 'watches' (shifts), day and night, in constant noise and heat, ear defenders on, no conversation, in a grey and dirty-white world of asbestos-lagged pipes, gratings and riveted steel that pitched and rolled according to the sea's mood.

We negotiated steel doors to the turbine room itself, the shriek of the fans now eclipsed by the turbines' din. Massive coiled pipes fed steam to the turbine blades. Aft, I made out one of the twin rotating propeller steel shafts, of shining steel, where it receded astern into a narrowing 'shaft tunnel'. We walked along its grating until we could progress no further. Above us was some 20,000 tonnes of steel ship. We were metres below the waterline and under the carrier's stern. The throb of the huge propellers on the ends of the shafts was noticeable. Afterwards, I would emerge on deck into air so fresh it seemed to sting, with admiration and respect for those who kept our floating home and air base functioning round the clock for weeks on end.

The accommodation for the junior sailors in HMAS *Melbourne* was appalling. Officers and petty officers lived in reasonable comfort in cabins that varied from tiny single units, to larger shared spaces with multiple bunks. However, home for many of the sailors was merely one of the ship's passageways. Bunks, three tiers high, lined the sides of many of the thoroughfares. There was little privacy. *Melbourne's* rudimentary air conditioning had been modified over the years, but it would remain inadequate for her crew, especially the sailors sleeping three bunks high in the hot and noisy passageways. The odour of bodies and sweaty clothing was strong. In the tropics, there would not be even the solace of a long shower after duty, because the engine room could only provide so much fresh water from the sea's salt. By order, showers were limited to thirty seconds. In tropical conditions, it felt as though you had not even showered at all. The thirty second shower was rigorously enforced for every officer and sailor.

Toilet arrangements remained virtually unchanged from the days of sail. The heads (toilets) were flushed with seawater and merely emptied straight into the sea. Whenever *Melbourne* was alongside, human waste and toilet paper could be seen floating about the hull; the niceties of a sewerage treatment plant were not a consideration when the British designed the vessel. The officers' heads were at the aft end of the ship and in rough weather, the crash of the descending stern forced gouts of saltwater back up the pipes and into the toilets, with revolting results.

The officers' wardroom boasted a bar that was almost always open, and meals were served in relative comfort. The petty and warrant officers used smaller but comfortable Messes where one could buy a beer and eat a reasonable meal. The junior sailors were fed cafeteria-style, and were restricted to a daily 'beer issue'. In the RAN, the Nelsonian 'rum ration' had evolved into two cans of beer per man per day, both cans opened on the spot by the issuing petty officers to prevent hoarding. After duty a sailor would enjoy his two cans of beer, then his thirty second shower. He would try to sleep in a hot, lurching passageway – amidst the body odour – with swearing, shouting men constantly passing up and down the deck just on the other side of his thin curtain. After a few hours of fitful sleep, it was back on watch in the boiler room, catapult space, hangar or on the flight deck. It was little wonder that a 'run ashore' for many of the junior sailors was a riot of drinking and carousing – a momentary escape from the awful living conditions on a small, ageing aircraft carrier.

For a while, I sat in the wardroom, its bar at one end tended by a steward, on an upholstered bench seat that ran along the angled side where you could lean back against the ship's roll and read, talk or solve a crossword. On a table lay several large scrap books: they were the 'Line Books'. Most military units of the day had a Line Book, and HMAS *Melbourne* and her squadrons were no exception. A Line Book comprised an eclectic mix of photographs, press cuttings, home-grown cartoons, ribaldry, and quotes from various unit characters. An older volume caught my eye, and I leafed through it. Fascinated, I looked at the black and white images of naval aircraft that had operated from HMAS *Melbourne* or HMAS *Sydney* in a bygone era: Gannets, Sea Venoms … One photo depicted an aircraft inverted and tangled in the aerials above a carrier's island. Then, another image caught my attention. It depicted the actress Ava Gardner, flanked by civilians and naval officers, walking through the hangar deck of HMAS *Melbourne*. In 1959 the carrier had been used for the filming of the movie version of Neville Shute's *On the Beach*, the novel that had fascinated me as a child and teenager. Gardner had played the Moira Davidson character, alongside Gregory Peck, and HMAS *Melbourne* had been substituted for the book's HMAS *Sydney*, which in the novel was laid up at Williamstown Naval Dockyard for lack of fuel oil after the apocalyptic nuclear war. Although diminished somewhat from the nineteen fifties and sixties, the Soviet threat was what we were still being trained to face. During my explorations of the old carrier, I would note remnants of her original system of water sprinklers, designed to wash off the radioactive fallout of nuclear detonations.

Later that day I stood hunched in my flying jacket, facing aft on an almost deserted flight deck, braced against the raw wind and the movement of the ship. Soon a helicopter would land on to fly our group back to Nowra. Low cloud scudded below an overcast as the grey steel of *Melbourne*'s flight deck heaved and rolled in the swell across a lighter grey sea and sky: up, tilt, down, tilt, up, in a ponderous corkscrew. I could almost sense the solidity of the metal that comprised the curved steel lip of the 'round-down', the very aft edge of her landing area, which lurched and canted against the horizon. I would have to land an eleven-tonne aeroplane carrying crew, aviation gasoline and possibly unspent weapons on this deck, and I would have to do it safely and consistently at any hour of the day or night, after a six-hour mission, and often out of range of any land airfield. Excitement and trepidation welled as I anticipated my first carrier landing.

In one of Great Britain's darkest periods German submarines, 'U-boats', ravaged the convoys of merchant ships that brought supplies and equipment to the country from North America during World War II. The U-boats operated almost unmolested in the 'air gap', an area of the mid-Atlantic Ocean that was too remote for shore-based patrol aircraft operating from either shore. Eventually, longer-range shore-based aircraft, and aeroplanes operating from escorting aircraft carriers closed this gap. This, along with increased numbers of navy escort ships (including the famous 'corvettes'), sensor equipment such as sonar and radar, and advanced weapons, made a dramatic difference in being able to deter, detect and destroy the U-boats that were targeting the convoys. But always, the possibility of a lurking submarine preyed on the minds of ships' crews. After World War II, submarines were armed not just with improved forms of the traditional torpedo, but with missiles: missiles capable of being launched from below the surface to deliver multiple, independently-targeted nuclear warheads. Nuclear power became the favoured propulsion; up until then, submarines regularly had to surface in order to run their Diesel engines to charge the huge batteries required for sub-surface progress.

The Achilles' heel of the submarine is its vulnerability after detection. At or near the surface, it can be attacked with depth charges or torpedoes, bombed, strafed with guns, or rocketed. When underwater, the explosion of a depth charge or torpedo will result in, at the least, damage to its sensors or, more likely, flooding that would send it to the bottom, or even 'implosion'. On the surface, although a submarine can make good speed, it can be picked up by radar from ships or aircraft, or by the human eye. Underwater a 'conventional' (non-nuclear powered) submarine is quiet but slow, limited by its electric motors and batteries. A nuclear-powered sub is much faster than its conventional cousin, but still its atomic reactor's machinery, turbines, pumps and propeller produce noise that is detectable by listening warships and aircraft.

A submarine captain will almost always rely on his vessel's stealth.

To intercept a convoy or naval task force, which itself may be travelling at speed, the submariner must get his boat (submarines are always referred to as 'boats', not 'ships') into the correct position. Attacking the moving target from 'astern' (behind) is difficult due to the sub's relatively slow speed. The possible area from which a submarine attack could come can be calculated by a surface commander, who will task aircraft to patrol it and be ready to pounce on any submarine contact. The possibility of detection is a significant problem for the sub's captain; the 'feather' of a periscope's wake can be spotted by crew or picked up by radar, making navigation and acquiring the target difficult for him. So the mere presence of an aircraft produces a first line of defence against a submarine attack: deterrence. But anti-submarine aircrew also need a means of detecting and destroying their quarry. During World War II, equipment to do this was heavy, unreliable and primitive, though sometimes effective. Still, the patrolling aircraft forced the U-boat commanders to stay submerged most of the time. Thousands of sailors' lives were saved, and precious merchant ships with their cargoes got through.

After the world war was won and the Cold War between the West and the Soviet Union escalated, the United States required an aircraft capable of both hunting and 'killing' enemy submarines. It would be packed with the latest sensors and able to carry depth charges, air-to-surface rockets and homing torpedoes. The Grumman Aircraft Engineering Corporation, noted for its famous carrier-borne aircraft such as the Wildcat and Hellcat fighters, and the Avenger attack bomber, was selected to produce this machine. The factory where it was to be made was known as the 'Grumman Ironworks', because its products had a reputation for toughness and reliability. The new ASW (anti-submarine warfare) aircraft would also have to be compact and tough because, like its famous forebears, it would operate from the deck of an aircraft carrier. In early 1953, the Grumman S-2F flew for the first time. It would be eventually named the Tracker. Royal Australian Navy aircrew would affectionately call it 'The Grey Grumblie' because of the muttering rumble of its piston engines at cruise power. The Americans invariably called it the 'Stoof' (from S-2F), and one version that was fitted with a huge radar dome on top of its stubby fuselage was known as 'The Stoof with a Roof'.

The Tracker was of all-metal construction, with a boxy, blunt-nosed body that was lifted by long, slender wings, mounted high on the fuselage, of a span significantly greater than the fuselage was long. A powerful piston engine was housed in a big 'nacelle' slung under each wing, which also contained sturdy landing gear and at its rear, stowage for 16 submarine-detecting sonar buoys (sonobuoys). Pods on the nacelles contained droppable, floating smoke markers, flares and more sonobuoys.

Because of the stubby fuselage, a broad tail fin towered high for stability, which carried high-set horizontal tail planes, also of an impressive span. Attached to the rear of the fin was a tall rudder that had an unusual arrangement: a big electrically controlled 'trim tab' was hinged *forward* of the rudder. For take-off, landing, and in the event of an engine failure, the pilot engaged the 'rudder assist' system, because failure of one of the Tracker's powerful engines at low speeds would result in dangerous amounts of asymmetric thrust. The rudder assist turned the whole trim tab and rudder into one control surface that was moved by a hydraulic ram. It was vital to turn this system off before manoeuvring at higher speeds to avoid excessive strain on the structure. I would later appreciate the training that I had received on the HS 748 in preparation to fly the more demanding Tracker when one engine was not running.

Relatively dainty twin nose wheels sat at the end of a stalky strut that sprouted from the extreme nose of the aircraft, but there was also a small retractable 'tail wheel' at the rear: a Tracker would sit back on this on the catapult or when heavily loaded, with its nose wheel in the air. To steer the pilot used 'differential braking' on each main wheel and the nose wheel just 'castored' freely; just like in the Macchi. The main wheels retracted into the engine nacelles at the end of legs that were twice as strong as those fitted to a land-based aircraft. The wheels themselves were also seemingly designed for an aircraft twice the Tracker's size, with tyres inflated to 190 pounds per square inch to absorb the impact of carrier landings.

Under the S-2's belly was a stout barb-like hook, over which the wire 'strop' would be looped to connect the aircraft to the aircraft carrier's catapult shuttle for launch. Under the tail was that hallmark of the naval aeroplane, the arrester hook. When extended by the pilot, the hook dangled beneath the tail to catch a carrier's arresting wire.

The Tracker's twin engines were brutes. They were Wright Cyclones, that had nine large cylinders arranged in 'radial' form like the spokes of a wheel. The advantages of the radial engine include relative simplicity, especially of air cooling (even for the most powerful radials), ability to take battle damage, efficiency for weight, and not to mention the wonderful sound of a radial engine running! Radials always have an odd number of cylinders, and the power strokes are sequential around the engine, resulting in smooth and efficient power transmission. There is no music quite like the throaty bellow of a radial engine at full throttle, which decreases to a purposeful rumble at its relatively low cruising RPM. Even the start-up of a radial engine can be spectacular when small amounts of accumulated oil in the lower cylinders produce puffs of greasy smoke from the exhaust pipes as the engine coughs, and slowly each cylinder 'wakes up' until they all fire properly to produce a warm, steady beat.

The Tracker's Cyclones were supercharged to force air into the cylinders at more than fifty-six inches of 'boost' at full power ('static' boost for a non-supercharged engine is around thirty inches). Special 115-145 octane fuel was used. Some 1,800 kilograms of it were carried in wing tanks inboard of the engines.

Each engine drove a big three-bladed steel propeller, its blades wide with sharp, square-cut tips. The propeller's, and therefore each engine's, RPM was controlled by a lever which hung down from the overhead panel between the pilots, each next to the twin throttles and fuel mixture levers.

A powerful generator on each engine supplied the sub-hunter's systems, electronics, sensors and radar. Unlike most piston-powered aircraft, these generators produced alternating current (AC) that required complicated constant speed drives (CSDs). Failure or overheating of a CSD could cause problems for the Tracker's crew. A double generator failure was an emergency because the Tracker was not fitted with batteries. A naval aircraft, it was assumed that external power from a ground unit or ship would always be available to plug in to the aircraft in order to start it. Electrical problems in the Tracker had to be dealt with correctly and with deliberate care.

The span of the Grumman's wings had to be reduced in order for it to be accommodated on a carrier's deck, deck lift (elevator), or in the hangar space below. The wings were hinged outboard of the engines, and hydraulic rams folded them like crossed arms over the top of the fuselage. This reduced the Tracker's impressive span to a little over eight metres. Wing fold and unfold was activated by the pilot using controls on the overhead panel. Unfolding for flight was an important operation! The consequences of a wing fold mechanism malfunctioning were obvious to Grumman's designers, so they made sure that the system was 'fail safe'. There was yet more complication in the wings: apart from the big flaps, vital to slow the machine down to carrier landing speed and the usual ailerons for roll control, large spoilers poked up from the top surfaces of each wing when activated by the pilot's yoke for control in roll (bank), which would destroy the lift over that wing, giving the Tracker a powerful response in 'roll', vital for maintaining the aircraft straight for landing on a rolling, corkscrewing carrier deck. 'Slots', rectangular openings just behind the front of each wing, allowed extra air to pass over the wing's top surface, which at low speeds, reduced the aircraft's stalling speed to allow a safe carrier landing.

From the starboard (right) wing, a Perspex dome protruded. It housed a powerful searchlight. Its beam could be steered by the co-pilot (TACCO) using a joystick mounted on the sill of his side window. A curtain would be slid out between the front seat crew to shield the pilot's eyes from the searchlight's blinding glare, in order that he could concentrate on his flight instruments, vital when manoeuvring at night low over black water. Even the tips of the wings were put to use. They comprised sensitive aerials that could pick up radar and radio signals from friend or foe. The Tracker's own powerful radar would often be turned off to avoid, in turn, giving the aircraft's position away to listening snoopers.

The Tracker carried four crewmen. Two sat up front: one pilot on the left, and a highly-qualified observer – a Tactical Coordinator or 'TACCO' – who also carried out co-pilot duties on the right. Two sensor operators, 'Sensor Three' and 'Sensor Four', were stationed in their own compartment some two metres behind them. The pilots sat facing a vast main instrument panel, and there were more instruments and controls on the ceiling between the pilots, and above the Tracker's distinctive little eyebrow-like windscreens. Unusually, the engines' throttle and propeller controls, along with levers for the landing gear, wing flaps, arrester hook and wing fold, were located on the ceiling panel. This left space for more equipment on the box-like console that sat between the pilot and TACCO. It hinged up to allow them to enter or leave their seats. A large square plastic grid, the tactical plotter with its selectors and coloured buttons beneath, dominated the centre of the main instrument panel. Banks of duplicated engine instruments sat next to a comprehensive matrix of warning lights. Above each crewman was an escape hatch. In the event of a ditching he stood on his seat and clambered up and out through it. The forward hatches could be opened in flight. Row after row of circuit breakers studded more panels behind each pilot. There were dials, levers, knobs, lights and switches just *everywhere*.

The Tracker's interior was a sombre grey, relieved by the matt black of the panels with their white legends and coloured dial markings. There was the grey-green of the soundproofing material and the meagre upholstery on the seats, and black rectangles of anti-skid material were laid on the grey metal floor. Always present was that whiff of 'avgas' – the aviation gasoline on which the Cyclones ran – stored in the wing tanks above and behind the crew, mixed with the aroma of oil, stale flight suits and occasionally, the sickly smell of hot heat-sensitive paper from the sensor station. Light struggled in through the tiny side windows of the sensor operators, but for the pilot and TACCO, there was a glorious view to the sides through the goggling Plexiglas bubbles.

An archway in the riveted metal bulkhead behind the pilots led back into the rear compartment along a tight corridor formed by the racks of equipment that fed the operators' panels. On each side of their compartment, next to the tiny window by their elbows, the sensor operators sat, their panels reaching to the ceiling. By craning across, they could peer down the passageway and through to the cockpit, to obtain a grudging view ahead through the inverted forest of engine controls and the other levers that sprouted downwards from the overhead panel.

A Tracker crew entered the machine through a small door in the starboard side of the fuselage, under the wing. A step led up into the sensor operators' area, and the 'front seaters', clutching their helmets and flight bags, would push their way up the small corridor from the sensor stations to squeeze through the archway, clamber into their seats, strap in, and lower the folding centre console to the floor between them. All crew rested their backs on parachutes, but the presence of these was of little comfort, because a Tracker routinely operated at altitudes too low for a safe bail out. There were no ejection seats. A serious fire in the aircraft would probably result in an urgent ditching into the sea. In the event of a ditching, a four-man life raft could be deployed from its well in the upper fuselage. To save weight, the engines were not fitted with a fire extinguishing system. Crews would always be aware of the 1,800 kilograms of high-octane aviation fuel that was stored inside the wing just behind the crew compartment. They had only one small handheld extinguisher.

Beneath the floor on the port (left) side of the fuselage was a weapons bay, capable of holding two homing torpedoes. Behind the sensor operators, the Tracker's boxy fuselage held the big radar antenna that rotated inside its radar dome, or 'radome'. It resembled a giant inverted thimble. When airborne, the radome was lowered through a gaping hole in the aircraft's belly to give a 360-degree radar picture on Sensor Three's scope. The radar was powerful enough to pick up a submarine's extended periscope or antenna. Additionally, any 'conventional' (non-nuclear powered) boat would eventually have to extend its 'snorkel' or 'snort' tubes to run the Diesel engines in order to recharge its batteries. However, a Tracker crew were always aware that the aircraft's radar emissions could also be detected by a hostile submarine or surface vessel, giving away the presence of the hunting aircraft.

Further aft in the fuselage's interior were more racks of electronics and, finally, the retractable 'MAD' boom (the magnetic anomaly detector), which allowed close-range pinpointing of a target submarine. With the Tracker airborne, the MAD boom was extended back from the tail until the aircraft resembled a great fat bumblebee with a huge stinger. The MAD system detected tiny anomalies in the earth's magnetic field caused by the steel of a submarine lurking below the ocean's surface. Its indicator would 'spike' if the aircraft overflew any large metal object. The Tracker had to be flown at extremely low altitude for the MAD to work, so I would have to become proficient at flying the Tracker in 'MAD trap' patterns at one hundred feet off the water during the day, and at three hundred feet on the blackest of nights, banking up to forty-five degrees, totally by reference to instruments.

A 'MADman' was the sudden spike on the indicator, which pinpointed the moment when the hunting Tracker roared at low level exactly over a submarine. As a reference, a floating pyrotechnic marker was dropped by the crew at that time. Then an attack could be made. With the torpedo bay doors gaping open and a weapon armed, the pilot would haul the Tracker around into a steep turn back towards the 'smoke'.

The torpedo would soon fall from the Tracker's belly and race through the water at forty knots. Acoustic sensors in its head would lock onto the submarine as the torpedo spiralled in ever-decreasing circles around its target. The submarine's horrified crew would hear the scream of the torpedo while it made its final run toward their vulnerable hull.

However, there was much work to be done by the crew before they were at that point of attacking the submarine. Hour after hour, the Tracker rumbled along at 130 knots – or 240 km/hr – at about 500 metres above the ocean. Senior officers in tactical command would decide whether radar was to be used or not: was the mission one of deterrence, or was it a priority of surprising and destroying hostile submarines? During a radar search, Sensor Three would stare at his scope, looking for the tell-tale 'return' of a periscope or 'snort' amongst the 'clutter' caused by radar reflections off the waves. The submarine, however, would have a receiver on a retractable mast that could detect the Tracker's searching radar beam. At the first hint of a probing aircraft's radar, all masts and periscopes would come down and, like a rabbit scuttling into its burrow, the sub would go deep, making it almost impossible to locate.

However, this outcome itself could be beneficial. The sub would be forced to stay submerged for hours, denying its captain the use of his periscope and aerials. Also, he would be forced to move almost silently but at a greatly reduced speed below the surface, hampering his efforts to locate and attack his target. Submariners were terrified of being attacked from the air, and I would learn that an Anti-Submarine Warfare mission was mainly deterrence. With the presence of patrolling aircraft, surface vessels and land targets were less likely to be attacked. This had been dramatically borne out in the Battle of the Atlantic.

Besides radar, the most likely tool that a crew used to initially detect, then localise, a submarine was the sonobuoy. This was a narrow metal cylinder about one metre long and fifteen centimetres in diameter, dropped from their aircraft. In the water a 'hydrophone' (a sensitive underwater microphone) would fall on a wire from the floating buoy on a pre-set depth. Hydrophones picked up all manner of underwater noises, not only of marine life, but also the beat of a ship or submarine propeller and the whine of machinery. The hydrophone's information was sent through an antenna on top of the sonobuoy up to the aircraft, and displayed on a paper trace in front of Sensor Four. The result was a graph that showed him the frequency of the detected noise in the vertical axis as the paper rolled along with time. This system was called 'Jezebel' ('Jez' for short). During training the new sensor operators, both officers and enlisted aircrewmen, spent hour after hour in the ASW school at Nowra analysing Jez grams for practice from a library of signatures from many types of warships and submarines. An operator could, with experience, look at a gram and deduce the type of vessel and its speed.

In the aircraft, a crew member could flip a monitor switch and hear the sounds picked up by a sonobuoy. I would get to hear the plaintive calls of whales, waves of ships' noise echoing through the depths, and the castanet-like clicking of 'snapping' or 'pistol' shrimp. Sometimes, I would even hear the brief muffled roar, transmitted down through the water, of our own aircraft flying over a sonobuoy at low altitude.

There was another type of sonobuoy. The one that has already been described was of the passive variety: its sensitive microphone just listened out for any sound in the ocean depths, including that of a prowling submarine. A submarine's crew would not know that it was there, listening for them. The other type of buoy was known as the active sonobuoy or 'pinger'.

A pinger was a miniature sonar. It sent out regular pings, and like ripples in a pond after a stone has plopped into it, circles of acoustic energy radiated out that would hit a submarine and reflect back. This had two major effects: the ripples of sound bouncing back to the sonobuoy gave the sensor operator a very accurate distance of the target from the buoy. However, the pings would be heard by the submarine's crew and the game would change. Alerted to the presence of hunting aircraft, the submarine captain would commence evasive action: course and speed changes; change of depth; use of the 'layer', a demarcation of different water temperatures in the undersea where sound waves get distorted or deflected.

The hunt for a submarine usually commenced with the dropping of passive sonobuoys in lines known as 'barriers' in the most likely area where the submarine could be. The Tracker would fly 300 metres above the water, while ejecting a sonobuoy at regular intervals from the tubes in the rear of its engine nacelles, listening for the sub. The TACCO would carefully plot the position of each in grease pencil on the tactical display, giving steering commands to his pilot and ordering each sonobuoy release: 'Drop now, now, NOW!'

A target passing through or near the barrier would give away its presence and, after the signal strengths from each sonobuoy was evaluated by the Tracker's sensor operators, the data would be passed to the TACCO, who would calculate a possible location for the submarine. It would now have to be 'localised': out would go the pingers (the active sonobuoys), each producing a 'range ring'. The intersection of several rings gave an accurate location for the target. The pilot would manoeuvre the Tracker more aggressively now as tight patterns of pingers were dropped. However, the pings would alert the sub's crew. Stung into action, aware that he was being hunted, the submarine commander would steer his boat to port, starboard, double back, dive deeper …

But there was generally no escape from an active sonobuoy pattern. With the target localised, the Tracker's crew could now 'pinpoint' the submarine with MAD and then attack it. Lower and lower the hunting aircraft would descend, banking steeply left and right to lay yet more sonobuoys and smoke markers. Terse commands would crackle over the intercom from the TACCO along with updates and target information from the sensor operators while the pilot manoeuvred the big machine just one hundred feet off the water. At last would come the sudden 'spike' from the MAD trace caused by the aircraft overflying the metal of the submarine. Sensor

Four would call 'MAD MAD MAD', and a smoke would be dropped, directly above the target. Then would come the final attack.

When competent in the tactics required to locate and attack submarines, a Tracker crew would have to be able to carry them out in all weather conditions, day and night, after being catapulted from a ship at sea. Afterward, the aircraft would need to be landed by its young pilot safely onto a pitching, rolling deck. In July 1978, I was issued with the manuals for my Tracker Operational Flying School, and once again I got to work.

9

'HOOK DOWN'

1978 – 1979

The white tabs of the mid had gone. Now I sported the solitary gold stripe of an acting sub-lieutenant. For flying, I was back in the green flight suit and yellow life jacket. I also wore a battered bone dome helmet that had white and red panels of reflective tape to help rescuers sight me if I ended up in the ocean. I was twenty-one, but still not really out of adolescence. I had had further incidents of unkempt uniform and immature behaviour. After the struggle of the air force pilot's course and then routinely and adequately operating the navy's Macchis and the HS 748s, some overconfidence had developed, all of it unwarranted. My girlfriend and I maintained a long-distance relationship with her stationed at an air force base now far away in Queensland. Every few weekends, she took air force transport to a base near Sydney and I was becoming distracted by a deepening relationship. I spent most other weekends driving along the beautiful south coast of New South Wales while the car's cassette deck blared out the hits of the 1970s. With the distractions of a car, girlfriend and money to spend, I had several lapses during the intensive ground and air training to fly the Tracker, which were forthrightly debriefed by the instructors.

Lieutenant commander Bob 'Windy' Geale was the Commanding Officer (CO) of VC 851 Squadron. A nuggety man with ginger hair and a beard, Windy was Canadian, and had commenced his service with that country's naval air arm. In the wardroom bar, he would talk in his soft Canadian accent of his experiences: firstly as a Telegraphist Air Gunner in Fairey Swordfish open-cockpit biplanes, and later as an observer in Barracuda and Avenger torpedo bombers: these aircraft were of World War II vintage. He had been in several crashes. He transferred to the RAN as an Observer, made Australia his home, and attained the pinnacle of a naval aviator's career: the command of a naval air squadron. An excellent administrator, Windy was respected as the squadron's CO, and he dealt with un-officer-like behaviour and occasions of saying the wrong thing at the wrong time in a discreet and fatherly manner.

At Nowra's School of Anti-submarine Warfare, I sat through lectures on weapons, tactics, and the Soviet Union's submarine and surface fleet. Australia's defence posture was directed toward the USSR, more than any Asian country or even communist China. A simulator, the Weapons System Trainer (WST), replicated the interior of a Tracker. We called it the 'Woost'. Its instruments wavered and indicated, and warning lights came on with simulated emergencies. Orange light even flickered through frosted Perspex to one side of the cockpit during the simulated engine fires. The Woost was invaluable for practicing the physical switch and control selections for engine starts, failures and fires, although the simulator itself did not move and there was no view outside. I could fly instrument approaches and anti-submarine tactics at the direction of the trainee TACCOs, with inputs from the sensor operators behind, who were also under training. Like the real aircraft, all the instruments and the panels in the Woost were lit in red to maintain night vision, and in its perpetual night, there was a synthetic replication of the rumble of a Tracker's engines, counterpointed by the faint background whine of the circuits of the intercom system.

I flew the real aircraft to an adequate standard during most of the training flights. It rumbled along at half the speed of a Macchi or HS 748, making it easier to stay ahead of the aircraft and, as usual, I generally did well at the instrument flying. I revelled in the views through the bulging bubble windows: the lush green hinterland of the Shoalhaven River, the sparkling blue ocean, the curve of Jervis Bay with its surrounding grey-green scrub dotted with its holiday towns, and the brown ramparts of the Great Divide to the west.

For the first time, I fired weapons from an aircraft. I was shown how to drop small practice bombs that simulated depth charges, and how to fire unguided rockets that sped from cylindrical underwing pods with a 'whoosh'. Weapons training was carried out at Beecroft Head Bombing Range, a rocky plateau formed by one of the massive headlands of Jervis Bay. For bombing and rocketing, the Tracker had a rudimentary sighting system: a stick with a bead that stuck up in front of the pilot's windscreen, and a graticule etched onto the windscreen glass. The little practice bombs were dropped from level flight. I achieved indifferent results with these, and my rocketing was worse. The Tracker would be flown level at 3,000 feet – or 900 metres – and with a smart 'roll in' towards the target marked on the bare grass, be put into a steep dive, ideally twenty degrees down. I had to allow for wind drift – and I always struggled to achieve the correct 'sight picture' – but fire! My thumb would stab a little button on the control yoke and – swish! A rocket would shoot from a pod and arrow earthwards, but rockets required accurate visual flying and good balance of the aircraft using the rudder at the time of release. Invariably, my projectiles were tens of metres off target … There was no time to dwell on it: I would have to smartly recover from the dive as the earth rushed toward us, the g coming on (the sturdy Grumman was allowed to 'pull' 3 ½ g) and skywards again, to turn downwind in the rocketing pattern. Then I would listen to the Range Safety Officer's assessment of my rocket, before I made another attempt – hopefully but rarely, an improvement – until the projectiles were exhausted.

I flew formation again; the big machine was surprisingly

manoeuvrable. Station keeping was relatively easy when in 'echelon starboard', with the leader to my left and easily visible. The piston engines responded quickly to the power changes required to keep the correct fore-and-aft position, but there was always a small rudder adjustment required. The 'echelon port' position, sitting to the left side, was more challenging. The reference points on the lead aircraft now had to be followed through the right hand window across the cockpit while I peered through the forest of controls hanging from the overhead panel and past the other pilot or TACCO.

The grey and white sub hunters looked solid and purposeful up close in flight, with their blunt grey noses and thickset fuselages and wide propeller blades beating. The cockpit crews were clearly visible through the side bubbles, their white and red helmets occasionally moving and nodding, one pilot's arm hanging from the overhead throttles. We banked over blue sea and green pasture, and then manoeuvred in a 'tail chase', where, as 'wingman', I would throw the big Grumman around to follow a twisting, diving climbing leader. We would later re-form into echelon to run in through 'initial' at Nowra, invariably at low level and at high power. The aircraft would bob in low-level turbulence above green fields dotted with the dairy farms that were scattered along the wide Shoalhaven River. We would pass Nowra Hill, green and conical in our peripheral vision, to make our run over the airfield. Although our base boasted Skyhawk jets, the roar of a Tracker formation running in at a few hundred feet at 250 knots – or 460 km/hr – followed by the subsequent break as each of the big machines fanned up and around into the landing pattern was always an attention-getter.

After thorough briefings, I flew Field Carrier Landing Practice (FCLP) flights in preparation for landing on HMAS *Melbourne*: tight, low circuits to touch down on the yellow square painted on one of Nowra's runways that represented *Melbourne*'s landing area … it looked so small! A Landing Signals Officer and a Mirror Landing System were to the left side of the square, which mimicked the landing aids of the carrier. I flew pattern after pattern until the instructors considered that I would be viable for an actual deck landing on a later occasion.

It was November 1978 and I was inspecting a Tracker before I was to fly it on my Final Handling Test to complete my Operational Flying School. Urgently, I summoned a maintainer to check on a perceived abnormality with the aircraft, which was, in fact, non-existent. Nervous about the test and jumpy after too much coffee, I had wasted his time and felt like a fool. I was also on edge because 'Beachball' was to join me at the aircraft to conduct the test. He was the Senior Pilot of 851 Squadron. A gruff lieutenant commander, he was a seasoned naval aviator who sported a black beard above the thickset frame from which his nickname was derived. He had flown helicopters with the Royal Australian Navy's detachment that operated with the Americans during the Vietnam War. He expressed himself plainly, and stood no nonsense. An observer was to accompany us in a back seat, ready to provide radar information, assist with any problems and to provide an extra pair of eyes if there was an emergency.

'Parachutes?' Beachball called.

'Fitted,' I responded.

'Mags?'

'Off.'

'Park brake?'

'Set.'

'Cowls, coolers, carb air?'

'Open, open direct …'

So started the lengthy Pre-Start Check List, the 'challenges' read by Beachball who was acting as co-pilot. With all the checks complete, it was time to start the left-hand engine. First, I checked clear, then selected the starter switch above my windscreen that would crank the big engine. Six blades sliced past my window, then I put the magnetos (ignition) on, and with another finger I intermittently operated another little sprung switch that pumped fuel directly into the cylinders from an electric primer pump. A few coughs emanated from the engine, and then there was a shake through the airframe as the Wright Cyclone came to life. Gouts of smoke blew from the exhaust pipes. It was time to push the engine's mixture control lever forward, release the primer switch and adjust the throttle to the required rpm. I checked that the engine's warning lights were out, then repeated the procedure to start the right-hand engine until the Tracker was properly alive, with both Cyclones settled into a steady beating idle. We completed the After Start Checklist and taxied to the run-up area, my hand hanging from the throttles to control taxi speed, feet on each toe brake to steer.

I followed through with the lengthy 'run-up' procedure: I had increased power and exercised each engine's propeller pitch change mechanism and checked the auto-feather system that would automatically feather the propeller blades in the event of an engine failure at high power during take-off. Then, I ran up the Cyclones to static boost. The engines' bellow was almost overwhelmed by the buzz of the propeller blades just outside each cockpit side bubble. I checked the small engine instruments that vibrated on the panel as best I could, then I brought the throttles back to idle. After another lengthy checklist, we were ready to depart for the training area over the Tasman Sea.

We were cleared for take-off. With the aircraft's nose pointing down the runway, I held the Tracker on the brakes and once again set static boost, this time on both engines. I was used to the roar of the machine as it vibrated and strained, wanting to fly. I released the brakes, and set full take-off power. The noise was overwhelming. Air was being forced into each cylinder at over fifty-six inches of mercury while the propellers bit the air at 2,800 rpm. Again I struggled to read the instruments as the cockpit shuddered and vibrated ... after night flights in the Tracker I knew that gouts of blue flame would be dancing around the exhaust stacks. While our lightly laden warplane accelerated down the runway, the whole base would hear the snarling roar reverberating from the iron hangars. When we lifted off and accelerated to climb speed, the noise would diminish to waves of rumbling sound as we turned towards the sea. We climbed in an azure sky east, towards a deeper blue ocean, and after passing over the coast, we carried out a few exercises including an engine shutdown and restart.

Beachball seemed satisfied so far. Now it was time to demonstrate my ability to handle the Tracker in its true element: close to the water's surface and manoeuvring in tight turns in the various anti-submarine tactical patterns. On this cloudless day I could descend to the sea visually. There was the usual fresh breeze over the open water, and the surface was flecked with whitecaps. I eased the Tracker down to one hundred feet from the water, scanning the radar altimeter – or 'radalt' – which is a device that bounces radio energy from the surface to indicate very precisely on a dial the aircraft's height. A standard aircraft altimeter is really just a sophisticated barometer that responds to air pressure, but that would not be accurate enough for flying low over water. There was an intermittent 'beep beep beep' through our helmets and a flashing red light generated by the Radar Altimeter Warning System (the RAWS), which was set to sound off continuously below one hundred feet. The sound pierced through the rumble of the Cyclones and the background whine of the intercom. I was careful not to let the tone sound too long, but to try and hold just above one hundred feet to keep the RAWS silent. Rippling blue water and frothing wave tops slid past my elbow at 130 knots – or 240 km/hr – after I settled at the low height scanning horizon, airspeed indicator, radar altimeter, horizon … Then Beachball directed me to turn, as would be required in a 'MAD trap' pattern, still at one hundred feet from the surface but banking steeply.

'Don't descend, whatever you do!' I said to myself. The tip of one wing would now be much closer to the sea. 'Watch that bank angle, watch the radalt …'

'OK, roll out there,' called Beachball.

I levelled the Tracker's wings, maintaining straight flight, still at one hundred feet, and concentrated on the horizon ahead and the flight instruments in front of me. I was hoping to impress Beachball with my accurate flying.

Suddenly, the aircraft yawed. My peripheral vision picked up needles on one set of engine instruments winding back. Engine failure! Stupidly, I blurted out, 'Is this for real?' and hesitated for a split second before I overcame the surprise and launched into the Tracker's engine failure drill by memory: rudder assist on, propeller levers at full 'increase', throttles up, check gear up and flaps up, and then, if required, jettison (weapons and fuel) ... Now, I saw Beachball's hand on one of the overhead throttles, but I had not heard the customary call of 'practice' to announce any simulated failure. In any case, no instructor had ever given me a simulated engine failure at just thirty metres above the water. I climbed the Tracker away from the surface with a leg straining against a rudder pedal to keep the aircraft straight. Not a good performer on just one engine, the S-2 crept upwards, its 'good' engine roaring at full power and the buzz of its propeller blaring through the cramped cockpit.

Now Beachball was shouting over the intercom: 'Of course it wasn't for real, you idiot! Keep the bloody thing climbing away and take us back to Nowra.'

'Mark, the cowl flaps are still open,' the observer in the rear seat called.

I had forgotten to close the 'dead' engine's cowl flaps (little cooling doors) in order to reduce air drag and, in this case, keep the idling engine – that Beachball had simulated failed – warm.

The Senior Pilot was furious at the well-intentioned crewman. 'Shut up! I was waiting for him to spot it himself! Just keep your bloody mouth shut.'

Once again, a final test had degenerated into farce.

I sat dejected at Beachball's desk while he told me, in no uncertain terms, that he was unhappy with the way that I had handled his unannounced, simulated engine failure. 'If that had been for real, what would you have done ...? Would you have just sat there, saying,

"Is this for real?" Just because you're at one hundred feet off the water, it doesn't mean that an engine isn't going to fail! And you wouldn't have got the cowl flap in if the observer hadn't told you. Use your bloody head and be ready for anything. It wasn't good enough, and I can't pass you'. Softening a little, he said, 'I'll give you a few flights with Killa and we'll see where we go from there. That's all'.

It was my final test at Point Cook, all over again.

'Killa' was a personable, outgoing flying instructor on the Squadron who, along with several others, had been charged with teaching a boy just out of his teens how to fly a navy warplane. I made several flights with him but, like my remedial flight at Point Cook, there was nothing much more that he could teach: it would be up to me to practise and get more comfortable with the aircraft in the hopes that it would free up some mental capacity to think of everything and react properly. On yet another flight with Killa, the infamous 'south-east drift' weather pattern had moved in from the sea to blanket Nowra and its surrounds in low, thick cloud that extended well above any altitude that a Tracker would fly. Positioned over the ocean by the observer with his radar, we descended through the murk to break out a few hundred feet above slate-grey sea, where Killa directed me through the usual ASW manoeuvres. There was no simulated engine failure until we were on our way back to Nowra, back in the cloud. I conducted an engine-out approach, and then we flew approach after approach in the grey gloom where Nowra's runway appeared each time only just at the minimum altitude. Killa 'pulled' an engine a few more times, and watched how I handled the aircraft, making sure that I applied all the required checklist items and was aware of what was happening.

Wrung out after the flight, I trudged across the tarmac under the overcast to the crew room for a post-flight brew. While sipping the navy's ghastly instant coffee, I was called over to the Senior Pilot's office in the adjacent hut, where Beachball was waiting.

'Killa tells me you did all right on the flights with him,' he said, 'especially today in solid cloud. I've got reservations, but I'm going to regard those trips as your Final Handling Test. But you're not going to the operational squadron yet. You're going to stay here on 851 Squadron where we can keep an eye on you, and you won't be going to the deck until we are satisfied with your ability. You'll have to keep putting the work in, and don't screw up. Anyway, congratulations.' Beachball shook my hand, and I was dismissed.

At last, my gold wings were confirmed, but unlike my course-mates who would go to the operational unit, I was to remain as a Staff Pilot on the training squadron.

I crossed the grass, still in my flight suit, back to the crew room. When I approached the door, two course-mates appeared on the old wooden building's iron roof, each wielding one of the navy's ubiquitous grey metal waste paper bins. Gouts of cold water splashed down from above.

'Congratulations, Marcus! About bloody time,' they called.

I was saturated, and the cold weight of the water pressed the baggy suit to my skinny body, but it also helped hide a few tears of relief.

'Eight Four Five Ball, Videan, twenty four hundred,' I radioed.

'Roger, ball,' came from the Landing Signals Officer, the LSO, on his platform that protruded over the port side of HMAS *Melbourne*. At his back, the canvas screen gave some protection from the wind over *Melbourne*'s deck while he and his assistants looked aft towards our approaching aircraft. Seated in the right hand seat of Tracker 'side number' 845, I had made the standard call to advise that the flying pilot, Lieutenant Alan Videan, had sight of the 'meat ball' and we had some 2,400 pounds of fuel on board. I was becoming familiar with the picture of the carrier approach, albeit from the co-pilot's seat.

After rolling out on final approach – the 'groove' – the ship appeared as a small, grey trapezoid at the head of a white wake. However, the orange meatball and its green datum lights on the carrier's port side were distinctive. An elephantine blue and white Wessex helicopter – call sign 'Pedro' – hung low over the water a few meters off *Melbourne*'s port quarter, its rotor beating, maintaining its station. Pedro would be on the scene immediately if we ditched into the sea. The carrier took on more features as it bloomed in the windscreen: there was its rounded grey stern with the cut-outs surrounding the ship's quarterdeck, topped with the horizontal steel knife edge of the 'round down' (the aft end of the flight deck). I tried to scan as I would be if I was flying the 'pass': meatball, line-up, airspeed, meatball, line-up, airspeed … In closer, and there was the whiff of stack gas from *Melbourne*'s funnel being sucked through the Tracker's open overhead hatches, the burble of the 'rooster tail': a trail of turbulence behind the hull and the ship's island, and now the flashing-on of the 'cut lights'. In response, Alan whipped the throttles back to 'idle'. Again I felt the jarring impact through my seat as the Tracker hit *Melbourne*'s deck. There was a surge of power and the engines bellowed as Alan pushed the throttles up to take off again for the 'touch and go' (really just a violent bounce back into the air). The ship's island flashed past to my right, the deck area ahead dropped away, and now there was nothing but sea and sky as we climbed away once more. Our arrester hook had been left retracted for the touch and go, the last of several that Alan had made as a demonstration. But the deck landing picture was very specific; landing on the carrier while flying from the right seat was forbidden. Alan could only demonstrate from the left seat while I acted as his co-pilot and watched. We flew away from the ship, engaged the Tracker's primitive automatic pilot, and hurriedly swapped seats in accordance with the special procedure.

It was time for my first carrier landing.

Since the shaky finale of my Operational Flying School on the Tracker, Windy and Beachball had kept a close eye on me as a Staff Pilot on VC 851 Squadron. However, with the pressure of the OFS over, I enjoyed the staff flying, which meant tasks such as observer and TACCO training, along with some pilot continuation training. There was usually a 'Friday Formation', which was an hour of formation flight over the coast and two, three or four Grumman Trackers rumbling along in tight 'echelon' or 'line astern' patterns, then cavorting in a tail chase before reforming to roar through 'initial' at Nowra. Later would be a hurried de-brief and then off to the wardroom bar for loud conversation, 'war stories' and a never-ending stream of glasses of beer handed around in the shouts. There was work with the ships: ASAC and PWO training. FCLP was scheduled every few weeks to assess my continuing suitability for operations at the deck. Most weeks, there was night flying, which included not just circuit and instrument work, but night FCLP. I would often find myself miles off the coast of New South Wales, at three hundred feet above the water in the black of night with no horizon, the intermittent beep of the RAWS cutting through the rumble of the engines, the faint whine of the intercom and the terse dialogue among the crew. I was now entrusted to be the only pilot on board, my three crew mates all observers or aircrewmen. For hour after hour, my world was the glowing ball of the attitude indicator and the red-lit airspeed dial, radar altimeter and the other instruments while I banked and wheeled the Tracker in anti-submarine exercises through the blackness. I worked hard to keep safe and accurate, not to exceed my capabilities, and, after reports from the more senior observers who I flew with including Windy, our boss, the Senior Pilot gained some confidence in my ability.

I made a parachute descent during a special optional course. I stepped off the open rear ramp of an air force Caribou transport that roared along a few hundred metres above Nelson Bay, near Newcastle. Wind blast hurled me out and I fell, my heart in my mouth until I felt the pull of the static line that had one end attached to the aircraft and the other end attached to the parachute's rip cord. A heartbeat later there was a shock and a pull at my harness, and I swayed gently under a glorious canopy, the bellow of the Caribou's 'double-row' radial engines receding skywards, but there was no time to lose: I had to undo the lower leg straps and be ready to slip out of the upper harness as my feet hit the water. Annually, we had practised recovery after being caught under a sodden parachute canopy in a swimming pool, and it was vital that an aviator had the know-how to get clear. However, parachute jumps and gaining confidence and competence were all very well. I had not yet landed on the ship.

Again, HMAS *Melbourne* was steaming into the wind in the placid water of Jervis Bay. Al Videan was now my co-pilot, checklist card in hand. I was in the left seat of the Tracker, and I was expected to get the aircraft safely aboard. Tense and excited, I turned towards the ship for my first carrier landing.

Approaches to HMAS *Melbourne* were flown from the 'Charlie pattern', which was the equivalent of the traffic circuit of a land airfield, but the Charlie was flown at just three hundred feet – or one hundred metres – above the waves by day, and a little higher at night. I flew upwind with the grey-green bulk of *Melbourne* sliding by to my left. After a short interval, I turned in front of her in a level-continuous turn onto downwind, airspeed dribbling back. The ship was steaming on her 'aircraft recovery course'. I had now established our Tracker on a short, downwind leg (short because the ship itself was moving ahead), and there was just enough time to carry out the pre-landing checks before another left turn towards the final approach path.

Not what one would normally do in a land-based aircraft, I had already slowed the Tracker to its landing airspeed of 95 knots and trimmed the controls – 175 km/hr. Before that I had extended the landing gear and set the large flaps to 'full'. But I had left the arrester hook retracted. This was to be a 'touch and go' landing on *Melbourne*'s deck. Now counterpointing the engines' roar was the buzz of the propellers set at high rpm in an unsynchronised 'rowrr, rowrr, rowrr.' This was standard procedure in order to have the aircraft set up for a 'wave-off', a touch and go or an unplanned 'bolter' where instant response and power from the Cyclones would be vital. The hatches directly above our seats were slid open as they were for all operations at the deck, in order to be able to escape after a ditching. Day or night, rain or shine, the open hatches gaped above our heads when we operated 'at the deck', with the blare of the engines and the buzz of the propellers even louder, and the buffet of the airflow above adding to the noise and distraction.

After mere seconds, I had to turn towards the carrier at the pattern's 'base' position (that the Navy called the 'one-eighty'), but strangely, it was from almost directly abeam the ship: I had remembered that *Melbourne* would move forward as I turned towards the approach to her deck. It was an odd sensation to be turning in from immediately abeam a landing point. With the aircraft set up and trimmed for its landing speed, I could concentrate on 'crossing the wake' and picking up the ball as the aircraft carrier steamed forward.

The instructors had emphasised that a landing carrier pilot had to positively cross the ship's wake in order to correctly align with the final approach track. *Melbourne*'s landing area was angled that five degrees to the left to enable 'touch and go' or 'boltering' aircraft to safely clear all those obstacles to its right: the grey and black towering steel of the island, the pack of chained-down aircraft, and any launching aeroplane at the catapult. The eye was always drawn to the arrow-straight wake, but this was deceiving because it ran from the fore-and-aft axis of the ship. With the landing area angled to the left, pilots had to positively *cross* the carrier's wake well to its right in order to line their aircraft up properly with the yellow stripe of the landing centreline. *Melbourne*'s captain, eyeing the wisp of steam leaking from the catapult track that ran to the bow, would have set a course so that the 'wind over the deck' comprising the natural ocean breeze and the airflow generated by the ship's forward progress would blow the white plume directly down the *angle* of the landing area.

In a level turn towards the ship at three hundred feet with the wake positively crossed, I picked up the 'meatball', which was the orange blur that, at that moment, sat below the green lines of the datum lights on either side.

'Eight Four Five Ball, Carr, twenty two hundred,' Alan radioed to the LSO.

'Roger, ball,' he replied. I kept the level turn going, nudging the throttles up to maintain that precious ninety-five knots. Now the ball was climbing towards the datum lights as I flew to the glide slope … I needed to catch it and come back with the power to descend with it and, at the same time, level the wings – a little blip on the elevator trim to compensate for the power change … Then, I had to watch that 'line up', which was critical, as there were only three and a half metres between the right-hand wingtip of a Tracker on the centreline, and the steel of the island, or less if you drifted to the right. After that, I checked the speed … The scan 'meatball, line up, airspeed' had been dinned into us. My gloved fingers 'walked' the throttle levers back and forth in tiny movements and the engines' buzz rose and fell while I 'flew the ball', keeping it centred between the green lights, catching it with power if it sank, more power to get it back to centre, and then a little power off to keep it there, an endless cycle of almost automatic movements as the glide path defined by the ball funnelled in. It was like flying formation on an aircraft that got closer and closer, the adjustments becoming smaller and more exact while the carrier loomed.

Airspeed was critical. Too fast, and the 'flatter' attitude of the aircraft as it approached the deck would cause the dangling arrester hook at the tail to be higher, increasing the chance of missing the wires: a bolter. In the event of an arrest, the excessive speed would place even more strain on the aging ship's arresting gear. Being slow was not worth thinking about: a more nose-up aircraft attitude, more drag, less control and excess power available. That would put speed near the stall: a potential disaster for a carrier aircraft and, indeed, the ship itself, hence the technique of having the aircraft at its landing speed prior to turning towards the carrier, requiring only small adjustments of trim with power changes, which allowed a pilot to concentrate on his approach.

I was now in the 'groove' (the final approach path), but the ball had sunk low.

'A little power,' the LSO radioed.

I corrected as I would have done during Field Carrier Landing Practice (FCLP) at Nowra, and the ball settled between the green lights while the ship bloomed, and then I backed off the power to keep it there, but not so much as before. I tried to block out the distraction of the open hatches and concentrated on the ball, the thick yellow stripe that marked the centreline of the landing area and the Tracker's air speed indicator. I was ever aware of the curved steel of *Melbourne*'s green-grey stern that was topped with the dark lip of the round down. To my left, the blue and white Wessex slid out of my peripheral vision as we closed towards the carrier's creaming wake and a stream of funnel smoke.

'Right for line up,' came from the LSO as I drifted a little to the left, seduced by the wake. Hurriedly, I corrected the aircraft to the right, making sure to keep the ball level with the green lights as the glideslope narrowed and became ever more sensitive. Now I was 'in close', and for the first time, I felt through the controls the 'burble' of the disturbed air near *Melbourne*'s stern. Fly the ball! There was the sulphurous smell of the stack gas. The deck loomed in the windscreen, grey sea beyond. Now the ball was dropping a little again. It was too late to put it where it should be, all I could do was to just stop it dropping further. Another correction for line up … still a little left, but now the 'cut' lights flashed on. I was to come aboard by smartly pulling the throttles back to idle while holding that nose attitude which would tend to drop, still watching the line-up. Ker-rashh! The Tracker fell and its main wheels hit the steel, the high-pressure tyres and shock absorbers soaking up the impact. The little nose wheels were forced onto the deck with a bang and a rattle just below our feet, then it was up with the throttles in an instant for the touch and go, ensuring not to over-boost those powerful engines. The Tracker leapt back into the air. The few metres of deck ahead fell away as the grey-green of the island with its black masts and radar flashed past our right, and again we climbed away over the marbled surface of the bay. It had all happened so quickly. I banked left for another pattern. There was more work on the throttles and trim to stabilise level at 100 metres from the water, and Alan set the propellers' RPM. While I made the turn, the ship had moved further into the wind, so again, 'downwind' was short. I set the Tracker up for landing as I had done previously, but now established in the 'Charlie' pattern, there were even fewer seconds of 'straight and level' before it was time to turn again towards the carrier as she steamed inexorably away. Three more times I would come aboard for a touch and go, the arrester hook staying retracted, but at last Flyco radioed, '845 hook down.' The arrester hook would be extended for one arrested landing. After that we would taxi up to the catapult, then launch for Nowra.

Again came the now-familiar burble and smell of sulphur as we neared the gently rolling stern of the ship. The 'cut' lights flashed, and I smartly pulled the throttles back to idle. The Tracker fell a few feet, its nose high, and the main wheels hit the deck, but just before impact, the dangling arrester hook at the tail caught a wire. The hook bit, and Alan and I were flung forward against our harnesses. Then the nose wheels crashed down with even greater force than previously, and the aircraft snaked a little as the wire ran out, the hook now horizontal behind, and the deceleration violent. In no time, we were rolling back slowly as the arresting wire rebounded. White-jerkined sailors rushed up to us, one giving frantic signals: 'brakes on' – now that the wire was clear of the hook – and 'hook up', so Alan pushed up the hook-shaped lever on the overhead panel into its niche behind the throttles. My feet trembled on the brake pedals as I maintained pressure on them to ensure that our aircraft did not move in the tight confines of *Melbourne*'s deck. I was mindful of the knife edge before a twelve-metre fall to the water. Now the 'bear' was waving at me to taxi forward with no time to be lost, because the carrier would soon have to be turned around in the confines of Jervis Bay. While I taxied, Alan called the 'challenges' of the checklist and I made the 'responses'.

Now we were at the catapult. The handler used little movements of his head to guide us in aligning the Tracker, its engines beating at idle, with the catapult track: the steaming rust-red slot in the deck that ended at *Melbourne*'s square bow. Unseen, other handlers looped the wire strop that joined the aircraft's belly hook with the catapult's shuttle. Sharp steel propeller blades would be slicing by just centimetres from their heads. A sailor slid one end of a frangible steel 'hold back' fitting into a slot under the Tracker's tail, its other end clipped to a fitting in the deck. The catapult would soon be 'tensioned up' by the 'stokers' of the catapult crew, who would gently nudge steam valves to move the huge pistons slightly to pull on the strop. Now that was done, and the aircraft slowly tilted and sat cocked up on its little tail wheel, the twin nose-wheels high off the deck. Under the tension on the aircraft's launch hook, we were now restrained only by the hold back fitting at the tail. Now, I doubly made sure that my feet were *off* the brakes. A petty officer had been standing just outside Alan's window directing the sailors with his signals, but now he stood clear, to be replaced by the flight deck officer, who was holding an incongruous little flag on a stick which he now waved in circles above his head. This was the signal for me to set full power. I pushed the throttles up and the gentle motion of the ship was now unnoticeable as the Tracker quivered at full power. The tall fin and the wide tailplane would be vibrating furiously behind. Noise blared through the open hatches as my right hand held the throttles forward at maximum permissible boost. I had two fingers curled around the pull-down catapult grip. I knew that the acceleration of the launch would be so violent, that gripping this little inverted T-shaped handle would prevent my arm from involuntarily pulling back on the throttles during the catapult stroke. We remained 'in tension' and at full power while I checked the instruments and warning lights in the vibrating panels as best as I could.

In the event of an engine fire or failure just before starting the take-off roll on a land airfield, a pilot can reduce the engine power to idle and sort things out. But not so when under tension on the catapult of an aircraft carrier. Then, there is no guarantee that the device will not fire should the launch need to be 'aborted': one of the unique hazards of naval aviation. Against all logic and survival instincts, in the event of a major problem, all a pilot can do is to remain at full power on what engines were available, violently shake his head, call 'cancel, cancel, cancel' over the radio, and hope that the impending launch can be stopped. A fire? Still, he must remain at full power in case the catapult fires and he is hurled from the deck regardless: he has to try to keep the aircraft flying clear of the ship for at best a diversion to land or, at worst, a ditching. Following a cancelled launch, only when the flight deck officer himself steps directly in front of his aircraft can a carrier pilot be reassured that the catapult will not fling his aircraft from the ship. The wire strop would have fallen from the belly hook after gentle movements of the deck shuttle under control of the catapult crew. Now the pilot can reduce power, plant his feet firmly on the brake pedals, and deal with the problem.

But this time there were no warning lights, and the engine instruments looked good. We were ready. I nodded at Alan, whose left hand backed up my right on the throttles. We pressed our heads back into the headrests and he gave the Flight Deck Officer the standard signal that we were ready to launch: a snappy salute. The FDO continued to twirl his little flag in the air as he checked *Melbourne*'s bow, which nodded gently in Jervis Bay. When the moment was right, his flag went down to touch the deck: the signal to the catapult crew to initiate the launch sequence. My fingers tightened further around the catapult grip. A heartbeat later, the catapult fired.

It is difficult to describe the feeling of accelerating from zero to flying speed in the space of thirty-four metres. A giant hand seemed to slam us forward and, momentarily, our bodies were subject to almost

3 g of force – three times our weight – but unlike the force that had crushed me down into my seat when manoeuvring the Macchi, this force was horizontal. I had sat through Alan's launches previously, but it was still a bizarre feeling as the Tracker accelerated violently down the deck, shuddering with a higher and higher frequency as the speed built up over just a few seconds. The increasingly frantic rattle of the landing gear could be heard over the noise of the engines and bizarrely, the flight controls instantly came alive in my hand. I concentrated on the horizon, with my helmet forced back into the headrest and making sure that I held that catapult grip to maintain those throttles at full power. With the carrier's steel deck having raced away beneath us, now there was nothing but water below and the horizon ahead – we were flying.

Simultaneously, we felt a 'thump': it seemed as if the aircraft had slammed to a halt in mid-air. But all that had happened was that the strop that joined us to the catapult had let us go. The cessation of the violent acceleration had fooled the body into thinking that everything had stopped. The momentary violence of the launch had flung us from a world of oscillating grey steel and white and yellow jacketed figures into a routine climb over the sea. We brought the Cyclones back to climb power, and turned for the shore.

On Nowra's tarmac, we clambered out of our aircraft, to the irregular ticking of cooling metal and the smell of hot oil. The usual stains of it streaked back from the vents and breathers along the sides of the nacelles, to be wiped off while still warm by the maintainers. A flight of Skyhawks screamed overhead to join Nowra's circuit: their pilots had also just been to the deck for their first carrier landings. For them, there been no demonstration beforehand by an experienced deck pilot such as I had been given. The special two-seat Skyhawk trainers were not able to operate from *Melbourne*'s tiny flight deck, as they could have done from a huge American carrier. An Australian Skyhawk pilot would experience his first deck landing solo, in a single-seat aircraft.

I plodded across Nowra's tarmac towards the crew room in

quiet relief. My first landings on HMAS *Melbourne* had not been outstanding, but at least safe; the LSO had radioed that I had made four 'no grade' passes but there had been one 'fair'. Thankfully, I had not been waved off. I had not boltered. The LSO had not had to dive into his safety net!

Before we walked away, Alan had been poking about under the Tracker's tail and now he handed me a small but heavy blue and yellow turned-steel cylinder, which had a torn, jagged edge at one end. Over the whine of the Skyhawks that were now taxiing in, he shouted, 'Here you go. It's the hold-back fitting from your first cat shot!' The fitting had restrained us while we were in tension on *Melbourne*'s catapult. Half of the device had stayed in its slot in 845's tail as we were shot from the deck and flew back to the land. It sits on my desk today.

10

'ROGER BALL'

1980 - 1981

I felt weightless for an instant as *Melbourne*'s stern crashed back into the sea after a lurch upwards. The throb of the ship's propellers changed as the screws once again bit into deeper water. The plunge reversed into another rise, then yet another fall. Slightly nauseous, I lay on the bunk of my tiny cabin, which was buried deep in the hull near *Melbourne*'s stern. The bunk doubled as the top of a steel drawer cabinet and tiny built-in writing table. A blank cream steel bulkhead was opposite, allowing just enough room to stand between it and the side of the bunk. A 1950s vintage petal-shaped lampshade cast a circle of light over the faded floral-patterned brown carpet that was laid over the steel of the deck. There was no 'scuttle' (porthole) and, therefore, no view out. In this lurching steel box I slept, read, studied and daydreamed. Through its thin metal door came the whirr of ventilation fans, the constant tramp of boots on the steel deck of the passageway outside, and the clang of hatchways. An incessant rising and falling whine penetrated from a hydraulic steering motor in its compartment nearby. Overwhelming it all was the throb and judder of *Melbourne*'s propellers below, which – when at high cruise or aircraft recovery speed – shook everything.

In early 1980, *Melbourne* was ploughing through Pacific Ocean swells. I was embarked with VS 816 Squadron, which I had just joined. My new unit's *nom-de-guerre* was 'The Fighting Tigers'. We were now in deep ocean, far from any land. I could stare into deep blue depths through smooth patches of water immediately behind *Melbourne's* quarterdeck before the frothing wake, which surfaced far behind the propellers. Shafts of sunlight disappeared vertically into darkening water kilometres deep. Only a few layers of man-made steel lay between us and a long cold plunge in darkness to the deepest ocean bottom on the planet. We lived, worked and flew in the layer between the ocean's dark blue surface and the lighter blue of the sky, usually studded during the day with 'streets' of fair-weather cumulus cloud. HMAS *Melbourne*, with her tiny Air Group, was on her way to to exercise with the U.S. Navy near Hawaii, thousands of sea miles away.

Apart from the flying as a Staff Pilot back on 851 Squadron, I had been subject to various other courses and duties considered applicable to a junior naval officer. There was 'Base Duty Officer': sleep-deprived nights of instant coffee, constant phone calls, and messages to check in the wooden hut at Nowra's gangway (like *Cerberus*, the air base was regarded as a commissioned ship: HMAS *Albatross*). 'Squadron Duty Officer' came around regularly, as did participation in the regular ceremonial parades, 'Divisions'. I had undergone a Base Flying Safety Officers' Course with the army, which was a prerequisite to yet another 'secondary duty' as a Squadron Flight Safety Officer. A few months later in October 1979, I found myself aboard an air force Hercules transport. It was difficult to read or talk in the noisy, windowless interior. All there was to do was to loll in the canvas benches that were strung along the sides of the hold and doze, or stare at lashed-down boxes and crates for hours on end. I called this 'Hercules Sensory Deprivation.' However, on this flight, I had much to think about. I was positioning to Darwin, where for a month I would operate with the detachment of Trackers that flew as part of Operation 'Seawatch', with the responsibility of finding and tracking refugee boats and foreign fishing vessels that entered Australia's waters.

I had experienced a taste of Darwin life (and my first flight in a Tracker) during that HS 748 trip that now seems ages past. The same wooden block, with its open, slatted windows, became home, and after some familiarisation flights, the standard three-day routine became familiar. On Day One, as I slept under the swish of the ceiling fan but still damp with sweat under a sheet, the telephone would shrill in the early morning darkness: 'Good morning, sir, it's the exchange. It's time to wake up.'

After a groggy shower, I would pull on the flight suit. In the heavy, still air – filled with the chirp of insects and still dark– I crossed the damp, tropical lawn to climb the wooden stairs of the old Officers' Mess, opened especially for us for an early breakfast. 'Changa', our TACCO, would join me, and soon we would drive the short distance to the Detachment offices in the RAAF Operations Centre to meet our Sensor Three and Four operators, a petty officer and a leading seaman, to be briefed on which one of the three standard patrols we would be flying today. The routes took various directions seawards from Darwin, and lasted for up to six hours.

With the sun just appearing and in the tropical morning calm, our Tracker usually used the same take-off runway, blaring at full power over the hapless residents of a nearby caravan park at five am. We turned seawards, then levelled at 1,500 feet – or 460 metres. Sensor Three extended the big thimble-shaped radome from the Tracker's belly and the search began: primarily with radar, but for Changa and me up front, also a visual scan of the sluggish sea, which was usually an oily calm striated with yellow stains of algae and floating seaweed: there were rarely any whitecaps. Often, sea snakes were clearly visible; their black and yellow stripes were very distinctive. Over the tropical water, the air was nearly always silk-smooth in near windless sky. The sensor operators took turns at the radar and competed to spot 'contacts' and steer us toward them, Changa craning forward, peering through special stabilised binoculars. If the contact was of no interest, we turned away, but if it was a stained, dilapidated vessel or an obviously Asian fishing boat, we would descend, to run alongside it at a low level, with Changa leaning into his side bubble with his camera to record its details.

We usually found and reported several Asian fishing boats each patrol, but refugee vessels were not common. Changa noted details and position of all contacts of interest, which we radioed to the shore authorities. These patrols were a revelation as to how responsible the TACCOs were for navigation. Soon after take-off, Changa unlocked and stowed the hefty co-pilot's control wheel in front of him using a special release handle, which gave him space to rest a wooden plotting board on his knees. Miles from the coast and from any navigation radio aids, the TACCO navigated the Tracker using just a pencil, dividers, a protractor and a paper map. He plotted course, wind and drift backed up by the occasional radar 'fix' passed by Sensor Three when we were close enough to pick up a prominent feature on the Northern Territory coast. There was no GPS, and we were too low and too far out to pick up any accurate navigation beacon from land. All navy observers had passed through the air force's School of Navigation at East Sale prior to completing an OFS back at Nowra, in a parallel process to the pilots, and they had undergone a course that was, in most respects, no less demanding.

For hour after hour the engines rumbled at 1,800 rpm, propelling us along at 130 knots – 240 km/hr – with the intercom coming to life from time to time with contact reports, radar fixes and occasional banter. There was a routine of checking fuel usage and engine indications, and regular 'burn outs': momentarily increasing the power on the Cyclones to burn any oil deposits from the spark plugs. Clad in flight suits, Mae Wests with survival gear and heavy helmets, for the crew the interior of the Tracker was stifling. There was no air conditioning, and the heat generated by the electronics added to the discomfort, but the TACCOs had devised 'air conditioning sticks', notched lengths of wood, that would hold an overhead hatch slightly ajar. This provided some welcome cooling airflow through the cramped cabin for us all.

Finally, it would be time for an expeditious return to Darwin; no 'run and break' this time at the end a long patrol. With the Tracker shut down at the 'Det', it was off to the showers and later the Officers' Mess to join other navy crews and support staff, air force base personnel and the occasional itinerant Hercules crew to slake our not inconsiderable thirsts. After that, dinner and an early night.

Day Two of the routine was easy: the same early call and breakfast in flying gear but this time we were the 'standby' crew to cover sickness, unserviceability or any other contingency. After the operating crew's Tracker bored out over the caravan park and turned north, the standby crew could relax in the air-conditioned 'Det' Operations Room. There, with any administration and secondary duties complete, the traditional American naval aviator's game of 'Acey Deucey' would begin.

Acey Deucey was a modification of Backgammon. Invariably, if a game was in progress any other aviators in the room would gather around to 'kibitz' (shout ribald comments, strategy suggestions, and general ridicule of the players' moves). A player would be in a tight spot; then, a roar would erupt from everyone if he threw a lucky 'ace-deuce' to reverse his fortunes. One pilot would remark, 'You know, they should put an Acey-Deucey set in our survival packs. It wouldn't matter where you came down; if you started playing a game, someone would always show up to kibitz.'

When the beat of the returning Tracker's engines' stopped outside on the tarmac, the standby crew's time was now their own until Day Three, which would be free of Seawatch flying, but there could also be continuation training, maintenance test flights, instrument flying practice, secondary duties and administration that would be followed by an early night. The telephone would shatter fitful sleep under the swish of the fan before dawn on the next morning for that day's patrol, and so the cycle would repeat.

There were social functions, usually involving large quantities of beer, organised by the sea-going navy. Darwin was a patrol boat base, and these boats responded to Trackers' sightings of illegal and suspicious vessels. It had not been so long since Cyclone Tracy had struck Darwin in 1974. HMAS *Melbourne* had been hurriedly dispatched there with her decks full of Wessex helicopters, and she was one of the first military units that could provide significant assistance to the inhabitants of the devastated city; thereafter, naval personnel were always welcome in the pubs, clubs and at civic functions. A borrowed car allowed me to explore some of what to me was alien territory: serried ranks of tropical growth topped with red escarpment, the heat and humidity of the hinterland, the stench of road kill, the eccentricities and cultural variety of the Territorians, and middens of beer cans alongside placid waterholes ... Much of it was interesting but I was not entirely disappointed when the month's detachment was up and once again I was sagging in the dark hold of a Hercules, bored and restless, but at least heading south east. I had not fouled up in any great way during my flying with DET DAR. My long-distance relationship was ongoing, and it would be good to be together after the Hercules landed. But soon I was to go to sea with 816 Squadron in HMAS *Melbourne*, and if I could complete the 'cruise' safely and competently, I would be considered a true naval aviator.

We were 'working up' for the forthcoming cruise to Hawaii. Whitecaps studded the Tasman Sea under a cloudless sky as HMAS *Melbourne* steamed on her recovery course. With the now familiar crash and rattle, the Tracker's main landing gear, then the nose wheels, fell heavily to the deck and, as usual, we were hurled forward into our harnesses as the hook engaged an arresting wire. There was the now familiar routine of the rollback – 'brakes on, hook up' – and then the frantic marshalling of us to go forward by the handlers. The deck gently oscillated as we quickly completed checklists while we expeditiously taxied forward to the catapult. Now we were in tension. The Tracker was shaking at full power ... heads were jammed into the headrest, followed by the salute, and ... 'wham!', the violent acceleration of the catapult shot and, in an instant, we were flying again, on course to make an almost-immediate left turn ... level out at 300 feet, barely one hundred metres ... but don't roll wings level, keep the turn going for another pattern! The ship had moved forward, and we were already at the 'one-eighty' – still in the turn! After a confirmatory 'hook down' call from Flyco, we completed the landing checklist and continued the original turn to pick up the approach to the carrier again ... *call the 'ball' ... now we are 'in the groove' ... fly the ball ... meatball ... line-up ... airspeed ... here's the 'rooster tail' of disturbed air from the ship ... meatball ... line-up ... airspeed ... in close now, stop the ball moving ... line-up, line-up ...* now the green 'cut lights' glared and we fell to the deck. Once again, we were 'in the wires' and had to repeat the exercise, a session of multiple 'arrest and cats' (catapult shots), in order to obtain the required numbers prior to being considered as 'carrier qualified' for the deployment.

Today, it had been 'the sport of kings'. A summer ocean, good 'wind over the deck' and just enough ship movement to give experience in evening out the oscillations of the meatball. There had also been a shore diversion, Nowra, our 'home plate', available in case of a problem. Later, in the quiet of my cabin there, I could even discern a faint ache in my ribs from the multiple violent decelerations of the arrested landings where my bony chest had been flung forward against the harness. Yes, it had been a good day. A couple of OK passes, and the only wave-off by the LSO had been due to a 'foul deck' (another aircraft had blocked the landing area). I had gained some confidence, but another challenge loomed: I had to do it all again, but in an oceanic night.

This time, I was tightly strapped into a seat in the Tracker's rear compartment. Blocking any view directly ahead were the darkened instruments and switches of the sensor operator's panel. I could crane sideways and forward to look down the cramped passageway, beyond which the view was the now familiar overhead panels and engine controls, bathed in red light. Through the little eyebrow-shaped windscreens there was only black: nothing to see through those, especially from back here. The tiny window next to my elbow also revealed little of the outside world except for orange and blue flames that danced eerily from the engine's exhaust stacks. The routine patter of talk from the two pilots in front dominated the intercom. I could also hear the radio calls from HMAS *Melbourne*'s LSO and 'Flyco'. Then, 'Eight Four Eight, Charlie': the call from the ship to direct our aircraft to join the 'Charlie pattern', the carrier's 'circuit'. Minutes later, I could only sit and wait and stare out into the black from the side window as the pilot commenced his first carrier approach for the night.

The pilots called the ball. I could still see nothing.

'Roger ball,' replied the LSO. The engines' note subsided a little, then rose and fell as the pilot flew the orange ball of light to keep it level with the green lines of the datum lights on either side. I could feel the wings level out once in the groove, and through all this, the LSO's voice came through my helmet: 'Right for line-up ... a little power ... hold what you've got ... a little slow ... power ...' The LSO would be on his platform looking astern from *Melbourne*'s deck, focussed on a blossoming set of lights that would be our Tracker. A special light on its wing's leading edge would show various colours corresponding with the aircraft's angle of attack, showing the LSO the aircraft's speed in relation to the optimum for landing. His 'calibrated eyeball' would assess our approach angle and line-up in the night from the moving deck, and as our lights bloomed over the stern, if we were in his imaginary 'box' for a safe landing, he would press the button on his 'pickle switch' to give our pilot the 'cut' signal.

The LSO's voice became slightly heightened as we neared the

carrier. Suddenly, I made out a white streak of disturbed water through the side window: *Melbourne*'s wake. A heartbeat later, I heard the engines come back to idle. I braced myself against the seat and headrest. A few dim lights suddenly rushed by below and a second later, there was the impact of the landing but now the engines roared, and the Tracker leapt back into the night sky from a touch and go. The flames from the exhausts now leapt and dazzled as we climbed away and turned for another pattern. There were a few more touch and goes, then an arrest and catapult shot. Airborne yet again, with the aircraft established in the carrier's 'Delta pattern' for holding, I clambered up to the co-pilot's seat to observe several night landings by the instructor. And then it would be my turn.

I had flown many night patterns during the land-based FCLP training at Nowra on the dummy deck painted on the runway. However, during these exercises, in my peripheral vision there were always the lights of the base, the town and the farms that dotted the area. But now, I was flying on instruments over black water with no horizon. I made out two tiny points of light below and to our left. One was HMAS *Melbourne*, and the other, astern and to port, was the rescue destroyer ('RESDES'). There would be no patiently hovering 'Pedro' rescue helicopter available at night to fish crashed aircrew from cold, dark water. Coordination between the bridge crew of the carrier and the destroyer was vital: the two infamous and tragic collisions between HMAS *Melbourne* and HMAS *Voyager* and USS *Frank E. Evans* occurred when the respective destroyers were moving into the RESDES position.

I was descending on instruments to 800 feet – 240 metres – above the unseen sea and the tiny point of light that designated the carrier. The blare of the engines and propellers was even harsher in the cold night air, and cold airflow buffeted the tops of our helmets after we opened the overhead hatches in readiness for my first night carrier landing. The arrester hook was left up for a touch and go.

'848 Ball, Carr, one thousand four hundred.'

'Roger ball.'

This time we were descending from 800 feet with the glide path, not the daytime 300. The meatball settled between the green datum lights, prominent in the darkness. But where was I in regarding to the line-up? In the darkness, I could not make out the ship's wake. I used a combination of instrument flying and looking outside towards the tiny lights and the ball. I rolled the wings level to where I thought the centreline was, but there was no wake to be seen that I could use as a reference in the blackness before the smudge of light that was the carrier's flight deck. The meatball meandered left and right in the windscreen while I struggled to achieve the correct line-up.

I descended with the ball as the LSO called corrections: 'Right for line-up, hold what you've got, you're a little high ...' But now we were closing the carrier and the smudge of light began to take form: the ridiculously small trapezoid of the landing area, bathed in faint light, and some tiny lights embedded in the deck and on the stern that marked its centreline. However, because the landing area was barely one hundred meters long – even in close – there was little perspective to assess whether our Tracker was on centreline. I fought to stay lined up correctly. At the same time, I had to fly the ball and maintain the correct speed. I was ever aware of the bare four metres between the aircraft's starboard wing and the metal of *Melbourne*'s 'island' and masts to our right, and *that* was if the aircraft was lined up correctly. My right hand walked the throttles to fly the ball, but it oscillated up and down: was it me, or was it deck movement? In the darkness, I could not tell. The LSO encouraged me to even out the oscillations with some helpful calls. But this had been to the detriment of my line-up: my left hand worked the control wheel, fighting to stay on the landing course, which was starting to become a little easier with more perspective in close. But now, it was too late. The red wave-off lights glared and pulsed at the side of the mirror as the LSO radioed, 'Wave-off, wave-off.'

Smartly, I pushed up the throttles and locked my eyes onto the attitude indicator in front as I selected the climb attitude. The ship's lights below were gone in an instant as we climbed into the blackness ahead, the bellow of the engines and buffet of the airstream filling the cockpit. It was pure instrument flying to 800 feet on the radar altimeter in the left turn and level out for another attempt. The LSO gave a brief critique over the radio, explaining that he was unhappy with my overcorrections. Then I drifted to the left 'in close', so I was waved off. I would try again. Frustrated, I tried to calm myself as we again turned inwards towards the ship. This time, as I rolled out on the approach path, my eyes occasionally flicked to the sphere of the attitude indicator on the panel in front of me. As best as I could, I judged when I was lined up correctly and, at this point, the indicator helped me maintain wings-level. I worked on making my corrections smoother and smaller and, this time, the carrier's lights blossomed at about the right spot: I was lined up correctly, on speed, and the ball was near where it was supposed to be. The bright green cut lights blinked on. I chopped the throttles, held the Tracker's attitude, and we fell to the deck. A 'no grade' pass, but safe. After several more touch and goes, it was time to put the hook down. Almost getting the hang of it, I took the cut and once again we fell aboard, but this time we were slammed forwards into our harnesses as the arresting hook bit, and in no time came the frantic waving signals of the handlers: 'hook up, brakes off', and we were taxiing on the rolling deck, busy with checklists, forward to the catapult somewhere up in the gloom.

Even more so than in day operations at night, we were in the care of the 'bears' (the aircraft handlers). Melbourne's deck was only faintly illuminated, and beyond the weak pools of light was complete blackness with no distinction between ocean and sky. There were no barriers to stop our big aircraft from rolling over the unseen edge of the deck. The vigorous marshalling signals reduced to head nods and tiny gestures as we taxied forwards to the catapult and went through the drills made familiar by day. But this time, as we prepared for the catapult shot, there was no ocean horizon beyond: only black. Now, with the aircraft throbbing and straining, held by the hold-back fitting, the world was the attitude indicator in front of me well before the catapult fired, and soon came that familiar shove in the back, the rattle and clatter, but this time in total darkness after one or two tiny lights rushed by in my peripheral vision. I knew that rapid acceleration can fool the organs of our inner ears into making us think that the body is pitching upwards, and so low above the water, a reflexive push forward on the control wheel would be catastrophic. Indeed, the one Australian Tracker that had been lost had crashed into the water ahead of the carrier after a bolter at night, its pilot fooled by the acceleration into thinking that the aircraft was pitching up. Luckily all four crew escaped through the overhead hatches and were rescued, fortunate not to be run over by the ship. With this in mind, I stayed locked onto the attitude indicator during the assault on our senses of the catapult shot. I made sure that the aircraft was climbing away at the correct attitude into the night and this time, we turned towards the distant glow of the New South Wales coast for Nowra and home. Despite the initial waveoff, my night deck work had been satisfactory, because soon I was to fly a Tracker from Nowra to embark, with the rest of the squadron, for my first cruise in HMAS *Melbourne*.

Now, *Melbourne*'s bow creamed through oceanic swells north-east towards Hawaii. The ship was in unimaginably deep water: a floating, moving air base of steel – never dormant. The embarked squadrons of Skyhawks, Trackers, and Sea King helicopters were supplemented by a detachment of two Wessex helicopters. *Melbourne* was accompanied by HMAS *Supply*, a tanker as elderly as herself, and a pair of destroyers. Regularly, *Supply* would carry out a Replenishment At Sea (RAS) with the other ships. When *Supply* was cutting through the water just metres parallel to *Melbourne*, fuel hoses connecting the pair as the big ships steamed along, we expressed muted admiration for the bridge crews and seamen despite our youthful aircrew arrogance. The thousands of tonnes of the steel ships would be subject to a force trying to suck them towards each other as the water rushed between the parallel hulls. The ten to fifteen knots of speed multiplied the dead weight of each vessel into a huge amount of kinetic energy that required significant anticipation and control through steering and engine orders to maintain exact formation as ship's fuel oil was pumped aboard the carrier. And there was not only ship's fuel oil to replenish, but volatile aviation fuel. Stores and even personnel were transferred on lines between the ships and, at the end of the RAS, one vessel would swing away, usually *Melbourne*, heeling during the turn onto its into-wind course to launch or recover her aircraft.

I settled into the rhythm of life at sea, governed by the Flying Program and other duties. There was constant noise and heat, and sleep opportunities were sometimes difficult to come by. The ship was filled with bustling activity day and night. There were men everywhere: aircrew, maintainers, deck crew, ship's crew, cooks, air traffic controllers, weapons specialists, the admiral and his staff. The dull clump of safety boots rang up and down the passageways. The slap of the leather sandals worn by officers and seamen not involved with heavy equipment was incongruous on the steel deck plates. The pipes were incessant.

The ship seemed to never just cruise along towards Hawaii. There was always an exercise, a RAS, flying operations, emergency drills … and the vessel was not just an aircraft carrier but also a hospital ship, a storage ship, and a command and control ship. Like HMAS *Supply*, she could refuel other vessels. She had a mail room for her own complement and those of the accompanying ships. Now we were close to Fiji and my crew were tasked to fly ashore to Nadi International Airport and bring mail on-board. In good weather, I landed the Tracker at Nadi, but I kept the engines ticking over while the mail was exchanged: the Tracker had no internal batteries and therefore could not start its own engines. It was a new experience to appear at a civilian airport from a ship at sea.

For our crew, the flying routine at any hour of the day or night was to pull on a clean flight suit in the confines of our tiny cabins with the ship's propellers throbbing below, and then, with flight bags, we moved unsteadily along the oscillating passageways and up the ladders of the island to the theatre-like briefing room. There, we rested in the high-backed chairs to be briefed on the upcoming exercise or mission along with the weather conditions and the shore diversions, if any, that would be available in the event of an emergency. There were no computer displays in the early 1980s – an overhead projector was considered the height of technology. Our TACCO manually plotted the various points and courses on his paper chart, and then we would clamber back down the ladders to the safety equipment room at flight deck level, pick up our helmets that were covered in various patterns of white and red reflective tape, and don our Mae Wests. Tentatively, we ventured out of the island onto the flight deck – was there a Skyhawk landing on? A Tracker launch in progress? What about helicopter rotors and jet blast? Deaf in our helmets but with our heads swivelling, we moved carefully to our assigned Tracker to climb up and in through the little door on its starboard side. The Flight Deck Officer and his petty officers watched us intently, the courtesies of rank disregarded when they shouted and swore at any careless aircrew not paying attention.

After preliminary checks, it was time for the 'walk around' or external inspection of the aircraft. It was more like a 'clamber round' as – forever mindful of the nearby deck edge – we stuck close to the aircraft structure. The tripping hazard of a web of multiple chains, unseen at night, stretched between points on the aircraft to the ringbolts in the deck (the chains would be removed by the 'bears' after the engines were started). There could be the sudden whistle and bang of a Skyhawk impacting the deck just a few metres away, its pilot throttling up again, engine momentarily roaring until he was sure that he had caught an arresting wire, or the full-power blare of another Tracker at the catapult followed by the vibration and thump of the shot, discernible through our feet. We had to climb up out of the overhead escape hatches of the sensor operator stations and crawl along the upper surfaces of the high wings to check the

Grumman's fuel and oil filler caps, engine exhausts and antennae. In some parking spots, the water would be rushing by below the edge of the wing stub that projected over the deck. At night, all was black apart from dim red lighting from our torches and some very faint deck lighting; the ship's officers were always reluctant to show too much light and, during exercises where the carrier was to be unseen, the deck environment was Stygian. But the ocean rushing by beyond the deck edge was ever present. The flight deck lights would only be turned on immediately before a launch or recovery.

Our crew comprised me, our TACCO Ollie, Neale, a fellow acting sub-lieutenant, and Max, a leading seaman. We were to fly almost exclusively together for this cruise. Our respective skills had been honed during the ship's 'work up' off the New South Wales coast, but it was a first cruise for Neale and me, and we still had much to learn. The sensation of the catapult launch became familiar, and the mission would be anything from anti-submarine exercises at low level to Anti-Submarine Air Controller training, or weapons firing. For that, *Melbourne* towed a splash target on a long cable, which we attacked with practice bombs and rockets, but my weapons work showed little improvement. I imagined the derisive comments from the 'goofers' watching from high on the island or from the quarterdeck at the stern. I just did not have the 'feel' or visual acuity for accurate weapons sighting, and the instructors of VC 724 Squadron had been right not to recommend me to fly Skyhawks. However, luckily I had shown improvement and consistency in deck landings. We were now in deep ocean, Fiji was long past, and I had to get the Tracker and our crew aboard every time. There was nowhere to go in the event of failure to land on the carrier, apart from a ditching alongside before the fuel ran out. Thankfully, I was generally safe, and the greenie board in the crew room displayed my record of 'fair' passes with a smattering of 'OK's and only a few 'no grades' and wave-offs that were due to poor technique.

We were now under full tropical weather and the ship, designed for service in the North Atlantic, was a sweat box. With *Melbourne's* engine room evaporators struggling, showers were strictly limited to once a day for thirty seconds, under threat of charges being laid for transgressing. There were cycles of round-the-clock exercises: a routine of fitful sleep, briefing in an already clammy flight suit and, soon, the 'thump-rattle-thump!' off the catapult for long anti-submarine exercises, mostly at low level and often over unseen ocean in darkness. Always, especially at night, the thought that I would have to get us all safely back onto *Melbourne*'s deck nagged while I stayed locked on to the instruments for hours at just a hundred metres above the water. Ollie, our TACCO, was not a pilot, so I was manipulating the aircraft without a break and it was vital that I stayed sharp. Finally, there was the recovery to land onto HMAS *Melbourne* and, if late at night or the still-dark hours of an early tropical morning, the squadron Duty Officer would pass two cans of beer to each of us afterwards for consumption after the debrief. Later would be the fleeting luxury of the thirty-second shower and maybe a meal, attending to 'secondary duties', and then finally some more fitful sleep in our metal cabins amid the din of the hatchways, the electric whine of the pumps and motors, the tramp of boots on steel and the never-ending pipes.

As the carrier and the squadrons became fully worked up, the exercises became more demanding. Anti-Submarine Warfare is a cat-and-mouse game of trying to use sensors to detect the enemy. There was also the very important aspect of communicating with the controlling unit and reporting enemy contacts. But every time a radio transmitter button is pressed, or a radar sends out its probing electronic finger, these emissions can be detected, analysed and can reveal to a silent, listening enemy an approximate location of a threat and even what type of emitter is being used. In the mass of considerations of modern warfare, EMCON (Emission Control), is important. Strict EMCON rules were developed and, for these exercises, we were required to follow them. We could not use our radios or 'shine' our radar within certain distances of the carrier or other 'friendly' units: HMAS *Melbourne* would turn off her TACAN beacon, radars and other navigation aids; her air traffic controllers would not talk to us and with us all now reasonably experienced naval aviators, we were expected to find the ship, enter the landing pattern, and then fly the ball to a safe arrest without Flying Control or even the LSO having to transmit on the radio. This was called an EMCON Recovery. The LSO was only allowed to use the cut and wave-off lights. He was only allowed to talk on his radio in the case of an emergency. It was incumbent on us to fly our passes accurately and safely.

There were several important pieces of information that our crew had to have to find the carrier at the end of our mission, especially in darkness and in EMCON conditions: the Base Recovery Course, the Charlie Time, and an estimated latitude and longitude of the carrier's recovery position. These were given to us at the pre-flight briefing. The Base Recovery Course was the estimated direction that *Melbourne* would be steaming in order to have that vital 'wind over the deck' nicely down the angled landing area. The Charlie Time was the instant when our aircraft would have to be 'in the wires', safely on the deck, and this time was critical.

It was rare that the carrier and its accompanying fleet would be steaming in a direction that would place the prevailing wind 'down the angle' of the flight deck in order to safely launch and recover its aircraft. HMAS *Melbourne* and at night, her accompanying rescue destroyer, would nearly always have to detach from the main formation of warships in order to turn onto her recovery course. The extreme case was the recovery course being 180 degrees to that of the fleet's line of advance. Every second that *Melbourne* spent heading away from the fleet would have to be made up for later. With her propellers throbbing, she would fight to catch up; otherwise, the entire fleet would have to change course or speed. Therefore, the tolerance on our Charlie Time was thirty seconds. Any earlier or later and *Melbourne*'s deck would not be ready to receive us, resulting in a wave-off and delay while a further landing pattern was flown. If a crew missed their Charlie Time, testy messages would emanate from the bridge or the admiral's staff to FLYCO, then on to the squadron's CO for passing on, in a very forthright manner, to the offending crew. Conversely, to take a wire with the carrier swinging through the wind right on Charlie Time sometimes earned a 'Sierra Hotel' (Shit Hot), as the ship could then keep her turn going in a perfect circle, deck still heeling, while with the Tracker's wings folding, we would be marshalled to our tie-down spot. Then the carrier could straighten and steam ahead to re-join the fleet.

These recoveries were difficult enough requirement during an oceanic blue day, but on a pitch-black night, after some four hours of ASW manoeuvring or patrolling, the TACCO, using only his plotting board, would have to plan to arrive in the landing pattern of a moving, turning aircraft carrier that would be using no radios or navigation aids and, until the last few moments, showing no lights. Then, it was up to me to arrange the landing pattern to be in the wires as *Melbourne* passed through her recovery course. At three minutes to Charlie Time, a single masthead light illuminated over *Melbourne*'s island. Weirdly, the little light would often be close underneath us. When we turned cross-wind in the black sky to enter our landing pattern, we calculated that the ship would also be turning onto the briefed Recovery Course, and her turn radius would have to be allowed for. At one minute to Charlie, the feeble lighting of the landing area was switched on, and, thankfully, after we turned inwards at the one-eighty, I caught the familiar sight of the orange meatball and its green datum lights.

Fly a good pass … don't force the LSO to make any correctional radio calls … meatball, line up, airspeed … now, ker-rash! In the wires, brakes on, hook up, flaps up, wings folding … hurried marshalling to one's 'spot' … watch the handler's signals … don't lose concentration, it's not over yet, one wheel is very close to that deck edge as the carrier heels in the turn …

With our Tracker now safely chained down onto the ship we shut down the Cyclones and we emerged onto the steel of the flight deck. Warm, tropical wind tugged at our sweaty flight suits. We carefully made our way to the base of the island to clamber up its ladders for a debriefing, then those two cans of beer that wouldn't touch the sides ...

The cliché 'well-oiled machine' does not do justice to the level of coordination and discipline required to operate an aircraft carrier, especially one whose structure strained under the weight and speed of aircraft its designers never envisaged. During a busy session of flight deck operations, a Tracker would recover, its wings folding while it was frantically marshalled towards its spot clear of the landing area, while a flight of Skyhawks would shriek past on the island side, the first one already pitching left towards the 'one eighty', now down it comes toward the deck, its air brakes deployed like outstretched hands from its rear fuselage and now the Tracker is just clear as the grey and white jet takes a wire, with a momentary roar as its pilot momentarily slams his throttle up in case of a bolter ... but he's caught the wire and the engine rapidly diminuendos back to its idling whine as the Skyhawk smartly clears the landing area with two of his 'flight' coming in close behind. No sooner are they all on deck, there is another Tracker taxiing toward the catapult for launch, while the rotor of a big Sea King helicopter 'turns up' aft. The Tracker's off the 'cat' now and the deck lurches as the bridge officers turn to make headway back toward the main fleet, but this time blue and white 'Pedro', the elephantine Wessex rescue helicopter, needs to land on ... a hole gapes in the deck as one of the lifts descends with the clang-clang-clang of its warning bells, a Skyhawk chained down on it, dropping to the cavernous hangar deck below which is also crowded with chained aircraft and equipment. The choreography of flight deck crew, ship's crew, the bridge, Flying Control, catapult room, arrester crew, lift operators, the aircrew, all built up over decades of experience on lurching decks, on blue oceanic days or in the black of night far from land was exquisite, but unforgiving of the slightest lapse of concentration, timing or organisation.

In Hawaii, HMAS *Melbourne* docked at Pearl Harbour, the scene of the attack that I read so much about as a child. Incongruously, a Japanese warship lay next to us. During the morning Colours ceremony on the flight deck, Melbourne's band played Japan's beautiful national anthem, 'Kimigayo' as protocol dictated, along with Australia's national anthem, and that of our host nation. Later, I watched our sailors returning from their runs ashore. Weeks of confined, hot, noisy and smelly living conditions were forgotten in the seedy bars. Later, many would drunkenly sway up *Melbourne*'s gangway from dockside, some ripped off, penniless, and others bloody from fights.

Back at sea, I saw, firsthand, the size of an American aircraft carrier. 'Wacka', our Senior Pilot, was to take a Tracker to land on the U.S. carrier *Constellation* for a mail exchange, and I was fortunate to be assigned as his co-pilot. Approaching the American carrier in the Pacific vastness, even above the rumble of the Tracker's radials, we heard a momentary roar from overhead and behind. *Constellation*'s Carrier Air Patrol (CAP), two U.S. Navy Grumman Tomcat air superiority fighters, had swooped down to identify us. Their twin afterburners blinked on like malevolent eyes as the jets pulled up in echelon to disappear into the blazing sky. The Royal Australian Navy routinely used the American 'NATOPS' standardisation procedures, so we flew the standard pattern and I called the ball as Wacka approached the American ship, a darker grey than *Melbourne* and far bigger. We caught one of its arresting wires to decelerate us at a seeming leisurely pace on *Constellation*'s huge landing area: it felt like a 'field arrest' at Nowra. We kept the engines running as the mail and documents were exchanged with the American flight deck crew, and we swapped seats. I was to fly the take-off from *Constellation*, and it *was* a take-off. The U.S. carrier had a more advanced catapult system that was not compatible with our old bird, so while our engines roared at full power, 'Connie's' Flight Deck Officer touched his flag to the deck and there were echoes of World War II carrier operations as

I released the brakes for a non-catapult launch.

While *Connie* steamed into the wind, we rolled towards the deck edge, smooth blue swells beyond, but as the rim of the deck loomed, I gaped as I saw only sixty knots on the airspeed indicator, which was well below safe flying speed, but nothing for it, we had to keep going. Now we were over the lip, and towards the water we sank. Fortunately, *Constellation*'s deck was far higher than *Melbourne*'s, so gravity aided us, as did the unfailing power of the Cyclones while we dropped to a few metres from the waiting sea. We staggered up and away.

Later, we speculated that *Constellation*'s crew had underestimated our take-off weight. Unused to relatively antique piston engine Trackers, they had assumed that we were an empty 'Trader' cargo version, and even though we had advised them of our weight, the ship's speed had provided barely enough wind over the deck to 'free deck' launch our heavier aircraft.

After the giant U.S. carrier, *Melbourne* looked miniscule. Wacka called the ball and later we recounted our free deck launch in the wardroom bar as the duty-free beer flowed. With no night flying programmed, the usual hijinks began. There were raucous games of Acey-Deucy and Liar's Dice. On other evenings, the drinking mats might have come out. Each squadron had one, embroidered with its emblem, and they were defended zealously. VS 816's had its Tiger motif. On later cruises, 816's mat would be supplemented by a large painted-plywood cartoon tiger, standing on his hind legs in a cocksure pose, propped up with a stand and holding a frothing stein of beer in one paw. On the back of the tiger was scrawled, 'THIS TIGER WAS A PUSSYCAT UNTIL HE STARTED DRINKING WITH 816.'

In the centuries-old tradition of pathetic puns and jokes of the navy, the mascot had been christened 'Sub Lieutenant T. [Terry] Iger'. Terry was the first name of our squadron's boss of the time. In semi-formal 'Red Sea Rig' (black trousers, white short-sleeved shirts and cummerbund), we stood on our mat or around our tiger, while aircrew of the other squadrons conspired to deprive us of our mascot while we plotted strategies to obtain their mats for ransom later. Passing sailors shook their heads, bemused, when one melee spilled out into the main passageway with naval officers in Red Sea Rig engaged in a tug-of-war at each end of a plywood tiger. Sometimes, a truce would be called, and the 'birdies' would instead take on the ship's officers, the 'fish heads'. Each group would try to outdo the other in noisy song. One evening, one of our pilots had had enough of us being drowned out by the ship's officers: he returned from his cabin with an electric guitar and an amplifier, and for a few minutes we had them overwhelmed with the volume of our squadron songs until a ship's engineer tracked down and pulled the fuse of the wardroom's power supply. Most of us were in our twenties, and, furtively, the older Senior Pilots, Senior Observers and Commanding Officers egged us on. They were proud of squadron morale and encouraged their boys' letting off of steam after intense round-the-clock carrier operations. Occasionally, non-aviator members of *Melbourne*'s crew had to be flown ashore for one reason or another, strapped into the back seat of a Tracker to be catapulted from or, landed on, the carrier. After their experience, many quietly confessed that they would not wish to repeat it, and that aircrew's flying pay, extra leave and wardroom horseplay were entirely justified.

On this cruise I was a 'young' twenty-two, and one instance of my impetuous behaviour raised eyebrows. Detailed to fly a 'fish head' commander to a shore base, I recalled a bar story about a U.S. Navy Tracker pilot who applied a small amount of aileron before his aircraft was thrust down the catapult stroke, which threw the aircraft suddenly into a turn as it was flung from the ship's bow. I thought that it would be a good idea to try it for myself. Tensioned up on the catapult with the engines at full power, I held a smidgen of right aileron as the TACCO saluted the Flight Deck Officer. I felt the familiar push in the back, then the slam at the end of the stroke and the Tracker was airborne. Sure enough, it whipped into a snappy right-hand turn, which happened to be the direction of the shore base that the commander, strapped into one of the back seats, was to be delivered.

With a 'mission accomplished' feeling after the very efficient departure from the ship, I landed back on *Melbourne* to be greeted by the Senior Pilot, who delivered a severe verbal 'rocket'. Also, my even more thoughtless choice of right aileron instead of left had the aircraft turning hard across the carrier's bow, causing consternation on the bridge. I was assigned extra stints as Squadron Duty Officer to encourage me to reflect on my misdemeanour. Much, much later, the same Senior Pilot confided to me that he thought the launch was 'shit hot'.

Melbourne left Hawaii for more exercises, and then turned homewards towards Australia, pausing for a 'show the flag' exercise at Honiara, in the Solomon Islands. We swung off the 'pick' (anchor) in Honiara harbour while hundreds of locals were barged out to the carrier, gaping at this alien, floating metal world and its warplanes. All too late, *Melbourne*'s crew realised that most of them were barefoot under the blazing sun and the deck scorched the soles of their feet as the poor islanders hopped from one foot to the other. Lines of them stood in the meagre shade of Trackers' outstretched wings that were ranged for display on the flight deck until they could be taken out of the sun, massed on the hot steel of a flight deck lift. Coincidentally, a large Soviet trawler lay near us in Honiara harbour, and we suspected it had been trawling for more than fish.

As Australia neared, we experienced the 'channels' (an ancient Royal Navy term for the anticipation of home and loved ones as the ship neared England). Ashore, there would be relief from the constantly-moving world of the sweaty, swearing men, the lack of sleep, the lurching ship, and the pulse of its propellers in pervasive heat. My first 'cruise' would be complete, and I could finally consider myself a true naval aviator. However, back in my cabin at Nowra, the silence was weird and the building felt strange in its steadiness and quiet. For nights I found it difficult to fall asleep in the silence. Also, I had to remind myself to 'flare' the big Grumman for runway landings, because I was so used to 'flying the ball' and then the 'taking the cut' to impact the carrier's deck with no finesse required to soften the touchdown.

Again came the routine of 'staff flying' and generally work-free weekends of shore-based life. I looked forward to the long drives to family and friends in Victoria over leave periods. I experienced a tinge of regret whenever I left the state to drive north-east back to Nowra. But soon there was talk of another deployment, and finally it was announced for July.

A full Sub Lieutenant, no longer Acting, I had generally stayed out of any further trouble. For this second cruise, my TACCO was 'Mini Mac'. There were several 'Macs,' even in the small Fleet Air Arm, and two of them were differentiated by their stature: 'Big Mac' and 'Mini Mac'. Mini and I got on well, and we shared a slightly more commodious cabin that was tucked against the slope of the inside of the carrier's hull. Sometimes, we could just discern the sound of warships' sonars rattling against the hull like handfuls of thrown gravel; it was not the echoing, hollow 'ping' of the war movies.

This cruise would be long, especially by *Melbourne*'s standards. The carrier and its escorts would range through the northern and eastern Indian Ocean, exercising with other naval units, carrying out surveillance missions with its aircraft, and showing the flag in a few ports. In August 1980, HMAS *Melbourne* sailed from Sydney's Garden Island dock, this time with the Air Group aboard after work-up and the aircraft proudly ranged on deck. Families and loved ones thronged the dock in the classic farewell to sailors, the ship's band playing, and all available crew lined up along the decks at the ceremonial 'Procedure Alpha' used for arrivals and departures.

My parents were dockside to see the ship sail, but I was in

misery, prostrate in our cabin with an extreme case of influenza. It had knocked me flat, and later *Melbourne* and her little convoy were caught in a storm in the Great Australian Bight. Mini Mac had relocated to another cabin to avoid my germs. The ship pitched and rolled horribly in the Southern Ocean swells: they were monsters. I was still feverish and congested, but now I was nauseous from the ship's motion. But I couldn't help myself: I *had* to drag myself out of the cabin along the lurching passageway to the quarterdeck and view the angry, grey sea for myself. A few hundred metres away, a destroyer plunged and rolled. As violent as *Melbourne*'s movements were, I was grateful not to be aboard the smaller vessel.

Suddenly, the carrier's stern plummeted, and the entire destroyer completely disappeared behind a mountain of grey water marbled with white foam, and then reappeared as the carrier rode the rolling mountain upwards. The wind howled through the quarterdeck and, feeling awful, I staggered back to my cabin. The ship's motion became even worse, and soon a pipe from the bridge rasped through the thin, steel door of my cabin.

'Do you hear there, do you hear there, all weather decks now out of bounds to non-essential personnel.'

While the carrier lurched and plunged, in my stupor I could feel the occasional impacts of her bow thumping into even bigger Southern Ocean swells. They began to jar the ship so much that I could feel the aft end of the vessel, where I was, bounce up and down with vibrations of decreasing amplitude as 20,000 tonnes of carrier flexed after the shock of each impact. Then there would be a few lesser plunges and lifts until – bang! Another sickening impact from the bow and an audible, creaking, 'wonk-wonk-wonk-wonk' as the ship's structure vibrated with the shock.

Most things happen relatively slowly at sea. As we rounded the southwest tip of the Australian continent, the sea settled gradually, and so did I. We were on our way to calm waters in Fremantle harbour. The destroyer that had accompanied us had been damaged in the swells and put into Albany for repairs. While alongside in Fremantle, the memories of Pearce and 2 FTS flooded back, especially on runs ashore into Perth.

After flying in various exercises off the Western Australian coast, and a voyage north-west, I experienced my first Asian port in Jakarta, Indonesia. We glided in calm, oily water under a sultry, grey haze to reach Jakarta's port. In dock, there was little for aircrew to do, apart from stints as Officer of the Gangway, secondary duties, and to play Acey-Deucey in the wardroom.

I became the Squadron Flying Safety Officer, and there was administration associated with this duty. However, there was ample time for runs ashore. I had just turned twenty-three, but found Indonesia a little intimidating with its masses of people and vehicles. The cloying aroma of clove cigarettes was ever-present. I was always glad of the company of my squadron mates when I went ashore. Along the rough road into town in a grubby taxi, we stared at the people living in wooden shanties alongside filthy canals. I recall a vignette of naked children frolicking in green stagnant water and a woman defecating into it not far from them. We straggled between the bars and restaurants, most of us young and awkward in an alien land. We were short-haired westerners who mostly sported beards. I too had been granted 'permission to cease shaving'.

Again, there would be more desultory activity on-board the following day including letter writing. This was before the age of internet, email and mobile phones, let alone 'global roaming'. Then would come that evening's 'run ashore'. Occasionally, my turn came up for 'Officer of the Gangway', a duty foisted on us aircrew by jealous seaman officers who were determined to see us doing something. It was a mind-numbing four-hour stint, usually finishing into the early morning, of standing at the forward sailors' 'brow' (the head of the gangway at the ship's deck), chatting to the duty petty officer and, fighting to stay awake, trying not to glance at one's watch too much. We watched the sailors fall out of taxis onto the wharf, to stagger up the gangway, some held up by their mates. Periodically, local people emerged from the darkness to rifle through large dumpsters that sat on the dock whenever the cooks and sailors descended the gangway to empty bins full of 'gash' into them.

We flew in various exercises during a short voyage to Singapore, where the ship docked for two weeks. The old carrier was maintenance intensive, and the joke was that she spent just as much time in port as she did at sea. Her aircrew – useless with the ship alongside – would facetiously refer to the 'floating hotel', and that wonderful vessel that conveyed them from one party to the next. After the ship came alongside at Sembawang, on the north shore of the island state, the old hands remarked on the creeping modernism and development that was working its way from Singapore's south side, but over the weeks it was still a similar routine to that in Jakarta but in a cleaner, better organised city. The avenues and 'married quarters' of the now-Singaporean naval base oozed colonial British gentility, but outside were still canvas-covered shanties that were often the last port of call for returning ships' officers and sailors for a chilli crab or noodles washed down with Tiger beer. 'Jenny's Side Party' came aboard: elderly Chinese women who, in twelve-hour stints broken only by occasional tea breaks, scraped and painted the ship's steel and even climbed into the funnel casing to clean it out. Eventually, the shopping and runs ashore came to an end, and it would be a short voyage to Colombo, Sri Lanka. But on the way, there would be trouble.

With the carrier thirty-five nautical miles north of the Indonesian island of Sumatra, while I was below decks dealing with paperwork, the Commanding Officer of the Skyhawk squadron, 'BH', clambered up the long boarding ladder and into his jet's high-set, cramped cockpit. He was to fly a training mission in the little fighter. After BH completed a few careful checks, the Skyhawk was tensioned up on the catapult, the engine roaring at full power. After giving the signal to launch – the salute to the Flight Deck Officer – BH felt the violent but familiar slam of the launch. But no sooner had the jet been flung into the sky, the RPM gauge wound down – the engine had failed!

The delta-winged jet fell towards the sea. BH ejected, the

'Escapac' rocket-powered ejection seat blasting him up and out of the Skyhawk's cockpit. Unlike in the Macchi, a Skyhawk's pilot could eject with the aircraft stationary. Clear of the carrier and after struggling to free himself from the parachute harness, BH floated free and 'Pedro', the Wessex rescue helicopter, was in the hover above him in an instant. He was back on *Melbourne*'s deck, unhurt, just four minutes after his jet had hit the water!

With one of her fighters at the bottom of the Andaman Sea, HMAS *Melbourne* crept into Colombo – in the now-familiar oily Asian windless water. Multitudes of rusting cargo ships lay about her at anchor, some listing, others down by the bow or stern. We lay alongside for the familiar rounds of runs ashore, secondary duties and turns of Officer of the Gangway. Sightseeing tours were arranged to various scenic spots in Sri Lanka, as was some charity work.

There were diplomatic duties, such as the hosting of local citizens at our ship's Sunset ceremony. Then, *Melbourne*'s hangar deck was cleared and cleaned. In our long, formal whites, we made polite conversation with local dignitaries. Conversation stopped when the lights were turned down and attention was drawn to the steel slab of one of the massive lifts, stopped halfway down into the hangar from the flight deck above. A single floodlit grey and white Skyhawk was chained down on it as a backdrop to *Melbourne*'s band. With stirring music, they performed the Sunset ceremony, lowering and folding the illuminated White Ensign to a hymn. Then the band marched off to applause, and the buzz of resumed polite conversation continued.

Later, word was passed around that, due to simmering political instability in Sri Lanka, HMAS *Melbourne* was to anchor offshore. For a few days, the carrier swung 'off the pick' in Colombo harbour until she departed on a short voyage to Cochin, on the south-west coast of India, where the routine was repeated until we sailed again, this time for a long stretch at sea.

Only one day out from Colombo, another Skyhawk was lost – the fighter had been on the catapult preparing to launch. Naval aviation is unique in that systems intimately associated with the operation of aircraft are in the hands of non-aviation people. Unknowingly, a steam valve that controlled the catapult had not properly closed. The Skyhawk's pilot was nicknamed 'Blemish' because he had an older brother with an impressive physique known as 'Bruiser', who also flew Skyhawks. He was completing last minute checks prior to giving the usual salute to the Flight Deck Officer to indicate that he was ready to launch. But with the steam valve open, the jet began being dragged along the catapult track towards *Melbourne*'s bow, at nowhere near the acceleration that would see it safely airborne. Reflexively, Blemish's feet shuddered on the toe brakes of the Skyhawk's rudder pedals in an effort to stop. However, the overwhelming power of the catapult's steam pistons slowly and inexorably dragged the shuttle and attached jet with its locked wheels toward the bow's abrupt drop-off.

'Eject, eject, eject!' burst over the radio from the alert officer in Flyco as, simultaneously, Blemish fired his seat.

An instant later, the ballistic spreader snapped his parachute open and seconds later, the pilot was in the water. *Melbourne*'s bridge crew reacted instantly, stopping the ship's engines and swinging the stern to starboard, away from the sinking aircraft and the now floating pilot. The carrier's engines were stopped, but not put into reverse to stop the ship quickly: the huge blades of the ship's twin propellers rotating at full reverse would be a hazard to floating aircrew. But, even after the 'all engines stop' order from the bridge, the inertia of tonnes of rotating metal propeller do not dissipate easily.

(Decades earlier, the pilot of a foreign Tracker suffered the same result of a 'cold' catapult shot, and the Trackers were not fitted with ejection seats! Along with his crew, the pilot pushed himself up and out of an overhead hatch while the aircraft sank. But, by the time he struggled clear, the Tracker was underneath the ship. With his Mae West inflated, the pilot shot up towards the surface, but he watched, horrified, as a massive shadowy blade of one of the slowing ship's propellers sliced down through the murk of the water and impacted one of his legs. The rapid response of the rescue helicopter delivered him back on deck alive, but his leg could not be saved.)

Fortunately, Blemish had passed clear down the port side of the swinging, slowing ship, and he floundered in the water astern. Soon, 'Pedro' was hovering over the young pilot. There was anxious tension in the air as the churning wake from *Melbourne*'s still-turning propellers sucked him down, entangled in his parachute lines. He fought back to the surface and, after help from the Wessex's rescue diver, the helicopter crew had him back on the deck in minutes, his back sore from the violence of the ejection, but otherwise unharmed. The rescue diver was the same crewman who had assisted Blemish's Commanding Officer, BH, after his ejection three weeks earlier.

Operating relatively modern aircraft, the ageing carrier was always at the limit of its capability. Several Skyhawks and a Tracker had been lost from the ship over the years but fortunately, all of the crews had survived. Years before, another Skyhawk had suffered a bad catapult shot. Its pilot attempted to eject; the canopy came off but the seat failed to fire. He was still strapped in his aircraft when it violently impacted the water, ahead of the carrier that was now bearing down on him. The pilot's first instinct was to undo his harness and get out of the sinking fighter but then came the realisation: a 20,000 tonne ship would steam over the sinking Skyhawk ... and there would be the ship's propellers, still turning! After he heard the churn of the props pass above him, he struggled clear of the cockpit to surface astern from very deep water. He was fished out by 'Pedro'.

We remained at sea for nearly a month, exercising and patrolling in tropical heat with the exacting rhythm of carrier operations. This time, there was a sense of importance: we were there to 'show the flag' while a few Soviet units cruised the Indian Ocean. Mini Mac, my sensor operators and I flew our share of long surveillance flights of identifying merchant ships and, in particular, plotting and photographing the Soviet ones. During very low passes at a prescribed distance past the vessels, Mini's camera drive whined and snapped. Back on-board, he would hand his film over to the ship's intelligence officers.

Both *Melbourne* and her personnel began to feel the effects of the relatively long time at sea. On board the small, ageing carrier, again there were shower restrictions, constant sweat, and irritability from round-the-clock operations. Once, a ship's engineering officer lay sedated in *Melbourne's* sick bay, temporarily insane with heat stroke from the brutal environment of the engine room. He would have had little respite in his tiny, humid cabin when not on watch below. The ship's food stores began to run down, and for our long aerial patrols, our in-flight rations became sandwiches made from ship's bread filled with just lettuce and boiled eggs, green with age. They were washed down with cups of ship's 'limers'. An antiscorbutic, lime juice had been served up on naval vessels since the days of Captain Cook.

As well as on the Skyhawk squadron, the long deployment in the Indian Ocean had taken its toll on the old carrier, so once again she would return to Singapore for more maintenance and much needed re-victualling. Our crew and two others had flown Trackers off the ship prior to docking, to the Singaporean Air Force Base at Tengah. Then after another two weeks of maintenance, *Melbourne* was finally Australia bound, firstly to the seas off Perth, where we flew in formation above the city in a flypast. Once again I would see the sparkling buildings set alongside the turquoise waters of the Swan River and Indian Ocean from a gin-clear sky. While I held station off the boss's wing I reflected on my struggles at Pearce; then the base itself flashed past in the corner of my eye as we overflew it, appropriately at low level and high speed, to show the air force that it wasn't the only service that flew warplanes, and to motivate the navy students there. After we landed back on *Melbourne*, we watched from the goofers' platform as the navy instructors from Pearce flew out to the carrier in air force Macchi trainers to fly deck landing patterns. At the last minute, they 'waved off' without actually touching down. Navy students or RAAF instructors would have watched from the back seats, in awe of the tiny size of the carrier's landing area.

Afterwards, to my excitement, it was decided that because our Perth flypast had been so successful, we would repeat the exercise over the city of Melbourne.

The carrier steamed across the Great Australian Bight again, this time eastwards, and I revelled in the cool air and deeper blue sky of temperate latitudes. Now the seas were just lazy, smooth swells that gently rolled the ship. Once again the channels brought on anticipation of land, home and family, especially with a stopover in Melbourne. In the warming weather of December 1980, we steamed through the Port Phillip Bay heads, and I would once again fly in that sky that I had gazed at as a boy in Mornington, but this time from a carrier in the Bay itself.

Our Senior Pilot obligingly not only assigned me to fly in the formation of Trackers that would overfly the city of Melbourne, but also authorised the formation to pass over Mornington. But during the pre-internet and -satellite telephone age, it was impossible to tell family and friends of a planned flypast from a ship at sea. Eight Wright Cyclone engines rumbled as four gull-grey Grummans wheeled in a diamond formation over the vast suburbs of Melbourne, and then we circled my home town. As I concentrated on holding an especially tight and steady position on the boss, my eyes darted downwards momentarily to glimpse the green of Mornington High School's ovals and the grey masonry and iron roofs of the classrooms. Later, I found out that few of my friends – many now working in various parts of Melbourne – had seen us, and my family members had all been indoors. My sister had heard the noise of our engines but did not come out to look as she had 'thought it was the police helicopter.' Still it had been a satisfying moment, and I reflected on the journey it had been from leaving the school, to wheeling in a formation of navy warplanes in the sky above it just five years later. We landed back on in placid waters and summer sky in Port Phillip Bay and immediately the ship turned shoreward, towards Station Pier. But soon we were called to the briefing room. The Port of Melbourne's tugboat crews were on strike and, somehow, the ship's officers had to get the carrier alongside. They would use a procedure called the 'windmill' or 'pinwheel'.

The scene ahead through the little eyebrow-shaped windscreens of our Tracker was surreal. I looked down at a large crowd of people, dockside, on Station Pier. I knew that my parents were among them, but I was concentrating on other matters. Our aircraft was bucking and straining with the Cyclones bellowing at full power, and often my eyes flicked down to the duplex cylinder head temperature gauge as the readings approached their limits. The Trackers were so powerful that when chained to *Melbourne*'s deck with their engines running, four of them could move the 20,000-tonne aircraft carrier with its 1,300 men and its aircraft alongside the pier. Instructions were relayed from the bridge to Flyco, then by radio to the aircraft, and the pilots set power as ordered. With a pair of aircraft each facing outboard at the ship's bow and stern, we easily turned, and then pushed the carrier the last few metres to lie neatly alongside. But the air, already hot under the blazing sun, was now thick with exhaust fumes and the unmistakable odours of hot oil and metal. Finally, the order came to idle the Cyclones and then shut them down. Many engines' temperature limitations had been exceeded. Later, pilots vociferously complained that the Trackers' engines had overheated and should be overhauled immediately. But the ship always came first – that was the way of the navy. Aircrews and aircraft came second, whether it was being required in wartime to identify and report an enemy contact at sacrifice of themselves, or to stress aircraft engines while chained to the deck on a hot day in order to dock their ship. But notwithstanding that, we hoped that some of the striking tug crews would have been idling about the wharf to then incredulously watch an aircraft carrier dock, despite the withdrawal of their labour.

My second cruise in *Melbourne* was coming to an end. A few days later, VS 816 Squadron would 'fly off' its aircraft back to Nowra. We all posed for photos on the flight deck with Sub-lieutenant T. Iger, our two-dimensional drinking mascot. He flew off with us while the empty carrier plodded towards its home in Sydney. For me, it was back to the routine of shore-based flying, secondary duties, and the occasional weekend visiting my girlfriend. But we were growing apart. Our long-distance relationship had survived the long Pacific Ocean and Indian Ocean deployments, but now the prospect loomed of yet more months away, this time in the South China Sea. Despite my time at sea, I was still immature and had also become somewhat arrogant and selfish. We were still young and before I embarked on this third voyage, the relationship would be over.

The second Skyhawk loss during my second cruise was the last straw for the RAN. It was decided that operating high-performance jets from an ageing aircraft carrier designed to operate piston-engine aircraft of the 1950s was now an unacceptable risk. Skyhawk operations from HMAS *Melbourne* came to an end. The versatile jets were to become land-based strike aircraft. But the Trackers would stay at sea. With the fighters now 'on the beach', we considered our hulking sub-hunters as the elite aircraft on board. We lorded it over the boys who flew the big Sea King anti-submarine helicopters, the Wessex crews and, of course, the fish heads. With the reduced number of aircrew on board, I occupied a large, comfortable cabin all to myself.

In late April 1981 the old carrier was again ploughing westwards towards the Great Australian Bight. Off Adelaide, we launched on a mail run to RAAF Edinburgh, the air force base north of Adelaide. This time, there was no thoughtless stunt off the catapult. We caught up with the ship as it steamed on a course that would eventually see us dock at Fremantle, but this time it would not be the only carrier there. An American carrier would also be lying off Perth: USS *Midway*. The two navies would then cooperate in various exercises, then *Melbourne* would set course alone for the South China Sea.

Midway, although also old and conventionally powered, was immense. Her flight deck was twice the height of *Melbourne*'s, and her landing area alone was almost as long as the entire length from bow to stern of our old British carrier. Seemingly, an entire air force was ranged on *Midway*'s flight deck, with more aircraft lashed down below in cavernous hangars. I noted with interest and envy the squadron of Grumman Intruder attack jets. The Intruder had a bulbous cockpit canopy that afforded its crew a stunning view, and twin engines of the same type that powered our single engine Skyhawk. Multiple racks for fuel tanks and weapons bristled beneath their folded wings. The Intruder carried a pilot and, seated beside him, a Bombardier/Navigator (B/N). The B/N controlled the sophisticated weapons system, similar to that fitted to Australia's F-111C bombers. But, unlike the land-bound F-111, the Intruder could be on the scene of an attack within minutes from its carrier lying off a hostile coast. The Intruder could also refuel other aircraft in flight and could receive fuel itself, under the 'buddy' system, as could our Skyhawk. A group of us befriended some Intruder crew during a visit to *Midway*. We Aussies felt like country cousins as we gaped and enthused over the huge American carrier and its aircraft. Almost apologetically, we invited the Americans to visit our little *Melbourne*, with its out-dated aircraft and faded British gentility. The Intruder boys made polite noises as they crawled through our Trackers, but condescension turned to amazement after we invited them to *Melbourne*'s wardroom for beer. Alcohol was prohibited in ships of the U.S. Navy.

At sea once more off Perth, exercises began. We had a real submarine to try to find: an Australian 'O-boat' (an *Oberon* Class submarine). We had no hope of locating it or its periscope in the rolling seas among the whitecaps. These conventionally-powered subs were extremely quiet – quieter than any nuclear boat – and I was later presented with a photograph of our vainly circling Tracker, taken through the 'scope.

The Americans, too, had been embarrassed. A Royal New Zealand Navy frigate was also taking part in the exercises, playing the role of the enemy. One night in choppy seas, the frigate launched its tiny Wasp helicopter. The torpedo-carrying Westland Wasp was of British design, and it stood on four stalky undercarriage legs with tiny wheels that swivelled on the ends. The helicopter was reminiscent of a hospital trolley supporting the cabin of a compact car with a rotor on top. In the darkness of the ocean, the little Wasp sneaked in at low altitude towards *Midway* – its minimal radar signature lost in the sea's clutter – and rumour had it that the Americans only knew it was there was when the Wasp's crew lit up the *Midway*'s bridge with the helicopter's searchlight. There would have been some consternation and possibly some choice language from the Americans.

Suddenly, the whole exercise halted. USS *Midway* reported a man overboard. Everybody began searching for a human bobbing in the vast sea. An American destroyer was rebuked for continuing to ditch gash, because floating bags distracted the searching units. Four Trackers were detached from HMAS *Melbourne* to Pearce air force base, from where they searched and searched until, the crews exhausted, the aircraft were flown back to the carrier by fresh pilots, which included me, having been positioned to the air force base by the ever-dependable Wessex helicopters. Terry, our boss, expressed pride after we received a 'Bravo Zulu' (a 'well done') from *Melbourne*'s captain after the Trackers' work and an expeditious late-night recovery made back to the carrier. Four Trackers had roared in turn through the 'slot' on the starboard side of the ship, 800 feet off the water, until, one-by-one, they smartly broke left to turn downwind into the landing pattern. With the exercise called off, *Melbourne*'s bow turned northwards towards Singapore.

Once again, Jenny's Side Party came aboard there as the old carrier underwent maintenance. It was the familiar round of secondary duties, Officer of the Gangway and runs ashore for the aircrew. Singapore's modernisation had crept even further north towards Sembawang dockyard but most of our old haunts were still there including the infamous Bugis Street, where Australian sailors sat around steel tables that were festooned with bottles of 'Tiger' beer outside the restaurants. Some shouted ribald comments to the drag-clad transsexuals who frequented the area, while others drunkenly dared each other to do the 'dance of the flamers' on the concrete roof of a decrepit toilet block. The dance involved squatting down and waddling along with their trousers lowered, with one end of a roll of newspaper wedged in the cleft of their buttocks. The other end was lit on fire by their mates, and the aim was to duck-walk to the end of the concrete slab before the fire burned close to private parts. Then with the maintenance complete and the crew sober, the carrier sailed north east to Hong Kong.

We lay alongside Hong Kong's HMS *Tamar* (the Royal Navy base) right in the heart of Hong Kong harbour. The then British colony was like a beehive – there were people everywhere. The city never seemed to sleep. Tall, narrow buildings clung to precipitous green hillsides. Even *Tamar*'s dockside administration building was a skyscraper. Our little Australian aircraft carrier was wildly popular. American carriers were far too big to come alongside, so they always had to swing off their anchors, well away from shore. The ship was thronged with visitors, mostly expatriate British, and many of them attractive girls. Receptions and wardroom functions never seemed to stop, and British Royal Navy personnel were everywhere. But they were not the only military visitors. British Army helicopters landed on Melbourne's flight deck to fly a fortunate few of us to their base at Sek Kong, north of the harbour in Hong Kong's New Territories. We sat in a tiny Westland Scout (the army version of the navy Wasp of *Midway* fame) while the warrant officer pilot flew us over and around Hong Kong's many islands. Near the Chinese border, the pilot pointed down. On vast mud flats below, a figure was propelling itself over the ooze on a plank that had a handle sticking up out of it; the primitive conveyance was a 'mud scooter', which enabled him to cross the flats towards the nearest settlement. The man was an 'I.I.' (Illegal Immigrant), who was fleeing Communist China for the perceived riches of the West. We had already noticed blue dots in the hundreds littering the shore lines of the New Territories. These were discarded cheap inflatable mattresses that I.I.s were using to cross the border at high tide. The British Army helicopters were tasked to detect and report immigrants and, occasionally, to hoist their drowned bodies from the muddy water or shorelines. We enjoyed the hospitality of the British Army in their mess at Sek Kong before being flown back to our carrier to contemplate the next social function. But, eventually, it was time for the ship to head south for the Philippines, and then homeward. The paid holiday in Hong Kong had ended, and the deployment was far from over.

'Bolter, bolter, bolter!'

The LSO's urgent call came through my earphones. I had already begun to push the throttles up, and I rotated the Tracker to the launch attitude. Dim lights on Melbourne's island flashed past to our right, and then everything outside was black again. My world was the attitude indicator in front of me as Keith, our TACCO, carefully set climb power. We routinely carried out touch and go landings on the carrier, leaving the hook up, to fall onto the deck after the cut to then seemingly bounce off it, with the application of maximum power and the climb away for another pattern. But there was a psychological quirk that, with their arrester hook down for a 'trap', pilots always expected to be slammed forward in the harness as the hook engaged, the aircraft fishtailing to a halt, caught in one of the wires. A 'bolter' (when the hook missed the wires) was *always* a surprise, despite being half-expected after a marginal approach or an excessively rolling or pitching deck.

I was not the only pilot having trouble getting aboard tonight. The problem of landing on an aircraft carrier in rough seas was one thing: we became experienced in averaging out the oscillations of the ball as the deck pitched and rolled. Sometimes we would be 'talked down' by the LSO's (who sometimes seemed to mentally put themselves in our own cockpit), and to make multiple attempts to catch a wire in rough weather. But tonight was different. Now, the seas west of the Philippine Islands were dead calm under a moonless, windless sky. But these conditions had created different problems for us. Firstly, the old carrier had to steam at maximum speed in order to produce sufficient 'wind over the deck' to safely launch and recover its aircraft. As I turned for another landing attempt, I knew that *Melbourne*'s propellers would be throbbing hard. Her decks would be vibrating underfoot. Plates, cups and glasses would rattle in the wardroom. Some twenty knots of wind would be blowing along her flight deck, thanks to her speed. Because there was no natural breeze, the wind generated by the ship itself was 'axial': fore-and-aft, not blowing down the ship's angled landing area. The induced wind whipped around the slab of the island, causing more than the usual turbulence for pilots 'in close', disturbing even a nicely-flown approach. Also, with the poor old carrier at full power and with no natural wind, the aircraft moved faster relative to her deck. Dangling arrester hooks tended to skip and miss the wires. Approach angles seemed flatter.

Over the unseen windless, waveless sea, several of us, including me, made more than one attempt to get aboard. Later, as we savoured our two cans of beer, I found that I would be flying in similar conditions again tomorrow, but at least it would be in the light of a late tropical afternoon.

Late the next day, were tensioned up on the catapult. The sea was still the hackneyed millpond, and the carrier was rock-steady under deepening blue sky. The far horizon was indistinguishable in haze. Soon, the catapult fired and we were airborne. Even in daylight, I had always focused on the attitude indicator on the instrument panel in front of me immediately after a catapult shot, and this time I was glad that I had. There was absolutely no horizon. We climbed higher and higher into an eerie blue world. The sea was a mirror, with the deepening sky reflected in it. Even in these conditions, a pilot would normally see the distant knife-edge of an oceanic horizon – that external reference he would use to tell the attitude of his aircraft – but this time, because of the haze, there was none. We were suspended in what seemed an opalescent fish bowl. There was no up or down: the deep blue of the horizonless sky was reflected back in the mirror of the flat sea. It was still broad daylight, but I had to fly on instruments. This fishbowl effect increased further as the sky darkened, and I flew a shaky 'no grade' pass back onto the carrier, lucky to catch a wire. The dash of the 'no grade' pass would sit among the 'fairs' and 'OK's next to my name on the 'greenie board' in the briefing room until the end of the cruise. Still, I marvelled at what nature could throw at an oceanic aviator, and soon it all would be forgotten on the runs ashore in the Philippines.

In blazing heat, a group of us crossed a bridge spanning a canal, which stank like a sewer (it probably was a sewer). That morning, HMAS *Melbourne* had docked at the huge U.S. Navy base at Subic Bay. The volcano that brooded nearby, Mount Pinatubo, would not erupt until years later: the eruption coinciding with the end of the Cold War, when American forces would leave the Philippines and its vast bases. The U.S. Air Force's Clark Field would be covered in volcanic ash.

But today, we were crossing the bridge into the infamous Olongapo City, the place of recreation for thousands of U.S. sailors. In the crowded bar district, a huge American passed, towering above the throng of Filipinos, a monkey on a chain sitting on his shoulder. We gawked at another, his tee shirt depicting a human head through the cross-hairs of a sniper's rifle scope, captioned 'U.S. Special Forces: You'll Never Know'. Each bar we entered was trying to outdo the others with wild gimmicks and debauchery. Later we would straggle back to the ship across the same canal, but in the darkness attractive girls in colourful dresses stood on rickety canoes that floated in it, lit by lanterns. Boys would dive into the filthy water to retrieve coins thrown by the sailors passing overhead. The next day we would visit the American naval air station, Cubi Point, and would be awe-struck at the huge Officers' Club (wardroom), perched in tropical greenery on the side of a hill. Each squadron had its own large wooden carving on the wall, elaborately carved by Filipino craftsmen, which depicted their squadron symbol, motto and aircraft. Stunning wooden models, made and painted to order, of U.S. Navy aircraft were everywhere. Locals in immaculate dress served at the bar and in the dining area.

A few days later *Melbourne* sailed into Manila Bay to dock in Manila itself, where the runs ashore redoubled to any number of bars and restaurants. On the way back to the carrier, a group of us – several with guitars – sat near a fountain and sang our squadron songs, much to the consternation of the locals. With the entire squadron on an organised night out at one restaurant, a cavalcade of gorgeously dressed, attractive girls arrived. They split into groups and descended on our tables. They did not appear to be prostitutes but reasonably educated women, who had paid an agent to be introduced to westerners, in their desperation to get married to one and escape grinding poverty in the Philippines. There was a flurry of address taking before we left. Months later, after many exchanges of letters, someone in our group actually married one of the ladies.

There was more flying as the ship steamed on the long voyage homewards: surface surveillance, weapons exercises and deck landing practice. I was now twenty-three, but occasionally I still did thoughtless things. One night on an uneventful flight, out of boredom and curiosity I climbed our Tracker up to 10,000 feet – over 3,000 metres – and then slightly higher just to say that I had done it – a stupid thing to do without an oxygen system, and I was found out. Once again, my credibility and fitness as a naval officer were brought into question, and there were extra stints as Duty Officer as punishment. Beforehand, I had shown interest in becoming a Landing Signals Officer (an LSO). Wardroom chats with Willie and Larry, the LSOs on this cruise, had piqued my interest, especially when they went into detail about the course that a prospective

LSO would undergo courtesy of the U.S. Navy. After experiencing American hospitality and their awe-inspiring equipment on USS *Midway* and in the Philippines, I was excited about becoming an LSO, and particularly about the prospect of flying a U.S. Navy Skyhawk jet, which was part of the training. Australian LSOs would be required to 'wave' both Skyhawks and Trackers aboard their own carrier.

I had already done my share of 'writing' for the LSOs at sea. Every 'pass' by every pilot was graded and later debriefed. To aid this, the LSOs 'writer' stood next to him, the two men facing aft on the little platform that jutted over Melbourne's port side, the canvas windbreak flapping behind their backs. We wore the Mickey Mouse-eared cloth helmets to listen to the carrier landing radio frequency, and the LSO of course had his microphone. Pickle switch in hand, the LSO would dictate a quick appraisal to the writer after each aircraft 'trapped', touched-and-went, occasionally boltered or was waved off: 'Smith, low in the middle, a little fast, flat at the ramp, no grade, four wire'. Then, the next aircraft would call the ball and again the subsequent pass would be critiqued and graded: 'Jones. A little long in the groove but OK, three wire.' Scribbling on a pad on a wind-blasted platform was difficult for the writer, so a shorthand notation had been developed: letters, loops, squiggles and signs described the pass. For example, brackets meant 'a little'. A musical 'b', meant the 'flat' symbol. The aircraft was *flat* in attitude: too fast, and less likely to engage a wire. Therefore, the derisive 'FU♭AR' denoted 'Fucked Up, Flat At the Ramp'.

Through this cruise I had spent much time on the LSO's platform watching and writing and, on one occasion, with a steady deck I was allowed to 'wave' some Trackers aboard myself, thinking of that imaginary box in the sky astern of the carrier through which the aircraft must pass to successfully land. I was shown how to judge an approaching Tracker's speed by its nose-up attitude: if correct, the tips of the aircraft's wide tailplanes would just be visible above the wings. Too much tailplane: he was fast. Can't see the tailplanes: the pilot was too slow. But the illegal climbing episode had blotted my copybook.

While I continued to show interest in becoming an LSO, hints were being dropped that I was being considered for a non-flying job on the carrier: possibly the Assistant Aircraft Control Room Officer.

Nothing was said officially. But even though I was a young and now somewhat-conceited naval pilot, I knew that sea postings were important to one's development as a naval officer and to gain experience for higher rank. I had always liked ships anyway. So, resigned to what I had heard, I periodically visited the carrier's Aircraft Control Room (the steel compartment in the base of the island) to see what I was in for the next time HMAS *Melbourne* went to sea. I watched the sailors and petty officers moving the wooden scale models as if in a casino, over the table-sized representations of Melbourne's flight and hangar decks. It was the giant chess game that determined where aircraft would be moved, chained down, or raised and lowered on the elevators. The moves would be relayed to the white-jerkined bears who moved the actual aircraft to where it was required to be. The vast game was overseen by the ACRO (Aircraft Control Room Officer). On an aircraft carrier that worked round the clock, he required an assistant, and various buzzes around the ship indicated that the next one would be me. But after several visits to the ACR, the 'Carr to be Assistant ACRO' rumour died down. It seemed possible that maybe the whole thing had been a hoax: several squadron mates were notorious for 'duff' postings and practical jokes. Perhaps my naivety and resignation had turned the tables on them. They would have expected me to be bitter and disappointed to be moved away from flying, and to rail against the forthcoming posting. Perhaps, my positive attitude to the unglamorous job had caught the perpetrators by surprise.

We disembarked, and later in the weird quiet and stillness of a cabin at Nowra, I reflected on both the ship's, and my own, good fortune over three cruises. HMAS *Melbourne* had had the reputation of being a jinxed ship after her disastrous collisions with *Voyager* and *Frank E. Evans*. But neither had been her fault. The elderly carrier had operated high performance Skyhawks, heavy Grumman Trackers

246 WRITTEN IN THE SKY

and big Sea King helicopters for years without the loss of any aircrew. For naval aviators of our generation, at least, she had been a lucky ship, and I had been fortunate as well to not have damaged an aircraft or hurt anyone, despite my occasional thoughtless actions.

Home from the sea, again there was leave in Victoria. But my parents' marriage was coming under strain, and I was uncomfortable staying in the family home in Mornington. I spent some time with Yvonne, my platonic college friend and her welcoming family in their small town north east of Melbourne that nestles against the foothills of the Great Dividing Range. With leave over, I was back to the routine of land-based flying, which included surveillance flights around the oil and gas drilling platforms of Bass Strait. RAN Trackers were to provide a visible presence in the face of unspecified terrorist threats against the rigs. Keith was still my TACCO, and we would spend time at the RAAF base at East Sale with our aircraft for these missions. At East Sale navy, army and air force flying instructors were trained by the RAAF's Central Flying School (CFS) to instruct on Macchis and CT-4s. The base was also home to the RAAF's 'Roulettes' aerobatic team and the School of Air Navigation, which trained navy observers and air force navigators. Sale was cool and green under quiet grey skies, but soon it was back north to Nowra in anticipation of my next posting. I knew that after three deployments on the carrier I would be moved on, and I had made it known far and wide that I was very interested in becoming an LSO. Lately, the senior officers of VS 816 Squadron had indicated that I might have a chance of becoming one if I kept my nose clean.

'Marcus, Commander Kavanagh wants to see you,' someone called through the crew room doorway.

Kavanagh had been seeing officers throughout the morning, advising them of their new postings. Mine would be the LSO's course in the States! Once again I sat facing 'Clump' Kavanagh, no longer as a nervous seventeen-year-old in a cheap suit, but as a seasoned carrier pilot, although a 'young' twenty-three and of average ability. I was excited and incongruously cocky about my upcoming course in America. I hurriedly exchanged pleasantries with him and then, impetuously, I blurted, 'Well, Sir, when's my LSO's course?'

Kavanagh raised his eyebrows, sighed and replied, 'Maybe you should think of broadening your horizons to other areas?'

My heart sank. I was not to be an LSO. A desk job in Canberra? A sea posting? The stupid things I had done: aileron down the catapult; climbing above ten thousand feet … Was that Assistant ACRO job not a hoax after all?

In a breaking bad news kind of tone, he said, 'You're going to Central Flying School at East Sale for a flying instructor's course. Then, you're going to instruct at 2 FTS on the Macchi.' He paused, uncertain of how I would react, because many operational military pilots were not interested in instructing, and most navy pilots were happy and settled at Nowra.

But I was delighted.

Kavanagh smiled wanly as I enthused, 'Thank you, sir, that's outstanding news.'

As I left his office, my mind raced. I was was going to fly the Macchi again! Firstly, on the flying instructor's course with the air force at East Sale. Then, provided that I passed the demanding course, I would be teaching others to fly the little orange and white jet in the golden West!

VIPER FOUR SEVEN

1981 - 1984

Once again I faced a senior officer. This time the mood was tense, and I was rigidly at the 'ho', along with my air force and army course-mates who were at 'attention'. We were 'paraded' in his office. He was an air force wing commander, the Commanding Officer of Central Flying School. He had been considering whether or not to send students on our flying instructor's course back to their original units in disgrace. Now we waited as to what the wing commander would decide.

The flying instructor's course, conducted by elite instructors at Central Flying School (CFS), RAAF East Sale, Victoria, was intense. These 'instructors of the instructors' also flew as the 'Roulettes', the air force's jet aerobatic team. They trained student instructors on both the CT-4 Airtrainer and the Macchi. The course comprised several months of concentrated lectures, examinations, and naturally, lots of flying and associated tests.

The first task was to relearn the Macchi and familiarise myself with the landmarks and airspace of East Sale. After the study of the flight manual and several flights with a CFS instructor, I exuberantly threw the Macchi solo about the sky over the green fields of Gippsland. The little jet seemed so simple after the massive Tracker with its panels of levers, instruments and switches, and the crew who had to be interacted with. But this joyous flight was a rare opportunity. The workload was intensifying, with academic work in the classrooms, and acquiring the skills of flight instruction. To be able to train young students in operating a single-engined jet, my flying had to be of a high standard, and there was an extra complication for a Macchi instructor: on anything other than instrument training flights, he had to fly the aircraft safely and accurately from the back seat. In modern jet trainers, the rear (instructor's) seat is stepped up, allowing the back seat pilot to see ahead over the front occupant. However, the Macchi had been designed in the 1960s when such niceties were considered unimportant.

After my solo flight came my first 'back seat' training session. I was on approach to one of East Sale's long runways. The broad fields edged with lines of trees grew closer on either side of the cockpit as, once again, a little Viper engine warbled behind me, near idle thrust. But where was the runway? Blocking my view ahead was the mass of the CFS instructor's ejection seat topped with the yellow and black loops of the firing handles and his white helmet. I craned left and right to squint through the curved sides of the Macchi's canopy – the transparent upturned boat – and a few features of the runway area became discernible, distorted in the thick Perspex. Somehow I got the aircraft over the runway threshold and I could now use my peripheral vision to judge when to 'flare' the Macchi. I also had to keep the jet on the runway centreline as I rolled along for a few heartbeats before I was to push the throttle up, check the engine's response, then raise the nose for a touch and go. I craned my neck left and right under the heavy helmet and oxygen mask, trying to stay on the centreline, until the Macchi leapt back into the air.

Flying from the Macchi's back seat had its advantages. The rear cockpit was more spacious. Thanks to the basic 'attitude flying' that had been drilled into me as a student, and many nights at low-level over unseen black water, I religiously flew 'attitude': not chasing the instruments. From the jet's rear seat, pitch angles were easier to judge. Aerobatics seemed easier from the back with the added length of the cockpit in front. But the lack of a view ahead was always a problem. After having attained a reasonable standard of flying from the rear seat, I had to show a good standard of doing it all at night. I flew circuit after circuit in the still, night air. Runway lights danced and blurred, then disappeared beneath us as I stretched to peer past the dark shape of the front seat and its occupant as we flew down the glide path to a landing.

I was now a lieutenant in rank – a second gold ring had joined the first on my winter jacket, and I was maturing a little. After my youthful and at times awkward moments of intense carrier flying, flying from land in this simple little jet was a joy, apart from the workload of the instructor's course associated with it. I must not fail! If I did, there would be no flying the Macchi in Western Australia – it would probably be a desk job or sea posting, and I may never fly again. Again, I studied diligently and carefully prepared for every flight. Along with the day and night flying, the ground school was intense: particularly the advanced aerodynamics and high-speed flight theory. There were exercises and critiques in instructional technique and briefings. Most weekends were reminiscent of Pearce: I was usually 'in the books', preparing for the inevitable exams and the 'readback' (assessment) flights, while other more talented course-mates let off steam in the Officers Mess. But every second weekend I found time to drive to Melbourne, and I began going out with Yvonne, the music student who had been among my small circle of friends at University College.

I was the only navy student on this flying instructor's course group. The rest were air force and a pair of army pilots. There was also a Malaysian Air Force officer. Half of us, including the army pilots, were training to instruct on the CT-4, destined for basic flying training at Point Cook. The other half were learning to instruct on the Macchi. We all shared the academics and ground exercises.

Some of the RAAF pilots were less than enthusiastic about becoming flying instructors, particularly those assigned to teach basic students on the CT-4, the 'Plastic Parrot', at Point Cook. Several of them had come from front-line fighter and strike squadrons. On a boozy night in the Officers' Mess 'Back Bar', a group of student instructors sang a derogatory song that one of them, a talented musician, had written about the instructor's course. Sung to the tune of 'Folsom Prison Blues' made famous by Johnny Cash, and accompanied by Charlie's guitar, the song began:

> *'They took us from our squadrons, where we could operate*
> *And sent us down to CFS to learn to masturbate*
> *Oh, I'm stuck in fucking Sale, I hope to God I pass*
> *I'm stuck in fucking Sale, you can stick it up your arse ...'*

The ballad continued with more obscene verses, and for future reference they penned the lyrics behind a picture on the wall of the Back Bar. Unfortunately, the pilots' picture-straightening ability was not up to standard and the following morning the bar staff discovered it, were rightly offended, and the entire course were subsequently to be paraded in front of the incensed Commanding Officer.

On learning of the incident, the CO had summoned the senior member of our course, a talented flight lieutenant who would be destined for very senior rank in the air force. The CO told him to find out those responsible – they would be thrown off the course. Even for those pilots who did not want to become instructors, being 'scrubbed' from instructor's course would be a severe blot on their records. Our course leader hurriedly gathered us all together in a classroom: 'Right, I need a cross-section of every service on this course to come with us to the CO's office. I don't care whether you were in the Back Bar at the time or not. The CO is considering terminating everyone involved, but if the navy and army say they were in on it, it might be harder for him.'

So there we stood in front of the wing commander, all of us having taken responsibility for the misdemeanour.

He made his decision: 'I'm disappointed to see that some of you from the army and the navy were also involved. I would have terminated the offenders, but due to the involvement of the members of the other services, this would be politically difficult. Instead, the entire course is confined to base for the next three weeks. The weekends will be spent repainting and redecorating the Back Bar. Dismissed.'

Once able to fly the Macchi satisfactorily from the back seat, we had to learn how to instruct in it. The technique was 'Demonstrate, Direct and Monitor': demonstrate the manoeuvre, for example, by completing a loop (from the back seat, of course); direct, by talking the student through his first attempts; and then sit back and monitor his further efforts, offering guidance and – mostly – criticism. Training flights were delineated as 'Gives', where the CFS instructor demonstrated instructional techniques. Following those were the 'Mutuals', where we flew with a course-mate, (our 'crash buddy'), and practiced instructing on each other. After that there would be the 'Readback' flight. On those, with a call of 'Bloggs on', the CFS instructor role-played as a mythical and clumsy student pilot called 'Bloggs'. However, Bloggs would sometimes throw a curly question at us, which we would have to answer convincingly. We had to show our ability to demonstrate, direct and monitor Bloggs' efforts at, for example, circuits, formation flying, navigation or instrument work. We used our voices to 'quack' or 'patter' instructions and observations to Bloggs while we demonstrated or critiqued the various manoeuvres and sequences. The CFS instructor knew only too well the common mistakes that a stressed or untalented young man would make in a single-engine jet during the high-pressure pilots' course, and he would replicate them convincingly. At 'Bloggs off', he reverted to a CFS instructor to give criticism and advice.

In the tandem-seat Macchi, the only tools an instructor could use to teach a young man how to fly a jet were his ability to demonstrate, direct and monitor, his tone of voice and his choice of words. There could be no body language, pointing, facial expression or thump on the student's arm or helmet. Instrument flying training was carried out with the instructor in the front seat of the Macchi, and the student occupying the rear cockpit, enclosed in the instrument flying hood: the dirty white tent that blocked his view outside

Despite the work and the pressure, there were opportunities to revel in manoeuvring the orange and white Macchi about the Victorian sky. Ninety Mile Beach was an impressive 'line feature' – a ruler-straight edge of surf and sand between grey bushland and the rippled waters of Bass Strait far below – which aided accurate aerobatics. While my crash buddy, 'Freo', flew instruments with me on a 'mutual' under the hood in the Macchi's back seat, I could look out over an undercast of snow-white cloud below, that spread to the horizon. Freo would fly an instrument approach and practice the 'patter' to me over the intercom: after we sank into the layer beneath us on final approach, the greyness would eventually give way to feather-light wisps of cloud until the flat green fields, in beautiful contrast to the orange of the Macchi's wings, would appear, and there would be the long, black runway ahead. I would take over for a touch and go (it seemed so easy from the front!), the main wheels chirping onto the asphalt, nose held high and then up with the throttle, climbing away back to the cloud, until I said, 'Handing over, Freo.' He would take the controls to 'quack' further approaches until our fuel ran low. On the next flight, it was my turn 'under the hood' (in the back).

I eventually got the idea of not only teaching the basic flying of the Macchi but teaching the 'use' of the aircraft as well: instrument flying, formation, high level and low-level navigation. An enjoyable exercise for me was to teach one of the CT-4 student instructors to fly the Macchi to a level where he could fly one solo flight in it – he would have had flown the jet on pilot's course himself and it was really a 'refresher', but still, he was my first 'student'! Dolefully, he unstrapped himself from the jet after his solo, knowing that he was to fly nothing but the CT-4 for the next two years at Point Cook. Likewise, I flew a CT-4 on one flight, after my counterpart had re-familiarised me with the 'Plastic Parrot'. It now seemed so much easier as I made a few aerobatics and practice forced landings and circuits in the little trainer, the piston engine rattling in front. But the memories flooded back as I climbed out of its cockpit that still smelt of fuel and vinyl: the nausea, thumps on the arm from Clough, the sick feeling as Rocky flew us back to Point Cook. And, of course, that magically still, blue morning where I fluked the practice forced landing that saved my 'scrub ride' on the last day. But, where I was going, there would be few cold, grey days in a raw wind, no salt seaweed smell from the Bay, no whiff of the sewerage farm, no creaking wooden buildings, and no snarling CT-4 engines with their buzzing little propellers.

When the end of the course neared, the workload eased. The Back Bar had been repainted and I could afford to spend more weekends with friends, family and Yvonne in Melbourne. Some of the air force student instructors on our course had been paired as crash buddies with the army pilots, who were to be trained and sent 'solo' on the Macchi as an exercise by their air force counterpart, their one and only flight alone in a military jet. When an army Nomad tactical transport aircraft visited East Sale, my army course-mates organised a group of us to fly in it, even to fly a couple of 'circuits' under the supervision of the visiting pilot. I took the controls of the Australian-designed Nomad, marvelling at the view from its cockpit, and the power and instant response of its twin turboprop engines. Its propellers – unlike those of the HS 748 I had seemingly flown a lifetime ago – could be placed into full reverse pitch: their reversed thrust quickly slowed the boxy little transport on East Sale's vast runway. Its controls were light and responsive and, although not familiar with the Nomad, we were able to land it passably under the guidance of the army instructor.

At the course's end, I flew a final test with the Commanding Officer. This time, my hard work was rewarded after I demonstrated the various sequences to an acceptable standard. After some leave I would again be travelling west. This time it would be as a jet instructor who would train advanced students who had passed through the ruthless sieve of Point Cook and were looking towards attaining their 'wings'. As a marginal student, I had never imagined this. I looked forward to the modern buildings and offices of RAAF Pearce, the cloudless skies, Friday afternoons in the mess, and the pomp of the course graduations. Near the end of the instructors' course, Yvonne and I had become engaged and together we set off on the long, hot drive to Perth, the western sky beckoning. She would return to Melbourne for a year to finish her music degree and to ensure that we were sufficiently committed. But I was to find that advanced flying instruction would have its own challenges, and at twenty-four I was still far from mature. Ahead lay several years of grinding hard work, but they would become some of the best years of my life.

The air force and navy required lots of pilots. The Soviets were active in Afghanistan, and course after course was being processed through Point Cook. Most students who got through the brutal initial training arrived at Pearce much as I had: relieved at having 'survived' 1 FTS, excitedly anticipating flying a jet for the first time and, who knows? With hard work and some luck, they would pass the course and become an operational RAAF or RAN pilot!

In early 1982, once again Perth sprawled ahead under blazing sun with the blue ocean shining in the background, as Yvonne and I drove westwards down the escarpment towards the city.

The 2 FTS instructors were each assigned a radio call sign for use when flying the Macchi: 'Viper', after the ever-reliable little engine that powered the jet to denote '2 FTS', followed by an individual number to identify the instructor. My call sign was 'Viper Four Seven'. After a few flights to relearn the training areas, and a final check by the standardisation pilots, I was let loose on the students; or, perhaps, they were let loose on me. Again, we wheeled and soared in the flawless blue sky with the deeper blue of the Indian Ocean to the west, but now *I* was the carping instructor in the back seat. Below lay the same grey-brown terrain of tan earth and stunted grey-green trees, and towards the eastern horizon, the immense white dry lakes of inland Western Australia. Perth's northern suburbs had crept further north during the years, but the deep blue of the Indian Ocean lay beyond the coastal strip of suburbia. I moved into a rented house in one of Perth's northern suburbs, living 'ashore' for the first time, while Yvonne worked and studied in Melbourne. For me, several years of work hard, play hard had begun.

It was difficult initially, keeping that one step ahead of the students. They were of mixed ability, but I eventually became more comfortable with my knowledge and ability to demonstrate, direct and monitor the various sequences. However, our workload increased as training stepped up. For each flight, in my blue-walled cubicle, I painstakingly drew out the briefing points with coloured markers on a whiteboard, then briefed the student (the 'stud'), as per the prescribed CFS technique. We would then both proceed to the safety equipment room, to pull on and zip up the tight fitting anti-g suits, don our Mae Wests, and waddle out, helmets in hand, to our allocated Macchi that would be waiting in the line of orange, white and silver jets in the shade of Pearce's huge, white car ports. I would follow the student through his pre-flight inspection and we would each check our ejection seats carefully, ensuring that their seven safety pins were in place, ready to be removed by the 'strappers' (the two airmen who attended us).

Soon after, we would be airborne with our breaths sucking and rasping through the live intercom, while I demonstrated the syllabus exercise and talked the student through until he had enough of a grasp to fly it with just the occasional comment from me. Not much older than most of my students (and, in some cases, younger), I conscientiously directed, demonstrated and monitored. Even too much, at times, especially in my first years at 2 FTS, and I became overly picky and sometimes aggressive and tense. I got on well with the more competent students, but not with the weaker ones. I think it was because I myself had once been the weaker student, so I picked, cajoled, briefed and re-briefed – sometimes excessively so. I spoke sharply and swore, frustrated at basic errors, which was ironically in an attempt to prevent them from falling behind and being 'scrubbed' from their course, as I so nearly had been.

My favourite syllabus flight at Pearce was 'General Flying 1'. The student, having completed the initial ground school, would fly in a Macchi for the very first time. Flying from the back seat, I would roll the jet onto the threshold of Pearce's runway, push the throttle forward, and gradually, the little Viper would wind up behind us. At lift-off speed I would raise the nose wheel, and after a little hesitation the jet would fly off. Normally, we would climb away. However, on this flight, I would not immediately raise the nose to gain altitude, but I would hold the Macchi down above the remainder of the runway, letting it accelerate to around 300 knots – or 550 km/hr. Then the nose would go up, up, up and we would zoom skywards – the ground noticeably receding below us – and then I would pull a hard turn with the g coming on and staying there, until I would snappily roll wings level to head towards the training area, climbing and climbing. My mind's eye usually visualised an exclamation mark above the white helmet bobbing about in the front seat. Most of my students would exclaim: 'Wow, a bit different to the CT-4, sir!' Or, 'It goes up like a rocket, sir!' Or, just plain 'Yahoo!' However, there was the occasional student who reacted little to his first flight in a military jet: no comment, no imaginary exclamation mark. I found that most of these 'low reactors' would have difficulty with the course, as they struggled and were uncomfortable. Some were excessively nervous, whereas others suffered the slow realisation that they would not be able to cope with advanced jet flying training. A few, as I had been, were marginal candidates who had only just scraped through Point Cook, but could improve sufficiently to obtain their 'wings'.

Soon came the day to send my student on his first jet solo. The straps and pins of the rear ejection seat were 'safetied' by the ground crew, while I watched and listened high in the control tower at Pearce's satellite airfield, Gingin, which lay fifteen nautical miles – or twenty-eight kilometres – to the north of the main base. Gingin's single runway sat in a sandy rectangle, cut out from the low, scrubby grey-green bush. The field was ideal for initial student solos because it had little traffic. As I myself had done just a few years before, my 'stud' came back elated after having flown alone in a single-engine jet. After giving him a handshake and a debrief, I had the rare pleasure of flying us both back to Pearce. With the engine roaring at its 'maximum continuous' thrust setting, I would hold the aircraft down low over the grey-green scrub as we jolted through the turbulence. Just minutes later, we would belt through a low 'initial' to a hard pull-up and pitch-out onto downwind to land, with my student still on a high. Lots of beer would flow for students and instructors alike in the Cadets' Mess later that evening, all paid for by the solos!

I flew three, sometimes four, training 'sorties' each day, with night flying several times per month. I generally enjoyed the night flights: that mix of instrument flying for immediate aircraft control, but looking outside for visual circuits and landing. The blaze of light to the south that was Perth was spectacular, and the air was cool and smooth after a hot Western Australian day. Initially, the student would have to master night circuits and landings in the Macchi that, like the initial daytime work, was done at the quiet and remote runway at Gingin. However, by the very nature of its remoteness, Gingin at night comprised just a thin, lit rectangle of the runway and a few dim taxiway lights. Complete blackness surrounded the field, unlike at Pearce, where lights emanated from the base, the town of Bullsbrook, the Great Northern Highway and the homesteads on the escarpment. From Pearce, there was also that blaze of Perth itself to the south. At

Gingin, it fell on the instructors to demonstrate landing the Macchi at night from the back seat: the jet's nose was high at its approach speed, our necks stretching and craning to see past the dark mass of the ejection seat and helmet in front as we tried to maintain the correct 'picture' of the runway ahead. Its white lights were distorted and dancing in the sides of the windscreen and the upturned Perspex 'boat' of the canopy, while we 'pattered' over the intercom the correct technique and what was to be achieved. Then, on edge initially, we directed and monitored the student's efforts until the circuits were satisfactory. Then would come the time to demonstrate the 'flapless' landing in the dark with the Macchi's nose tilted even higher as it flew down its final approach. Also, the jet was more 'slippery' to fly without the drag of the flaps. Ironically, a slight cross wind was a boon, because with the aircraft 'cocked off' left or right to allow for drift on approach, more of the runway could be seen, although distorted, to one side of the windscreen and the canopy. With the jet's nose attitude so high in the air, the 'night flapless landing' demonstration on Gingin's runway was one of the more demanding exercises to demonstrate from the back seat. It was usually a relief for the instructor to hand over to the student for his attempt, from the much clearer vantage point of the front seat.

The social life at Pearce was hectic. Most instructors were in their late twenties to early thirties and many were newly married with babies. 2 FTS was seen as a stable posting, ideal for young families, the men home nights, rarely working weekends and no extended deployments away. There was always time for a beer or two in the Officers' Mess several times per week after flying, before the long drive to our rented home in a northern suburb of Perth. Drink-driving laws were in effect, but were more often than not 'honoured more in the breach than the observance'. After night flying there was always beer, consumed still in our flight suits at the Back Bar, and every Friday afternoon was the obligatory drinking with the students in the Studs' Mess.

During my student days at Pearce, I did not imagine that in a few years *I* would be one of the instructors capering to the actions of the animals in a bawdy version of 'Old MacDonald Had a Farm' or singing raucously along to 'The Neptune Song'. Bemused students watched, listened and tentatively joined in. But aside from the hilarity, the studs listened intently to their instructor's war stories and banter. In the Mess, many a 'wet debrief' took place where a young prospective navy or air force pilot took away with him a lesson or information that would stand him in good stead later. Invariably, his instructor would enthuse about the operational aircraft types that he had flown. As a navy pilot, I spoke of the disciplined madness of day and night carrier operations. There were the 'Dining-in Nights', both the formal ones in the Officers' Mess, but then there were others held in the Students' Mess for 'Postings Night' and Graduation.

The 'Postings Dining-in Nights' could be particularly wild. Never 'mixed' affairs, where wives and girlfriends could attend, these nights began formally as would navy Mess Dinners, with instructors and students in Mess dress sitting at long tables in the massive students' dining hall, and perhaps a small brass ensemble playing discreetly in one corner. At the meal's end, the Loyal Toast would be made. Then would come the highlight of the evening: the students' postings (on the assumption that they would gain their 'wings'), would be read out: to a fighter squadron, 'trash hauling' (transports), helicopters, the VIP transport squadron … The drinking redoubled as students celebrated being awarded their preference, or accepted their posting philosophically to a transport or helicopter unit, or were just happy that they were still on course to warrant a posting at all.

At the end of the night, the Mess games would start: 'St George and the Dragon' or the occasional cry of 'Dead Ants!', where everyone within earshot had to fall to the floor and lie on their backs, wiggling their arms and legs in the air. Last one down bought the next round. Then would come the time for 'Fan Stopping'. Those cadets posted to helicopters were helped up onto a chair and an instructor turned on a ceiling fan. The player had to use his head to stop the fan from rotating. The more inebriated victims stuck their heads straight up into the whirling blades only to be knocked off the chair, often with angry cuts to their heads, to cheers and roars from the men below. The correct technique was to use the top of the scalp to gradually slow the blades down, as would sometimes be demonstrated by an instructor, in the spirit of correct CFS technique. However in this case, a colleague would surreptitiously turn off the fan's control knob just before he showed the students how easy Fan Stopping was. Then the power would be reinstated for the student's attempt. Later, our small cadre of navy pilots would lead the way with 'Carrier Landings'.

I left one Postings Dining-in Night in the small hours of the morning, this time to sleep it off in the Officers' Mess, still clad in a tablecloth toga. A ring of car headlights coned the Students' Mess as shouts, singing and the occasional sound of crashing emanated from within. Upon hearing the chaos, the RAAF Service Police had surrounded the building, but they were powerless to enter unless ordered. We were only having fun. A student, with assistance from the instructors, had managed to get his 'Mini Minor' car into the Mess foyer, while in the meantime we navy pilots had been demonstrating the British 'ski jump' carrier launch technique on the parquet floor with the aid of bicycles and tilted coffee tables. Damage to the Mess would, of course, be paid for later by us.

After the Queen's health had been drunk at one affair, Scotty, a fellow RAN instructor, and I decided that the 2 FTS Commanding Officer's speech was boring. We had heard about 'roof running', so we decided to try it and, against all protocol, we slipped out of the Mess Dinner early, and somehow climbed onto the roof. We could faintly hear the hilarity from below as we periodically ran up and down the galvanised iron, while the CO attempted to complete his long-winded congratulatory speech to the students amid the waxing and waning 'tromp tromp tromp tromp tromp' from above. Then, there were more irregular noises from above as we searched in vain for some sort of manhole in order to exercise our plan to climb through it and drop down from the ceiling and land somewhere amid the multitude inside.

Among all this play, the pace of flying at 2 FTS became frenetic. With the Soviets still active in Afghanistan, more courses than ever were being put through, and most of us had 'secondary duties' – mine was Programming Officer. In addition to three or sometimes four flights in a day, it was my responsibility to produce the next day's flying program, which involved slapping and sliding magnetized labels representing students and instructors around a huge 'white board' in a dedicated office. I juggled students, their instructors, times and test requirements. There were no computers, let alone spreadsheets, then. Several 'waves' of training flights were launched each day, and each had to be programmed. Then I had to plan the night flying program, retests, and reschedule missed sorties due to weather, sickness, student failure or unserviceability.

I was also the 'Quiz Officer'. During the routine Morning Briefing of the assembled students and instructors, the 'QuizzO' asked questions relating to aircraft operation, emergency drills, limitations, and regulations. After a student's name was called, the cadet or midshipman would rise and stand to attention to answer the question. An incorrect response would result in the contemptuous 'Remain standing'. The landmarks and boundaries of the training areas had to be known by heart.

On one occasion, bored with the duty, I asked students of the senior course, who now thought that they knew it all, 'What ground feature lies at this bearing and distance from Pearce?' I gave them the coordinates. With no clue, several students were standing. 'Right. That's the Wanneroo Lion Park. I would avoid ejecting over that if at all possible. It would be a pity to survive an ejection to then be looking down from your parachute with the lions looking up watching their lunch descend from on high.'

Flying several sorties a day in the height of a Western Australian summer could be onerous. The Macchi was a European aircraft designed in the 1960s. At low altitudes, its primitive air conditioning system was overwhelmed by the heat and the Western Australian sun blazing through the Perspex. Under the canopy pilots sweltered clad progressively, in underwear, Nomex flight suit, Mae West, g suit, harness webbing for the ejection seat and parachute pack, heavy helmet and rubber oxygen mask. Low-level navigation exercises were flown at 240 knots – or 440 km/hr – and, at just 200 feet – or sixty metres – mostly over the hot wheat belt north and east of Perth. Invisible waves of heat billowed into bumpy 'thermals' making the jet jolt and fishtail as the huge tawny fields, off-white dry lakes, scrubby trees and the occasional tiny, siloed wheat town slid below. Back at Pearce we would unclip our rubber oxygen masks that were slimy with sweat, and unstrap and clamber out of our Macchis with our flight suits wringing wet with perspiration. After a debrief off to the showers, change into a fresh flight suit, and then prepare the briefing for the next student. Stress from heat and workload was severe at times; it was fortunate that most of us were in our mid- to late twenties. An air force doctor visited on one occasion to research the effects that heat stress had on us. One instructor was tasked to swallow a capsule that transmitted his body core temperature to a remote reading unit, but no positive action resulted as a result of the study. We just flew, and flew, and sweated, and I am ashamed to say that many of us came to regard a student being 'scrubbed' as being a welcome easing of our workload.

In September 1982, Yvonne and I were married back in Victoria in the chapel set in the parkland of HMAS *Cerberus*. I had just turned twenty-five, then at twenty-six, I became a father when Avalon, our daughter, was born. There was more study and a flight test in order to become a Category A-2 flying instructor. With a family, a heavy flying programme, ground duties, and the social life with the other young air force and navy families and the mess functions, life was hectic yet satisfying.

My RAN colleagues and I at Pearce were administered from HMAS *Leeuwin*, a navy training base south of Perth. On occasion, I took the long drive down there to attend to administration. We also had the opportunity to relearn the operation of the work-boats that were based there. There were Mess Dinners and other functions held at *Leeuwin,* and at HMAS *Stirling*: the operational naval base at Garden Island, even further south. Navy instructors at Pearce were sometimes expected to attend them. But most of my friends were air force, and I had begun to absorb the RAAF culture as I had while on pilots' course. *Leeuwin* was a training base, there were no aviators there, and I found the Mess Dinners stuffy and uninteresting. Dining-in Nights at Pearce were far more enjoyable to a young military pilot.

However, things were looking promising regarding the future of RAN air power. After a final short 'cruise', once again with no Skyhawk jets aboard, HMAS *Melbourne* was finally retired and it was mooted that a British carrier, the relatively new HMS *Invincible*, would be sold to Australia to replace her. It was a bizarre situation: Britain, an island nation with a glorious maritime history, had decided that aircraft carriers were expensive, vulnerable, and replaceable by land-based (that is, air force) air bases. Any future war would be fought with missiles, or with land-based air power supported by air-to-air refuelling. However, in 1981 Australia's conservative Liberal Party government under Malcom Fraser still considered that, for Australia, with its vast coastline and integration with the U.S. Navy, carrier-based air power was important. The buzz around the tiny RAN Fleet Air Arm was that *Invincible* was coming, maybe even with Sea Harrier 'jump jets' and anti-submarine helicopters flying from her deck. But what about the Trackers? *Invincible* was not a conventional carrier. She had no catapult or arrester gear for launching and recovering fixed-wing aircraft. She did, however, have the flat deck of a carrier and a 'ski jump' ramp was fitted to her bow. The Sea Harriers, with their 'vectored thrust' jet nozzles, would launch themselves off the ramp, but no other type of fixed-wing aircraft could operate from *Invincible*. The speculation about what would happen to the Trackers was that they would operate as coastal patrol aircraft from shore, but it was just that: speculation.

Along with the future of the Grummans, I also pondered my future with the navy. I did like ships. I considered the navy as a superior service to the air force in mess standards, tradition and the calibre of its senior officers. Even air force fighter pilots went quiet when a naval aviator spoke of landing on a carrier's pitching deck at night. RAN aircrew were encouraged to go on to gain their bridge watch-keeping 'tickets' – sea-going qualifications – in order to progress up the promotion ladder beyond commander rank. What about flying helicopters? I had been taken low-flying in helicopters on several occasions, which were unforgettable. On the other hand, the RAAF operated the mighty four-engine Lockheed Orion maritime patrol aircraft, which was about four times the weight of a Tracker and three times as fast, but did essentially the same job. Also, the entire air force was geared around aircraft, while senior naval officers seemed to regard them as just another weapons system. Transfer between the services was not unheard-of, and I already served at an air force base. In the meantime, I worked hard as I wondered what the future might bring.

A few months before Yvonne and I married, events occurred in the South Atlantic Ocean that had serious implications for the future of air power in the Royal Australian Navy. In April 1982, Argentine forces invaded the Falkland Islands. The British Government responded by sending a naval task force to retake them, which included two aircraft carriers: HMS *Hermes* and HMS *Invincible*. Britain's Royal Navy Fleet Air Arm starred in the conflict, its carrier-based Sea Harriers shooting down attacking Argentine aircraft. Also based on the carriers, Royal Air Force Harriers and pilots supported the ground forces. In June, the Falklands were liberated, and it had been overwhelmingly the Royal Navy's war. Naval pilots worldwide joked about the solitary bomb that a lone land-based Vulcan bomber of the Royal Air Force had managed to place on the Port Stanley runway after a gruelling crew effort and a ridiculous number of air-to-air refuelling sessions to get one bomber to the Falklands – the refuellers had to be refuelled in the air themselves! The atmosphere was now electric around the RAN; here was a pivotal event that demonstrated the importance of carrier-borne air power. But after the events in the South Atlantic, the British decided to retain HMS

Invincible for themselves. So what carrier would the RAN get now? Perhaps one of the smaller American types, not in the league of their huge nuclear-powered vessels, but the U.S. and some other countries produced capable and more affordable ships. However, a dark shadow suddenly appeared over the Royal Australian Navy, cast by Australia's changing political landscape.

It was March 1983. Australia's conservative Fraser government was becoming tired, though still effective in countering the socialist Labor Party opposition that appeared to have weak electoral support with its leader of the time. However, with a federal election looming, the Leader of the Opposition was suddenly deposed by Bob Hawke, considered more charismatic and intelligent than the man he replaced. After flying ended on the day the news broke, rather than go to our homes, a group of us gathered at the Senior Naval Officer, Murray's, house in Perth's northern suburbs, where most of us lived. As we drank Murray's beer in front of his television, we watched the news commentators crowing about the charismatic Hawke and his prospects of winning the election, and therefore the Prime Ministership. Labor governments were notorious for their neglect of the armed services. With a sense of foreboding in the air, we watched the images of Hawke in the interviews and the opinion pieces from various television journalists. We were unusually quiet for a group of relaxing military pilots. Later that day, I drove home with my mind in turmoil. What was going to happen to our navy? Our carrier? Surely a Labor government would see sense in retaining and indeed enhancing Australia's naval air power, particularly after the lessons of the Falklands War? There would still be a future in the Fleet Air Arm, right?

It was now late 1984, and a life-changing message was in my hand. It stated that in January of the following year, I was to proceed to RAAF Edinburgh, the huge air force base north of Adelaide, South

Australia, for conversion training onto the Lockheed P-3C Orion patrol aircraft. After six months' training, I was then to take up duty as a co-pilot with the famous No. 10 Squadron, RAAF. The news was not unexpected. For most of the year I had been wearing the blue uniform of the Royal Australian Air Force. I was now one of the 'crabs'. I no longer belonged to 'Pusser's'; I was at the beck and call of 'Ronnie Raff'. I went to the 'toilet' instead of the 'head'. I went 'off base', not 'ashore'. I saluted with my palm outwards, like one of the comic Benny Hill's characters. I ate 'dinner', not 'scran'. I no longer made jokes about air force officers in their blue uniforms being asked for twenty dollars' worth of 'Super' by little old ladies at petrol stations. However, my air force friends and even the CO and the Flight Commanders still called me by my nickname, 'Admiral', and they were not surprised when I expressed my preference for flying Orions, which had just been duly granted.

Now, the fixed-wing Fleet Air Arm was no more. HMAS *Melbourne* had been decommissioned in June 1982 by the Fraser government in anticipation of a new carrier being purchased. But Hawke's Labor government, after being in power for just over a year, had virtually given Australia's navy Skyhawks to New Zealand's air force. The Trackers had been withdrawn from service and left in the open at Nowra, unprotected, the metal of their airframes and engines relentlessly corroding in the salty coastal air. The Macchis had been transferred to the air force and hurriedly repainted to remove all traces of their navy heritage. There would be no new carrier. The Labor government's actions hit the navy and the community of Nowra hard. Fleet Air Arm officers and sailors alike were furious at the arbitrary destruction of their careers and the uncertainty of their futures after years of service, including duty at sea, which had not been without hazard. The RAAF, which had always been resentful of the navy having effective fixed-wing air power, gleefully stepped into the vacuum. It promised that it could take up the Fleet Support role that the Nowra based Skyhawks and Macchis had carried out. Naval aviators regarded this undertaking with great cynicism.

Decades of expertise in carrier aviation had been lost overnight. Expensive and capable aircraft were rotting in the open, or had been given away. The two HS 748's would soon go. The navy now only had its helicopters. Naval aircrew were given the options of staying in the RAN to fly helicopters, go to sea as 'fish heads', or transfer to the RAAF. Another option was to transfer to Britain's Royal Navy, which, unlike Australia, was now actively expanding its Air Arm. For me, the latter option was not appealing. With no fighter background, the chance of my flying the amazing Sea Harrier, the star of the Falklands War, would be slim. I would probably end up flying RN helicopters in a grey country on the other side of the planet. I had a new wife and a baby, I was already working with the air force, and I had always considered the Orion an impressive aircraft. So, after night flying at Pearce on my last day in the navy, the beer flowed profusely in the Back Bar, and later the lads sat me down in a chair and off came the full navy beard, leaving a thin air force-style moustache. Next morning, with Yvonne and the baby still asleep as usual, after nearly eight years' service with the Royal Australian Navy, I donned a new khaki summer air force shirt, slipped on the 'slides' that bore two dark blue stripes, denoting that I was a flight lieutenant of the Royal Australian Air Force, and pinned on the heavy pewter RAAF wings. On the long drive to the base, my face felt strange and sensitive without its naval beard. But after some crew room banter followed by the routine morning briefing, just another day of hectic flying began.

I couldn't sleep, but the inability to drift off did not worry me. My family and I were on a long but interesting journey. We occupied a tiny compartment on the famous Transcontinental train that was taking us from Perth to Adelaide. Our car rocked on a flatbed truck at the end of the train. The bunks gently swayed to the clack of the train's wheels and, thankfully, Avalon was asleep. After we moved to Adelaide, we would be within a day's drive of friends and family in Melbourne. A friend from 2 FTS and a fellow instructor, Al Fraser, would be with me on the Orion course. Adelaide was a nice city, from what I remembered of it. And the Orion was 'operational'. There would be some serious flying involving intelligence gathering, hunting Soviet submarines, and overseas detachments ... but never again would I look out past orange and white wings and the black faces of a Macchi's tip tanks to a cloudless Western Australian sky and a deep blue sea. No more roaring through 'initial', cavorting in a 'tail chase' at the end of formation flight, or beer and song with the students under a golden west coast sunset outside the Mess. I recalled our formation of Macchis, flying to a training camp at the 'bare bones' base of RAAF Learmonth on the north west coast of Western Australia, dropping down to orbit Mount Augustus, a monolith bigger than Uluru. And, of course, I would no longer 'fly the ball' onto a carrier, or hear the roar of twin Cyclones at full power. But long-range patrol and anti-submarine warfare operations would be interesting, and so far there had been no sign of the Hawke government attacking the capability of the air force.

While the train rumbled towards Adelaide, the memories rolled on. A British Hawker Siddeley Nimrod anti-submarine jet belonging to Britain's Royal Air Force had visited Pearce during an exercise. A derivative of the pioneering de Havilland Comet – the first practical jet airliner – the British had tacked on a bulge underneath its fuselage as a torpedo bay. Other excrescences covered antennas and radars and a big fixed MAD boom projected from the Nimrod's tail. The aircraft was painted a strange brown colour called 'hemp' by the RAF, but it looked futuristic with its four jet engines buried in the wings, not slung underneath them in pods. Its nose sloped down bluntly like the front of an old-style Diesel locomotive. We had taken the British pilots flying in our Macchis, and in return I would sit on the 'jump seat' of the Nimrod's cockpit on a flight. The interior was impressive: roomy and packed with technology. There were huge screens and tactical displays, computer keyboards and banks of sonobuoy sensor stations that made the Tracker look like something out of the 1960s – which it was.

But then I entered the cockpit to take my place on the jump seat behind the pilot and co-pilot. It was reminiscent of the cab of a steam locomotive! The cockpit interior was black, with instruments, switches, levers, knobs and wheels everywhere, just like the original Comet, flown in the 1950s. The Nimrod's cockpit windows comprised the tiny multiple panes of the Comet, and the view outside was poor. For pilot awareness of the anti-submarine warfare 'plot', the Tracker had had the tactical display, prominent on the instrument panel between the pilot and the TACCO, and the Orion had an electronic screen on its panel, but the Nimrod's cockpit didn't seem to have anything.

'As the captain, how do you know where to steer and what the tactical situation is?' I asked the pilot who sat in the left hand seat.

He pointed to a small instrument similar to the ILS indicator on the old HS 748, with its two little cross hairs. 'The chaps in the back send the steering commands to this,' he replied. 'And we just keep the tactical plot in our heads.'

This was in a four-engine jet derived from an airliner, manoeuvring at low-level over the water, possibly at night over a stormy North Atlantic Ocean.

'And, by the way,' he said, 'I'm not the captain of the aircraft. It's "Spock", down the back.'

This Nimrod crew were operating under a peculiarly British system where the captain of the aircraft was not necessarily the pilot. I recalled accounts I had read of the fluttering two-seat reconnaissance biplanes of World War I, where an army officer would be in command as the 'observer', taking photographs and mapping enemy activity, while the pilot would often be an enlisted man, regarded as merely the 'driver', under the direction of the officer. In this case, Spock, an Air Electronics Officer, and also the Commanding Officer of the Nimrod's squadron, had 'signed for' the aircraft and it was totally under his command.

'What happens if you have an emergency?' I asked the pilots, incredulous.

'No problem, Spock will just say to take care of it, but as captain he will make the decision where to land and all that.'

We were now airborne in the Nimrod and climbing to 38,000 feet, higher than a Macchi could fly. The 'First Pilot' promptly got out of his seat and invited me to take the controls. It felt heavy but I was able to fly it reasonably accurately. There was a change in the control response as the Flight Engineer made an adjustment to something the crew called 'stabilizer gearing'. He was seated facing sideways behind the pilots and occasionally he manipulated clunky switches on his panel. Under Spock's direction, we reached the exercise area over the Indian Ocean, and dropped down to just a few hundred feet from the water, where the pilots generously allowed me to manipulate the big aircraft. It was interesting to be at low-level again over the sea, but with no vibration from any propellers or piston engines. Back in his seat, the First Pilot dutifully flew the manoeuvres commanded from the cabin, and after a few hours we climbed away, now in darkness, to return south to Pearce.

On the way back, I chatted with the flight engineer. A problem jet engines have is that, at low altitude, they consume lots of fuel. But with the Nimrod's clean design, it could shut an engine down and save some. I remarked to the engineer that the Orion could do that as well, but its propeller would have to be 'feathered' (its blades turned edge-on to the airflow to reduce drag).

'The advantage of the Nimrod,' said the flight engineer, 'is that it's a jet. It's simple. You don't have to feather a hole!'

While the train clanked and rocked, I recalled climbing out of Pearce's Search and Rescue Caribou, grey with airsickness at the end of a flight in it. A storm was battering Perth, and a huge oceanic drilling platform had broken loose from its tow, with men aboard. I was detailed to go in the back of the Caribou as a lookout, and as we approached the rig, the aircraft's rear ramp opened and, restrained by a 'monkey harness', I leaned out as the green transport circled over the rig. We lurched and jolted in the gale under a light grey cloud deck, the sea a more angry grey flecked with white. Below, the huge rig heaved and rolled. It had four giant retracted 'legs' that protruded hundreds of feet above each corner of its square deck. My nausea was forgotten, as while the Caribou orbited overhead, I watched one of Pearce's Search and Rescue Iroquois helicopters hovering over the platform, dodging the gyrating legs as it winched the rig's crewmen to safety one by one. The helicopter crew would later receive awards for their action that day.

There would be no more family breaks at Rottnest Island, where the army provided partly-used barracks available for hire by defence force families. Gone were the alcohol-fuelled hilarious nights with the pilots' courses in the same barracks: young men who were letting off steam after helicopter winching training in the water off Rottnest that was done towards the end of their course. I thought back to the flight I had had in a visiting Orion, the aircraft on a whole new scale above the Tracker. I recalled the view from its beautiful flat cockpit windows, but there were waves of vibration and noise from the four huge propellers, and its crew were multitudinous – there were even two flight engineers! Derived from an airliner, the Lockheed Electra, the Orion weighed many tonnes, had four powerful turboprop engines, and rack after rack of electronic equipment was arrayed down the airliner-sized cabin. Above all, I recalled the tiredness. Keen to experience the much-vaunted Orion, I had gone along on a flight that departed Pearce late at night, and in the small hours of the morning, we landed back there after a long night surveillance mission, my eyes gritty and my ears ringing. Unlike the British Nimrod pilots, the Orion's crew had not invited me to occupy a control seat, much less fly it at any time. I was pretty much ignored. I just sat or stood fighting sleep, trying to make sense of what was going on, and scanning the banks of dials and switches, trying to work out what each was telling me. There was nothing to see outside in the blackness over the Indian Ocean until the sun rose during the long transit back to Pearce.

Finally, I drifted off for a few hours in the swaying bunk while the train rolled eastwards. I had to find a house for my family somewhere in Adelaide. And the task of learning to operate and eventually command and 'fight' the complex Lockheed Orion, over six months of training, lay ahead.

THE GREY AND WHITE KINGSWOOD

1985 – 1987

For a few months in early 1985, we lived in a hotel room in Adelaide, partly paid for by the air force. The city, although well laid-out and with its beautiful old buildings, became cloying after I returned to it each day after a long drive through Adelaide's sprawling northern suburbs from RAAF Base Edinburgh. The room was small and there were no cooking facilities. I shared it with my wife and baby, and I also had to study at night. After going house hunting, we finally found an unpretentious house in a northern suburb. The solid-brick cream-coloured house was located on the side of the escarpment to the east of Adelaide and faced west, looking over the civilian Parafield Airport. The view was spectacular, even more so with the lights at night, but the neighbourhood itself was unremarkable. Other RAAF families lived in the area and Al Fraser, my friend from Pearce, lived in the next suburb. I scraped together a deposit from our meagre savings and committed to a bank loan to purchase the little house – our first – at the age of twenty-seven. I knuckled back down to the Orion course, which would last six months. It started with weeks of lectures, conducted by pilot instructors and flight engineers, on the aircraft's systems.

The design of the Lockheed P-3C Orion was based on the company's Electra airliner. A giant compared with the Tracker, but as the much smaller Grumman had been, it was built for the United States Navy. Australian crews sometimes referred to it 'The big grey and white Kingswood', after a popular family car in the 80s, because the aircraft, like the vehicle, was regarded as solid and reliable. Its gull-grey with white-topped fuselage was an airliner-style tube over thirty-five metres long, and its cabin was pressurised to airliner standards. The stubby grey wings ended with blunt squared-off wingtips and they spanned some five metres shorter than the fuselage was long, making the Orion look lean and purposeful in planform. However, the rounded tip of the grey vertical fin betrayed the aircraft's heritage from the 1950s vintage Electra, although it towered to nearly twelve metres above the tarmac. But the stand-out feature of the Orion was its four engines and their massive propellers: they were monsters.

Each Allison T-56 turboprop produced 4,600 horsepower, and was essentially a jet engine coupled to a long shaft that led forward to a massive gearbox. Suspended from this gearbox was the biggest propeller that I had ever seen. A huge black conical 'spinner' from which the four fat propeller blades sprouted concealed highly complex pieces of machinery that controlled the pitch of each propeller blade. Like most turboprops, the propeller spun at an almost-constant RPM as the angles of the blades were adjusted to provide the desired thrust. Like the little Nomad I had flown at Sale, an Orion's propeller could reverse the pitch of its blades on the ground to help slow the aircraft. The P-3 could even taxi backwards: while doing so, pilots were careful to place their feet flat on the floor, away from the brake pedals on the rudder controls, as a sudden jab of the brakes would tip the big aircraft onto its tail. An experienced Orion pilot rarely used the brakes while taxiing the big machine because the propellers gave total control over speed and braking. A significant portion of the Orion's truncated wings was covered by the air blast from the huge propellers, enhancing take-off and climb performance. Extending back from each engine was a gaping jet-like exhaust tube that blasted the hot gas over troughs in the upper rear surface of each wing in a blur of heat haze and with the occasional puff of black soot.

The dull black propeller spinners concealed a multitude of devices. There were, of course, the normal mechanisms to adjust the pitch of the propeller blades with the pilots' power demands. But the consequences of a propeller getting out of control ('running away') would be disastrous. The blades would tend to 'fine off', creating the effect of a four-metre diameter 'flat plate' on the wing. One device was a 'pitch lock' that, in the event of the hydraulic oil that controlled the propeller being lost, would lock the blades at their current angle. There were feathering mechanisms and their pumps. There was a Negative Torque System, which prevented the propeller from 'windmilling' and driving the gearbox, thereby damaging it. There was a 'pitch lock reset', (the purpose of which I have long forgotten) and as a protection of last resort, a 'de-coupler', would disconnect the propeller from the engine in the event of a runaway. All that was multiplied by four to comprise the entire propulsion system of the aircraft.

The Orion's engines drove hydraulic pumps to power the flaps, the brakes, the landing gear retraction and extension, and the huge belly doors of the torpedo bay. There were also electrically powered hydraulic pumps that could provide pressure. The electrical demands of the aircraft systems and the Anti-Submarine Warfare equipment were prodigious, so each engine drove a powerful generator. The landing gear was massive, again based on the airliner design, with twin main- and nose-wheels.

Even with its engines not running on the tarmac, the Orion required such a vast amount of electric and hydraulic power that an Auxiliary Power Unit was fitted on one side of the forward fuselage. This was essentially a small jet engine that could be started on the ground. It powered its own electric generator to provide electrical power to run the aircraft's systems and pressurise the hydraulics through an electric pump. It also provided the high-pressure air needed to start the massive engines: electric starter motors for the Allisons would be impractical.

The Orion was packed with fuel, enough to easily fly missions lasting over ten hours, in multiple tanks, the feed from which was carefully managed by the flight engineer. For long missions a 'dinette' and galley at the rear of the cabin were used. Orion crew could heat their 'frozos' (frozen meals) in the galley oven, eat them at the dinette area, then take a nap in one of the two bunks that were fitted! It was a far cry from stale sandwiches and a swig of ship's limers while strapped into the seat of a Tracker. But, during my rare breaks from the controls, I usually found the dining and sleeping facilities already occupied by either one of the two flight engineers, a navigator, enlisted sensor operators (AEAs), or AEOs (Airborne Electronics Officers, or 'Airborne Eating Officers', as they were sometimes called).

However, the provision of these amenities did not detract from the grim purpose of the aircraft. Like the Tracker, the Orion was a warplane: a serious long-range maritime patrol and strike aircraft, with some of the detection and weapons capability of a navy frigate. Along with more modern computerised versions of the Tracker's sonobuoy system, radar, MAD and electronic support measures, the P-3C Orion carried an infra-red detection system (IRDS) in a little retractable turret underneath the forward fuselage, which sent TV imagery to the crew in day and night conditions. Leading the back-end crew was the TACCO, in tactical control of the aircraft as our navy TACCOs had been, but he sat in front of a massive screen at his own station on the left forward side of the main cabin. Across the aisle to his right sat the navigator, also with his screen. These screens were fed with navigation and sensor data, while 'waypoints' and steering commands were fed to a smaller, simpler round screen on the pilots' main instrument panel. A broad console covered with switches and panels sat between the pilots, which was so wide that duplicated sets of the four 'power levers' that controlled the mighty Allisons were installed, one on each side of the console for each pilot. An Orion's captain occupied the left seat, while his co-pilot assisted from the right. Behind and between the two pilots sat the flight engineer, facing forward. With the complexity of the aircraft's engines, propellers and systems, the flight engineer was an integral part of the flight crew. For long missions, the second engineer was carried.

As you moved aft from the pilots' seats back into the cabin, you passed between rows of electronic racks, the TACCO and navigator stations, more racks, and sideways-facing grey consoles of sonobuoy analysis panels with screens and keyboards along one side. This was the domain of the specialist AEOs and AEAs, the sensor operators. There were more racks of electronics on the other side. The cabin floor, sidewalls and ceiling were a dirty cream colour, which gave the interior a fairly light and spacious feel, despite the scarcity of windows. Further back was the radar operator's station and the MAD console. Unlike the Tracker, whose radar scanned from its retractable radome that extended underneath in flight, the Orion had two fixed radar antennae: one facing forward in the nose cone, and the other facing aft under the tail. The two were electronically linked to provide one continuous 360-degree scan. Likewise, the P-3's imposing MAD boom was fixed in place to extend back permanently from behind the base of the tall tail fin, like a giant insect's stinger.

Further aft, before the dinette and galley, there was a sonobuoy rack, from which buoys could be loaded into a dispenser by crewmen, ready for release. These were in addition to externally loaded sonobuoys, ejected from holes under the curve of the rear fuselage. Most aft, there was a toilet compartment that housed a chemical commode. Who would empty the 'honey pot' after a long flight was variously decided by a roster system, reversed seniority, as a penalty for some mistake, or for getting on the wrong side of one of the senior crew members.

A P-3C with a full weapons load was a formidable war machine. I was familiar with most of its capability from my Tracker operations, but it was on a vastly greater scale. A 'bomb bay' occupied the bottom forward section of the fuselage under the cabin floor, enclosed by two large doors. The capacious bay could carry four homing torpedoes, against the Tracker's two. Like the Tracker, the Orion could drop depth charges. The Orion could also drop an apparatus called 'Lindholme', which was a container that would deploy a life raft with survival equipment and rations to survivors in the water. The aircraft could also lay mines and it could deploy another potent weapon that made the Orion more than a killer of just submarines: the Harpoon missile.

An Orion could carry four Harpoons, each mounted under a rack beneath the stubby outer wings. The Harpoon was a 'cruise' missile designed to destroy surface vessels. One thinks of a missile as a 'rocket', but the Harpoon was actually a miniature four-metre long, unmanned *kamikaze* jet aircraft. On launch from the Orion, the missile fell from its rack and then its little jet engine started as it dropped towards the sea, skimming along just above the surface until it automatically 'popped up', switched on its radar, acquired its target, and slammed into the target vessel with devastating effect. Trainee crews practised feeding the approximate position of the 'target' into the Harpoon system. The pilots would then drop the Orion to low-level and race over the sea at over 350 knots – or 650 km/hr – to the 'launch' point. There, easing back on the control yoke resulted in the big machine soaring skywards, the sea receding, trading high speed for height until it was within the Harpoon's launch 'window'. After the weapon launch, the Orion would make a hard diving turn away and down towards the safety of the ocean's cluttered surface to race away from the scene.

With its sophisticated central computer system, state-of-the-art sensor suite and its formidable weapons, the Orion, typically captained by a flying officer or flight lieutenant in his twenties with his equally young crew, was essentially a naval frigate in capability. But it moved at over ten times the warship's speed. The aircraft cruised effortlessly at 380 knots – or 700 km/hr – at up to 30,000 feet, or nine kilometres in the sky. I wondered why Australia's Orion force was based near Adelaide, central and high in the soft underbelly of the continent, far from the perceived threats to the north of the country. I came to realise that with its speed, a P-3 could be anywhere around the Australian coastline within about three to four hours' flying from Adelaide.

The conversion course was intense. Although I was to be posted to the famous Number 10 Squadron, for now I belonged to 292

Squadron, the training unit for all Orion crew. I was initially to be a co-pilot until my performance would be evaluated after I gained experience. However, the course was a 'left-hand seat' conversion: to be trained to operate the aircraft from the captain's seat, and to be competent in all manoeuvres and emergency procedures from there. It was also my first taste of a proper flight simulator: a box mounted on hydraulic rams, on which screens were mounted that even with the primitive computers of the 1980s, displayed convincing simulations of the world outside the cockpit windows: runways, the horizon, clouds, the sea, rudimentary landscapes. The Orion simulator was a far cry from the primitive WST in which I had spent hours at Nowra, learning to operate the Tracker.

I worked in the simulator under the guidance of an instructor, and after mastering normal operations, training for emergency situations began. With four engines and massive complicated propellers, these were numerous. I learned to interact with the flight engineer, who routinely handled engine start, propeller checks, power and fuel management, pressurisation and a myriad of other tasks. Communication between myself, the co-pilot and the flight engineer were important, especially while coordinating our actions during the simulated emergencies. The now embedded concept of Crew Resource Management in aviation was embryonic in those days, but instinctively most of us grasped the importance of clear communications and a methodical approach to problem solving.

Unique to the Orion, the 'FE' (the flight engineer) handled the engines' 'power levers' (throttles) at all times of flight right up until the flare for landing. The philosophy was ship-like, we guessed, because the Orion was designed for use by the U.S. Navy. Also in betrayal of its naval origins, the Orion's cockpit or flight deck was referred to as the 'Flight Station'. Established in the simulator on the long final visual or instrument approach that larger aircraft usually flew, the FE handled the four levers while I called for the appropriate power settings in torque units: direct measurements of the power of the Allisons. If a little fast, I called for less power, then when 'on speed', another call to maintain. If the approach had been accurately flown, just before the flare above the runway the call was 'Pilot's power'. After the FE responded 'Pilot's power', my right hand grasped the bank of four power levers to reduce the power on the turboprops, while at the same time I raised the Orion's nose to cushion the touchdown. Then I was to retard the power levers further, placing the propellers into reverse pitch to slow the aircraft on the runway. The pilot handled the power levers during taxi, with use of the wheel brakes minimal as he regulated the big machine's speed with gentle touches of forward, neutral or reverse power, provided by the ever-changing pitch of the propeller blades and their watch-like mechanisms. The Orion's brakes had to be used carefully because they were not fitted with the 'anti-skid' system that was usually fitted to big aircraft.

After some months, my family and I could move out of the hotel room, and we settled in our modest house at Para Hills. Although it was small, it was pleasing to live in our own home. Very early one morning I stepped out of our front door and as usual paused to take in the lights of Parafield Airport and, further away, Port Adelaide twinkling before the dark expanse of the Gulf of St. Vincent, before I set off on the long drive north to RAAF Edinburgh. But today, finally, I was to fly the real aircraft, not the simulator.

The banks of instruments danced and blurred in front of us. The flight engineer had set high power on the engines, carrying out the routine checks on the propeller systems that were made before take-off. We wore headsets, not helmets, and the noise blared into our ears: not the high shrill of the HS 748's Darts or the bellow of the Tracker's Cyclones, but a dull, thudding low buzz from the huge propellers counterpointed by a low, hollow whistle from the Allisons' turbines. The aircraft shook and strained against the braked double main wheels. The noise subsided a little and I could just make out the FE's litany of checks while he recited them over the intercom, then we ran through the final checklist required to take the big machine into the sky. Soon we were climbing north to the training area, over the upper reaches of the Gulf of St. Vincent. I occasionally stole a look down at the unremarkable light tan country by its shore punctuated by countless hothouses, a few straggly trees and long, straight dusty roads. The view from the large, flat side window was excellent. The Orion jolted in the heat-driven turbulence, even at 15,000 feet, or four and a half kilometres in the sky, while I got the feel of it: surprisingly manoeuvrable, especially in roll, thanks to its stubby wings.

A young pilot officer, fresh from pilot's course, waited for his turn at the controls – the two of us were being trained together. Later during his turn in the left seat I would lurk in the cabin, or stand behind the flight engineer in the roomy Flight Station, somewhat nauseous from the incessant bumps. There was a large un-upholstered box structure behind the left-hand pilot's seat that could be sat on, and later I would find that it held the magnetron for the forward radar. I wondered if the jokes told by the AEO's about the electromagnetic radiation you would absorb from it had a degree of truth. The Orion's wing was not only short but relatively stiff, not ideal for absorbing the shocks of turbulence, and the aircraft bounced and lurched. The propeller tips thudded past the fuselage a few feet behind us, with waves of vibration through the structure as the automatic synchronisers minutely adjusted the propellers. The low moan of the turbines and the whir of equipment cooling fans came from further aft. While the noise and vibration gave the impression of a slow lumbering giant, the truth was that the Orion was cruising easily at 380 knots – or 700 km/hr. Its maximum specified speed was 405 knots – or 750 km/hr – which the aircraft could easily achieve in level flight, faster than any Macchi could fly in anything other than a dive. Folklore had it that the Orion's power would provide even greater speed and that the limitation was due to the strength of the windscreens in the case of a 'bird strike'. Now, the old Tracker's leisurely 130 knots – or 240 km/hr – patrol speed seemed positively snail-like. As the dull patchwork of off-white and tan below us slipped by deceptively quickly, it became apparent that I had much to learn about managing sixty tonnes of aircraft, its large crew and its complex systems. Moreover, as with the Tracker, I would have to become competent to 'fight' the P-3, this time as a fully-fledged RAAF 'Maritime Captain' anywhere on the planet, manoeuvring the airliner-sized machine in low, wrenching turns at just one hundred feet – barely thirty metres – from the water in sub-hunting patterns, or managing a flight cruising high at airliner levels between countries and continents.

There were hours of thorough and exacting training, including engine shutdowns, restarts, and simulated emergencies. Like all airliners, including the HS 748, the Electra-derived Orion was operated so that an engine failure could occur at that decision speed on take-off, 'V1', and the aircraft would continue to accelerate down the runway and still lift off and fly away. Especially if an outboard engine, Number One or Number Four failed (or was simulated failed), it was important to keep the aircraft tracking straight, and once again my left or right leg quivered on a rudder pedal as I strained to keep the machine tracking true. At heavy weights the ground run after the 'failure' seemed interminable but with the call 'rotate' by the other pilot at the given speed, the Orion would still lift ponderously into the air and fly away on three engines.

There was approach after approach by instruments into Edinburgh and, more interestingly, Adelaide International Airport. Adelaide had an ILS: an Instrument Landing System, that accurate system of crossed beams that would guide an aircraft down to just 200 feet, or just sixty metres, to land on the runway ahead. I dredged up the much-faded memories of the very few ILS approaches I had flown in the navy's HS 748 and we flew ILS after ILS, often with one or even two of the Orion's engines idling at 'zero thrust' – simulated failed. While the other trainee flew, I had time to take in the views of Adelaide, its north-south sprawl hemmed in to the east by the Mount Lofty range and further down the approach to the runway, the city buildings and the red-roofed houses that crowded so close to the airport boundary. Ahead stretched the runway with Glenelg beach at its far end, and then the horizon of the Gulf of St. Vincent, as sharp as a knife in the clear sky. As well as instrument approaches, we flew visual circuits back at Edinburgh: 'normal', simulated engine-failed; 'flapless' simulating a failure of the flap system that would have normally allowed a lower landing speed; and spectacular 'low level' circuits where we hurtled downwind in the airliner-sized machine, houses and roads slipping by only a hundred metres below. The standing joke was that the residents beneath must like aircraft, or had bought their cheap real estate over a weekend, when circuit flying at Edinburgh, particularly low-level ones, was rare.

We practised a 'windmill taxi start'. The Orion was a warplane and the U.S. Navy catered for all wartime contingencies, including being able to start one of the Allisons of a sorely needed maritime patrol aircraft that had its starter system failed. We accelerated down Edinburgh's runway with three engines at take-off power. Using a carefully coordinated drill, at a certain speed the flight engineer started the fourth engine by 'unfeathering' its propeller blades, which began to spin in the rush of air and, at the specified RPM, he introduced fuel and ignition to start the engine. Meanwhile, the pilots intently assessed the remaining runway available to stop in as the far end loomed. If all had been done correctly, the fourth engine would be 'winding up' just as the pilot carefully but firmly applied the brakes and full reverse thrust on the 'good' engines to bring the Orion to a shuddering stop in time. The aircraft could theoretically then taxi back to carry out a normal take-off on all four engines. The flight manual even contained a drill for using the hot jet and propeller blast from an Orion to start the disabled engine of a second P-3 in a similar manner, which would be parked behind the first, but this was not practised.

After mastering the flying of the aircraft, it was time to learn to operate it in its combat role. Much of the tactical training was at low-level over the sea, flying the anti-submarine patterns familiar from my Tracker flying, but the speed, size and complexity of the P-3 added new dimensions. We hauled the big machine around the patterns at one hundred feet – or thirty metres – for daylight operations and 300 feet on the radar altimeter at night. Often nauseous myself when not at the controls, I felt for the trainee 'back end' crewmen. As the aircraft bounced and jolted at low level with the g coming on during the steep turns they had to stand, unrestrained, to load sonobuoys into the chutes at the rear of the lurching, windowless cabin. Simultaneously there was the sulphurous smell of the sonobuoy launch charges and the periodic aroma of burnt copy-paper from the teleprinter as it automatically clattered out its reports. Use of sick-bags or hurried dashes back to the toilet were frequent by the 'back enders'.

One squally day we were flying these patterns at low-level over the Gulf of St. Vincent. While the Orion bumped and banked low over choppy sea under grey stratus cloud, the navigator came up over the intercom: 'Pilot and TACCO, we just got a message about a yacht in distress off Victor Harbour. We've been tasked to find it and shadow it as it tries to make port.'

'Roger, give us a fly-to point and an altitude so we can get there ASAP,' the instructor replied.

The TACCO inserted a 'fly-to' point into the system, a small green symbol displayed on the round monochrome display in the centre of the instrument panel, and I banked the Orion around to head towards it. Also, we began to climb.

Because the situation was urgent, the instructor and TACCO decided to fly to Victor Harbour at the lowest practical altitude.

'What's our Safety Height, Nav?' the instructing pilot asked.

The navigator responded with the altitude. Knowing the Safety Height was vital because a hilly peninsula of land lay between us and Victor Harbour on the coast to the south-east. Safety Height was ascertained from a map: the highest terrain or obstacle along the track of the aircraft was noted, and 1,000 feet – or about 300 metres – added to that figure in order to provide a safe clearance for the aircraft to overfly. I continued the climb to the navigator's altitude then accelerated the P-3, now jolting even more. We were blind in cloud and rain. All of us were re-thinking our new task: communications, fuel state, sensor use … I felt a twinge of excitement about being diverted from a routine training exercise to carry out a search and rescue.

But a little later, the instructor came up on the intercom: 'Nav, what was that Safety Height again?'

The navigator confirmed the figure.

Then the TACCO burst through: 'Christ, you need to climb NOW! The Nav hasn't added the safety margin. He's just given you the actual height of the terrain!'

The trainee navigator had made a dangerous error. Distracted and excited by the 're-task', the junior crew and the other trainees, along with myself, had taken the navigator's altitude for granted.

Clear of the land, we descended until clear of cloud over the Southern Ocean. No longer sheltered by Kangaroo Island to the south, a south-westerly gale whipped up white foam that almost obscured the roiling grey seawater. The Orion rocked and bounced even more, but then one of the observers scanning from one of the four oval windows spotted the yacht. I turned towards it until we saw it through the Flight Station windows. The boat was white-hulled, heeling with its mast broken and a scrap of sail set and, thankfully, it was being blown towards shore. We set up an 'orbit' above it and the instructor took over while I was given the task of managing communications: there were several helicopters approaching, Air Traffic Control had to be advised, and all that time, the Orion lurched and bucked in the gale over the furious white ocean under grey overcast. The flight engineer grabbed for a bag and vomited. I struggled to write call signs and frequencies on my note pad in the turbulence. For several hours we circled while the yacht was blown towards shore and its relative shelter, until finally a helicopter advised that it would take over and that our presence was no longer required.

In the quiet of the evening, with Yvonne and the baby sleeping, I reflected on the day's events. While having a sense of achievement after the safe arrival of the yacht into port, the Safety Height incident replayed in my head. I was no longer flying a Macchi, responsible for my own navigation, or in the intimate milieu of a Tracker crew, in the company of an experienced, trusty TACCO with his maps next to me, over open sea on carrier operations. The Orion flew to and from land. It had numbers of crew members directly involved with the safety of the aircraft, but they were remotely located back in an airliner-sized cabin. Fortunately, the experienced instructors had picked up the mistake. If they had not, our Orion could have come dangerously close to impacting terrain that day. Why did I not think of preparing and checking my own map?

Almost six months after beginning to fly the Orion, tactical training was nearly complete. I had been run through the anti-submarine tactics in day and night, weapons delivery profiles, Lindholme drops and the familiar drill of 'loitering' the engines. Patrol aircraft flew basically two profiles: either the best power and speed for 'range'; that is, covering a maximum distance for a minimum amount of fuel, or for 'endurance': staying in the same area for the maximum amount of time that fuel would permit. For endurance flying, high speed was not desirable, and with four powerful engines, an Orion crew could save significant amounts of fuel by shutting down one or even two of them, to enable the aircraft to 'loiter' in one area. But pilots are pessimists: they always consider the effects of a further failure. With one engine 'loitered', what if another one failed? Well, the Orion had so much power that two engines would safely keep the aircraft airborne. However, prudence would dictate that the 'good' loitered engine be started as soon as possible. So a comprehensive brief was given by the flight engineer, a memorised litany that detailed the actions that he would take to re-start a loitered engine should the need arise. With its impressive power, the pilots would barely notice the effect on performance with one engine shut down, just the changes in rudder trim with any speed or power variation. The Orion would be in its element, the huge blades of an outboard propeller feathered against the airstream for hour after hour while the aircraft circled and swooped and dashed from contact to contact, or between sonobuoys or smoke markers.

At lighter weights, the *two* outboard engines could be 'loitered' for maximum endurance. However, failure of one of the operating inboard power units would result in the Orion flying on one engine! Because of this, the lowest allowable altitude was 1,000 feet – or 300 metres – above the water, which would give just enough time for one of the loitered outboard engines to be started while the aircraft slowly descended towards the surface, the remaining running engine throbbing at full power. The flight engineer's brief for this was even more comprehensive, with no time for hesitation should an emergency restart be required.

Now the end of the course was in sight, which would be an international deployment. But first, our course group was to visit Nowra, as it was here that some theoretical anti-submarine training was to be carried out. A joint Anti-Submarine Warfare training school was still located there, despite the Fleet Air Arm being eviscerated by the Hawke government. The navy still had its Sea King ASW helicopters, and ASW was also a role of its frigates. Another Orion crew dropped us off at my old home. As the low hum of its Allisons receded to the west, the silence struck.

I had not been to Nowra for over three years, after my time at Pearce and Edinburgh. Now I was wearing an air force uniform, its blue colour and its cut cheap-looking. There was nothing flying. No shriek of a Skyhawk through 'initial' or the wheeze and howl of a Macchi's engine starting. No throb of helicopter blades or the growl of a Tracker flying the 'pattern'. However, the Skyhawks would soon come back to Nowra as Royal New Zealand Air Force aircraft, rented by the Australian taxpayer, to carry out the fleet support duties that, unsurprisingly, the RAAF had found it could not do. A few hundred metres away, the Trackers sat forlorn in rows out in the open with canvas covers flapping loose in the wind, tied down to concrete bollards to ensure that they would never again be airborne, even by accident in a gale. Later a solitary grey helicopter would start up, the 'whup-whup' of its rotors echoing around the almost empty tarmac and closed hangars.

The wardroom was almost deserted, apart from our course group.

Only a few of the navy faces there were familiar, and my assigned cabin smelt of mould. I sat through the tedious lectures and presentations, much of which was already familiar from my Tracker flying: but I was now air force, and their system could not make allowance for previous training. I drank and joined in the banter with our group in the wardroom at night, but I looked forward to going home to Adelaide and getting the training over with. This would be after I was deployed with my instructor and my course-mate to Cocos Island in the Indian Ocean, after which we would operate from RAAF Base Butterworth in Malaysia for a week. We would then fly to a U.S. Navy base on the island of Guam in the Pacific, make an overnight flight non-stop home to Edinburgh, and then training would be complete. The P-3C was a potent warplane and I now belonged to a service for which aircraft were its *raison d'etre*. I had a family and my own home at twenty-seven years of age. Providing that I kept out of trouble, I would be an Orion captain in a year or two, operating all over the world with my own crew. But through the time of this visit to Naval Air Station Nowra, a pathetic shadow of its former self, the memories flooded and the dismay and resentment at what had been done to our Fleet Air Arm burned raw.

I was sitting in the dinette near the rear of the Orion's cabin, almost at the tail, with just whiteness outside its two little round windows. We were in transit from Butterworth to Guam, a U.S. territory and island in the Pacific Ocean, east of the Philippines. We were crossing over the Philippine island of Luzon. The other student pilot was at the controls with the instructor in the Flight Station. Suddenly – 'thump! Whoomp!' The aircraft bucked, as if a giant had grasped it and waved it bodily up and down. My stomach rose and fell. Now, there was a juddering noise and the aircraft shook violently. I felt the tailplane vibrating just behind us – hell, this was pre-stall buffet! Equipment flew about the cabin and my heart raced. The buffet stopped and after one more lurch, the violence stopped as quickly as it had started, and the whiteness in the window had flicked away. Now there was blue, but there was also blue liquid from the toilet spread over the floor, and food and gear everywhere.

The instructor's voice rasped over the PA system calling for a damage report. With the pilots blind in layered cloud, the radar operators had not picked up an embedded cumulonimbus cloud ahead and the Orion had blundered into it at 380 knots – or 700 km/hr – the cloud's first massive downdraft flinging the aircraft down, then the central updraft reversing the forces on the machine, and another reverse when the P-3 hit the downdraft on the other side. Even at cruising speed, the storm cloud's vertical currents had disrupted the airflow around the Orion's stubby, stiff wing and almost caused it to stall. Shaken, I helped clean up. I had never experienced anything like it, and even from the rear of a big aeroplane, a lesson had been reinforced: cumulonimbus clouds are deadly monsters and man's flying machines are insignificant against their violence. I had heard and read the stories of aircraft penetrating storm clouds, never to emerge from the other side in one piece, flung about and then broken up, and now, that could have happened to us had the cloud been more violent.

Sharp words passed over the intercom between the instructor and the radar operator. The upper reaches of most of these storm clouds are just ice crystals, which show up on a radar screen poorly, if at all. The operator should have been 'tilting' the radar's antenna down as it scanned back and forth, in order to pick up the tell-tale 'return' on his screen of the liquid water droplets in the warmer, lower reaches of the thunderstorm. I contemplated the incident for the rest of the flight. With no cockpit radar display, relying on a non-pilot down the back of the aircraft for weather avoidance had its challenges. The Orion had nearly stalled, blind, kilometres above the earth in thin air and bad weather, in the violence of the encounter. The short duration of the turbulence had been fortuitous, with the aircraft popping out the other side of the cloud, back under control, but its crew shaken. This and the safety height incident reinforced the importance of being aware of the limitations of relying entirely on other crew: check, cross-check, and question everything.

Our Orion had travelled from Edinburgh to familiar ground at Pearce. Then, we went on to Cocos Island, lonely in the Indian Ocean. From there we had flown in to Butterworth, which was a joint RAAF-Royal Malaysian Air Force base on the Malayan Peninsula's west coast, opposite Penang Island. A 2,700 feet – or 833 metres – peak dominated the island, which would be invisible in the usual afternoon cloud or thunderstorm. It glowered over the water only a few kilometres west of the base, and we were ever-aware of its presence. We carried out our first surveillance exercise: a transit westwards from Butterworth at the Orion's normal cruising level to the area of interest before turning around and dropping to the optimum radar search height of 1,500 feet – or 460 metres. Like a grey and white airborne shark, we patrolled at this low altitude with one engine 'loitered', on the long route back towards Butterworth. The radar operator and his trainees called any 'contact', towards which we would smartly bank the big machine until 'visual', usually called by the flight engineer who faced forwards, peering through binoculars, behind and between the pilots. Most of the ships were called as 'no interest', in which case we turned back towards our planned track. Any contacts of interest, primarily Soviet and Chinese merchant ships – more so, any military vessels – were photographed. We ran close abeam the targets at low-level, the whine and click of the motor drive of the camera held by a navigator or AEO audible behind us as he photographed the vessel through the special round optically flat window. I had carried out these 'rigging runs' many times in Trackers with the TACCO snapping away through his side bubble. However, in this heavier, faster aircraft, manoeuvring at low-level during these runs had to be done with more planning and care. For hour after hour, we meandered along our track. Careful to avoid the mountain on Penang Island, we landed after this first epic ten-hour patrol. The following day was a training exercise where we flew from

Butterworth to Singapore to inure us to the system of airways and the unstable tropical weather, with several instrument approaches at airports along the way. It was a far cry from the relatively simple 'blue water' operations from HMAS *Melbourne*, where we rarely had to consider foreign air traffic control, extremely high terrain and tropical thunderstorms.

Several crews from the operational Orion squadrons were stationed at Butterworth, rotated through for 'detachments' of several weeks. I found that they also worked hard and played hard. After the transit to Guam came the overnight flight direct to Edinburgh from the remote Pacific island. Eyes stinging, I walked into our house in a cold, grey dawn. But at last, training was complete. Soon I would join an operational crew on Number 10 Squadron.

Ian was a tall, rangy Maritime Captain, quietly spoken but authoritative. Now on 10 Squadron, I was his new co-pilot, but we shared the flying equally: I was in the left seat as 'flying pilot'; while Ian, who was 'right seat checked' as captain, carried out co-pilot duties but could also operate the aircraft from that seat. 10 Squadron RAAF had a proud history dating back to World War II, when it operated the famous Sunderland flying boats from a base in the United Kingdom. Its role had been to patrol for and sink German U-boats, and to escort Allied convoys. Now, the squadron had a deep sense of history and considered itself superior to the other operational Orion squadron, Number 11, also based at Edinburgh, in the manner of high-morale military units the world over, who regard similar 'outfits' as their inferiors.

After a few training exercises, our crew were off by way of Kwajalein Atoll in the Pacific to a U.S. Navy base, Barber's Point in Hawaii, along with another P-3. At last, we were to 'play with the big boys' in an anti-submarine exercise. At Barber's Point it was ironic to see Orions with 'NAVY' emblazoned on their fuselages: the aircraft had been designed for that service, not an air force. I had settled into the routine of the preliminary exercises, then the long, long ocean transits high up, weaving between the thunderheads, with occasional procedural talk and banter over the intercom. We would land, with our bodies seeming to still be buzzing after hours of the beat of the propellers. That was alleviated by quantities of American beer in their Officers' Clubs. I discovered that an operational Orion crew could be an instant party: a van would be made available to us by the accommodating Americans, and there was sometimes a day free between long transits or exercises.

Operationally, we found the Americans disappointing with the tasks that they allotted us, so our Flight Commander arranged a further transit to the Canadian base of Comox, on the east coast of Vancouver Island. I had never been to North America. The vast coniferous forests and snow-capped mountain chains were wondrous after flat, red-brown and olive-green Australia and damp, palmed tropics. The Canadians were more accommodating with their tasking, and for the first time, I participated in a high-altitude surveillance operation, the Orion's interior almost bearably quiet as we sat monitoring our dropped sonobuoys with both of the outboard Allisons shut down: there was only the subdued whistle and hum of the two running engines and the whirr of the cooling fans of the electronics. The aircraft slouched in clear, smooth air over a marbled blue North Pacific. We listened for Soviet submarines but found no trace of one; however, the 'Cold War' feel of the operation, to me, was a highlight of the deployment. A few days later, it was back to Hawaii and a party after arrival with Americans who always seemed to be so loud when relaxing, but we got caught up in the mood: officers in uniform plunging into a hot tub; a woman shouting in her American accent, 'You Aussies sure can party hearty!'; cartons of Australian wine, carried all the way on a special pannier in the Orion's torpedo bay being shared out; and performing our squadron song:

'The sexual life of the camel,
is stranger than anyone thinks
At the height of the mating season,
he tries to bugger the Sphinx
But the Sphinx's posterior passage,
 is blocked by the sands of the Nile
Which accounts for the hump on the camel,
And the Sphinx's inscrutable smile.

Ten Squadron ever, Ten Squadron ever more!
A submarine we have never seen,
And we'll be sober no more ...'

An introspective day followed in preparation for our long flight home to Adelaide via Kwajalein Atoll and Townsville, Queensland. Despite my naval background, the deployment across the vast Pacific had been a new experience and a classic work hard, play hard military operation.

Captain Ian was nice to fly with, quiet and competent, and he shared the flying equally. I had flown navy Trackers, I was a Macchi QFI, had completed the Orion conversion and thought I knew it all, but there was still much to learn about the operational Orion flying. I absorbed how Ian, still a lowly flying officer in rank, handled the aircraft, the crew and the multitude of administrative considerations that came up. Running a four-man Tracker crew that operated just a few hundred miles from all the facilities of an aircraft carrier was one thing, but the large crew in the Orion – co-pilot, two flight engineers, sometimes a spare pilot, navigator, TACCO and the numbers of sensor operators – would require quiet, competent authority, especially as a lone crew on the other side of the planet, far from its operational control in South Australia.

After some more exercises from Edinburgh, we were set to deploy to Butterworth, Malaysia, as part of Operation Gateway. If I thought that the Pacific deployment had been a case of 'work hard, play hard', the Butterworth detachment, over a month long, would make the Pacific operation seem like a school excursion.

We were gathered around a battered piano in the Officers' Mess at Butterworth, in Malaysia. We sang to the tune of 'Waltzing Matilda':

> 'Once a jolly trishaw driver camped by a "monnie" drain
> Under the shade of a Durian tree,
> And he sang as he sat and spat into that monnie drain,
> You'll come a-riding a trishaw with me.

Then came the chorus:

> 'Riding a trishaw, riding a trishaw
> You'll come a-riding a trishaw, with me
> And he sang as he sat and spat into that monnie drain,
> you'll come a-riding a trishaw with me.

> 'Down came a gecko to drink at the monnie drain,
> Up jumped the trishaw driver, who grabbed him with glee,
> and he sang as he stuffed that gecko in his makan bag,
> you'll come a-riding a trishaw with me.

[Chorus]

> 'Down came the constable, mounted on his bicycle,
> Up jumped the church police, satu, dua, tiga!
> "Where's that jolly gecko you've got in your makan bag?
> you'll come a-riding a trishaw with me".

[Chorus]

> 'Up jumped the trishaw driver, and sprang into the monnie drain,
> "You'll never take me alive," said he,
> And his ghost may be smelt as you pass by that monnie drain ...
> You'll come a-riding a trishaw with me ...'

Trishaws were three-wheeled pedal-powered taxis that were a common form of transport in South-East Asia. A 'monnie drain' was a deep monsoon (storm water) ditch. These drains lined most of the streets in Penang Town (George Town), and the drains were renowned for their mud and smell. The Durian tree bore a pungent-smelling fruit, a delicacy in much of Asia. *Makan* was food. The Islamic 'religious' or 'church' police, as we called them, regulated the moral behaviour of the Muslim population in Malaysia.

Our crew was very fortunate in that, not only was one of our AEOs a teetotaller, but he also played the piano. Inevitably, he also wound up driving the van allotted to our crew. Gathered around the piano with mugs of 'Tiger' beer in hand, the officers of our crew and the others sang 'The Trishaw Song' among other, some unprintable, ditties. But we would stay on the base this evening: there would be no 'traps run' to Penang tonight, and despite the beer and song, we had a relatively early night in preparation for a long day tomorrow. Our crew had been on a 'traps run' the night before: it started with a rattling, fuming local bus, then a ferry to Penang town, and then into a bar that was both a ritual and an uncanny experience.

The Hong Kong Bar was the invariable meeting point in Penang Town for the Orion crews. The bar was run by cheerful Malaysian ethnic Chinese people who, when a European customer or group walked in, whipped out a Polaroid camera and took a snapshot. Rows of photo albums lined the shelves in the Hong Kong Bar, and it was easy to look up any previous visit in the meticulously labelled volumes, some of which were dated years before. The barmaid always asked, 'What crew you on?' if she suspected that one of us was in the air force, because each Orion squadron was organised into set numbered 'crews'. I often wondered who else would be perusing these albums with their photographs and crew details after-hours in the Hong Kong Bar, and whether if I were in charge of the detachment, I would have put it 'off limits'. RAAF personnel were not the only regulars. The Australian Army also operated at a base near Butterworth, and invariably there would be a group of very young Australian soldiers in various degrees of drunkenness and, also invariably, the juke box would be playing one of two songs: 'Khe Sanh' by Cold Chisel or 'I

Was Only 19 (A Walk in the Light Green)' by Redgum. The two songs alternated with little else played on the blaring jukebox.

For us, the Hong Kong Bar was merely the starting point before we all jumped into the trishaws waiting outside for us to head off for a meal served on a stainless steel table outdoors, washed down with lots of Tiger or Bintang beer, while the trishaw drivers obligingly waited. At the end of the evening, some aircrew would tell the trishaw men to climb into the backs of their own taxis, where they lolled and grinned, while Australian airmen pedalled them in races against others back to the ferry.

We had already been flying for hours, having been woken very early in the morning. I had slept fitfully in the bare, windowless room that four of us shared at Butterworth, alternately broiling and freezing from the lone cranky, rattling air-conditioner. We could make out the south coast of the teardrop of Sri Lanka, green in the early dawn, as we descended back towards the sunrise on a long, low-level patrol inbound towards Sumatra and the Malay Peninsula. The Orion dropped to the standard radar search height of 1,500 feet – or 450 metres – from the water. With one engine loitered, we would cruise the 'iron highway': the endless line of ships that steamed between the 'bottom' of Sri Lanka and the 'top' of Sumatra, where they would turn south-east to sail down the 'slot' between Sumatra and the Malay Peninsula for Singapore, or onwards to enter the South China Sea. This route was familiar from the training sortie I had flown as a student, and once again we cruised like a shark about a reef, turning this way and that towards the 'contacts' called by the radar operator. A flight engineer scanned ahead through the flat central pane of the Orion's windscreen with his stabilised binoculars: if he called 'No interest', we turned back towards track.

If the engineer called 'Chicom' – a Chinese Communist cargo vessel, its red star prominent on the funnel – or 'Soviet' – a freighter with its hammer and sickle – we continued toward it and dropped down to photograph it in the now-familiar 'rigging run'. Hour after hour, Ian and I took turns manipulating the big aircraft at low-level, snaking between the various contacts and muscling the aircraft around and down for the photography runs, then up again. Of most interest were any military vessels, rare but important, and we manoeuvred around these vessels with great care. We had to respect the Rules of Engagement, which were laid-down distances and procedures that had to be applied in order to avoid international incidents. Later, the showers and thunderstorms would build, and we would weave between those. At low altitude, we could usually fly visually between the shafts of rain and occasional lightning bolts that lanced down towards the grey oily sea. When we were blind in heavy rain, the radar operator, metres behind in the cabin, tried to steer us through the worst of the weather.

After eight or nine hours airborne, we entered the 'slot' between Sumatra and the Malay Peninsula, and headed south-east towards Penang Island and Butterworth, always aware of the terrain inland from each coast and the 800-metre high mountain of Penang Island that lurked near our base. The lesson of the Adelaide terrain incident was still with me. The 'back enders' welcomed the surge of power after we started the Orion's Number One engine that had been shut down for hours. Wrung-out, there was no 'run' into Penang that evening; beer and local food at the nearby boat club would be more than sufficient. We would all meet at the Hong Kong Bar the following night. Then after more Gateway missions and having completed a month on the 'Det', we headed south east through Darwin, and back to families and homes.

At the beginning of 1986, my time on the operational 10 Squadron had totalled six months, and that would be all. With my previous instructional experience, I was given a hurried 'Maritime Captaincy' qualification then an instructing revalidation by Central Flying School, and now I was an instructor again: on 292 Squadron, the Orion training unit where I had been a student myself just six months previously.

292 was not like a typical squadron. It did not operate its own aircraft: it took what was available from the pool of 10 and 11 Squadron Orions. A constant flow of trainee pilots, flight engineers, navigators, TACCOs and sensor operators streamed through the unit. 292 was sometimes derisively called 'The Cockroach Farm' by the operational crews because of the milling masses of trainees that would stream in and out of their P-3, along with the instructors, themselves a large number because of the various specialisations. The squadron's Commanding Officer was a navigator, with the senior pilot of 292 Squadron being my Flight Commander. However, the pilot instructor colleagues were familiar friends, including Al, with whom I had instructed at Pearce.

However, instructing at 292 Squadron was unlike the routine at 2 FTS. There was no daily Flying Programme with its constant two, three or sometimes four flights per day with the several students assigned to me. I was assigned my first two students, fresh from pilots' course. I put six months of my life into just these two individuals. Unlike at Pearce, the QFI also ran the students' ground school on systems and procedures in conjunction with the flight engineer instructors. He then trained his students in the flight simulator before their introduction to the aircraft, as I had been just one year earlier. After the comprehensive training in flying and operating the Orion, the instructor took his two students on the end-of-course deployment to Butterworth, the students were then assigned as co-pilots on an operational squadron.

There was other flying apart from the pilot training: specialised flights to train flight engineers and 'back enders'. The training area was south of Kangaroo Island and on most days, flawless blue seas and skies were the norm. Hour after hour we hauled the big machine around the various patterns: radar searches, sonobuoy drops, MAD traps and the occasional Harpoon profile, where we skimmed the sea before hauling the Orion up into the sky in the 'pop up' manoeuvre. When we turned, I could glance out and down at the huge propellers, sunlight dancing on the silver blades as blue sea and whitecaps slid beneath them. The props made more of a purr at low-level rather than the thudding buzz of the high altitude transits. It was demanding work with a young student in the left seat as I carefully monitored his height control and bank angle over the water in such a big aeroplane. I found my first two students a challenge: one had flown extensively in General Aviation as a civilian prior to joining the air force and felt that he knew it all. The other lad plodded along, but was to leave the air force soon after his training. There were occasional 'airline style' flights where personnel had to be delivered to various bases around Australia, which I relished. There were night ASW exercises, with my concentration heightened even more, and of course the awareness of the terrain that would lie between the ocean and our base, from where I would arrive home in the early hours of the morning to a sleeping family.

Along with the trainee 'back enders' I took the two students on the standard end of course deployment that included a 'Gateway' patrol and other exercises, a challenge for me because they were to do most of the flying, while, apart from supervising them and being in command of the entire crew, I was the 'super co-pilot', communicating with Air Traffic Control. This was particularly difficult around Malaysia, where we entered and left 'controlled airspace' several times during our missions. Clearances had to be negotiated over crackly High Frequency radio with an operator on the other end, where English was not his first language. Thunderstorms and high terrain had to always be considered and I never really relaxed in Malaysian airspace until past the Philippines en route to Guam, where it was a straight high-level transit, followed by a relaxing day off at the U.S. Naval Air Station Agana. Agana sat on the rocky island that was almost totally covered in low but impenetrable tropical growth. The following night I was awake throughout the long flight home that passed over the high terrain of New Guinea. I looked out for thunderstorms as I monitored the students through the night

I was about to turn twenty-nine, and I was climbing the seniority ladder as a flight lieutenant. On this large operational base, there were many pilots, their pewter-coloured wings large on their uniform shirts, who did not fly: they sat deskbound in offices and operations centres. I knew that the possibility of a 'ground job' was looming towards the end of my second year on 292 Squadron, and even more so should I ever become promoted to the rank of squadron leader. Even the squadron leaders on the flying units seemed to be mired in paperwork and rarely flew. Some of the navigators and AEOs, the majority of officers on the squadron, were difficult to deal with, and I did not get on particularly well with my own Flight Commander, who was a pilot. I had found my first student Orion pilots hard going at times. I was never really comfortable in Butterworth and Malaysia in general. And the air force was notorious for posting their people away every two years. Having just established a house and with a young child, a move was inevitable for us later, if not sooner.

I had always wanted to settle in Victoria. Also, it seemed that every other day I heard of yet another air force pilot resigning to join Qantas or Australian Airlines. Al had been posted to one of the operational squadrons. His replacement was an easy-going, dry-witted instructor with whom it was a pleasure to share an office, but now it was an office that I rarely seemed to get out of, even with syllabus training and instructional flights. But an airline pilot did nothing but fly, his medical condition permitting, into his fifties. The Australian military retirement package was poor compared to those of the airlines, unless you were able to stick it out for twenty years. If I joined Australian Airlines, or even Ansett Airlines, I could live in Victoria. With Sydney-based Qantas, 'staff travel' was available cheaply, and with them I might even fly the mighty Boeing 747. I could even live in or near Nowra if I wanted! There was also a trickle of pilots joining Cathay Pacific Airways, based in Hong Kong, whose pay cheques and bonuses were legendary. It was time to start working on a civilian Senior Commercial Pilot's Licence. I also wrote to some airlines and waited to see what transpired.

Between tasks at Edinburgh, I plunged back into the books. Although my military experience qualified me for a basic civilian Commercial Pilot's Licence, the airlines would require 'Senior Commercial' subjects, which were more appropriate to large jet aircraft. This required detailed knowledge of flight planning, meteorology, radio-navigation aids and other subjects. The work was reminiscent of my teenage days of study, but with the added requirements of a family and, of course, work and the occasional deployments away with 292 Squadron. Motivation and a purchased correspondence course got me through, along with exercise after exercise, flash cards, past papers, carefully presented workings, endless summaries ... The Flight Planning examination was particularly demanding, requiring 'first approximations' from tables to achieve a second accurate figure for the fuel burn of a mythical jet transport, with distances and times, and emergency diversion calculations. In those times, the exam was not multiple-choice. I had to write narrative answers, and all workings and diagrams were scrupulously checked by the marker. I found it tough, but I scraped through.

The journey seemed endless. I was on an overnight bus that was traversing the 1,300 kilometres from Sydney to Adelaide. My Flight Commander had refused to grant me the following day off after my first-ever airline interview, which had been in Sydney, (though, soon enough he would be off to join an airline himself). With no flights leaving Sydney to allow me to get to the base at 0800 the next day for duty, the overnight bus was the only option. While it rumbled and whined through the night, the interview I had attended in a Sydney hotel room that morning replayed in my brain.

With my fresh Senior Commercial Pilot's Licence, I had sent my CV to Qantas, Australian Airlines (the government-owned domestic carrier), and Ansett Airlines. In addition, a friend and fellow instructor from Pearce, Steve Nelson, urged me to also apply to Cathay Pacific Airways Limited in Hong Kong. Unlike Steve, I had misgivings about moving my family to Asia. Also, Cathay's standards were notoriously high, and they would require a civilian Instrument Rating before joining, which I did not have. But I wrote to them anyway. Surprisingly, they responded immediately and the interview I had just attended had been with a white-haired, plummy-accented Cathay Pacific management captain.

It had not gone particularly well. I was stuffed up with a cold, and some of the captain's questions were obscure and vague, even patronising, though I had tried to prepare for what I thought I would be asked.

Later, the letter arrived: 'We are unable to offer you a second interview at this stage, however, we encourage you to apply again in another twelve months.'

It felt reminiscent of my first attempt to join the Fleet Air Arm! However, there were other pebbles on the beach: Australia's two domestic airlines and Qantas, who were all recruiting. Anyway, I had experienced enough of Asia during my naval and Orion flying.

Soon, an invitation arrived from Qantas for an interview.

It was now May, 1987. Here I was, at the beginning of another end-of-course deployment with my two students and, of course, the plethora of back-end instructors and their protégés. However, there was a different atmosphere about this one. I had just completed an interview with Qantas. It had gone well after I had prepared assiduously for the simulator exercises and questions. I was confident in front of the selection board, even in a new cheap suit, and especially because I now had experience in long-range flying as an Orion captain. I went through a medical examination and a flying assessment in a light twin-engine aircraft from Sydney's Bankstown Airport. The laconic Qantas pilot who assessed me had not said much, but I had made no major errors in flying the unfamiliar little aircraft under his supervision. I also had to fly the Qantas flight simulator, that of the Boeing 747, but with most of its panels covered to leave just basic flight instruments in view. The Jumbo felt surprisingly light, but stable, and I managed to carry out the basic manoeuvres that the assessing captain asked for. An engine 'caught fire' and I applied common sense, asking for the fuel to be cut off and its fire extinguisher to be operated. Carefully, I flew a three-engine approach, but then I was directed to 'go around' off the approach without landing. The captain 'repositioned' the simulated aircraft on an approach again and said, 'OK, just go ahead and land.' I heard an audible relieved outflow of breath from him after I asked for the landing gear to be extended. I had heard horror stories of failures at this stage of the selection process where candidates had 'landed' the simulator with the wheels still retracted.

After the Qantas interview process, there was something exciting in the air. I couldn't put my finger on it, but I went on this deployment with an inkling that this would be my last. Normally serious and sometimes a little 'tense' on these trips, I departed with my crew, relatively relaxed and full of anticipation.

Unusually, we had a young Administrative Officer along for the ride, who was very keen and could not do enough for us. He, instead of myself and the other instructors, would be instrumental in organising meals, accommodation, allowances, and other minutiae. My two students were excellent both in attitude and flying ability (they would later leave the RAAF to join airlines). Another crew deployed with us in a second Orion, whose pilot instructor was 'Monty', another friend from Pearce. Monty was British, ex-Royal Air Force, who had transferred to Australia's service, and he regaled us with tales of flying the Avro Shackleton and other 'full of character'

British aircraft, and life on the British bases in Europe and the Middle East. Monty thought outside the box, and this time he suggested that we reverse the time-honoured ritual of Edinburgh-Pearce-Cocos Island-Butterworth-Guam-Edinburgh. Therefore, the first leg of our journey was from Adelaide to Guam.

As usual, we landed and were accommodated at Agana, the U.S. Naval Air Station. Like the previous visits on our rest days, our crew drove in the ubiquitous van to the huge U.S. Air Force base, Andersen, which also sat on the island. The magnet for us was the base 'PX', a huge canteen the size of a department store. It sold just about anything at tax-free prices, and was even more attractive with the high Australian dollar of the day. Outside Andersen AFB sat its 'gate guardian'. At most bases, this was a small fighter or perhaps a medium-sized aircraft. But Andersen's gate guardian was an enormous Boeing B-52 eight-engine bomber.

At Andersen I never tired of watching the B-52s lift off, trailing black smoke and thunderous noise, seemingly levitating skywards, their fuselages level because of their unusual tandem main landing gear under their bellies, the wings set at a higher 'angle of incidence' to the main body of the aircraft. But now we were in the PX, snapping up anything from vinyl records (CDs were only just entering the market) to kettle-type barbecues, to be lashed down in the Orion's empty torpedo bay. A U.S. serviceman's child laughed uproariously at our Aussie accents. Then came the noise I will never forget. On the vast American air force base, the sound would have heralded the beginning of a thermonuclear war. It was the alert siren. 'Siren' is probably the wrong word. The sound was a continuous, unmodulated ear-splitting raucous, throaty roar. Personnel in the building dropped everything and rushed out, including those clad in olive-green flight suits. We followed to watch military police cars prowl with their muted sirens growling, while other vehicles dashed to various buildings, flashing lights everywhere. Nuclear-capable B-52 bombers were based here, and 'Alert' crews were always ready to launch in response to a Soviet attack. After some minutes the noise stopped and, with no subsequent smoke and rumble of a fleet of eight-engine bombers starting up, we assumed that this had been one of the base's innumerable drills.

I couldn't help but say to our group, 'Fellas, we've just heard what the end of the world will sound like.' I thought of Shute's *On The Beach*.

Later, we landed at the familiar Butterworth, Malaysia, where we discovered segregated areas in the Officers' Mess for the Muslim Malaysian officers (Malaysia is a mixed-race nation of predominantly indigenous Muslim Malays, but with a sizable proportion of ethnic Chinese and Indians). We drank with the Chinese and Indian officers, who to a man were planning on leaving their air force. 'Low Initials' (low passes into the circuit) had now been restricted due to demands from the mosque just outside the base. Butterworth, once a bustling joint RAF/RAAF establishment, was now becoming 'localised', with noticeably less traffic. A highlight of our patrol from there would be the detection and photographing of a Soviet *Kara* class cruiser, grey and bristling with guns, missile tubes and exotic-looking antennae, and we were careful to follow the Rules of Engagement with regards to distance from the vessel and the number of 'passes' we could make. It was the first Russian combat unit I had encountered. I caught a fleeting glimpse of the sailors, staring at us, but one of them waggled his buttocks at us as the impressive grey and white Orion with kangaroo markings flashed past them just a few hundred metres away. And no doubt we were being photographed as thoroughly as their cruiser was being imaged.

Our Butterworth task had now ended, and Monty had added another change to the training flight routine – we would transit home via the Indian Ocean's Christmas Island, not Cocos. We landed there from a conservative approach to the island's runway that sat high on a plateau. Birds were everywhere, so there was no 'low initial' this time due to the risk of a damaging 'bird strike'. While Cocos is a typical coral atoll, low in the ocean around a lagoon, with coral sand beaches and palms, Christmas Island is a rocky block that juts from the Indian Ocean with few beaches. It is relatively close to Indonesia, and is hot and very tropical. The locals were hospitable. Orion visits were relatively rare and they took us on a tour of the island's interior: variously a moonscape of rocky pillars left from the mining of phosphate (huge amounts of guano that had accumulated over the centuries) or jungle that was bizarrely totally free of leaf litter due to the voracious millions of red land crabs. We then patrolled in to Learmonth, Western Australia, where we gorged on the local prawns. At last, we set course for Edinburgh and our families. For me, there were two weeks of leave to take.

My wife was expecting again, and the three of us stayed in quiet army holiday accommodation: little cabins near the mouth of the Murray River at Goolwa, South Australia. I drove home, relaxed, actually looking forward to going back to work. But, in our little house in Para Hills, the telephone shrilled not long after we walked in the door. It was one of our flight engineers at the Squadron.

'Mark, we've been trying to get hold of you for days! We took two messages for you, one to call someone from Qantas.' This would be the news of success or failure! 'And the other message is that there's a lady from Ansett Airlines who wants to speak to you. They couldn't get you at home, so they called the Squadron.'

I stood, open-mouthed, for a second. Somehow, staff from two airlines had tracked down my office at a military base, in the days when mobile phones were non-existent and even answering machines were rare.

'Thanks, Mick, I'll get straight back to them. I really appreciate your help.'

I called the gentleman from Qantas. He told me that I had been successful with my application, and he obligingly gave me a start date of three months' time (the air force required three months' notice). I sat, dazed, for a few minutes, then made the second call to the lady from Ansett Airlines, my mind racing. Ansett had been far from my thoughts with the overshadowing considerations about Qantas. It was also folklore that Ansett took few military pilots, in contrast to its government-owned domestic counterpart, Australian Airlines, that had been re-invented from the old TAA. But I had just been invited to an interview in Melbourne with Ansett.

Now that an airline career could be a reality, I lay awake that night, my thoughts churning. I loved the military. I had just been notified of my forthcoming promotion to squadron leader rank at the age of twenty-nine. But then I visualised myself as a desk-bound squadron leader and, later, a wing commander, my trousers polishing an office chair in the 'Grey Sponge': Russell Offices, in Canberra ... A new posting every two years, with two children and their schooling to consider ... One more flying job if I was lucky ... But, then there had been rumours of 'specialist aircrew', where one could fly with the air force permanently but with limited promotion prospects. I would have leapt at it. But these were only rumours.

However, now I could be a Qantas pilot flying 'wide bodied' jets internationally, no desk jobs, a good salary ... On the other hand, there would be a lot of time in expensive Sydney, the airline's base, where most of its training was done. I would join as a second officer, the third pilot in the hierarchy of the Qantas flight deck, but that would be on the Boeing 747 or 767, flying internationally. It would be several years before I would be a first officer (co-pilot). A second officer was just a 'seat warmer' for the other pilots while they rested during the cruise. I would not take-off or land the aircraft until I was a first officer. I had worked hard to be in the position of being offered a job with an international airline. But now that it was a reality, I had to be absolutely, positively sure that I was doing the right thing for my family and myself. In the morning, red-eyed and groggy, but with my brain still racing, I called a senior officer at Edinburgh and told him that I would be submitting my resignation from the Royal Australian Air Force. The wing commander had flown with us on a previous training deployment, and he had been congenial and supportive. And even with this news there was no rancour or snide comment.

'OK, Mark, I was just working on a posting for you. I won't bother now. Thanks for letting me know.'

The Rubicon had been crossed.

The forthcoming position with Qantas overshadowed everything. I had submitted my three months' notice of resignation, and I had also managed to get time off to attend the interview with Ansett Airlines, which would be in Melbourne, the airline's base. The Ansett assessment process, held over two days, was far simpler than that of Qantas. I produced my logbook and answered questions in front of a selection panel. I told them I had already resigned from the air force and had a job offer from Qantas, which raised eyebrows. One of the interviewing captains remembered my father from his monthly visits to the airline's headquarters to see Sir Reginald and other executives regarding the Mornington Racing Club (Sir Reg had now long retired). Then there were the psychometric and aptitude tests, but far simpler than Qantas's tests with their larger recruiting organisation. The next day was the flying assessment. There would be no light twin flying, but there would be an exercise in a flight simulator.

While I flew the Ansett flight simulator for the Boeing 727 tri-jet airliner, the assessor, Captain Ed Field, was courteous and helpful as he talked me through what was expected. His manner was reassuring and friendly. I flew the simulator as accurately as I could and handled a few basic 'emergencies'. We chatted after the exercise and Ed showed interest in my military experience. We shook hands, and soon I was on the short flight home to Adelaide. But my head was still full of Qantas, and Ansett rarely took military pilots, didn't they? The prospect of flying for Ansett, Melbourne-based and straightaway a first officer rather than a 'dogsbody' second officer with Qantas, seemed too good to be true.

To use a worn cliché, you could have cut the air with a knife. I had called the Qantas Recruiting number and, coincidentally, the same chap who had cheerily offered me a job with them had answered. I told him that I would not be joining Qantas and that I was going to fly for Ansett. There was silence for a few seconds. It was almost unheard-of for any pilot to refuse a job with Australia's international carrier. He brusquely acknowledged the news, and hung up. But I was delighted. I could live anywhere around Melbourne and there would be family support for my wife and soon-to-be two children. Houses were far cheaper in Melbourne than in Sydney. I was joining as a first officer on the famous Fokker Friendship twin turboprop airliner. OK, the Friendship was old, but eventually I would move on to fly the Boeing 727 or 737 and later, Ansett's wide-bodied 767. I threw myself into preparations for civilian life and planning for our move to Melbourne. We decided that Yvonne and Avalon would remain in Adelaide while I was training with Ansett, and then we would decide where to go from there.

Ansett! I would not have thought I would end up flying for them while growing up on the Mornington Peninsula, with Sir Reg visiting the racecourse weekly and that visit from Cal, his helicopter pilot. Also, domestic pilots could fly until sixty years old, in contrast to the then limit of fifty-five for international flying with Qantas. Melbourne Airport would be my base after fond memories of visits as a child and teenager. I remembered the scream and buzz of the Fokkers, powered by Rolls Royce Darts just like the HS 748, which serviced Wagga Wagga, after the DC-3s were retired. Already, I felt a bond with the famous old airline, started by one man with one aircraft, and I looked to the future with great anticipation.

Weeks later, I clattered down the steps of the crew ladder that was unfolded from the Orion's doorway with an experienced Orion pilot, who I had been refresher-training. As we walked towards the tarmac office, figures suddenly appeared, dragging a hose. The other pilot departed the scene rapidly as a jet of water saturated me: I was being 'hosed down' as was tradition at the end of a 'last flight'. Then we drank beer, right there on the tarmac. There were a few days of administrative 'clearances' until the Friday afternoon, where a large group was gathered in a big suburban Adelaide tavern. Earlier, I had taken off a military uniform for the last time, after twelve years of service with the navy and the air force. There were always personnel being posted away from this large base, and a combined farewell had been arranged. At the time, pilots were leaving the air force in numbers, mainly to join Qantas and Australian Airlines, and my departure was not considered momentous. My brief farewell speech was merely a lame joke about an airline pilot. I didn't drink much or stay long: soon I left for home, and that was it.

Tomorrow morning, Saturday, I would wake up as a 'civvie', and that would also be the last day with my family for some time. On Sunday, I would drive to Victoria to stay with my paternal grandmother in Bacchus Marsh, west of Melbourne, ready to report to the Ansett Airlines training centre at Melbourne Airport first thing on Monday. My wife's mother had kindly travelled from Victoria to Adelaide in order to help Yvonne while I was away. I would leave my heavily pregnant wife and Avalon in Adelaide while I studied and worked for months yet again, not just to master yet another aircraft, but a completely different world of aviation. But, if I made the grade, I could live in Victoria and, above all, *fly* for the rest of my working life, an Ansett pilot!

1 3

THE DUTCH WHEELBARROW

1 9 8 7 – 1 9 8 8

Waal … ya gotta like chicken.

The response from a grizzled American airline captain being interviewed on a global news network when asked: 'What advice would you give to a young aspiring airline pilot?'

In 1987 I sat with the other pilots of my Ansett Airlines 'intake' on a Monday morning, having left my family behind in Adelaide. Being 'at work' in civilian clothes, not uniform, felt odd. We introduced ourselves while we waited for the first instructor or management representative to enter. I was the only ex-military pilot. The others were a mixed bunch, most of them with 'outback' flying experience. Some had flown business jets and 'commuter' turboprops. One or two came across as rough diamonds. Many had flown around the indigenous missions and settlements of northern Australia in the challenging conditions of the wet season. At twenty-nine, I was the oldest on the intake after a chap who had moved from one of Ansett's subsidiary airlines to 'mainline'. Most of my intake knew each other from the peripatetic world of General Aviation, which involved working your way up, usually in isolated bush environments, from single-engine aircraft. Then there would be the achievement of an instrument rating, then that first 'twin', and at last the precious 'turbine' endorsement; much of this, if not all, paid for by themselves through mine work, bartending, stacking shelves … one of my intake had worked in an abattoir.

After the introductions, the talk turned to something called 'The Integration'. The other pilots seemed quite disturbed about this, and I asked what it was all about.

'Haven't you heard?' one replied incredulously. 'Last Friday, Ansett bought East-West and Skywest Airlines.'

That Friday had been the day of my farewell from the air force in Adelaide. They were referring to Ansett's takeover of two smaller regional airlines that operated in northern New South Wales and Western Australia, respectively. I had heard it on the evening news, but thought little of it.

'Yes, I know about it, but isn't that good news?' I asked.

'You've got to be joking! This will really affect our careers! They will "integrate" the seniority lists. Today is our 'Date of Joining' Ansett. There are hundreds of East-West and Skywest pilots and we will end up junior to them all. This affects us big-time. Some of them are even Ansett rejects.'

I tried to grasp the implications. Just two days out of the military, I had little idea of how seniority among airline pilots worked, and how it affected almost every facet of a pilot's career and even his or her life. On this first day with Ansett, I assumed that I would be training alongside keen young pilots who were embarking on an exciting and lucrative airline career after the 'hard yards' of General Aviation. But all they talked about was 'seniority' – I thought they would have other priorities. Unfazed, I decided I would find out what this was all about later. I was keen to start training.

The chatter was cut short when the Head of Flight Operations came into the classroom, who made an appropriate speech of welcome. He fielded our questions, but they were mainly about this sudden and recent takeover of the two smaller airlines. His answers were optimistic and, as I expected, he stated that this would be good for every employee. I thought, 'What's the problem?' But it was the second person who stood in front of us that caused me some surprise. It was not another Ansett manager, perhaps the one in charge of training, or of the Friendship fleet management, to welcome us. It was not an administrative assistant or a technical instructor. They would come later. This individual was the union representative.

After introductions, his first statement was, 'I assume that you are all in the Federation?' Every head nodded except mine. He directed his attention to me. 'You're not in the Federation?'

'No, I'm just out of the air force,' I told him.

'Right, I'll give you the joining forms. Fill 'em out and get them in as soon as possible.'

The 'Federation' to which he was referring was the Australian Federation of Air Pilots, the AFAP, a union that I had vaguely heard about. It represented all 'domestic' pilots in Australia in a strict 'closed shop' system. The Qantas pilots, being 'international', had their own separate association. Hmmm ... so the second person to formally visit our group on joining a major Australian airline was the 'union rep'.

He passed out our contracts. The binders thudded onto the desks with their thick contents. He fielded questions about the integration from our group, but gave noncommittal responses. The pilots from the smaller airlines that had just been taken over were *also* members of the AFAP. But, foremost in my mind at the time was getting to grips with the famous Fokker Friendship.

The Fokker F-27 Friendship first flew in the Netherlands in 1955, two years before I was born. Ansett staff called it 'The Mouse', from its long sharp snout, or 'The Dutch Wheelbarrow', because its wings were mounted on top of the fuselage, spindly main undercarriage legs stretched down to small dual main wheels, and a large single nose wheel was prominent under the pointy nose. Some just called it the 'Friendly'. The Friendship had been flying throughout Australia for some twenty-eight years, and it was as tough as nails. The Ansett aircraft were painted white all over. Above the line of passenger windows, and in large rounded blue letters, '*ANSETT.*', with a prominent full stop, was emblazoned, as if the name alone was a statement. The tall, squared-off tail fin sported a stylised Southern Cross on a blue background, with coloured streaks fizzing back from each star. All Ansett aircraft of the time were in this livery, and in comparison, the aircraft of the rival government-owned domestic airline, 'Australian', recently rebranded from the famous Trans Australia Airlines, TAA, looked dowdy in a sickly blue, green and gold scheme.

Unlike its rival government airline, Ansett Airlines had been founded in pioneering circumstances. During the 1930s, a young Reginald Ansett had a road transport company that operated between western Victoria and the city of Melbourne. However, it was the heyday of the railways and his business became so successful the powerful government-owned Victorian Railways felt threatened. The resourceful Ansett sidestepped the pressure that was being applied by the state government: his company began *flying* passengers to and from Melbourne in a single-engine Fokker 'Universal' monoplane. With Reg Ansett's persistence and acumen, his airline flourished. I felt it fitting that the first Ansett type that I would fly had also been produced by the historic Dutch company.

During the ground school I found that the F27 was broadly similar to the HS 748, and memories of my early naval flying flooded back. The Friendship had the Rolls Royce Dart turboprops. It was of a similar size and was designed for the same purpose: a reliable short haul airliner. It droned along at about the same speed of 220 knots – or 400 km/hr. However, there were some differences from the British aircraft. The obvious one was the Fokker's 'high wing', mounted on the top of the fuselage. With the passengers sitting beneath the wing, large oval windows gave them an excellent view of the earth beneath. Another difference, not obvious to the outside observer, was its pneumatic system.

The HS 748 had used typical hydraulic systems, pressurised by pumps driven by the engines, just as the majority of aircraft have today. Hydraulics powered the landing gear retraction and extension, nose wheel steering and brakes. But the Dutch decided to use a different medium to operate the Friendship's vital components. They used air. High-pressure air provided by engine driven compressors replaced the more usual hydraulic fluid. Air ran through the pneumatic lines at high pressure on the Fokker to operate the landing gear, nose wheel steering and brakes. It hissed and puffed through a 'pneumatic cupboard' where various air valves were located, situated behind the pilots where the radio 'crates' had been on the 748. The noise was audible even over the scream of the Darts, especially when the nose wheel steering was operating: 'ktchh … hissss … ktchhh', reminiscent of the cab of a steam locomotive. I asked the Ansett technical instructor why Fokker had used pneumatics rather than hydraulic fluid. With the common perception that the Dutch are very thrifty people, he replied, 'Probably because air's free.'

Ansett had inherited a mixed bag of F 27 variants from various airlines it had absorbed over the years, so there were differences between individual aircraft, all of which had to be learned. They all had autopilots, a few reasonably modern, but the oldest Friendship was fitted with an ancient Sperry 'Gyropilot', which pilots referred to as the 'Hijack Box': it was likely to take you somewhere you didn't want to go to. But despite the Friendship's foibles, I looked forward to flying it, and soon 'line training' began.

I had flown from an aircraft carrier. I had instructed in single-engine jets and multi-engine heavy turboprops. I had captained Orions all over Australia, Southeast Asia, the Indian Ocean and the western Pacific, and in the airways system where the airliners cruised. I thought that I had experienced most of the different ways of operating an aircraft. But I was quite unprepared for just how different airline flying, particularly with Ansett, would be. I found my feet, but slowly.

Getting used to the way that Ansett operated the Fokker under the supervision of the Training Captains was a lot of work. It was another world. Almost everything in airline operations was regulated; now, military flying seemed like a free-for-all. An Orion crew was given a task, but it would usually be left up to the crew how to achieve it. I had considered the military manuals I had used were well laid-out and unambiguous, but Ansett's publications were works of art. They laid out in crystal clear fashion every action required by their pilots in almost every situation – normal and abnormal. On some runways, 'special procedures' were laid out in case of engine failure, regarding tracks to fly and altitudes to climb to. These had to be memorised. But unlike the tedious amendment process of the military manuals, an Ansett pilot merely had to swap the new section for old. The Ansett manuals were separated into separate sections in order that applicable parts (for example, emergency procedures) were small enough to slip into our flight bags.

There was no flight simulator for the Friendship, except, incredibly, a World War II vintage 'Link' trainer that creaked and groaned as it tilted and pivoted on the pneumatic bellows that moved it. The Link was purely a 'procedural' trainer for certain instrument procedures, so we were rostered for 'base training' in the real aircraft in the coming days. A group of us flew with a Training Captain to Avalon Airport, not far from Point Cook on Port Phillip bay, where we took turns to fly the Friendship in circuits, instrument approaches and simulated engine failures during take-off, where the old girl staggered away but still climbed, the 'good' engine throbbing at full power, the 'failed' one at idle thrust, my foot juddering on a rudder pedal to hold the airliner straight. The Fokker felt heavy but its solid feel inspired confidence in the old machine, and for the first time I heard the hisses and puffs of the pneumatics when the landing gear, brakes or nose wheel steering were operated. The landing 'flare' had to be judged carefully. Due to the high wing of the Fokker, there was little cushioning 'ground effect' that would normally salvage a rough landing.

Once again I wore a blue uniform shirt. After several months of 'ground school' then the base training flight, it was my first line training 'sector': a normal 'revenue' flight with passengers aboard. Mal, an easy going but highly competent Ansett Training Captain, occupied the left seat. A 'safety pilot', an experienced first officer, sat behind us in the 'jump' seat. Unlike most airlines, Ansett had chosen to deck their pilots out in light blue shirts, rather than the ubiquitous white. Their reasoning was that in Australia's sunny skies, blue shirts would cut down some of the reflected glare in the flight deck. Also, it made Ansett crew easily distinguishable, and they were called 'blue shirters' by pilots from other airlines. But wearing a blue shirt was where any commonality with the air force ended. An Ansett first officer (FO) was just that. There was no role change with alternate flights as we had done on the Orion, where the co-pilot would fly the aircraft as if he were captain. Ansett's head of flight standards, although respected, had decreed that FOs would have set duties that would not change on each sector. An Ansett FO could take off, fly en route and land the Fokker, but he was not permitted to start the engines, taxi the aircraft or operate certain controls on the autopilot panel. In addition he had administrative duties in the flight deck and, bizarrely, he had to select and call out the Friendship's lengthy checklists even while manipulating the controls on 'his' sector. This was a challenge on a 'tight' circuit at a remote airfield in the black of night. The Fokker's checklists were epic, printed on a roller blind affair mounted on the coaming above the instrument panel. While wrestling with the heavy controls, the FO twiddled a knob to scroll through the litany, calling out the 'challenges' and checking the captain's response. At last I flew an aircraft with a weather radar display in the cockpit, but it was difficult for the FO to use it; the primitive display was closer to the captain, and surmounted by a rubber hood that the captain would periodically peer into when there were storm clouds about. Ansett required to have the two radios on the same Air Traffic Control frequency in case one radio failed, so with each frequency change, there were two radio dials to adjust. Then, the navigation aids. On top of that, there was the complicated 'descent profile' …

Mal had patiently followed me through the plethora of procedures and checks as we flew my first two 'line' sectors, firstly from Melbourne to Canberra, then into Sydney. I had operated into both airports with the military, but the busywork of operating the old Friendship added a new dimension. It was a bittersweet arrival at Sydney after my very first airline 'line flight'. A buyer had committed to our house in Adelaide and, in turn, we had committed to purchase a home in Melton, then a 'satellite' town west of Melbourne. Staying with my maternal grandmother in Bacchus Marsh, further to the west, I found that Melton was convenient to the airport and was good value for money. But there had been a significant fall on the stock market, and my meagre payment from the Defence Force retirement fund had lost value. It had been committed to the deposit for the new property. Now doubts had been raised whether the purchasers of our Adelaide home would in fact have access to sufficient finance. In hindsight, it was a storm in a teacup, but with a second child imminent, a new career, learning to operate the Fokker and now fretting over perceived financial problems, I was almost oblivious to the white Rolls Royce, uncharacteristically allocated on this occasion by the hire car contractor, that collected us at Sydney Airport and delivered us to a newly built hotel with a stunning view over Sydney Harbour. It was only us pilots: Ansett policy was to accommodate the cabin crew in separate hotels where possible, and cabin crew nearly always changed from flight to flight with different scheduling requirements. The Friendship carried two flight attendants.

Despite my anxieties, I marvelled at the difference from the military: no crew van taking us to noisy, Spartan dormitory-style accommodation. The airline paid allowances to cover meals (and a few drinks) when on a 'layover' (overnight stay). Everything was organised, and there were no 'secondary duties' … it was a different world. I just had to put financial concerns aside while I worked on passing 'line training'.

A later flight was to Tasmania. I had a new Training Captain, and I was considered competent enough not to require a Safety Pilot. Over Bass Strait, under an arching blue sky, reflected in rippled blue water with occasional whitecaps beneath, the Darts moaned in their pencil-like nacelles behind while I finished my duties: flight log, checklists, tuning the radios … Instead of the plethora of flimsy paper charts that we used in the Orion, with the routine 'airways' system of airline flying, Ansett used 'route data cards' that had all the information a pilot needed to know: just lines with altitudes, tracks and, importantly, the 'DME steps'. DME steps gave minimum altitudes versus distance read from the Distance Measuring Indicator on the instrument panel, tuned to a specific beacon, and could be likened to irregular steps on a staircase. These steps kept the aircraft in the appropriate airspace for the arrival sector and clear of any high ground. There was a data card specific to each route. We had maps stashed in our bags, but these were rarely used.

We were en route to Wynyard, on Tasmania's north coast, and the Training Captain discussed the 'descent profile'. Like the HS 748, the Fokker descended at a very shallow angle at relatively high speed. I remembered that the Dart engine did not 'like' negative torque, where the propeller 'windmills' at low power settings and drives the engine. But eventually, the aircraft would have to be slowed down for landing, so the descent had to be carefully judged and managed. Another FO duty was to 'trim up' the engines by adjusting two 'blipper' switches to regulate fuel flow as the aircraft descended. This was done by reference to a rotating knob and scale fixed to the instrument panel. This further increased the power being produced by the Darts. Some terrain around Wynyard complicated the situation further. Here, there was no radar control like Melbourne, Canberra or Sydney, so the 'steps' were important – we were responsible for our own terrain clearance. My shaky grasp of managing this shallow, high speed descent slipped further when the Training Captain reached into his bag and produced a sheet of graph paper that unfolded and unfolded again across the flight deck, annotated with heights and distances for the arrival, in order to explain what was required. There was still much to learn.

At the end of 1987 I was thirty, and the financial anxiety was finally over following a successful house sale. In September the phone had rung very early in the morning in my grandmother's unit, where I was still living. Yvonne had gone into labour. I rushed to the airport and availed myself of a contractual free ('space available') Ansett flight to Adelaide and I was able to be present for the birth of our son, Rohan, at Modbury Hospital after a taxi dash from Adelaide Airport. Leaving my wife's mother looking after Avalon, I was soon back in Melbourne to make arrangements for a removal and to get on with the study and training.

On one flight, I landed pleased and relaxed. I had just completed my initial 'check to line' and the Check Captain had been a gentleman. It had been another Tasmania flight.

On the flight home, the flight attendant had come in to the flight deck with a platter of Tasmanian seafood for us. The Check Captain said, 'Come on, Mark, we can't both eat the seafood. It's all yours.'

Due to the risk of both pilots being incapacitated due to food poisoning, only one of us could eat it. The flight attendant placed the platter on the pillow balanced on my lap. I knew then that I had passed, and I was now a fully-fledged Ansett pilot!

After the check would be a full month of flying, known as a 'consolidation block', routinely assigned after initial training. 'Blocks' were the monthly schedules of assigned flights. Pilots would bid for whatever blocks they preferred, then the blocks were awarded in accordance with seniority. The best blocks were those with desirable destinations, extra flying that would be rewarded with lucrative additional payments above the 'base rate', or a combination of both. The worst blocks comprised the bare minimum of flying hours, and mainly 'Reserve' (stand by) duty, and only basic pay. At the bottom of the seniority list, I found that decent blocks of flying would be unattainable. But for at least this one month that provided lots of flying, I could settle into the routine of a line first officer.

My first 'line' flight following the check flight was memorable. I arrived in the Ansett crew room and met my captain. He appeared keyed up.

'G'day, Mark,' he said, 'this pattern is my final Command check, and it's with Captain Smith.'

This particular Check Captain had a name about the Fokker fleet for rigid and uncompromising standards, along with a highly developed ego. This was the young captain's final check flight after being promoted from first officer for command training. This flight would determine whether, after many years in the airline, he would wear the coveted four gold bars of an airline captain.

'I hate to tell you,' I said, 'I've only just finished training and this is my first line flight.'

He rolled his eyes. With Smith watching like a hawk from the jump seat, I got on with my job as best as I could. It was another Tasmania flight, and an instrument approach was required to descend below low cloud at the destination. With the landing gear and flaps down, and the Darts' whine subdued, we descended through the murk to our minimum altitude. Nothing seen! The weather forecast had not been accurate. The prospective captain pushed up the throttles and I raised the gear and flaps, attempting to make the all the appropriate 'calls' of height and speed according to the manual. We then circled and made another attempt to land.

'Not visual,' the candidate captain called once more. Then he made his decision, 'OK, we've got fuel for one more attempt before we divert.'

On the third attempt, the cloud had broken a little and we landed, the captain visibly relieved that there would be no busy diversion with a 'rookie' first officer. The checker had said very little to us throughout the flights. After arrival back in Melbourne, he picked me up on a few minor items, then continued with the candidate captain's debrief, but passed him.

Subsequent flights were less stressful as I got into the rigid rhythm of airline flying with regular 'line' captains. After arriving at the airport, the captain and I would proceed to the flight planning office. New to my experience, standard routes were laid out in a book of tables that gave time and fuel burn for the particular route, with various options to cover headwinds or tailwinds. The captain decided which wind 'component' to use, added any required fuel reserves, and filled out the fuel order. The relatively small Fokkers were invariably parked on remote stands on the tarmac, so along the terminal 'finger' we walked until we passed outside onto the tarmac, with its whiff of burnt kerosene (jet fuel) that had excited me as a child during airport visits. Sometimes there was the low whine as the starter motor kicked in on a neighbouring Friendship, which would build up to the familiar metallic scream of its engine, counterpointed by the 'rowrrr' of the propeller at 'flat' pitch. I would soon be in the cabin of our own aircraft checking equipment, then checks and 'panel scans' in the flight deck. The scans were laid out exactly in the manual: sequences of switch selections and instrument checks. The captain would return from his 'walk around' and then the passengers, forty or so, would stream aboard, climbing the small stair unit at the Fokker's rear entrance door. I would obtain the airport weather and runway in use, and consult a book of tables to calculate the Friendship's take-off speed and power setting. In Ansett, this was always the FO's job whether it was 'his' sector or not. I also had to obtain the clearance from Air Traffic Control.

With the passengers aboard, the captain carried out the engine start, and with the building whine of the starter motors subdued this time because we were inside, I would leave my seat to make my way down to the back of the aircraft, the metal blades of the propellers flickering through the deep oval windows. There was no warning light in the Fokker's cockpit to indicate that any passenger or cargo door was not securely closed; while the captain started the engines, it was my responsibility to check that the doors were properly locked. As I made my way down the aisle, a smart alec passenger would sometimes comment, 'Look, the pilot's bailing out.' However, the Friendship was well known to the travelling public. It had flown Australian skies for decades and it had a reputation for dependability.

I would clamber back into my seat, strap in and obtain taxi clearance from ATC. The captain always taxied, and I was now used to the 'kssshhh … sptt … kssshh' of the pneumatics as he steered the nose wheel and operated the brakes. There would be check of the flight controls and then the lengthy scroll through the roller-blind checklist, talk to ATC and setting the radios. If it was 'my' sector, the captain would open the throttles, the metallic shriek of the Darts now overshadowed by the buzz of the propellers, and I would take over the flying controls as we accelerated. Airborne! Even while flying the aircraft I had to set the pressurisation control, adjust the air conditioning and read yet another checklist as we climbed away. I would eventually engage the autopilot, but for altitude selections Ansett procedure required first officers to always ask the captain to set the appropriate figure on the autopilot panel. Climbing towards Tasmania over the Mornington Peninsula, there might be time for a quick glance down through the small side window to make out the ovals, buildings and quadrangle of Mornington High School, easy to spot a few blocks in from the beach. I would wonder if any other air-minded girl or boy was looking up at our Fokker laboriously climbing out towards Tasmania, as I had done.

When established in the cruise, it was time to check-cycle the wing's de-icing boots: black rubber inflatable panels that pulsed with compressed air in sequence, driven by a mechanical timer. Droning along at 220 knots – or 400 km/hr – at about 15,000 feet, four and a half kilometres high, there may now be a few minutes to relax and eat a meal, precariously balanced on a pillow while the big control wheel wobbled this way and that under the autopilot's commands. I calculated the descent point and gave a comprehensive brief to the captain about the DME steps, then, even though it was my sector, obtained the destination weather and called on the 'company' radio frequency to advise arrival time and any special passenger requirements (including hire car bookings!). I would also have to calculate the landing speed, and brief any special procedure for a missed approach.

Descent point! At about sixty nautical miles – 110 km out – I eased the Fokker's nose down but barely touched the throttles as we descended at near the maximum speed, hoping that I had correctly calculated to 'clip' the DME steps to keep us in the correct airspace and clear of terrain. I scrolled through more checklists as we descended, then 'trimmed up' the fuel with the commensurate increase in power from the engines. If I judged things correctly, I held level at a lower 'step', and the speed would wash off so that we could extend the landing flaps and undercarriage. In suitable weather in northern Tasmania we flew 'visual' approaches. Now down on the runway, I would check certain lights near the throttles: it was vital that the propellers be put into the 'flat plate' ground pitch configuration to brake the aircraft and to avoid a disastrous 'overtemp' of the turbines. Straightaway after every landing, the captain had to reach back to a large, awkwardly located handle behind his seat in order to lock the flight controls, which would also allow the propellers to fully reach their 'ground fine' position. His other hand would fly to the nose wheel steering tiller with the familiar hiss of the steering and brakes. He was now in control of the aircraft, and my duties reverted to those of every sector when on the ground: checklist, an after-landing 'scan', and dealing with ATC. While the propellers slowed and the passengers were being shepherded across the tarmac, our checklists complete, I thought about my arrival, particularly the descent. One captain commented, 'Yes, the Friendship sure is slippery going downhill. The fastest slow aeroplane I ever flew.'

On northern Tasmania flights, there was not the engineering or operational support that a Friendship crew would receive in Melbourne, Canberra or Sydney. Very early in the morning a taxi delivered us to Wynyard or Devonport airports, and it would be up to the crew to get the aircraft ready to fly after having been parked overnight. Often, a blustery gale would be blowing in from Bass Strait. While the captain was in the flight planning office it fell to the FO to remove 'cleats' that held the ailerons steady and prevented them from flapping about in the wind and being damaged. Because of the Fokker's high wing, a telescoping wobbly pole was used to unlock and remove them from below. Then came the infamous fuel drain: a sample of fuel had to be taken from each tank, located in the high wings. The same pole was used, which wobbled and waved in the wind blasting off the Strait, until it could be located into the underwing drain cock. Then, push up, and 'sploosh!' Down the fuel ran, inside and outside the tube, some of it to collect in the sample jar, the rest to run down the sleeve of my uniform jacket. A whiff of kerosene pervaded the flight deck when I took my seat, adding to the aromas of burnt jet fuel, rubber, grease, leather and Bakelite plastic – that evocative smell of a classic European or British flight deck.

In the climb, we usually burst through the Tasmanian overcast into a blue sky and, with duties complete for a while, we could enjoy a hot breakfast and coffee served by one of the flight attendants: a far cry from an air force tinfoil 'frozo' eaten in the Orion's dinette clad in a smelly green flying suit. With the Fokker parked at Melbourne, with the final checklist complete, I would be on the road towards my family.

After that one month of regular flying, life at the bottom of an airline seniority list began to wear thin. Now most days were spent on Reserve duty. The lawn was mown whether it needed it or not. I was paying off a hefty mortgage and supporting a young family and even on the improved airline salary compared with that of the air force, there was little disposable income left. Ex-military, I was inured to going to work every day and giving one hundred per cent to the organisation to which I belonged. But I was now grasping the implications of having little or no seniority.

The seniority system has been the cornerstone of airline pilots' lives since the 1930s. Like capitalism, it has many undesirable attributes, and aspects that are just plain bad, but it is the only system that works, despite its many faults. Most airlines are 'promotion driven': a pilot joins as a first officer. Under the seniority system, they must wait their turn before they are able to train to become a captain. Also, with multiple types of aircraft in an airline, seniority determines when a pilot is upgraded to a bigger, faster aeroplane. It allows more senior pilots to bid for blocks of flying to their preferred destinations, or flights that yield generous overtime payments. But seniority ties a pilot to the one company. If a senior pilot leaves their airline, they start at the very bottom of the seniority list at the next. It is as if a medical professional left one hospital as a surgeon but had to start at the new hospital emptying bedpans. Therefore, airline pilots are very industrially aware and occasionally militant: tied by the shackles of the seniority system, they are committed to their airline for life. However, for all its faults, seniority prevents favouritism and ensures that all pilots receive, in turn as vacancies arise, an opportunity for a Command (captain's) course or to fly bigger, faster aircraft. Those on the bottom of the seniority ladder take the crumbs allocated to them. Conversely, those with high seniority, whether a captain or first officer, can almost 'write their own roster' with preferred bids for flying, overtime and leave.

A seniority number is allocated to an airline pilot based on the date of joining the company. The pilot moves slowly up the list with retirements and resignations, and achieves a 'pad' below as new pilots join. This is important, because with any downturn, retrenchments start at the bottom of the list: 'last in, first out.' With my low seniority, the only blocks I was 'awarded' after bidding were those with lots of Reserve duty. Most of my scheduled flights were short, and of the bare minimum number required to keep me legally 'current'. Mobile telephones were not around in those times, so day after day, stuck at home on Reserve, I mowed, painted, helped with the children and made model aircraft, waiting for that 'callout' that rarely came. I began to realise what my course-mates had been on about on that first day of joining the airline. Now, it had become official: the East-West and Skywest pilots were integrated into the Ansett seniority list, and the date of their new seniority was the Friday of my farewell from the air force in Adelaide! And I had resigned from the air force with promotion imminent, and had refused a job with Qantas! Because our intake joined Ansett on the following Monday, we were junior to all of these newly-integrated pilots who would eventually be able to bid across to mainline and take the jet and captain positions ahead of us. Those three days had changed our lives.

As it had originally stood, it would have taken those from our intake twelve years to achieve a Fokker command at the current rate, let alone how many to captain a jet. I would have been around forty-two. Now, these new pilots piling in ahead of us would blow this figure out for years more. I did not want to wind up as an elderly first officer, conceivably sitting next to a captain who had been unsuccessful in getting into Ansett Airlines in the first place, there just because of good fortune.

I tried to explain our intake's plight to a captain who was active in the Federation. He began railing about his own loss of seniority during a previous integration: 'Yeah, I lost *fourteen numbers* when they took over Airlines of New South Wales.'

'Well, I've just lost 235,' I replied.

'Jesus Christ!' was all he could say.

Our intake took legal advice. We appealed to the AFAP but there was little solace there, because the union also represented the interlopers. I scraped money together in order to contribute to a fund that our intake set up in order to hire a Queen's Counsel to fight the situation in the Industrial Tribunal. Our argument was that we had been offered and accepted a position with Ansett prior to the takeover of the subsidiary airlines. Our application was refused.

We were granted an interview with the boss of Ansett Airlines, Sir Peter Abeles. Years ago, the pudgy, white-haired old man's company had taken over control of the airline from Sir Reginald himself in acrimonious circumstances. He was not well-liked by most Ansett staff. Still, we met with him and, predictably, he lisped in his Hungarian accent that the takeover would be '… goot for efferybotty and ze new airlines vould bring more flyink for all.'

But we left his plush office unconvinced.

Restless and bored on Reserve duty in flat, hot suburbia, I was always keyed up for that phone call. Very occasionally the phone did ring – great! A notification of a 'duty': a flight to northern Tasmania, Canberra or Sydney. Our seniority situation notwithstanding, I was still motivated and eager to fly, if barely once a week. The airline had to maintain Reserve coverage for illness or schedule disruptions. When I did drive to Melbourne Airport to fly the lowly Fokker, I often thought of the visits to Wagga Airport and my first sight of a Friendship as a small child, nervous from the shriek of the engines and its physical size. I had thought that the long pitot tube on one wing tip was a gun and became even more apprehensive! I recalled an advertisement for Airlines of New South Wales, now an Ansett subsidiary, and its catchy theme song on our black and white television: a girl with her mother in a rolling field pointing up at a Fokker, '300 miles an hour in pressurised, air conditioned comfort!' said the voiceover. And now I was actually flying the classic old airliner, if not as often as I would have liked.

The interface between man and machine on the Fokker Friendship was reminiscent of the navy's HS 748s. There were no computers. Everything was mechanical, and a human pilot carried out some functions that, even at the time, could have been readily automated with existing mechanical technology. For example, the 'fuel trim' function carried out manually by the Friendship's pilots had been achieved by a mechanical valve system on the Allison engine of the Orion, a product of the same era. I had never operated a machine that was so dependent on a human-mechanical relationship, but I still feel privileged to have flown it. But Ansett's very thorough and regimented method of operating the Friendship made flying it even busier than some pilots considered warranted.

'This mob operate it like it's Concorde,' one commented.

Yet, whenever Ansett pilots got together, despite what they had flown, the talk would revert to memories of their Friendship days. But soon, my time on the aircraft would be over. Thankfully, the East-West and Skywest pilots would remain with their own companies for another eighteen months while details of their integration were being worked out. If expansion continued, this might just give our intake an opportunity to become established as jet first officers before we would be condemned to sit in the co-pilot's seat for decades. And now a new development of the Fokker was on its way to Ansett Airlines, which would at last replace the venerable Friendship model. It was called the Fokker Fifty, and I left home for the first day of another ground school, newly-motivated and keen to learn about and fly the new type.

From a distance, the Fifty looked painfully similar to its predecessor with its high wing, stalky main landing gear and mouse-like pointed nose. But as you approached the aircraft, smaller twin nose wheels became apparent – this was no 'Dutch Wheelbarrow'. But the salient point was the engines: no longer would there be the scream of the Darts. The Fifty was powered by American Pratt and Whitney turboprops that were quieter and more powerful. They drove futuristic six-bladed propellers that felt and looked like they were made of plastic. Inside the new Fokker, things were even more different. The F 27's large oval windows had been replaced with more pedestrian squarish ones, but the Fifty carried more passengers and was much quieter inside. It cruised sixty knots; one hundred km/hr – faster, and flew higher and further. And in the flight deck, things were really new.

Most of the F 27's 50s-era switches, dials and levers were gone. For the first time, I experienced a 'glass' cockpit. Attitude, airspeed and altitude were displayed in a new presentation format on small Cathode Ray Tubes (CRTs), in addition to compass and radio beacon information. There were still a few 'back up', old-school-type instruments. The engines and propellers were controlled by computers that were commanded by simple thrust levers, and the pilot could select full 'reverse thrust' after landing, as we could in the Orion. The cockpit was quiet, well laid-out and far easier to manage. The Fifty had a 'normal' hydraulic system to operate its services: no more quirky, noisy pneumatics! Pressurisation was automatic and a system of gentle chimes and warning lights gave the pilots good warning of a malfunction. The days of clambering aft past the passengers to confirm that the door was closed were gone. The flight deck lighting was superb.

It was April 1988. There was no simulator for the Fifty, and I thoroughly enjoyed 'base training' in the aircraft at Avalon airport. The aircraft felt smooth and jet-like. But due to lack of resources in Melbourne, I was to go to Sydney for 'line training' in the new aircraft, courtesy of an Ansett Airlines' subsidiary: Airlines of New South Wales.

The support structure for the Friendships that flew out of Melbourne was similar to that of the jets, particularly in the area of keeping track of passenger loads and 'trim'. The loading, or 'trim' of large aircraft is a critical consideration. Especially with an airliner's long fuselage and variable passenger, cargo and fuel loads, it is vital that the aircraft is balanced with respect to the aerodynamic forces on it. The point where all the weight of the aircraft is assumed to act is its Centre of Gravity, or CG. If the CG is too far forward, the aircraft will not handle correctly, or may not even lift off. Too far back is even more dangerous: the aircraft becomes unstable, and disasters have occurred with incorrect loading, or shifts of an improperly secured load (huge freighters and military transports rearing up after lift off, then stalling, dropping a wing and plunging to earth to explode in a monstrous, ghastly fireball). I had received little exposure to calculating load distribution, or 'trim', because this was handled by the flight engineers in the Orion, and by specialised staff at Melbourne who produced the 'trim sheet' for each flight, even for the little Friendship. But Airlines of New South Wales (ANSW) did things differently: load distribution was calculated and arranged by the first officer, in addition to his or her other duties. They had to produce a Trim Sheet document for each flight, and I struggled to keep up.

ANSW flew from Sydney to airports in rural New South Wales including Narrandera, Griffith, Moree, Cooma, Merimbula, Ballina and my birthplace, Wagga Wagga. Many of these flights were 'triangular', for example Sydney-Griffith-Narrandera-Sydney. The FO was expected to 'run' multiple trim sheets, allowing for those passengers disembarking at the first stop and those getting on, the same at the second stop, and so on. Most of the airfields were 'uncontrolled' with no control tower, and ANSW pilots had to watch for traffic, navigate and land the aircraft, and calculate fuel loads at each stop. The FOs had to ensure the aircraft was loaded and balanced correctly. For multiple stops, old hands advised to run the trim sheets for the next sector ahead of time. ANSW procedures were that this was the FO's responsibility even when it was 'his' sector; that is, manipulating the aircraft. And with all this, I was flying a new type of aircraft in a network I had not flown before. The intermediate stopovers were very short and I found myself out of my depth, struggling with the trim sheets, and behind the operation. My Line Check on the Fokker Fifty, thankfully with an understanding Check Captain, was ironically through Wagga. But there was no time for sentimentality. With a rapid aircraft 'turn-around' after landing there, I concentrated on the job in hand, getting the aircraft efficiently into Sydney using the correct procedures, and I think that all were grateful, especially myself, that I would be going back to mainline in familiar Melbourne. I admired the ANSW pilots who had operated the even busier Friendship in the same circumstances. In addition to all the preceding considerations, they would have also had to calculate quantities of water-methanol, a liquid injected into the Darts to increase power for take-off in hot weather, on these multi-stage flights with restrictive maximum weights in an aircraft of far lower performance.

With the Fifty's speed, it was sometimes used on flights other than the staple Canberra-Sydney and northern Tasmania services from Melbourne. But my regulation 'consolidation block' of flying on the new Fokker was now complete and once again, we had the best-kept lawn in Melton. However, I was 'called out' for one memorable flight: Melbourne to Adelaide, which even in the new Fokker was still far longer than in an Orion. But rather than going back to the squadron office to catch up on 'secondary duties', as I would have done in the air force, it was straight to a city hotel. Also, I had just received great news: my bid onto the Boeing 737 jet was successful. To my relief, the East-West and Skywest pilots had still not been officially integrated. Early in the coming New Year, I would start training on the Boeing. But once established on the jet, after the integration took place, I would stay there for years: a first officer, co-pilot seemingly for life.

There was another cloud on the horizon. Australia's 'Two Airline Policy', where Ansett and Australian Airlines were tightly regulated as to when and where they could fly, was to be dismantled in a forthcoming deregulation of the industry. Rumblings of discontent began among the more senior pilots, not just of the Ansett group of airlines, but Australian Airlines as well, who felt that a pay rise was warranted, to 'lock in' before deregulation took effect. Inflation was running at over seven per cent. Also, just before Christmas, which would ensure little attention from the public, Australia's Federal politicians awarded themselves a thirty-six per cent pay rise.

Emboldened, in 1989, the Australian Federation of Air Pilots would demand a near-thirty per cent pay rise for every domestic pilot in Australia.

14

WORLD WAR III

1989 – 1990

Two turbofan engines hummed along with the 'husshhh' of the airflow passing over the flight deck. Captain Bob, who was training me to fly the Boeing 737-300 jet airliner, was knowledgeable and we got on well.

'Look at that,' he exclaimed, as the autopilot, coupled to the Flight Management System, crossed us over a ground beacon perfectly: the waypoint 'sequenced' at the exact moment that the 'raw data' needle pointing at the beacon swung 180 degrees, signifying that we were exactly overhead. 'Pure magic!' In 1989, this was new technology, and even Bob was in awe of the electronics fitted to the Boeing.

The Boeing 737 has been in continuous production since 1967. It is the best-selling airliner in history. At the time of writing, over 9,500 have been produced in various versions, with thousands still on the order books. The Boeing 737-300 model delivered to Ansett Airways was a quantum leap from the original 737: efficient 'high bypass' turbofan engines replaced the old noisy jet units that looked like stovepipes. It retained much of the old 'dial' type instrumentation but its biggest improvement, apart from the new engines, was the fitting of a Flight Management Computer, or FMC. The 737-300 was longer, and carried more passengers over greater distances using less fuel. We cruised at 35,000 feet – or 10,700 metres – high, in deepening purple skies between Brisbane and Cairns. This was my first 'line training' flight on the Boeing after 'base training' at Avalon. The Base Training Captain had a reputation for being difficult on 'check' flights, a member of Ansett's notorious 'Gang of Four' Check Captains who had a name for themselves among the pilots. But with his 'training hat' on at Avalon, his directions had been clear, concise, and the experience was enjoyable.

I had never flown a swept-wing jet. The Macchi had straight wings with only a slightly angled-back leading edge. A swept wing 'fools' the air into thinking that it is going slower relative to the wing because it is at an angle to the airstream. This delays the onset of 'compressibility', a symptom of high-speed flight, when the local airflow becomes supersonic. Compressibility can cause handling, performance and structural problems. Because the wing 'thinks' that it is flying slower than it really is, at slower speeds a swept-wing jet will sit noticeably nose-high. This restores the lift required by increasing the wing's angle of attack. So, in the cruise – and even on descent and approach to land – jet airliners sit nose-high. Because of this characteristic I had to become familiar with and memorise new, more nose-high attitudes for take-off, climb, descent, and especially approach and landing, after thousands of hours in 'straight wing' aircraft. Also, if a swept-wing pilot over-controls the rudder, the swept wings swing, lift increases on the outboard side because that wing is 'straighter' to the airflow, and the aircraft can roll sharply. Because of that, rudder control in a jet transport is kept to a minimum, and when used, the pilot must be gentle with inputs and be ready to compensate for the roll, particularly in the case of an engine failure or crosswind landing. Also, if a swept wing aircraft gets too slow, drag increases rapidly. This, combined with the initial slow response when throttling up the turbofan engines, requires the pilot not to tolerate any trend of the aircraft coming below its optimum speed. Conversely, the descent has to be carefully managed because the jet is so 'slick,' and even at idle, jet engines produce thrust. Speed brakes were fitted to the 737: panels extended from the upper wing to create drag in order to slow down, descend, or both at once. At last, after hard study on yet another ground course, then simulator work and base training (my third aircraft 'conversion' in eighteen months), I was first officer of a jet transport with 120 passengers aboard. They were being looked after by four flight attendants. Between tasks, I watched the darkening sky, the electronic screens full of colour and data, and the lights of the Queensland coastal towns strung like gems on velvet far below.

—✈—

The 737-300 could lift off at approximately the weight of a fully loaded Orion, powered by its two CFM 56 turbofan jet engines, which were jointly produced by American and French companies. The CFM 56 is still in production, and some 30,000 of them have been produced at the time of writing, which is an indication of their reliability and efficiency.

The design of the engine is called 'high bypass' because the turbine drives a broad fan at the very front of the engine. The fan directs some air through the various compressor stages behind it, then through the combustion chambers and turbine, but the rest of the air is 'bypassed' around the engine through a wide front cowling. High bypass engines are quieter, more powerful and more fuel-efficient than their turbojet predecessors. Another feature new to me was the automatic thrust system or 'auto-thrust'. This relieved the pilot of constantly adjusting the thrust levers to maintain the desired speed. The closest thing I had previously to an auto-thrust system was the Orion flight engineer adjusting the power levers as required, and sometimes without being asked! After landing, the Boeing's engines could be put into reverse thrust, where the rear cowls would 'translate' back to expose vanes that directed some of the cooler air from the front fan slightly forwards to help decelerate the aircraft.

Fuel was carried in wing tanks and in a tank located in the centre fuselage. Unlike in the Fokkers, the flight controls were powered by the aircraft's hydraulic systems, with an artificial 'feel' system for the pilot. Likewise, the landing gear, flaps, brakes and thrust reversers were hydraulically powered. There were also 'slats' fitted to the leading (front) edge of each wing: panels that opened to increase the wing's curve and, therefore, its lift, for take-off and landing. The main landing gear was unusual for a jet airliner in that both the double-wheel units retracted inwards towards the fuselage, but there were no doors to cover and streamline the wheels, which merely sat flush with the lower fuselage. Round covers were fitted to streamline the exposed main wheel hubs. 737 pilots were often the butt of jokes from others: 'My, what shiny hubcaps you have!'

The -300 flight deck was a mix of the old and the new. Round airspeed and altitude indicators were fitted and the overhead console was a clutter of clunky 1960s-style switches that controlled the electrical and fuel systems. The centre console between the pilots was dominated by the twin thrust levers, air brake and flap levers, wheels and knobs for flight control 'trimming' and the radio and navigation aid panels. But, in front of the pilots on the main panel, were two large Cathode Ray Tube (CRT) displays and below them, on the forward edge of the centre console, the keyboards and screens of the Flight Management Computer (FMC).

Apart from the simple Macchi, Auster and CT4, all aircraft I had flown required a bulky Flight Manual to be carried on board. The manual comprised a technical description of the aircraft, how to fly it, and its emergency procedures. Also, a good chunk of the publication was page after page of graphs, charts and tables that enabled the pilot to calculate the aircraft's performance: speeds, heights, take-off and landing distances, fuel consumption … Also, on every aircraft I had flown, paper maps and charts were essential for navigation – an Orion crew carried wads of them. Another special book gave details of airfields, airspace, Air Traffic Control frequencies and procedures.

But the FMC in the new Boeing was revolutionary. It carried all the information these publications contained inside a computer database. The FMC knew where it was by inputs from an inertial navigation system: a sophisticated device that navigated by using sensitive gyros and accelerometers. The FMC's position could also be updated by reference to ground radio beacons.

The pilots could load a pre-planned route, such as this night's Brisbane to Cairns, into the FMC, which drew an electronic map with the route shown as a bold magenta-coloured line on the Navigation Displays in front of the pilots. The 737's autopilot could be coupled to this. Waypoints along the route (imaginary points defined by a latitude and longitude), could be modified, deleted or new ones added via the FMC's keyboard. Airfields and ground beacons were shown on the display. For situational awareness, this was a quantum leap. However, it was drummed into all pilots converting to this technology that it was still important to monitor 'raw data': the old-style pointers on the screens, and the round gauges along with airspeed and altitude. The FMC was fallible – 'map shifts' could occur where the magenta track of the aircraft drifted from the actual track, so right from the start it was drummed into us to monitor the raw data. Later generations of new airline pilots would sometimes derisively be called 'Children of the Magenta Line' after several dreadful accidents caused by inexperienced or inattentive pilots blindly trusting the system. However, with proper monitoring, the FMC was – and is – a very useful piece of equipment. Paper maps were still referred to as a crosscheck, and it was still a requirement to refer to paper charts for approach and departure procedures.

While we sat in the glow of the instruments and screens, the Boeing was getting along at Mach 0.75, three quarters of the speed of sound, tracking to Cairns at 430 knots – or 800 km/hr. 'This is the fleet to be on', I told myself. Ansett's 737s flew almost everywhere on the network, not just mired in the triangle of Melbourne-Sydney-Brisbane like the bigger jets. But with the East-West and Skywest pilots about to join our seniority list, I would remain a 737 first officer for decades. And ahead lay the uncertainty of industry deregulation and, ominously, the AFAP was becoming increasingly aggressive in its push for the near-thirty per cent pay increase.

Once again, our lawn was the best-kept in the street. Training on the Boeing was over, as was the regulation 'consolidation block' of flying. It was early 1989 and again I was assigned only the minimum amount of flights required to keep me legally 'current', because I did not have the seniority to bid for proper blocks of work. I was perpetually on Reserve duty. The mobile phone had still not made its appearance in society, so I was tied to my home in Melton – and the house phone rarely rang for that 'callout'. This would be the status quo for years after the East-West and Skywest pilots pushed in ahead of our intake. After military service, I found the inactivity hard to take. Moreover, my ex-RAAF instructor friend Steve Nelson, already a captain with Cathay Pacific Airways in Hong Kong, had been in touch. Cathay Pacific was still recruiting. But the thought of a life in Asia still did not appeal, as did the prospect of yet more study and training. I had a young family, and our daughter had just started school. Cathay Pacific Airways required their pilots to hold the equivalent of a British Airline Transport Pilot's Licence (ATPL), because Hong Kong was a British colony. The requirements to obtain this were draconian. I would have to pass all of the exams as if I was a novice pilot, within two years after starting with the company. There were no exemptions for existing qualifications and experience. Cathay Pacific's standards were notoriously high. But the salary was the best in the world if a pilot could make it through their system. I could be flying either the Lockheed TriStar three-engine 'wide body' airliner that flew regional Asia flights, or the mighty Boeing 747 to Europe and North America. After yet another round of lawn mowing, I wrote to Cathay Pacific to advise them that I would like the opportunity for another 'first interview'.

I also missed military life. On the rare overnight stops with

Ansett, I sometimes shared a meal and a few drinks with my captain or other crew members who were in town. But on arrival back at Melbourne, everybody just went to their homes, scattered about the more affluent suburbs of Melbourne's sprawl. There was no mess life, or groups of pilots 'lobbing' at a friend's house after a hard day's flying to raid his beer fridge (an 'alpha strike'). I felt isolated in Melton: no other pilots that I knew lived in or near this working class western suburb. The rigid discipline of airline flying was a contrast to the 'just get the job done' freedom of a mission in a military aircraft and the work hard, play hard ethos. Then a thought crystallised: 'Why not join the Air Force Reserve?'

There was a Reserve squadron in Melbourne. OK, there would not be any flying, but I would be back in uniform with some military camaraderie and a more active social life. There were provisions in place for Reservists to be granted leave of absence by their employer for military duty. I was hardly flying anyway, so why not join? After a call to Air Force Recruiting, a few weeks later I once again wore RAAF uniform and wings at Number 21 Squadron at RAAF Laverton, from where I had flown the navy Macchis working with the destroyer over Port Phillip Bay. Coincidentally, my Flight Commander was Squadron Leader Jerry, now also ex-RAN, who had led us over the thunderstorm in our Macchi formation from Laverton to Nowra. 21 Squadron's Commanding Officer was an ex-fighter pilot. I was the only Ansett pilot on the unit, but Jerry and several other 21 Squadron officers flew for the government-owned Australian Airlines. The other personnel were administrative, nursing and engineering staff. I discovered that 21 Squadron, in conjunction with the RAAF Museum at Point Cook, operated a Macchi and, amazingly, an airworthy classic British Vampire jet trainer! These aircraft were flown by the CO and Jerry. Now the future was looking very bright and active: the salary and conditions of an airline pilot, but also being a 'weekend warrior' with the air force squadron. Perhaps *I* might fly the Macchi one day! But industrial tension between the AFAP, the airline managements and the government was increasing, and a sense of foreboding arose in me and many other pilots.

In the meantime, Cathay Pacific Airways had responded promptly to my letter, inviting me for another interview in Sydney. With my sparse flying roster and Ansett contractual 'staff travel' privileges, I did not need to ride the overnight bus back from this interview! I was questioned by the more practical Chief Pilot of Cathay's TriStar fleet, rather than the previous sniffy management captain. The interview seemed to go well. I explained why I was frustrated with all the time at home with Ansett and the long time to a captaincy. And I now had a proven track record of airline flying. But I didn't let on my misgivings about living in Hong Kong and the hoops that I would have to jump through. Before joining Cathay Pacific I would require a full Instrument Rating: a test carried out in a light twin engine aircraft at my own expense. For first officers, Ansett only required a 'Second Class' rating, earned in the simulator, and apart from the perfunctory flight during the Qantas selection process, I had no experience in civilian light twins. Then there would be the British ATPL exams, the rigorous Cathay Pacific training, the relocation of a young family to Hong Kong, and leaving the RAAF Reserve ... If I was granted a second interview by Cathay, I would see how the land lay from there. With a brewing industrial dispute and the implications of the East-West and Skywest pilots integrating, applying to Cathay Pacific seemed like good insurance.

In the meantime, the Air Force Reserve work nicely broke up the strings of days off in suburbia. But I always looked forward to Ansett flights: the usual early morning drive to Melbourne Airport; planning the flight with the captain; the aroma of hot coffee and breakfast heating in the galley behind as we prepared the flight deck ... then, airborne to Sydney, Brisbane, Adelaide, Cairns, Canberra, Hobart ... For the first time, I flew into Alice Springs, the red and grey of the McDonnell ranges were prominent. Then we flew onwards to

Darwin, this time to stay in a modern hotel, not a wooden, open-slatted building at the air force base.

We busily hopped from Brisbane to 'ports beyond', as the departure boards in Melbourne put it: Rockhampton, Mackay and onwards to layover in Cairns. And the jet was 'busy'; not so busy as the Fokkers, but first officers still had to check the cabin, calculate take-off data, read the checklists and tune the radios, even if it was their 'sector'. The jet moved so much faster: I had to stay ahead of the rapidly-moving aircraft. The very occasional long Perth flights were satisfying, but I had pangs for the Macchi flying and the social life that we had enjoyed there, now almost five years past. There had been so much water under the bridge since …

One morning a letter arrived. It was an invitation to undergo a 'second interview' with Cathay Pacific Airways Limited, in Hong Kong. With travelling time, it would be five days away. As bad luck would have it, I was rostered to fly during the days stipulated for the assessment. Meanwhile, Tiananmen Square in Beijing had erupted with protests against the repressive Communist Chinese government, and violence in the rest of mainland China was possible. British-ruled Hong Kong was due to be handed over to the Chinese in 1997. It was an agonising choice: decades as a first officer with Ansett, or the 'big bucks', rapid promotion and international flying with Cathay Pacific. But there was the RAAF Reserve with a prospect of flying the Macchi. I could 'go sick' with Ansett in order to free up the days needed to attend the assessment in Hong Kong. But after a sleepless night, I put pen to paper: 'Due to work requirements with my current employer, I regret that I am unable to attend this round of interviews.'

Had I burnt my bridges? However, the Hong Kong airline responded promptly: 'We understand your commitment to your employer. Please advise when you are able to attend an interview.' Cathay Pacific Airways rose in my estimation; they seemed to appreciate my loyalty to my organisation that was ingrained in me after twelve years with the military.

In August 1989 I was in Townsville, north Queensland, over 2,000 kilometres from home. It was the annual 'training camp' for 21 Squadron, held at the RAAF base there. We attended and gave lectures, practised drill, and underwent weapons training. As a pilot with nothing to fly, I had little else to do except enjoy the military activities during the days and sit outside the Officers' Mess drinking with squadron mates in the tropical evenings. My friend from Pearce and Edinburgh, Al, had joined Australian Airlines and was coincidentally based in Townsville. There was ample time to visit him and his family at their home. But as the days wore on, we became glued to the evening television as news reports of the government and airline reaction to the AFAP's bid for the massive pay rise unfolded. Memories of the gathering at Murray's home in Perth after Bob Hawke assumed leadership of the Australian Labor Party, with our forebodings for the future of the navy's Fleet Air Arm, flooded back. The Hawke government was still in power and it had made a deal with its power base: powerful trade unions, to agree on a 'Prices and Incomes Accord'. The unions agreed to restrict wage demands. In return, the government would minimise inflation and among other things, increase spending on education and welfare. However, the AFAP's claim for a near-thirty per cent pay increase was well outside certain guidelines for any Accord wage increase. The pilots' union had not just infuriated the domestic airlines' managements, but had taken on the mainstream union movement and the Australian Government as well. One afternoon my wife called the Townsville Officers' Mess and I was called to the phone.

'Mark, a white van has just delivered a letter from the Prime Minister,' Yvonne said.

It was a begging letter from Hawke urging individual pilots not to follow the path that the Federation planned on taking.

Events escalated. Australia's prime minister publicly referred to the domestic pilots as 'glorified bus drivers'. The AFAP responded with, 'All right, the pilots will work bus driver hours.'

So, while I drank Al's beer and watched events unfold on his television, thousands of kilometres from job and family, Australia's domestic airline pilots were directed to refuse to 'sign on' before 9 a.m. daily and not to work after 5 p.m.

Days later, with no concessions from the AFAP, Prime Minister Hawke declared, 'It's war.' Australia's Industrial Relations Commission cancelled the pilots' work award, and the airlines sent letters to all their pilots requiring them to return to work by the 22nd of August, or face dismissal. Australia's domestic airline system was in chaos.

On the 24th of August, Al and I watched the evening news, aghast, where the head of the AFAP announced that all domestic pilots in Australia had resigned their jobs! The head of Ansett, Sir Peter Abeles, had mooted the serving of writs for Breach of Contract on individual pilots, and while we were isolated in Townsville, the majority of Australia's domestic pilots had filled out letters submitting their resignation from their respective companies! This was in response to legal advice to the AFAP that a person could not be sued if they were no longer an employee. On that same day, Hawke authorised the RAAF and international airlines to carry domestic passengers. The gloves were off.

Yet again, I slouched in darkness and noise in the hold of a Hercules, en route back to Laverton with the training camp over. I just wanted the interminable flight to end while my mind churned … surely the two sides would see sense? The AFAP was a 'closed shop' union and a powerful and wealthy organisation, but surely it would make some concessions? How could the airlines survive a shut down like this? And the government? Would somebody not step in and mediate after Hawke's rhetoric? Could I end up unemployed, with a large mortgage and young family? All the years of work, exams, aircraft conversions … forsaken promotion with the air force, rejecting a job with Qantas, which was ironically not affected by the dispute … I was anxious to return to my family and to also receive some direct communication from the AFAP. The 'Herc' droned on and on, the thud of its propellers pounding in my brain.

Once again I faced an agonising decision. I had heard that a handful of domestic pilots had *not* resigned. Still holding the military ethic of loyalty to one's employer, I could see both sides of this insane situation. But the AFAP was powerful, it encompassed all domestic pilots in Australia and aviation was, and still is, a relatively small world. The epithet 'scab' was already being applied to those who did not resign or who 'went back', that is, crossed the line. There was the question of loyalty to my fellow pilots. So, hoping against hope that the Pilots' Dispute would be resolved, I made my decision. A day later, I walked into the AFAP building in Melbourne and was pounced on by Association officials.

'Have you put in your resignation yet?' one of them asked.

'No, that's what I'm here for,' I said.

'OK, boys, we've got another one.'

Then with the stroke of a pen, I rendered myself unemployed.

Australia was in turmoil. The tourism industry, hotels and other businesses were grievously affected by the shutdown of the nation's domestic air carriers. Nightly, the television news featured family separations, missed weddings, ruined holiday plans, business failures … There were rumours of military personnel, who would normally travel on a domestic airline for various requirements, travelling on RAAF Hercules with a domestic airline ticket still paid for by the government. International airlines ran extra domestic sectors. Despite some conciliatory moves from the AFAP, the dispute wore on, unresolved.

The airlines' managements put up an intimidating grey wall of non-communication with the AFAP and resigned pilots. Chartered aircraft flooded in from overseas. The airlines offered new contracts for any pilot willing to break ranks and return to work, which included, ironically, a significant pay rise, pretty much what the Federation had been pushing for! They offered car leasing arrangements and other perquisites. A bounty was offered to returned pilots who persuaded friends and colleagues to cross the line. There was further irony in that under the new contract, previous seniority counted for nothing and the returning pilots were no longer unionised, so the effects of the previous integration of the East-West and Skywest pilots on our intake were no longer relevant. For all intents and purposes, the situation had turned into a 'lock-out' of the resigned pilots.

Foreigners swarmed into the country to fly for Ansett and Australian Airlines, with immigration rules relaxed by the government. For many of the resigned pilots, financial situations became dire. There was pressure from wives and family to go back to work. Marriages came under strain. I was so lucky now that I had bought my home in a relatively low-cost suburb and I had some meagre savings to fall back on. Picket lines and demonstrations by pilots were organised. Jerry, my boss at 21 Squadron, was similarly affected, and I will be forever grateful to him after he arranged extra work for myself and the other Air Force Reserve pilots at Laverton. This kept a very modest income trickling in while we waited for some resolution of this crazy situation.

The weeks wore on. In these pre-internet days, a 'telephone tree' was organised by the AFAP. Every evening I received a call from Ted, a senior but now ex-Ansett captain, who would apprise me of the day's developments, few of them encouraging. The trickle of pilots returning to work was steady and the foreigners kept coming. One cold, grey day at Laverton, one of the ex-Australian Airlines pilots announced that he was returning to work. I remained tight-lipped, but his colleague roundly abused him. The other pilot would himself break ranks and return to work weeks later. Ironically, there were lots of social gatherings among us unemployed pilots: I attended more than any time before the dispute. At one, a wife proudly announced how in the local supermarket, she had encountered a woman whose husband had broken ranks and returned to work. 'There's a *scab* in this shop!' the wife had called out loudly for all to hear. The bitterness and division was growing daily.

A few weeks later, I received a letter from Ansett Airlines that demanded the return of my uniform and Boeing manuals. It felt strange driving to my old place of work to hand it all back. At the Ansett building, I encountered an ex-RAAF pilot from my Orion days who had later joined one of Ansett's subsidiaries.

'G'day, returning your manuals, are you?' I asked.

'No, I've gone back to work,' he muttered.

I had little to say as I threw a black garbage bag full of manuals and uniforms on the massive pile. For me, the returning of work accoutrements and pilot against pilot defined the end of the road of a career with a once proud and famous airline, founded by one man with a vision and one aircraft, his airline now changed forever. Even if the dispute would be magically resolved the next day, Ansett Airlines would never be the same.

I looked out and down momentarily at our shadow that streaked over the ground. It was odd, bat-like. I was flying the Vampire! Jerry was one of the few pilots authorised to fly the Air Force Museum's precious Vampire, based with 21 Squadron. The classic training jet was the epitome of a British-made aircraft: good looking, but quirky in design, with the ergonomics and comfort of the cockpit an afterthought. The fuselage – or, more accurately, a pod that accommodated two pilots side by side and the large-diameter engine behind – was partly made of wood! The engine, with its howling 'centrifugal flow' compressor, exhausted between the twin tail booms that each held a dainty vertical fin, and these were joined by a rectangular tail plane.

Jerry and I were intimately squashed together; the original Vampire cockpit design had not catered for the bulk of the twin ejection seats that would be fitted to later versions of the aircraft.

Trussed up in my seat in the cramped cockpit, I felt like the hunched polystyrene pilot figure from one of my Airfix models. Black paint in the cockpit was profuse with knobs, trim wheels and other controls scattered everywhere. But I didn't care. The experience was a great tonic during the grim Pilots' Dispute, and I found the classic British jet solid yet responsive to handle. Its engine produced more thrust than the Macchi. Jerry allowed me to fly a few circuits at Laverton, the classic old jet pleasant to fly and easy to land, but there were some engine-handling considerations, as certain power settings had to be avoided due to vibration regimes. Later, Jerry arranged a flight for me in 21 Squadron's Macchi. Flying it from the rear seat, memories of Pearce and fondness for the little jet flooded back. Again we flew a few circuits, the orange and white wings with the matte black of the wingtip fuel tanks familiar on each side, the Viper warbling away behind us on downwind as I carried out the checks, still in my brain after all that had happened since: 'Speed below one fifty, speed brake in, landing gear down, three wheels, flasher out ...' That did it. I had to get back in the air. In despair over the prospect of any resolution of the Pilots' Dispute, I wrote again to Cathay Pacific: I was more than ready for an interview in Hong Kong. There would be no problems with getting time off for it now! Also, although it was a crazy idea, I wrote again to Qantas. If anything, they could only say 'No'.

Almost by return post, a letter arrived. It was from Qantas, inviting me to an interview in Sydney! I was flabbergasted. After refusing a job with them, here they were inviting me back! And this would be only an interview; no need for another aptitude test, medical or flight test. A ticket on a Qantas Boeing 747 to Sydney was enclosed and, days later, I sat on a flight deck jump seat, watching the operation with interest. With me on the flight was a fellow ex-Ansett pilot who had also applied.

The next morning I rode in a taxi after checking out of a seedy hotel, travelling to the interview at Sydney Airport. Sharing the cab were two domestic passengers, and they were railing against pilots – they were trying to get somewhere in the chaos that still reigned. I did not let on to them that I was an ex-domestic pilot. And I felt awful: the fellow ex-Ansett pilot had tempted me to meet him in a pub the previous night, and we had drunk too much while we relived the events of the bitter dispute. I felt stupid. Sick and pale in my trusty interview suit, I gathered myself and strode in to the interview room, expecting an aggressive stance because of my previous refusal of their job offer.

Incredibly, the first words from the interviewing captain were, 'Mark, we understand why you're here, and you stand a good chance of being offered a position with Qantas.'

Expecting a grilling then a rejection, I could not believe my ears. After some chit-chat I was dismissed, and I walked out suddenly physically better, relieved with the glimmer of hope of resuming an airline career. And, when I arrived home, a letter from Cathay Pacific was waiting. I had been invited to Hong Kong for an interview with them!

Yvonne and I returned home from the Cathay Pacific interview process, which had been held over three days in Hong Kong. Wives were encouraged to accompany their husbands in order to experience Hong Kong during the interviews, and Yvonne had demonstrated a positive outlook during the infamous cocktail party. Management and even the company doctor were present at this function, where they assessed the social attributes of the applicants and their spouses, and their attitudes to the prospect of life in the crowded Asian city. They immediately picked up on the slightest hint of negativity: pilots with miserable wives were not likely to remain with the Asian airline for long. I had plugged away at the aptitude tests (almost familiar after the ones I had sat with Qantas and Ansett), flown the simulator acceptably and handled the 'problems' with what common sense and airmanship I could muster, and made a reasonable impression at the final interview. A very significant factor in my favour was my original application made to Cathay Pacific before the Pilots' Dispute began; therefore, I was not regarded as a refugee from the upheaval in Australia. I had been in an established airline flying Boeings, and had international experience and exposure to Asia with the navy and air force.

On an evening at home in West Melton a few days later, I answered the phone to a very British female voice: 'Mark, I am pleased to advise that we are offering you a position as a first officer with Cathay Pacific Airways. Your start date will be the 27th of January. Now, you need to finalise your Australian Command Instrument Rating, which will be a requirement before you start. You will also need to do the "Performance A" exam. A package will be mailed to you with study material and ...'

I felt a mixture of elation, relief and trepidation. I now had a position with what at the time was the world's highest paying airline, but the generous salary was paid for good reason. Cathay Pacific demanded very high standards from its flight crew. Hong Kong could be a difficult place for a western family in which to live, and housing was extremely expensive in the crowded city. We had two small children and faced an international move. What possessions could we take? What sort of accommodation could we afford? What schooling would be available for Avalon and Rohan? What would Yvonne do in an Asian city while I was away for days on international flights? Then there was the prospect of the handover of Britain's Hong Kong to Communist China in 1997. There was the infamous British 'Performance A' exam, which would have to be passed prior to joining. Later, I would need to complete the equally notorious U.K. Airline Transport Pilot's Licence exams. I had to study for an Australian 'Command' instrument rating exam, and arrange and complete a flight test in a light twin-engine aircraft prior to leaving Australia. And this was all additional to the training by Cathay

Pacific, renowned for its very high standards, on the Boeing 747 or the Lockheed TriStar. Kai Tak airport was famous for being one of the most challenging airports in the world. And there was typhoon season and the vicious thunderstorms that battered Asia during summer ...

However, eclipsing these concerns was the prospect of flying a 'wide body' airliner on international flights, financial security and maybe even a captaincy in four to eight years as opposed to decades with Ansett. I was now thirty-two, and the prospect of a far quicker command was very welcome. Steve Nelson, my friend from Pearce and a Cathay Pacific Boeing 747 captain, would be there to offer help and advice. Phil from my pilot's course was also a Cathay Pacific pilot. I could leave Australia, Melton and the chaos of the bitter Pilots' Dispute – or 'World War III', as some had called it – for a shining fresh start. And because I had applied to Cathay Pacific prior to the dispute, I was at the head of the queue of hundreds of unemployed Australian pilots who were only just now applying to Cathay and other airlines. Ironically, the Australian Pilots' Dispute had become a godsend for many expanding airlines that were short of crew: not only Qantas, but airlines in Singapore, Malaysia, the Middle East and Europe. Hundreds of experienced jet-qualified pilots were up for grabs. I would not be alone in uprooting my family for a new life overseas.

Several days later, the phone rang. The caller was the same gentleman from Qantas, who two years earlier, I had told that I was joining Ansett instead. Once more, he cheerily congratulated me on being selected for Qantas. He gave me a start date just two weeks away. I explained that this time I was joining Cathay Pacific Airways. After a long silence, he said, 'Right', and hung up in my ear. Now I was committed to making a success of my opportunity with the Hong Kong airline. Yet again, I had much work to do.

I studied for and scraped through the Command Instrument Rating written exam. I hired a light twin-engine aircraft with the remainder of our savings, and thankfully an understanding examiner talked me through an 'endorsement' on it, then observed me flying instrument approaches into various airfields around Melbourne. We agreed that I would never fly in Australia using that instrument rating again, unless I redid the flight test. A supportive ex-Ansett senior Check Captain who had carried out my last simulator check signed off a few extra items required for the 'command' rating. I studied for the notorious British 'Performance A' examination, then Cathay Pacific flew a group of us 'new joiners' to Hong Kong, where we sat it. The British used 'penalty marking': leave a question blank and you lost the marks for that question. But answer the question and get it wrong, you lost *double* the marks. While we worked at the paper, a rank of dark-suited Chinese officials from Hong Kong's Independent Commission Against Corruption stood along the wall behind us. There had been allegations of cheating on previous exams but I found it hard to believe how and when this would have been possible; perhaps they were just making work for themselves. Outside, jet engines roared and whined while we wrote the exam in the noisy room above the terminal at Kai Tak. I had been sick the previous evening after a bad meal, and still felt terrible.

After an anxious overnight flight home to Melbourne, a few days later I found that I had passed 'Performance A'. However, more exams, training and checking lay ahead. Yvonne and the children were going to remain in Australia for a few months until my initial training was complete. During that time I had to find a flat and arrange a school for Avalon before they could join me. Days later I boarded a Cathay Pacific 747 to commence employment in Hong Kong. For my family and me, at least, the bitter Pilots' Dispute was over but, through the eight-hour flight to Asia, my mind churned, wondering what the future would bring.

QUEEN OF THE SKIES

1990 – 1992

Cathay Pacific Airways only operated 'wide-body' passenger jets: those with cabins broad enough to accommodate two aisles between the passenger seat rows. The airline flew Boeing 747 and Lockheed TriStar jets to destinations from its Hong Kong hub. There would be no need to work my way up through a succession of smaller aircraft to Ansett's only wide-body, the Boeing 767. Cathay's TriStars served Asian ports while their 'Jumbos' ranged further afield to London, Frankfurt and Vancouver. Both types were presented in an elegant livery: white fuselage top, 'CATHAY PACIFIC' in red letters above a pleasing green 'cheat line' at window level, with the usual grey or silver metalwork beneath. The scheme was topped by horizontal white stripes on the green tailfin, known by the pilots as the 'cucumber sandwich'. A discreet British Union Flag adorned the tails. But unlike most national airlines or 'flag carriers', Cathay Pacific Airways was not officially backed by any government; it was a public company and its controlling shareholder was Britain's Swire Group. Swire's background was shipping. The company's fortunes rose with lucrative trade with China through the course of the second half of the nineteenth century. Over the decades after the first Hong Kong office was established in 1870, Swire would grow to become one of the *hongs* (or large established companies) in Hong Kong.

Swire had not always controlled Cathay Pacific Airways. The airline was born immediately after World War II; it was set up by two ex-military pilots, American Roy Farrell and Australian Syd de Kantzow. Over drinks in a Manila bar, Farrell and some pals discussed a name for a proposed airline. They wanted to include the word 'Cathay', which was from 'Air Cathay', a fictional airline from a popular action comic strip of the time. Cathay is an anachronistic but romantic name for China. They added 'Pacific' to make the airline's name even more exotic, and presciently, in the event that the airline one day might actually fly the largest ocean on the planet.

Here were echoes of the pioneering spirit of the founding of Ansett in Cathay Pacific Airways, even more so because de Kantzow and Farrell had been pilots of World War II's Burma 'Hump'. The Hump was the perilous air route between northern Burma (now Myanmar) and Kunming in south-west China, flown by military and civilian pilots in the piston-engine airlifters of the time. This supply line was essential to keep the Nationalist Chinese forces, who were fighting the Japanese, supplied from British India and unoccupied Burma. Day after day de Kantzow and Farrell braved almost every aviation hazard that a pilot would have to cope with: first, huge mountains: the Himalayas lay north of the route, and the Hump pilots had to claw their way to altitude to pick their way through a 'lesser' 15,000 feet – or 4,500 metre – high mountain range as they initially headed north-east towards the Himalayan foothills before swinging south-east to China. The aircraft, most of them redoubtable DC-3s or their military counterparts, C-47s or 'Dakotas', were maintained under wartime conditions, unpressurised, and their heating was primitive. Next to challenge the Hump pilots was weather: the torrential monsoon rains and violent thunderstorms of the Asian summer, and mountain snow, fog and mists of winter. Icing was always a problem at altitude in the overloaded, piston-engine machines. Vicious turbulence snatched and clawed at the aircraft as upper air wind streams arced over the mountain ranges and ripped through the passes. Then there were the Japanese fighters, almost an afterthought after the natural hazards. And bailing out or crash landing after trouble and ending up in the hands of the Japanese did not bear thinking about …

After the war's end, Roy Farrell picked up a weary surplus C-47 in the United States, flew it to Shanghai in China, then flogged it between Australia and Shanghai as his 'export company' aircraft. It was laden with all manner of consumer goods for wealthy Chinese who were still starved of material comforts, even with the Japanese gone. Eventually, Farrell met up once more with de Kantzow, his fellow Hump pilot, and, with China being wracked by political and social instability (Mao and his violent revolution would explode upon the country in a few years), the pair established themselves in the British Crown Colony of Hong Kong, geographically a pimple on the rump of the Chinese mainland, but a disproportionally stable and wealthy city under British colonial rule. Cathay Pacific Airways Limited was incorporated there in 1946, and later the Swire Group achieved control of the company as the young airline grew.

On that first morning in Hong Kong I awoke in an airport hotel room, and dragged the curtains open. In late January of 1990, it was winter in the northern hemisphere. The room overlooked the crowded tarmac of Kai Tak airport that sprawled under a smudgy grey sky. Training was commencing the next day. I watched Cathay's green and white-tailed Boeing 747s and aircraft from other airlines push back and taxi, departing for destinations planet-wide. I thought about Farrell and de Kanzow, military pilots who must have had nerves of steel but also a sense of enterprise, and how this would surely have worked its way into the present-day culture of the airline that they had founded. I pondered this second chance that glistened through the chaos of the Pilots' Dispute: straight into the first officer's seat of a 'Jumbo Jet'! If I met the standard, there would be a 'Command', or Captaincy, within five to eight years. During the 1990s, Cathay Pacific's pilots and flight engineers were among the highest paid in the world. Also, Cathay crew were represented by an 'association', not a union. Membership was voluntary, and there appeared to be no militant pilots or union officials to lose *this* job for me. Relations with management seemed cordial enough. However, a pilot was expected to meet the airline's high standards and, occasionally, to go above and beyond what was written in their contract, which was merely a booklet, not the weighty tome that had thumped onto my desk on Day One at Ansett. This was a quid pro quo for the generous salary, allowances and leave. There were a large number of ex-military pilots in Cathay, many I knew personally from Australia's navy and air force. There were also other ex-military pilots from Canada and the United Kingdom. Most military pilots are used to going that extra mile for the organisation that they fly for.

I recalled being aboard HMAS *Melbourne* when she had docked in Hong Kong in the early 1980s. Memories of the verticality of the tall, thin buildings, the throngs in the streets, the swarming red taxis and the British accents of the chic expatriate girls flooded back. The place had been reminiscent of a beehive. Now, barely a decade after, Hong Kong was home for me and my family. Hard yards lay ahead, but the work would be rewarded far beyond my previous expectations. My thoughts also went back to the Pilots' Dispute. It still raged, and the bitter gulf that divided those still resigned and those who had gone back to work was widening daily. Many other ex-Ansett and ex-Australian Airlines pilots were now on their way to join Cathay Pacific. At Ansett, there had been the notorious 'gang of four' senior Check Captains. Two had crossed the line back to Ansett, but the other two would later join Cathay Pacific, ironically junior to me in seniority on our new airline's list. Time and place were so important in this profession.

Other ex-domestic pilots, horrified at the thought of having to uproot their families to live overseas, stayed in Australia. But if these pilots wanted to keep flying airliners in their home country, their only options were a successful application to Qantas or the odium of 'going back', to fly for an airline now a shadow of its former self. Many foreigners had flocked in to take the vacant positions available in the attractive land 'down under'. The presence of these foreign pilots did not sit well with many Australian pilots, even though Australians had themselves crossed the line. The interlopers now occupied seats on the flight decks in which old colleagues had sat. The British, European, African and North American accents would have sounded alien on the flight decks, and for years after, they would jar over the radio frequencies of Australia's domestic air routes. Now there was no seniority system in Australia's domestic airlines, or industrial representation. Things were chaotic as the airlines rebuilt, and there was that stigma that the returned pilots had, rightly or wrongly to themselves and others, capitulated and crossed a line. Many resigned pilots left aviation altogether to start new careers, or languished in early retirement. Some ended up divorced and bitter, while others waited for their starts with other carriers. As a United Airlines 747 pushed back and started engines preparing to cross the Pacific Ocean, I thanked my lucky stars that I had applied to join Cathay Pacific before the dispute began.

Later, a quietly spoken Australian on the room telephone said, 'Hi, Mark, I'm Ed. I've just joined and I think we are together for our training on the Jumbo. Would you like to meet up for a beer?' When we met in the hotel bar, I found that the voice belonged to Ed Field, the captain who had carried out my simulator assessment prior to joining Ansett Airlines. A Fleet Manager and seasoned aviator, Ed had resigned from Ansett with the vast majority of the pilots. I learned that the pressure on Ansett's management captains had been immense during the dispute, but despite this and after investing decades of his life with the airline, he had not wavered. I had left

Ansett as a lowly two-year first officer. Now a management pilot and I were joining a foreign airline together as first officers at the bottom of a new seniority list. Aviation can be a strange world and the old adage 'be nice to people you meet on the way up, because you may meet them on the way down' came to mind.

The Boeing 747. The 'Queen of the Skies'. The 'Jumbo Jet'! It rates as an invention apart from the aeroplane itself. This monstrous aircraft brought affordable flight to masses of the earth's population, who could now travel to the other side of the planet in around twenty hours. One Jumbo could move 400 passengers across oceans and continents. The machine would cross-pollinate humankind like nothing before and affect the geo-political events of the entire world. My mind strayed back to a poster pinned to the classroom wall at Kooringal School in 1969, an artist's impression of the soon-to-be launched Jumbo Jet in Qantas livery. I had often stared across at it and dreamt of being a Qantas pilot while the teacher droned on in the heat. Now I was to fly the 747, not for Qantas, but for Cathay Pacific Airways, which was expanding rapidly in its Hong Kong hub that sat within three hours' flight time of two thirds of the world's population.

Over the next few weeks, Ed and I sat in a dim cubicle that smelled of mouldy carpet, working through the primitive 'computer-based training' modules that taught us about the huge Boeing. A bland American voice slowly enunciated information about the multiple hydraulic and electrical systems, We studied diagrams of the massive undercarriage layout that included 'body gear': four-wheeled steerable bogies that supported the bulbous fuselage in addition to the more typical wheel sets that supported wings and nose. The monster needed eighteen wheels to support its bulk. The training covered the four Rolls Royce RB-211 jet engines, of over 40,000 pounds thrust each. The RB-211 featured separate 'low pressure', 'intermediate pressure' and 'high pressure' compressors and turbines, each with its own shaft, or 'spool'. This three-spool design, exclusive to Rolls Royce, allowed a more gradual compression and exhaust through the turbines, let each stage run at its optimum speed, and it reduced the overall length of the engine. On the other hand, there was a weight penalty and added complication with this layout. Aerospace design is always a compromise. In a few respects the 747 systems and design was reminiscent of the smaller Boeings that Ed and I had flown, albeit on a far larger scale.

The cockpit (Cathay Pacific still used the manly term 'cockpit' rather than 'flight deck'), high in the famous 'hump' of the fuselage, even had a telephone directory. The pilots could dial either of the door stations on the upper deck, the eight doors on the main deck, or the galleys. Cathay Pacific operated its 747s with fourteen cabin crew to look after almost 400 passengers in First, Business and Economy Classes. These early Jumbos also accommodated a Flight Engineer in the cockpit, seated sideways behind the first officer facing his panel to the right. He controlled the engine, hydraulic, electrical and fuel systems. He also managed the 'bleed air' system that pressurised the cabin, controlled temperatures, and started the engines. On the ground, electricity, starting air and air conditioning was provided by the Auxiliary Power Unit in the tail cone. Imagine providing electricity, heating and cooling for almost 420 people – even the 747's APU was of a class of its own. Above that towered the 747's fin, adorned with the cucumber sandwich, its tip nineteen metres above the tarmac.

With systems training and the inevitable exams complete, we began training in the flight simulator. We found the cockpit cramped for such a large aircraft: smallish windows angled in towards the point of the roof. The Jumbo's instrument panel, however, was impressively raked, deep and low under a massive coaming. But there were no Boeing 737 cathode ray screens here; in fact, the pilots' instrument layout was reminiscent of the old Orion. A grudging nod to modernity was two monochrome navigation computer screens on the centre console, one for each pilot. These controlled the Inertial Reference System (laser gyros that calculated the aircraft's position). Even these were the same model as that of the Orion. I had flown the Qantas 747 simulator briefly during their assessment process, but when I could I took the controls, the simulator (simulators are notorious for being twitchy to fly) once more gave the impression of a gentle giant. The massive wings, sixty metres in span, banked with the help of two sets of ailerons and multiple spoilers, while in pitch the manual trim wheels on the centre console between us flicked and whirred when I operated the small electrical switch on top of the yoke to trim out the elevator forces. When at the desired attitude and power setting, the huge jet sat like a rock: predictable and stable.

International 'heavy' aircraft almost invariably flew drawn-out ILS approaches, unlike the usual slick, expeditious arrivals of Ansett aircraft into familiar regional airports. But at over 200 tonnes at landing weight, the 747 used mile after mile of 'track distance' to both descend and slow down. Most airports that it operated into were busy – some the busiest in the world. Its pilots had to think well ahead. Extending the landing gear and the massive 'slotted' flaps that resembled a giant's Venetian blinds rolling out from the wings' trailing edges was a drawn-out affair. The speeds at which each configuration was selected rolled back slowly during the deceleration: 'Flaps five … flaps ten … flaps twenty … gear down … flaps twenty-five … flaps thirty …' In level flight, the Jumbo's nose attitude was lifted higher and higher as the aircraft slowed down, raising the angle of its sharply swept-back wing well above the horizon in order to maintain lift as the speed washed off.

I had to study for and train in landings in fog (Low Weather Minimum Operations or LWMO), because Cathay Pacific Airways operated into airports in Europe, North America and North Asia in the depths of the northern winter. There was the inevitable emergency training: depressurisation, fire, one engine out, two engines out, hydraulic failures, electrical failures, combinations of these ... then, finally the Instrument Rating test, which I had thoroughly studied for and thankfully passed, and now it was time to fly the beast itself.

A small group of new Cathay Pacific pilots would board the real aircraft and fly the short distance for base training to the Chinese airport of Guangzhou (or 'Canton', when Anglicised), which lay further up the Pearl River into China. In charge was a Base Training Captain, British and stereotyped with double-barrelled name, fruity accent, pedantic manner and crisp long-sleeved white uniform shirt. He conducted us through the external 'walk around', but the aircraft was so huge you could only inspect the engine pods, the landing gear and the lower fuselage and wing surfaces. The bulbous dull aluminium belly squatted low over the two sets of 'body gear'. The struts that attached the 'wing gear', (similar bogies that lay just inboard of the inner engines) towered up into the lower structure of each wing that obscured the sky above us. The Jumbo's body looming above was reminiscent of a metal building before we climbed the tarmac steps to an entry door. I paused and looked far back towards the tail that appeared incongruously small because of the distance from our position at the top of the steps, to the far end of the seventy-metre fuselage. Behind and below, the vast left wing extended, swept back to its tip, which again seemed so distant. We entered the First Class cabin on the main deck for another climb up the famous spiral staircase to the Business Class upper deck, then forward to the cockpit. I occupied one of the two jump seats while one course-mate flew us out under supervision of the Base Training Captain. He and the others would carry out the required number of landings at Guangzhou, after which I would take my place in the seat for my own circuits and – as luck would have it – fly the return to Hong Kong. I craned towards the side window. Merely sitting level on the ground, the cockpit was over seven metres from the concrete: flying the 747 simulator was one thing, but I had to show competency and consistency in judging a landing from even higher above the runway, the nose cocked high in the landing attitude.

My turn came, and I flew ILS approaches to Guangzhou's runway in bleary off-white cloud, my brain working as I followed the captain's directions and coped with the new aircraft and the Chinese metric altitudes. The radio squawked and brayed as the Chinese air traffic controllers and local aircraft communicated in Mandarin. There were checklists and briefings to complete, and there was the flight engineer to interact with, who patiently monitored his panel and called the checklist challenges. We were assigned metric altitudes in broken English, each of which had to be converted to feet using a table as we climbed or descended. A small altimeter showing metres was scanned as a double check. At 1,500 metres – about 5,000 feet – in zero visibility we were assigned radar 'vectors' (headings to steer) around the 'pattern'. We never once saw the ground until almost at the minimum altitude, where we broke out of slate grey cloud and smog with old Guangzhou airport's single narrow runway ahead. To assist the pilot, high above the concrete at the start of the landing 'flare', the flight engineer called out readings from the radio altimeter, which was calibrated to read 'wheel height' above the ground. In normal conditions, if the pilot flared by means of a gentle increase in the aircraft's attitude just before the 'thirty [feet]' call, 'ground effect' from the Jumbo's massive wing would cushion the touchdown to a standard that would flatter almost any pilot's ability, even at the maximum allowed landing weight of almost 250 tonnes. I did as I had been trained in the simulator and far below us, the four landing gear bogies, then the double nose wheels clattered on Guangzhou's rough concrete runway. There were glimpses of dirty brown-grey buildings crowding both sides of the airport while the Training Captain reset the elevator trim and set power for the touch and go. For its size, the huge aeroplane was beautiful to fly, solidly stable yet responsive – even more so than the simulator. But the inertia and momentum of almost 200 tonnes of mass could not be ignored, and anticipation was important. After several reasonable landings, we climbed back into the miasma for the final time, because now we were to return to Hong Kong for another experience, my first 'IGS'.

Hong Kong International Airport's single runway protruded as a rectangular cleared area south-east from the cramped urban area of Kowloon. Its landing directions, regarded as separate runways, were numbered '13/31'. 'Runway 13' pointed south-east, as the direction was 136 degrees 'magnetic'. While taking off or landing the opposite way, the aircraft was heading 316 degrees, north-west on 'Runway 31'. Hills and buildings on Hong Kong Island towered to the west, up to 550 metres high at Victoria Peak, while to the east the terrain was a little lower but still significant. A narrow sea passage between the mountains, the Lei Yue Mun Gap, enabled aircraft to gain height straight ahead after taking off from 13, or to approach straight ahead onto 31. But to the north-west of the airport, Lion Rock was prominent among the other peaks, its silhouette unmistakably that of a crouching lion, crags to one side of its peak forming an unmistakable mane. An airliner's crew had to avoid terrain when departing on 31 or overshooting from a missed approach by making a left turn, but … the turn had to be made at exactly the correct point; turn too early or too late, and the aircraft would impact buildings or mountains. Grubby 'medium rise' buildings crowded the airport, pressing up its perimeter road and the first third of the runway that jutted out into the dirty water of Kowloon Bay, its end a rocky sea wall. Between the runway and the eastern shoreline lay the infamous Kai Tak *nullah* (or drain), where raw sewage flowed into the sea. A character in a famous novel set in Hong Kong had referred to the resulting stench as 'the smell of money,' among other phrases that would become clichés satirised by Hong Kong's expatriate residents. The smell usually washed through an airliner's cabin after touchdown at Kai Tak. During my first days there I heard the apocryphal story of a comedian, probably Bob Hope, who, after landing in, supposedly,

Hong Kong, turned to a companion and asked, 'What on earth is that smell?' His friend replied sarcastically, 'That's shit, Bob!' Hope retorted, 'I can tell that, but what have they done to it?'

When coming to land at a 'normal' airport, jet transport aircraft should be stabilised on their final approach path, lined up with the runway and at the correct height, by about ten nautical miles – eighteen kilometres – from touchdown. However, because of the peaks and buildings to the north of Kai Tak, an ILS (a normal Instrument Landing System) directly to the runway was impossible because of the tight, right-hand, low altitude turn that was required in order to remain clear of the hills and then line up with the runway. Another solution had to be found that would guide airliners to touchdown when landing to the south-east. This system and the procedure were called the Instrument Guidance System: the 'IGS'. The IGS was a normal ILS antenna system that provided both glide path and horizontal guidance by way of the normal cockpit instruments of any airliner, but it did not lead pilots on a straight path to the touchdown zone of a runway. The IGS beams led them towards the side of a cliff.

An almost-vertical brown rock face lay like a scar on steep green-scrubbed slopes at the foot of the line of peaks that curtained across the north and east of the airport area. Peaks over 1,500 feet – almost 500 metres – loomed beyond the face, with even higher ground further east. A red and white checkerboard was painted on the bare rock wall. Airliners crammed with people could fly down the IGS beam heading almost due east and, with the checkerboard visible, which had to be before the minimum altitude of 675 feet – or 200 metres – their pilots would continue descent but, at the correct point, abruptly turn right, still descending, being careful not to make the turn tight or too shallow. Their right-hand wing tip would now be scything through the air just a few metres from the roofs of Kowloon City. The aim was to roll out of the turn at just 300 feet – or one hundred metres – high, pointing south-east down the centre line of Runway 13, not far now from touchdown which would come just seconds later. In a Boeing 747, its right-hand wing tip was almost another fifty feet – or fifteen metres – lower still during the turn. As a passenger I would watch, fascinated, while the right-hand wingtip sliced past apartment block windows as we sank lower in the right turn, the engines' whine rising and falling to maintain speed. Lines of washing and even the blinking colours of the residents' television sets inside could be seen as the buildings flashed by. On one Friday night, a group of us Cathay 'new joiners' sat in a restaurant in Kowloon City and every two minutes, conversation stopped as a roar outside announced yet another Jumbo descending over the building to land off the IGS approach. The night being still, the front door of the restaurant wafted open and closed each time the vortices from the heavy jets' wingtips spun down to street level from just a few metres above one of the most densely-populated areas on earth.

The turn from the IGS altitude had to be judged perfectly: too early or too late, too shallow or too sharp, and the aircraft would not be correctly lined up with Runway 13. If badly misjudged and a 'go around' was not initiated, impact would be a possibility with either the high-rise of Kowloon or the rising terrain to the east. And then there were the threats of low cloud, or the vicious turbulence and crosswinds of the thunderstorms and typhoons.

Today, the weather was merely overcast, with the usual smog. I manually flew the Boeing down the ILS beam as I had in the simulator, and ahead was the checkerboard. On the captain's advice I modified my turn a little, drifting slightly wide of the flashing 'lead-in lights' that were laid out over Kowloon to assist pilots with this critical turn. This was a Cathay Pacific procedure to allow a little more time to finesse the final approach. I tried to convince myself that I was flying my body, not an aeroplane the size of a block of flats, to properly track it over the ground and to simultaneously descend to be at the correct place and height, with the goal of rolling the Jumbo's wings level and tracking straight ahead to the runway, regardless of the slight crosswind and turbulence. Through the windscreens, we could see that we would clear the buildings and terrain, but there was no room for inaccurate flying. What was this going to be like in bad weather? Quickly we were established on a very short, straight final approach, the special indicator lights at the start of the runway showing slightly 'high', the correct indication for a 747, due to the distance of the dangling wheels far below the pilot's eye level. The flight engineer called 'thirty' and once again I eased back on the yoke to raise the Jumbo's nose just a couple of degrees. The huge wings cushioned, then the main wheels rumbled onto the asphalt. I snapped the thrust levers back to the idle stop then lifted the four smaller knobs mounted ahead of them to select reverse thrust, in order to ease the brakes' burden of slowing the Jumbo down. The engines roared with the reverse and the nose wheels far below the cockpit fell to the runway – a little more firmly than I would have liked. Keeping straight as we slowed along the runway centreline stripes, I 'stowed' the reversers and the engine note became the now-familiar drone of idle thrust. Ironically, having landed the huge aircraft myself, I had to then hand control over to the captain. I had landed a Boeing 747 at one of the most demanding airports on earth, but Cathay policy at that time, as Ansett's had been, was not to allow first officers to taxi the aircraft!

Cathay Pacific was expanding so rapidly that its training system could not keep up with the task required to produce the numbers of 'line qualified' pilots that the airline needed. An opportunity arose. I had been in Hong Kong for three months, away from my family, working hard once again to learn yet another aircraft type and to fit in with yet another aviation organisation. But with the training delays, I could return to Australia until line training could start. It was an ideal opportunity to get to know my growing children once more and to prepare to move Yvonne, Avalon and little Rohan to live in Hong Kong. I had already resigned from the Air Force Reserve: colleagues on 21 Squadron were aghast that due to an industrial dispute, I had chosen to leave the country. Also, the Berlin Wall had fallen in late 1989, symbolically ending the Cold War, which had been such a large part of my life. Neville Shute's *On the Beach* became just alternate history; however, the uncertainty of the power vacuum left by the disintegration of the Soviet Union was apparent, even then. We sold our Melton house to a relative. A garage sale disposed of most of our furniture and possessions. We started again domestically in Asia because only limited removal assistance was offered and I had little idea as to what sort of flat we would live in.

Meanwhile, the remaining resigned domestic pilots of Australia had capitulated during the Australian autumn of 1990 and moves were being made by the Federation for 'an orderly return to work'. Ansett and Australian Airlines were continuing to receive government assistance in the form of the foreign pilots being admitted into the country, and ongoing support from the air force. During the dispute many civilian General Aviation and even some military pilots had taken the chance of a lifetime to walk straight into an airline job, and now there were people to train them: a few pilots who later 'crossed the line' and returned to work had been crucial Check and Training Captains. The airlines' managers knew then that they could rebuild.

The handling of the dispute had been disastrous on both sides. On one side had been the arrogance and industrial naivety of the Australian Federation of Air Pilots. The AFAP had been greedy, and it underestimated the cosy relationship between the socialist government and other unions with the airlines, one of them government-owned. However, the foolish statements from Hawke had inflamed the dispute and stung conservative, professional pilots, many of them family men, into unprecedented, uncompromising action. This same Prime Minister had presided over the emasculation of the country's Fleet Air Arm just a few years previously. Naval personnel and their families had had their lives changed forever, not to mention the squandering of all that expertise in naval aviation. Now the Pilots' Dispute had rocked the lives of many other Australians, particularly those whose livings depended on travel or tourism. But notwithstanding the capitulation of the AFAP, the airlines themselves would take years to recover, if ever, from the costs of the prolonged shutdown, the foreign charter aircraft and the training or retraining of their crews. I wondered how long either company would last.

Although I stood under clean, deep blue southern skies once more, I felt like a foreigner in my own land. I no longer worked for an Australian company, and I was preparing to move my family and a few possessions to Asia. After twelve years' service with Australia's armed forces, then two with what had been the nation's premium domestic airline and time with the Air Force Reserve, I flew out as a declared non-resident, disillusioned and glad to be gone. My family would soon follow. I wondered when, if ever, Australia would be home again.

Sixty-four steps led up from the front door of our first home in Hong Kong, known as a 'villa', to the highest of the five floors, and then further up onto the flat roof. The rented concrete structure was built into the side of a cliff in an area of mainland Hong Kong called Clearwater Bay. To an Australian, the area looked more 'normal' than the rest of Hong Kong Island, Kowloon and the 'New Territories', because of its low-rise apartments, some even with tiny gardens, which looked over either side of roughly sealed roads. These villas were far beyond the financial reach of the average Hong Kong citizen, and most expatriates unless they received rental assistance from their employers. Ours had the ubiquitous Hong Kong parquet floor on each level comprising only a small room or two. There was, however, a little garden on a terrace in front of the living area. Lots of expatriates resided in Clearwater Bay and the neighbouring Sai Kung. Many of them were Cathay Pacific crew because it was a reasonably short journey to Kai Tak Airport. Ed rented further down the hill and both of our villas boasted a spectacular view east over the South China Sea, where scattered, peaky islands could be discerned through varying degrees of haze. Most Hong Kong citizens lived in concrete flats in high-rise buildings, often three generations to a few square metres. Home ownership was rare; most locals rented as well, or lived in tiny flats provided by a government scheme. Our comparatively luxurious property's rental was heavily subsidised by Cathay Pacific, who at that time provided its expatriate crew some semblance of the standard of living that they would have enjoyed in their home countries. High summer was approaching, and the air was heavy with moisture as we trekked around the crowded city to source appliances and basic furniture. Shops that sold similar things tended to be located in the same streets. There were streets of electronic shops. There were streets of furniture shops. There was even a 'Wedding Card Street'. A friend joked that if you wanted a valve for your toilet cistern, you went to a 'Valve Street' miles away where the shops that sold them would be all located together. Ed and I had previously looked at a large housing complex, which comprised row after row of townhouse-style flats (the development derisively called 'Lego Land' by some). We were told that there were a couple of shops within the complex, which we assumed would sell food and a few of the other daily conveniences of life, because the complex lay a rough and winding bus ride along a busy road from any other shopping area. Contemplating living there, we took a look at the shops. One was a Mercedes car showroom, and the other sold radios for boats.

The new salary enabled us to afford a live-in helper. Our daughter and son were six and two years old respectively, and the boy was a handful. A 'girl next door' in Hong Kong who would babysit expatriate children was almost non-existent, and in any event there was the language barrier. Most Chinese people worked while grandparents looked after the children, in the Asian tradition. Middle and upper class local Chinese families also employed helpers from the Philippines for the same reasons. When I flew long-haul, I could be on the other side of the planet for days on end. There were few supermarkets that we could drive to, let alone park at, and a simple shopping trip could take half a day on public transport in the dripping heat, rain and humidity. Cleaning tasks were never-ending in the constant battle against mould. Dehumidifiers hummed night and day during the nine months of the humid season. Ruth, our new helper from the Philippines, eventually became a part of the family. There were occasional unsavoury reports about how the local Chinese and even some expatriates treated their helpers, and combined with the alien concept to Australians having live-in domestic help, Ruth was paid well above the stipulated wage and given more than the standard contractual opportunities to visit home, fares paid for by us. She sent most of her earnings back to the Philippines to support her extended family.

Oddly, expatriate life in Hong Kong could be reminiscent of that of residing in a small regional city or large town. A few hundred thousand Europeans and other expatriates lived and worked in the city-state of 6,000,000 Chinese, and of course a European stood out, usually taller, among the hordes of Chinese thronging the streets. It was not unusual to randomly encounter a friend or acquaintance in the teeming city. Although Hong Kong was a British colony, the language and cultural barriers between Europeans and locals were significant, and Europeans tended to primarily mix and socialise with their own background.

Hong Kong Chinese spoke Cantonese, a provincial dialect, not the national Chinese language of Mandarin, which was spoken throughout the 'mainland'. If one could read them, even the ornate Cantonese written characters were different to those of the rest of China. In the early nineties, 'home grown' airline pilots from Hong Kong were almost non-existent: the colony had no air force, and the cost of the limited private flying available in Hong Kong was horrendous. Also, aviation was not of interest to many young Chinese people, who were more inclined to a business or professional career. I rationalised things with the thought that we were specialist workers who provided a service that the locals of this developing city-state could not provide. We could not become Hong Kong citizens, but we had been issued with Identity Cards, subject to review, that entitled us to residency. If an expat kept his or her nose clean, after seven years a Permanent ID Card would be granted which would allow them to live in Hong Kong without restriction.

The parallel feel of a small regional city was also fostered by the entertainment available. The internet was not widely available in Hong Kong during the early nineties. The programming of the sole pair of English-speaking television channels was reminiscent of a regional Australian or American town. The evening weather report was something from the 1960s: a rather amateurish weather girl would read out the day's weather and temperature. On one channel, the next day's forecast would then be presented by 'Freddie'. He was a cartoon character who clip-clopped onto screen and invariably sighed 'Ahhhh!' then 'Ohhhh!' when a cartoon sun became obscured by cloud and smog. Alternatively, Freddie would get rained on or, if severe thunderstorms were forecast, 'zapped' in his rear end by a lightning bolt. Sometimes he was blown away by typhonic winds. The expat culture in Hong Kong was a melange of this small-town ambience alongside the prevailing British accents, conspicuous consumption, travel, and a relentless hunger for money.

However, I had little time to ponder life in the city-state. Flying the Boeing 747 was one thing, but now I had to become competent in *operating* the huge airliner as its second-in-command. 'Line training' loomed while I was busy with both settling my family and the study of routes, airports and procedures. The training comprised forty 'sectors', or individual flights with a Training Captain, and would go on for months, because most of the sectors were hours long. Most of these flights were 'regional': as far west as India, east to Japan and Korea, and to destinations in South East Asia. A few 'medium haul' sectors would be flown to Australia and the Middle East. I was now thirty-two, busy and somewhat stressed. I was settling my family as best I could in a foreign city, and simultaneously had to study the multitude of Cathay procedures, destination airports, flight routes, national rules and emergency actions. The rapacious Hong Kong landlords were not renowned for their fairness and assistance, and ours was no exception. Our villa comprised just the concrete and parquet rooms built into the hillside, with windows devoid of curtains or blinds, and no furniture or appliances to speak of. There was no oven or cooktop. The light fittings had no bulbs. Everything had to be sourced over time and transported through the traffic in our tiny car, or delivery laboriously organised to Clearwater Bay, which most Hong Kong people considered to be 'countryside' in comparison to Kowloon or Hong Kong Island. Rohan, at two years of age, was difficult and often distressed and angry after we moved into the Spartan rooms in the heat and humidity. It would be months before our efforts, along with Ruth's assistance, would make the concrete box into the semblance of a home.

I coped reasonably well with the Asian regional flights. My experience of operating the Orion in South East Asia was valuable. But unlike the Orion with its 'captive audience' of military crew, the Jumbo carried up to 400 passengers who had chosen to pay money to fly with the airline. The schedule, passenger comfort and fuel economy were paramount. I learned how the captains dealt with the multitude of issues that arose on every flight: air traffic clearances, weather, security, the thirteen or fourteen cabin crew, fuel uplifts, cargo loads and, together with the flight engineer, whether the occasional small defect was acceptable for the flight in accordance with the MEL (Minimum Equipment List), a legal document that had to be followed to the letter. Airliners have multiple systems, deliberately so, in order that – with one system or piece of equipment inoperative – the MEL *may*, with certain conditions and extra procedures, permit the flight to still depart and get the passengers to where they want to go.

Ranging further afield across southern China, Burma (now Myanmar), Bangladesh and into India, I found myself working to cope, ironically more so when acting as 'Pilot Not Flying' (or PNF), in other words, doing paperwork and handling the radio amid other duties, such as supporting the captain. Unlike Ansett Airlines, Cathay's in-flight paperwork was copious. A log was kept of every waypoint, along with times and fuel on board. Take-off weights, speeds and thrust settings had to be filled out on a card. In-flight, en-route and destination weather reports had to be written down, gleaned from scratchy HF broadcasts only available at certain times of the hour. A comprehensive Administrative Report had to be filled out on every sector. Fuel uplifts had to be calculated and noted, with the receipt and yet another form with the quantities converted to litres. All this paperwork was retained for checking by the airline after every flight, sometimes also for audit by the Hong Kong Government's Civil Aviation Department. Cathay's shortest 747 sector, Hong Kong to Taipei, was around one hour and twenty minutes' flight time with a relatively short cruise segment, far less with a winter jet stream tailwind, and a 'new joiner' would sometimes struggle just to get on top of the administration, let alone other duties. Despite its generous proportions, the 747 was the fastest airliner in the sky, apart from the supersonic Concorde. It normally cruised at Mach 0.85 (eighty-five per cent of the speed of sound), which covered ground at eight miles – or fifteen kilometres – per minute, and even faster when flying eastwards in a raging tailwind.

As the PNF, the radio work was a challenge until I got used to the system and what was required. Radar seemed to be used only by the military in some countries, and over Burma, Bangladesh and India, civilian separation was procedural: the controllers relied on radio reports from each aircraft to build a picture of where everybody was. I found that some countries had such primitive infrastructure that, for example, an air traffic controller in Calcutta, India, had no direct connection with his counterpart in Dakar, Bangladesh. In the '90s, it was still up to the individual pilots to communicate and coordinate their flights with the two air traffic 'agencies'; for example, when we were westbound over Bangladesh, after reporting to Dakar Control, we had to call Calcutta over another radio to advise them that we were over Bangladesh and approaching their airspace, along with our estimated times and, of course, our altitude. Usually, the aircraft's long-range HF radios – technology from the 1930s – had to be used to do this. On HF, all ground stations and aircraft talked over each other on the one static filled frequency, which hissed, squawked and popped in our headphones or through the cockpit speakers. Ground stations in India, Pakistan, Burma and Bangladesh also used the same frequency to pass traffic information to each other, where in the developed world, a landline or other separate communications link would be used. They often over-transmitted ('stepped on') other ground stations and aircraft. Old Cathay hands recounted heavily Indian-accented exchanges over HF, such as, 'Bombay, this is Calcutta. Bombay, this is Calcutta – *shut up, Delhi, shut up I am trying to call Calcutta!*' One had to jump into a break in the constant transmissions and then remember all the correct details to be passed to the ground, say, Rangoon Radio: call sign, flight level, departure point, destination, last position level and time, next position level and time, when we would enter their airspace, when we would leave their airspace, SELCAL code and check …

SELCAL was a special code that enabled ground stations to selectively call individual aircraft by way of a special two-toned beep. With a successful SELCAL check, there was usually a muttered, 'Thank Christ for that' from the pilots, because now they would not have to continuously listen to the static and chatter of the HF. A loud chime or buzz sounded in the cockpit to alert the pilot to select the HF monitor knob and to plunge into the chatter on the frequency to find out who was calling., Simultaneously, there were often separate calls on the two separate VHF radios that still had to be used.

There was not a lot of love lost between some Asian nations. India, Pakistan and Bangladesh, along with most Asian countries, had national military Air Defence Identification Zones. The navigation charts were festooned with 'ball flags' in these areas: little numbers that referred to special procedures written elsewhere, such as required position reports, often well in advance of entering new airspace, and to multiple agencies. Westbound over Bangladesh, the PNF had to simultaneously deal with Dakar on the VHF radio, 'close' with Rangoon on HF, pre-call Calcutta on the same HF frequency, and listen out to and make 'blind broadcasts' on yet another VHF frequency of position, routing and flight level. There would, of course, be a multitude of other aircraft that were also trying to get a word in to satisfy these requirements. International convention deemed Burma's airspace so primitive that the blind broadcasts had to be made as a last backstop to avoid, at best, a 'loss of separation' incident or, at worst, the catastrophic collision of two airliners. Then there was the paperwork as we overflew the relatively small countries of Southeast Asia at eight miles – or fifteen kilometres – every minute, dealing with each air traffic agency in turn. Now it was summer, and it was also the PNF's responsibility to get air traffic control clearance to deviate many miles from the flight planned route in order to avoid the thunderstorms that flickered and winked during the night in long lines ahead.

Hong Kong would seem pristine on the return from my first India 'pattern'. Outbound, we flew west towards the late afternoon sun to Bangkok for an hour's stop for more passengers and fuel, and then on through the black of night to Bombay (now Mumbai). Bombay airport sat close to the Arabian Sea coast in a miasma of wood smoke and the general smell of massed humanity. People ambled and dogs trotted about the taxiways and tarmacs as they pleased. The flight engineer had been issued with the routine bottle of Scotch whisky to ease the crew's processing through immigration. Then for an hour the bus thudded over potholes and crumbling asphalt through teeming streets to downtown Bombay, our teeth jarring and our bodies flopping about on the hard seats from tiredness. The racket from blaring horns was constant: trucks had the words 'Horn Please' incongruously emblazoned on the tailgates, exhorting other drivers to sound their horns as a warning when overtaking. They needed little encouragement. One pilot later recounted how he had had a bet with a Bombay taxi driver that he would pay double the fare if the driver did not use the horn. He did not have to pay up.

Sleep, even during the day in India, would be welcome, especially as the following night we were to operate an overnight shuttle flight from Bombay to Dubai in the Middle East and return; and so, we arrived back in Bombay similarly two mornings later to board the same bus. Coffee on the flight kept my brain awake for the interminable bus journey even though my body craved sleep. The sun was rising and vignette after vignette appeared in the bus window. Individuals and family groups slept on rags and cardboard in doorways; a naked man was casually urinating against a wall. There were other groups squatting and defecating in fields and open spaces holding cans of water or sometimes a toothbrush. A dentist's sign read: 'DENTAL SURGEON V. K. Singh B. D. Sc Bombay (failed)'. I assumed that even failed doctors and dentists in India had their place because poorer patients could afford their reduced fees. The hotel was relatively comfortable, however, many crew were still often sick. Later, a company doctor accompanied a crew on a Bombay flight to investigate what could be done. He caught a 'bait' himself. Drained and ill in his hotel room, Doc watched the maid polish up the toilet bowl, then give the drinking glasses on the basin a quick wipe over with the same cloth. We would get a day off in this hotel prior to two more night sectors back to Hong Kong via Bangkok, where I would walk the streets of central Bombay before returning to the hotel, worn down by the touts.

Another 'medium haul' training pattern was to Sydney for a layover there, then flying back to Hong Kong via Melbourne. We flew through the night, and arrived in Sydney in the early morning, tired and drawn. I felt like a stranger in my own land. There were a few Ansett and Australian Airlines aircraft in the air now, with most of their radio calls foreign-accented. However, it was an opportunity for me to visit a good old Aussie hardware shop: so much stuff that I had previously taken for granted, and all in the one store! My luggage was crammed with items that could be put to good use to make our Hong Kong villa a little more like what had been home.

Days later it was time for my first Europe pattern; however, we were not carrying any passengers. Cathay Pacific Airways operated several versions of the Boeing 747, including freighter variants. Apart from a huge door on the rear left side of the fuselage, the entire nose of the aircraft opened up like a helmet visor, allowing clear access to the completely bare main deck. The space was cavernous. Hundreds of rollers studded the bare metal floor, which allowed containers and massive pallets of cargo to slide along from the loading doors to their designated positions before being securely locked and strapped down. A clacking metal ladder led to the upper deck, where a galley and a Spartan rest area were located. Forward of the cockpit door the flight deck was virtually identical to that of the passenger Jumbo, with a few minor changes, mainly for the flight engineer. A critical system was that which indicated that the massive nose and side doors were correctly locked for flight.

The freighters carried an eclectic mix of loads. Among the myriad containers and plastic covered pallets ratcheted down on the vast main deck of the freighter could be luxury automobiles, racing cars or prize pigs. We carried racehorses, with their grooms accommodated in a small passenger area behind us in the 'hump' of the 747. After engine shutdown at Heathrow one evening with horses on board, the flight engineer commented drily, 'Those grooms will be OK for transport home.' The reader may be familiar with the classic American movie, *Top Gun*. The naval aviator hero, while in trouble with his superiors, is warned that if he does not shape up, he will end up 'flying a cargo plane full of rubber dog shit out of Hong Kong!' Well, here I was, an ex-navy pilot, doing seemingly just that! The famous line was fresh in the mind of most Cathay Pacific pilots during this time, and I would quip that I was also not above carrying rubber spiders or plastic vomit.

We flew non-stop, weaving among the winking thunderstorms through the August night, to Dubai for a one-day layover, and then we were onwards to Frankfurt, Germany. The route to Dubai was now familiar: we flew through southern China, Burma, Bangladesh, India and Pakistani airspace to the Gulf States. I found the Dubai to Frankfurt sector civilised because, after Iranian and Turkish airspace, Air Traffic Control spoke perfect English and radar control was used – so no more position reports! 'Direct' routings (short cuts) were almost always available. The volume of traffic around Frankfurt and the competence and calmness of the European controllers as they coped with it, were noteworthy. The crew hotel lay in the city of Mainz, on the Rhine. I had never been to Europe, and the washed-out, blue summer sky, the medieval buildings and the crowded beer gardens were a stark contrast to steamy, grubby and frenetic Hong Kong. But I was not there for sightseeing, I was under training and I had a lot to study about the busy European airports and air routes. It was also my first real taste of jet lag, which I would have to cope with for the rest of my career with Cathay Pacific.

The flight had also been my first taste of operating over the extremely high, mountainous terrain of Iran and Turkey. 'Escape Routes' published among our documents provided guidance for the crew as to where to turn and how to follow these special routes in order to descend to a safe altitude, should the aircraft depressurise or lose multiple engines. It was important to study these in advance, because getting onto oxygen, dealing with the depressurisation, emergency descent and checklists made for a frenetic situation. Over these mountains, a straightforward descent to 10,000 feet – or 3,300 metres – (the standard altitude considered where oxygen masks no longer needed to be used) would result in the jet impacting terrain.

Many Australians in the 1960s were culturally tied to Great Britain. As a child I had stood in the local theatre for 'God Save the Queen' and we celebrated Empire Day with the then-legal firecrackers, including the infamous 'bungers'. I hero-worshipped the Dam Busters, the Battle of Britain pilots, the British aviation pioneers and of course read books about any British aircraft. Many of my treasured books about flying had been written by Britons. The next day, we departed for London's Gatwick Airport, and at last I would set foot in the United Kingdom, a big event for me. We 'cleaned up' the 747 through its ponderous stages of flap retraction and climbed towards England.

I was PNF, and my hands flew around the cockpit on this short sector: checklists, paperwork, weather reports and the rapid-fire frequency changes as we passed from one busy air traffic control sector to the next. Soon, we were at cruising altitude, but only minutes later it was time to prepare for descent. But as the jet nosed earthwards at 300 knots – or 550 km/hr – I could steal a glance down in clear weather at the white cliffs of Dover. However, I found the rest of England was unexpectedly brown in the summer heat. The unflappable London air traffic controllers lived up to their status as among the world's best as we were vectored in heavy traffic to Gatwick's single runway, and I could not help but compare this with Australia's restrictive and inflexible air traffic control at Sydney and Melbourne: airports with multiple runways, overwhelmingly better weather and a tiny fraction of the traffic to deal with. I was compiling a mental list of 'things the British do best' and the first item on the list was 'Humour'. Now, I would add 'Air Traffic Control'. The next morning I added 'Breakfasts' as Item Three. But in this hot weather, I wouldn't have added 'Use of deodorant'. Eight days after we had left Hong Kong for Dubai we landed back at Kai Tak, which now almost felt like home. I suffered the effects of jet lag and fitful sleep but also exhilaration after travelling to Europe and England for the first time, which were no longer lines and colours on the maps I had pored over as a child. Over those eight days, we had travelled from Hong Kong to Dubai, then to Frankfurt, Gatwick, Heathrow, Frankfurt, Dubai and back to Hong Kong. My Training Captain, Stu from Kenya, had been delightful to fly with. Now I would have a few days off, followed by several regional flights with a new trainer, who, although pleasant, was more demanding. I could not relax for a moment. But by trying to meet his standards, I was well prepared for my initial 'check to line'.

***

The test was an overnight pattern to Jakarta via Singapore. As with most airlines, there were some oddballs among the cohort of Check Captains. In Cathay Pacific, the peculiarities of some of these captains were exacerbated by the various national characteristics and aviation backgrounds of the airline's recruitment base. One management pilot, small of stature, was renowned for waving an actual Cathay Pacific passenger ticket at assembled new joiners on their first day with the airline, exhorting, 'See this ticket? It's a one-way flight out of here if you don't come up to scratch …' But luck smiled, and I was fortunate to be checked by Ken Vickers, an Englishman who was legendary, not just for his outgoing personality and enjoyment of life, but also for his knowledge and competence. After the night flight south and a Jakarta layover followed by an early start, we flew northwards in clear skies towards Hong Kong after another transit through Singapore, the South China Sea uncharacteristically blue beneath. Insidious tension and anxiety had built up inside me since I committed myself and my family to a new life as an expatriate, which had been absolutely dependent on my meeting of Cathay's standards. It melted away on this last sector thanks to Ken's demeanour as we took it in turns to enjoy our lunch, balanced on the pillows on our laps. Ken gave me just a quick debrief in the cockpit at the 'gate' in Kai Tak about the inevitable 'training points', then shook my hand. Now, I was a Cathay pilot (albeit, a 'First Officer on Probation').

However, I had been in aviation long enough to know that passing a check flight is actually just a licence to learn. Until I was off Probation, I would not be completely in the fold. I would be assessed again on a 'Probationary Line Check' in a few months. The company always had a second look at their newly-trained pilots. But for a while, by 'flying the line' free of the minutiae and tension of training, I would be exposed to the strengths and weaknesses of the various captains and other first officers, to become more familiar with the Jumbo, Hong Kong and its IGS, and the ports of the network. There was a large variety in the captains of Cathay Pacific, even though at that time the airline only recruited Anglo-Saxon males from Commonwealth backgrounds: South Africans, Zimbabweans – previously Rhodesians – who were virtual refugees from their disintegrating country; and British pilots from the military, minor airlines and charter outfits. There were many Australians and New Zealanders, the majority from their respective air forces, but increasing numbers of ex-Ansett and ex-Australian Airlines pilots flocked to join in the aftermath of the dispute. There were a few Irish captains – one notorious for being argumentative and abrasive to fly with – another softly spoken, erudite and gentlemanly.

Equally among the first officers, the experience levels and variety of backgrounds were remarkable. Cathay Pacific had only just started recruiting Canadians who, like myself, were working their way through the first officer ranks. The Canadians also came from military and civilian backgrounds: many had extensive experience in Canada's white, frozen north and I found that they not only worked hard, but played hard. I still smile at the memory of one 'Canuck' (Canadian) on a Friday night of our initial training, being loaded by his slightly less inebriated buddies onto the long baggage conveyor belt that ran beside the walkway built over the road back to the Kai Tak Airport Hotel. There was the occasional conflict between relatively casual but competent and practical Canadians and some of the more rigid British, Australian and New Zealand Check Captains. Some British FOs had flown with the renowned Royal Air Force 'Red Arrows' aerobatic team. Many of the Africans had flown in war zones, such as Angola. An ex-Royal Navy pilot had shot down Argentine Pucara attack aircraft with his Sea Harrier during the Falklands War. Then there were the pilots from Ansett and Australian Airlines, some of whom had been in management positions, such as my friend Ed, all of them now first officers.

There were also the flight engineers, of similar demographics to the pilots. Most were ex-military of the various Commonwealth air forces, while a few had worked their way up through civilian engineering backgrounds. Unlike in the Orion, the 747 and TriStar flight engineers sat at sideways-facing panels behind the first officer, which meant that the FO could not see the panel directly; however, the captain could see it if he twisted around in his seat. From their years in the airline, the captains and engineers knew each other well, and would have flown together on many occasions. Therefore, a new first officer could feel a little cut out of the operation at times.

The flight engineers (sometimes referred to as 'ginger beers') were generally pleasant and competent to fly with. On the huge Boeing, the FE's duties included carrying out the external walk-around, and calculating the take-off data: speeds, flap settings, engine power to set and limiting weights, which had to be cross-checked by the captain or first officer. Most flight engineers were good company, technically knowledgeable and, importantly, knew the locations of the best bars and restaurants throughout the airline's network. A few were harder to deal with, and having this second crew member to interact with, along with the captain, especially at a busy time, could add to a first officer's workload. The FE's 'third set of eyes and ears' were invaluable, as was his ability to wade through the Minimum Equipment List. Because he knew the aircraft intimately, he could correctly interpret a small defect and apply the required actions and performance adjustments to keep the show on the road.

There were legends of flight engineers' exploits: two of them tried to lead a small pony that had been 'liberated' from a nearby travelling circus on a European layover into the crew hotel with the aim of knocking on the captain's door and leaving it outside as, late at night, the hotel lobby was deserted. They could not persuade the animal to walk up the stairs to the lifts, so they left the pony there and went to bed. One rotund Australian FE made it a tradition on departures from the Melbourne hotel to stop the crew bus at a bakery and buy a tray of meat pies for himself and the crew, to serve up later from the galley. There were tales of First Class passengers seeing the tray of hot pies and demanding one. A TriStar engineer persuaded newly-joined flight attendants that a toilet in the aircraft had an 'overheating flush motor' and it had to be flushed every ten minutes throughout the flight to save the aircraft from catching fire …

In all, Cathay Pacific Airways during the 1990s recruited 'the best of the best', and I would have to learn quickly and work hard to approach the standards represented by these talented individuals. Unlike in Qantas or Ansett, my captaincy was now a relatively short five to seven years away; however, Cathay's Command (Captain's) Course was notorious for its length, toughness and the dreaded final check flights.

In return for the high standards expected, Cathay Pacific's salaries and conditions of service were the best in the world. Hong Kong was regarded as a relatively alien place for a European to live with a family. There was also the looming handover of the British colony to China that would occur in 1997, just seven years away, which had spooked many prospective Cathay pilots. Therefore, the airline paid vast sums of money to subsidise housing and education to a European standard. Our daughter was enrolled in an English school in Kowloon and, at six years old, it did not take her long to start nattering away in a cultured British accent. A 'travel fund' was provided to enable expatriate employees to fly home on leave, and leave itself was a generous seven weeks per year. There was even a loan to enable a pilot to purchase a retirement property back home. But he would have no pension. The airline contributed to a 'provident fund', which was a cheque made out in Hong Kong dollars and provided at the end of a pilot's service. It was up to the retiring pilot to invest it wisely. I recalled my air force days with a young family in Adelaide, wondering how I would pay to replace a broken hot water system, and the red-letter days of walking into the local bank to deposit a few spare dollars after each fortnightly pay day if nothing else had gone wrong. Then there had been the eking out of the Air Force Reserve salary and savings during the grim, grey days of the Pilots' Dispute. I listened in on bar talk from senior Cathay captains, and the sums of money they spoke of regarding investments or real estate were, to me, jaw-dropping. In my early thirties, this was my final chance of obtaining financial comfort and stability and, despite the lucrative contract, I would try to live frugally and to invest wisely. Significantly, some cynical Cathay Pacific pilots would tell me, 'The best financial advice I can give you is to leave Hong Kong with the same missus you arrived with.'

However, there was that quid pro quo for all this company largesse: Cathay's pilots were expected to always go the extra mile: answer the telephone on a day off to crew a flight; go to the very legal limits of flight duty times; use a 'sharp pencil' when calculating fuel loads. The Boeing 747 consumed prodigious amounts of fuel to carry the weight of extra fuel. On long flights, well over half a tonne of fuel would be burnt just to provide an extra tonne for arrival at destination, such as when bad weather was expected. Crews were encouraged to 'press on' in typhoon conditions, to 'have a look at' an approach, on the chance that wind and visibility would be within the legal limits at 'minimums' to get the aircraft, crew and passengers to where they were supposed to be. Some of this weather was not for the faint-hearted. Standards would continue to be high for the regular simulator assessments, instrument rating renewals and 'line checks' in the aircraft. A pilot would still, well after training, be almost constantly in the books.

Until now I had only flown short and medium haul flights with Cathay Pacific. However, the pioneering spirit of Farrell and de Kantzow was still tangible with the airline, because then, Cathay led the world in long haul operations. Today, non-stop flights to almost anywhere on the planet are taken for granted, but in the early 1990s, although the Boeing 747 had revolutionised global travel, early models of the aircraft were less capable: most flights from East Asia to Europe, England or North America needed a fuel stop. But Cathay's 747-200s were just that slightly more efficient thanks to their Rolls Royce engines. The airline also employed top talent in its engineering and flight planning departments, and its motivated flight crew were a great asset. Cathay Pacific had, therefore, virtually pioneered long haul operations, and its non-stop services from Hong Kong to London and Vancouver were famous. The company's Business Class was named 'Marco Polo Class': marketing genius that invoked the spirit of the Venetian trader who travelled the Silk Road from Europe to 'Cathay' during the thirteenth century. The airline's television advertisements were set to 'Love's Theme' by Barry White's 'The Love Unlimited Orchestra'. One featured a 747 majestically cruising in a dusky sky, its beacons blinking almost as if to follow the beat of the music, the melody so appropriate that it could have been written for the company. 'Love's Theme' evoked romance so well but, in this case, that of travel and exotic destinations.

By the time I began my career with the airline, a few other long haul destinations had appeared on the rosters. My first was Rome, but the streets were wet under gloomy sky. Our captain had not been to Rome before, either, so we endeavoured to take in the sights. There were few overhanging verandas to walk under on the ancient streets, and rainwater dripped off the cornices of the buildings, most black with grime, as the Vespa ('Wasp') scooters snarled, beeped and belched smoke around us while we walked the ancient streets. We were accosted by gangs of pickpocketing gypsies and their hands were all over us as we pushed and shoved them away. The few Italian police who were around were uncaring as they strutted in their finery.

Long haul flights required more flight crew, not from charitable considerations of the airline's management, but from a legal requirement from Hong Kong's Civil Aviation Department. Crew members could not be expected to remain awake and alert for the entire time of a twelve to fourteen hour flight. Because it was long haul, a second flight engineer had been boarded for our Hong Kong to Rome flight along with another, more experienced first officer who was designated as the 'Relief Pilot' (RP). Ahead was yet another course to become an RP myself in a year or so, after gaining experience and further training in the classroom and simulator. I would also have to pass the British licensing exams. The RP was entrusted to act as the aircraft commander while the captain was taking his rest, and had to be immediately capable of dealing with an emergency, such as depressurisation or engine failure. Avoiding 'weather' (thunderstorms) was also the RP's responsibility. Most captains rested during the middle part of the flight, so the RP would also be responsible for obtaining the optimum altitude for the aircraft weight to ensure the required fuel margins were kept intact. On busy Asian air routes with primitive air traffic control, negotiating a higher, more efficient altitude to fly at was often a chore in itself.

Because of the statutory flight time limitations, the RP often became burnt out, which meant that at the end of his stint at the controls, he was considered a passenger because he had reached the end of his legal Flight Duty Period. The rest achieved by the captain and the other first officer could be credited towards an extension of their duty periods to the end of the flight to remain 'legal'. This resulted in the unfortunate RP enjoying only a few hours in the bunk at the start of the flight, then to come on duty for up to eight hours at the controls. With the end of the marathon journey in sight: he would get barely two hours' rest before landing while the flight attendants clattered away serving breakfast. The pair of flight engineers enjoyed a far better routine, they shared their duty periods equally.

When off duty, the resting pilot and flight engineer slept – or, tried to sleep – in green-curtained bunks in the 'hump' of the 747 behind the cockpit door. The area was draughty, noisy and cold from the aircraft's metal skin, a few millimetres thick, which shielded us from the far deeper cold of the stratosphere outside that was often below minus sixty degrees Celsius. I slept fitfully in the roar of the airflow around the upper body of the Jumbo and the background hum of the engines as the huge machine powered through the upper atmosphere, occasionally shaken awake by turbulence. Sleep was also fitful because of my inexperience: I would be keyed-up about the arrival (usually in the early morning) at an unfamiliar airport on the other side of the world. There was also the clatter of the passenger meal service, of which there were several on these marathon flights.

In late October 1990 came time for another flight to London, which included a longer layover. We lifted off and climbed smoothly through the Lei Yue Mun Gap in the stability and cool of the approaching pleasant time of the year in east Asia, before turning west towards Dubai for an overnight stay, and then a flight to Gatwick. However, only three of us were on board, because the aircraft was a freighter. Our captain was 'Killa', who had carried out the 'retest' of a young Acting Sub-lieutenant Carr, of marginal ability, in a Tracker only a decade ago. Such a small world was aviation! With the Cold

War over but the Gulf War raging, we were careful to monitor navigation and radios as we passed through Middle East airspace and into and out of Dubai. Strange military call signs in British and American accents came over the radio. It was ironic that I had spent twelve years in the Australian military without seeing a shot fired in anger, but here we were in a civilian freighter skirting a war zone.

I made a redeeming, acceptable landing at Gatwick, to my relief, and Killa and I reminisced over wine that evening. On the following days off I took the treasured opportunity to visit the museums, especially the Royal Air Force museum at Hendon, the Greenwich Observatory and the Imperial War Museum. I added 'Museums' to my mental list of 'Things the British do Best'. In my early teens I had assembled a small Airfix model of the famous 'tea clipper' *Cutty Sark*. Now I was aboard the actual preserved ship, black hulled, her tarnished coppered bottom supported in a dry dock. I strode the deck as I pleased, almost the only visitor on this cool, windy weekday. I gazed up at the white and black tracery of masts, spars and rigging etched against the blue and the white of a scudding-clouded Atlantic sky. The most compelling view was forward from the ship's wheel near the stern, with the three masts, their spars and rigging filling the sky ahead. Not so many decades ago, captains in sail had set out from here for eastern Australia, around the Cape of Good Hope, to then ride the 'Roaring Forties' westerlies, their objective the comparatively small gap between treacherous Cape Wickham on Bass Strait's King Island, and Cape Otway on Victoria's south-west coast, before passage onwards to Melbourne or Sydney. These ships were the nineteenth century analogue of a 747 full of humanity and goods bound for the other side of the planet. How the world had changed in just a century, yet we were doing similar work, but with almost zero risk and using technology that would have been unimaginable to Captains Moodie, Moore or Woodget of the *Cutty Sark*.

I had been with Cathay Pacific Airways for a year, which included the training delays, and the Probationary Line Check loomed. It was yet another freighter pattern to Europe, and the

Check Captain was Brian, a rather formal Caucasian West Indian: he spoke in an incongruous West Indian accent. He was also deeply religious. We operated from Hong Kong to Karachi, the main port of Pakistan. After sleeping off the tiredness from the overnight sector, surprisingly, Brian suggested a quiet beer in the hotel, an idea with which the flight engineer and I readily agreed. However, in this deeply Muslim country, the hotel staff took our passports to photocopy, then presented us with paperwork to fill out before we could order our refreshments. We duly signed the forms to certify that we were alcoholics, and that the alcohol was required for medicinal purposes. When we tasted the locally brewed beer, we wondered why we had bothered. Later, the captain – a little daringly, I thought – left the hotel in search of a Catholic church to attend, asking all and sundry if they knew where one was.

The next evening's flight was from Karachi to Frankfurt. We had a 'near miss' with another aircraft due to an air traffic control error as we climbed out of Karachi. Also, the arrival into Frankfurt was a first for me, because the forecast had indicated that we would be landing in fog.

Even into the twenty-first century, Australia lagged behind the rest of the world in providing facilities that would enable aircraft to land in low visibility: fog or smoke. The continent's generally good weather argued against the government of Australia's sparse population paying for facilities that enabled airliners to take-off and land in these conditions. The airlines did not think it was worthwhile to upgrade aircraft instrumentation and crew training for the few occasions of the year that fog would be a problem. But the rest of the developed world had moved on, and even then, many airliners were capable of flying automatic approaches and landings. All it took was an upgrade of the familiar Instrument Landing System (ILS), crew training, and rules to ensure safe separation and non-interference with the radio beams. En route to Europe, I mentally rehearsed my duties for Low Weather Minima Operations, for which we had trained in the flight simulator. This was my Probationary Line Check and I could not afford an error. The arrival into Frankfurt was the first 'blind' approach I had seen (well, not totally blind, as these early 747's could only fly down to 'Category Two' minima). The old freighter slid down the ILS beam in the early morning freezing grey fog, the autopilots 'coupled up' to the beam while I stayed glued to the instruments, monitoring and ready to call out any deviation. My tiredness from the overnight flight was swept aside. Brian clicked off the autopilots at just one hundred feet – barely thirty metres – above the runway; the special approach lights, bright spots that burned through the grey, had become visible to him in the nick of time. He just had time to flare the huge jet and eighteen wheels rumbled onto the runway; but my duties were not complete. I remained 'head down' following the ground chart, monitoring our assigned taxi route to the freight apron of this vast airport, a city in itself, where an incorrect turn onto an active runway or busy taxiway in fog could result in disaster. The worst aviation accident in history occurred on the Atlantic island of Teneriffe in 1977. Two Boeing 747s collided on the runway in fog. 583 people were killed.

After a night's rest, it was my turn to fly the aircraft from Frankfurt to London Heathrow, where we were driven around London to position at Gatwick. After another night, we flew non-stop from Gatwick to Hong Kong, this time four of us in the freighter after an RP joined us at Heathrow, riding the prevailing westerly jet stream winds. At Kai Tak, eyes stinging from yet another sunrise, I tried to absorb Brian's debrief of the check. He drew attention to several minor lapses, then he shook my hand – I had passed. I was no longer on probation. I should have been happy and relieved, but all I could think of was getting home to Clearwater Bay, and sleep.

However, the study *still* was not over: now I had to prepare for the exams for the British Air Transport Pilot Licence subjects. This was a requirement in order to operate as a Relief Commander and, later – I hoped – Captain. A few weeks of leave had been assigned, however, there would not be any trips home to Australia, or elsewhere, for me. Following weeks of correspondence study, a group of us clubbed together to fly a British lecturer out to Hong Kong to polish up our weak areas and to gain an insight into what to expect. We had studied diligently; there was much to absorb, including the characteristics and mathematics of 'air-driven gyros', 'Doppler navigation over the North Sea', and other subjects completely irrelevant to the operation of wide-bodied jet transport aircraft. We had to learn the arcane names and characteristics of various seasonal winds of the northern hemisphere: the Mistral, the Simoom, the Etesians ... Over three days, we sat two exams per day, all subject to that British 'penalty marking' system. The papers were the actual U.K. exams, however, to our frustration, 'NOT VALID UK LICENCE' was prominently stamped on the papers. After all this work, those of us who were interested in obtaining a British licence in addition to the Hong Kong one would have to sit all the exams yet again!

Operation Desert Storm, to evict Saddam Hussein from Kuwait, was in full swing, and it was considered too dangerous to transit the Middle East for yet another freighter pattern to Europe. We were planned to track north to Beijing for an extended layover, as there were only so many freighter flights and fresh crews, before operating on to Helsinki, Finland, for another overnight, then Frankfurt. Beijing in early 1991 appeared unexpectedly Westernised, apart from the masses of bicycles and other human-drawn, and occasionally animal-drawn, conveyances. Departing Beijing, we circled the heavy freighter overhead, 350 tonnes of it, in a procedure to gain height before heading north-west over the Great Wall and the mountainous country to the north. Then, we tracked over Mongolia and over the vastness of Siberia and Russia. Maps of the world had been pinned in my bedroom and in the classrooms at Kooringal School. The Mercator projection exaggerated the size of the far north and far southern lands, and now we were over those mysterious, distorted parts near the top of the world that I had stared at while the teacher talked, or while I idled on my childhood bed. But I only had so much time to contemplate as we carefully cross-checked and flew our metric altitudes, and attended to navigation and communications. Although the Berlin Wall had fallen two years ago, the Soviet system of air traffic control remained, which divided the huge empire into multitudes of relatively small Flight Information Regions, each with its own control authority and convoluted air routes to avoid military bases. There were the associated multiple radio frequency changes as the 747 roared westbound at eight nautical miles – or fifteen kilometres – every minute. The Russian controllers spoke to us stolidly in laboured English between bursts of Russian when they communicated with their own aircraft. Although English was the international language of the air, I had discovered that there were three major countries on Cathay Pacific's network that spoke their own language to their own aircraft: China and Russia (understandably, given the vastness and cultural isolation of their countries), but also France. A month previously, I had operated to Paris for the first time. The years of high school French classes stood me in little stead with the Parisian rapid-fire, colloquial French. More concerningly, we were unable to build a picture of what was happening in the airspace over France and around busy de Gaulle International Airport as the French controllers switched from using English with the internationals to French for their domestic aircraft.

Over unfamiliar Siberian terrain we carefully monitored en-route airports, their facilities and their weather, and we looked down on flat, snowy terrain that stretched from horizon to horizon, for hour after hour. At the usual cruising altitude of jet airliners, the horizon can be well over 200 nautical miles – or 370 kilometres – distant. Siberia and Russia were just *immense*.

After a night in Helsinki we flew in winter daylight to Frankfurt, then later to London. The threat from military activity in the Middle East had, in the meantime, been assessed as lessened, so days later we rode the jet stream westwards on the now-familiar route to Dubai, then on to Hong Kong. Over ten days away we had flown from

Hong Kong to Beijing, Helsinki, Frankfurt, London, Dubai, then home. It was a far cry from the usual minimum-hours once-a-week 'Melbourne to Canberra, then "passenger" home' routine of my last working months with Ansett. In my early thirties, having not seen much of Europe and with training complete, I thrived on it. And then time came to operate in the other direction across our planet – to North America.

I had not yet flown the North Pacific Ocean to Anchorage, Alaska or Vancouver, Canada. A system of air routes called the NOPAC (North Pacific) System comprised five closely-spaced parallel tracks that curved to the north and eastwards from Japan around to due east, north of the Aleutian Island chain, then over Alaska proper. A multitude of tiny 'ball flags' on the maps denoted special procedures to be followed. The NOPAC routes were busy, so most were designated 'one way', similar to streets in a city grid. Radar coverage and communications could be unreliable. In 1983, a Korean Airlines Boeing 747, Flight KAL 007, departed Anchorage for Seoul, Korea. Its flight crew had not connected the inertial navigation system to the aircraft's autopilot correctly. Relaxed in the blackness and just idly watching the 'waypoints' sequence on the inertial navigation system, they had not realised that the 'gates' that indicated the sequencing of each waypoint were miles wide, and that the 747 was slowly straying from its planned NOPAC route. The airliner penetrated Soviet airspace and was shot down by the paranoid regime. A Russian in a Sukhoi fighter did the deed, killing 269 innocent passengers and crew. After that disaster a special NOPAC procedure was instigated that required a positive distance and bearing check abeam one of the few ground-based navigation aids, with a confirming report by the flight crew to ATC.

We flew the NOPAC eastwards to North America, often in constant gloom, the sun sometimes dipping, then reappearing above the horizon. We truly were Tennyson's 'pilots of the purple twilight', and when we flew a freighter, we did indeed 'drop down with costly bales': the high-value airfreight that we would deliver. Through breaks in the cloud, tessellated off-white masses of frozen ocean were sometimes visible and, very occasionally, depending on the assigned route, one of the craggy, ice-covered Aleutian Islands. This flight was non-stop to Vancouver, the jet stream winds pushing us along. Later flights would be to Anchorage for fuel and crew change, then onto other cities. Anchorage was an official 'Sister City' to Australia's city of Darwin, and I saw why: a 'frontier' feel, a native heritage, extreme weather (one cold, one hot), isolation, and they were about the same size. Both towns boasted interesting local characters and man-hunting predators: Darwin's crocodiles, and in the Arrivals hall at Anchorage International Airport, a huge taxidermy polar bear reared on its hind legs, well above our heads.

On an Anchorage flight, as an unsophisticated Australian with no experience of operating an aircraft in ice and snow, I finally experienced it. My flights to Europe, although in the northern winter, up to then had operated from cleared runways and the weather had been just cold and grey, or crisp and clear. Not clearing an airliner's surfaces of ice and snow has been the cause of many horrible accidents over the years, and the reports and implications had been drummed into us during our training, simulator sessions and safety briefings. Entire company manuals were dedicated to Cold Weather Operations, and at Anchorage I would at last see the procedures for myself, each time different, because ice and snow on a tarmac was never the same on any two occasions.

Amid the laid-down procedures and rigid drills that cover most normal operations and non-normal situations, along with the technology, it still sometimes comes down to a captain descending the steps to the snowy tarmac, physically assessing the snow, its depth, its distribution, its 'wetness', and in conjunction with information from the airport and air traffic control authority, assessing what standard set of conditions the crew will use to determine take-off thrust setting, speeds and payload. The captain must also decide which de-icing procedure must be used to get rid of accumulated ice, snow and frost on the airframe; the type of fluid (there were various grades);

how long it would protect the aircraft from further surface freezing; and local de-icing procedures. No two airports are the same. Some require de-icing at the gate or after 'push back' onto the tarmac, where truck-mounted rigs drive to the aircraft to hose fluid over the body, wings and tail. At others, the aircraft taxies to a remote area and shuts down its engines, where a fixed gantry sprays the fluid.

Amid the laid down procedures and drills of airline flying, operations in ice and snow are almost the last bastion of a captain's subjective assessment of conditions based on his knowledge and experience. The human act of stooping to pick up a handful of snow is still part of the decision-making process in an otherwise automated and rigidly controlled industry.

I found that the time of protection that the fluid would provide to get the huge jet airborne (the hold-over time) varied wildly. It was presented on charts and ranged from a just few minutes to possibly an hour's 'window', depending on many variables. The crew had to get the jet airborne amid all the other traffic and weather, before the hold-over time expired, otherwise ... it was back for more de-icing. Any delay at a busy airport, and the departure 'slot' could be lost, or the crew's legal duty hours became compromised. Then there was an internal 'inspection' to be done just before take-off: a first officer sent back to the cabin, passengers bemused at the sight of a pilot peering out through their windows as a final check to see that the wings were 'clean'.

The northern hemisphere winter of 1991 had become summer, and the chaos of the last two years – the Pilots' Dispute, an international move, training in the new world of Asia-based global flying and settling a family overseas – had subsided. I still had a lot to learn and experience to gain: avoiding the thunderstorms of the Asian summer, getting familiar with more new destinations and, once I had seen the sights, coping with the routine of days away to then sleep off the jet lag or last night's overnight flight at home to the moan of the dehumidifiers, as once again the dripping South China humidity prevailed day and night. Some nights I lay awake while blasts of wind from the regular nearby typhoons pressed against our bedroom window, the landlord bizarrely refusing to protect his investment with proper protective shutters. I could finally take some leave, so Yvonne and I arrived back in Australia with small children and suitcases, and travelled among the relatives, savouring the space, clean air and fresh food. For the first time, we had some money to spend, thanks to a different, but lucrative, life in Asia.

Towards the end of 1991, with not even two years' service with Cathay Pacific Airways, I had to do more study, a training course and a simulator check, as I was now considered sufficiently experienced to be qualified as a Relief Pilot. The airline was expanding rapidly, and the company required as many 'relief qualified' first officers as it could get. One late afternoon I took over from the captain, who retired to the bunk for a few hours' rest while we flew the Pacific through the night, entering the NOPAC route, to be in charge of a Boeing 747 on the way to Vancouver. Primed with the knowledge of the initial critical actions following an engine failure or cabin depressurisation, I watched the weather reports and fuel log closely and was always aware of potential diversion airports, most of them far away and remote. But there would be no Vancouver landing for me. Towards the end of the flight, the captain would emerge and I would try to snatch a couple of hours' fitful rest before the thrust levers were eased back for descent while I watched from the jump seat. There was the problem, for years to come, of keeping the relief pilots – which I now was – 'current' with actual landings and take-offs. Regional flights were occasionally rostered along with the inevitable cycle of simulator checks to keep us reasonably current, but I had to try not to let my handling skills deteriorate with the frequently rostered 'relief duty'.

Later that year, more training loomed for the early months of 1992: the old 'classic' Boeing 747 was being pensioned off and replaced by a greatly improved model: the Boeing 747-400, often just called the 'Four Hundred'. It had a completely different cockpit and carried a far greater payload, but its increased range was a portent of even less 'hands on' flying. Once again, I was in the books. The airline was still growing at a feverish pace. However, now it had a new Chief Executive Officer, and Cathay Pacific's longer-serving pilots sensed that change on a wider scale, perhaps not all of it for the better, was in the wind.

1 6

FOUR HUNDRED

1992 – 1995

There was no flight engineer in our cockpit, just the captain and me, and electronic screens glowed in front of us as our Boeing 747-400 powered through mild evening skies from Hong Kong to Tokyo. Ed had once again been with me through the -400 systems course, then the simulator training, but now I sat with a Training Captain with 400 passengers and cabin crew aboard, on my first flight in the actual aeroplane. With experience on the old 'classic' 747, the niceties and expense of 'base training' in an empty 747-400 had been deemed unnecessary, because the new -400 simulator was considered sufficiently realistic.

The Boeing 747-400 was the world's first true 'intercontinental' airliner. Cathay Pacific's original 'classic' 747 relied on the jet streams that blow from west to east when making non-stop, long haul flights in that direction, eastbound, from London to Hong Kong or Hong Kong to Vancouver. But westbound from North America back to Hong Kong, or from Hong Kong to Europe, fighting the prevailing wind like a canoe being paddled upstream, the older 747s struggled to fly the equivalent journey with any reasonable payload. It was as if the aircraft had been optimised for the European and American airlines, which focused on the Atlantic Ocean. Often, the 'Classic' Jumbo required planned or unplanned fuel stops when returning across the Pacific. The fuel stops were expensive, annoyed the passengers and sometimes required a change of crew. At last, the improved 747-400 was capable of flying non-stop with a good payload in both directions, and this is how The Boeing Company achieved it:

They started with the engines, and cast around for more powerful and fuel-efficient models. Rolls Royce had upgraded the now-venerable RB-211 turbofans and these became an option, among other American makes, for fitment to the 747-400. Cathay Pacific, then a loyal Rolls Royce customer, naturally chose this new G model, festooned with sensors that fed a Full Authority Digital Engine Control (FADEC). The FADEC was an electronic means of controlling the engine and optimising temperatures, fuel flow and airflow through the engine via various 'bleed valves', and engine starting. The FADECs could also detect a developing problem and warn the pilots via indications on the Engine Interface and Crew Alerting System, EICAS (pronounced 'eye cass'), an upper and lower display screen in the centre of the main instrument panel. Thrust settings and engine data were displayed clearly in digital form on the upper EICAS. With simplified engine handling and monitoring, Boeing dispensed with the flight engineer's position, because the aircraft's other systems were likewise fitted with sensors that would alert the pilots if any parameter (a temperature, pressure or quantity) was not where it should be. The EICAS was, in effect, an electronic flight engineer who never felt tired and, importantly for the airline's management, never had to be paid, fed or accommodated. However, the EICAS could not tell a joke, cook gourmet meals in a freighter's galley or lead pilots to the best bars and eateries on layovers. And very often, we would miss the extra set of eyes and ears.

Boeing looked at the wings – how could they make them more efficient? It was not desirable to further increase the Jumbo's wing span of almost sixty metres, so their engineers added 'winglets':

uptilted miniature wings at the tips. These effectively increased the wing surface without a significant increase to the span, and smoothed out the drag-producing vortices that would spiral up and back around and behind the wing tips. Then, the Jumbo shed some weight. Of the 747's eighteen wheels, sixteen of them were fitted with brakes comprising multiple heavy steel discs (the nose wheels were not braked). The metal discs were replaced with carbon fibre units that were far lighter and could better withstand the heat generated after landing: a 747-400 freighter could land at an astounding 300 tonnes. Modern 'composite' materials replaced old metal in some non-critical parts of the aircraft, and cabin fittings were lightened and upgraded. With the new 747 lighter and with more powerful engines, it could lift more fuel. A fuel tank was added to the horizontal stabilizer: the tailplane, at the rear. The weight of fuel in the stabilizer tank could also be used to 'trim' the aircraft in the cruise, reducing the drag-inducing angling of the tailplane itself.

In the cockpit, the old style round 'clock' gauges had mostly gone, replaced with the EICAS screens, in addition to new Primary Flight Displays and Navigation Displays in front of each pilot. My short time on Ansett's Boeing 737s made me comfortable with these. And like the 737, there was a Flight Management Computer (FMC) for each pilot to greatly simplify navigation and increase situational awareness. The controls and panels were improved and simplified. The functional grey of the metal work, seats and panels of the old Jumbo were replaced, for a reason best known to Boeing, with a rather dirty brown colour, although the new warmer shade did make the cockpit feel more 'homey' in the dead of night. Cathay Pacific, desperate for more range and payload, had signed up for the -400 early, and had become one of the first operators of the aircraft; the long range, pioneering spirit of Farrell and de Kantzow was still with the airline.

After I 'checked out' on the -400, life settled back into the routine of 'flying the line'; well, as much routine as I could have when flying the equivalent of halfway around the planet several times each month. With the airline expanding, new destinations came on line: Amsterdam, Manchester, Los Angeles … all these ports involved east-west or west-east return flights from Hong Kong, nearly always through a night time with hours of time zone difference and, more often than not for me, 'relief' duty: the 'graveyard shift' on each flight, with broken and short opportunities for in-flight rest. A saving grace was the new facility for crew rest. With the flight engineer's position gone, Boeing thoughtfully installed a closet-like room at the rear of the flight deck, fitted with two bunks stacked one above the other, fore and aft along the cockpit sidewall. And Cathay Pacific introduced the second officer position, similar to what would have awaited me had I joined Qantas; the days of joining Cathay Pacific Airways directly as a first officer were now over. A long haul cockpit crew now comprised captain, relief first officer, a 'regular' first officer and a second officer, or yet another first officer until the supply of 'SOs' increased. The captain and first officer usually made up one 'team' while the relief first officer and the other pilot were the other. The big Boeing became a ship of the air with its captain not constantly on the 'bridge', but a capable first officer on watch while the captain rested. Even with the stuffiness of two sleeping pilots in a compartment the size of a walk-in wardrobe, it was a far better arrangement than the cold, noisy almost public space of the old 'Classic' 747. But still, I rarely slept well.

Most flights to Europe overflew southern China, Burma, Bangladesh and India before swinging north west over Pakistan, sometimes entering Afghan airspace and on into Iran and Turkey, or further north over the 'Stans', and then Russia. The flights invariably departed late at night Hong Kong time, and I would have tried to catch some sleep late in the day, amid the heat and family noise, before reporting for duty at Kai Tak to wade through the Notices to Airmen, study the weather, flight plan, payload and proposed fuel load. I was responsible for the aircraft, passengers and crew during the 'meat' of the flight: much of the cruise, so I paid particular attention to information and weather applying to that segment. The captain made the relevant decisions about fuel and payload weight, and then we were bussed across the busy tarmac, the driver inexplicably pumping the accelerator in the local style. After the jerky ride we clambered up the metal steps to the forward door of the silver, white and green aluminium 'whale' that loomed above, gleaming in floodlights. Noise assailed us: the shriek of the Auxiliary Power Unit, the roar of trucks and tugs, metallic crashing and banging as the light sheet-metal cargo containers were hustled into the cargo holds beneath, and then there was that aroma I will never forget: a combination of burnt kerosene (jet fuel), whiffs of the *nullah*, the smells of the garbage being removed from the previous flight, hot metal and on a still night, burnt tyre rubber from the touchdowns, not far away from us on the crowded airport. Airlines work on razor-thin financial margins, and a 747, worth about 150 million U.S. dollars in the '90s, would not be earning its keep on the ground, so the activity was frantic. The huge machine that had just moved 400 people a quarter of the distance around the planet would be on the ground for barely an hour before it would be off again, its sixteen brakes with barely enough time to cool after the previous landing.

In the cabin, swarms of Chinese in overalls cleaned, removed garbage and restocked the cabins and galleys, shouting in harsh Cantonese over the noise of the vacuum cleaners. They banged and crashed the galley carts into position with little subtlety and, in the holds below, the freight containers were slammed into position with a rumble and thump. Then, up another staircase to the upper deck, there was the business class cabin full of cleaners, and then forward to the cockpit. Even in the cockpit there was chaos. Often the pilots from the previous sector would still be there completing paperwork then gathering their bags and hats. There would be a quick exchange of pleasantries and any information about the aircraft, and we would take our seats, the sheepskin covers still warm from the bodies of the previous crew, to carry out our duties to get the machine 'pushing back' within, usually by now, about forty minutes. A queue of engineers, 'traffic' staff and cabin crew would be waiting at the narrow cockpit door to speak to the captain, as documents were passed back and forth ...

As 'relief', I would descend the steps again with my torch to carry out the 'walk around' of the huge aircraft, and go back to the noise and the aromas of the tarmac – sometimes in pouring, monsoonal rain – to methodically check what I could: the twin chest-high nose wheels, then look up along the curve of the forward fuselage, and walk down to the belly of the beast to check the usually-hot wheels and brakes, before briskly walking under the leading edge of the wing craning up to check the engine intakes and the big front fans with their black, pointed 'spinners' that slowly rotated and clattered in any kind of wind. Standing under the 'winglet' at the tip, I would look back along the massive wing, and across and up to the towering fin, as high as a six-storey building, then walk back along behind the wing, flaps, engine exhausts, and the plump rear fuselage along to the tail. The tailplane spanned twenty-two metres, equal to the entire wingspan of a small commuter aircraft. The rest of the walkaround, on the left side, was a mirror image of that on the right. I would clamber up the stairs once more to the now relatively calm cockpit, the captain and first officer now running through briefings and checks. While I was outside, the remaining fourth pilot would have checked various cockpit equipment and, importantly, made up the bunks in the crew rest area.

Later, I sat behind the captain as the aircraft, ponderously at first, gathered speed along Kai Tak's runway. The rumble of the nose wheels far below us eased when the nose tilted up at rotate speed. After lift-off, the pilots began the methodical process of 'gear up', setting 'climb thrust', acceleration towards climb speed, then retracting the flaps in stages. At about 15,000 feet – or 4,500 metres – in the slow climb to initial cruise altitude and with the aircraft heavy with over one hundred tonnes of fuel, the other pilot and I headed to the toilet, thoughtfully provided by Boeing exclusively for use of the cockpit crew, or the tiny crew rest area to change. A track suit was the order of the day for most of us, but some senior British captains actually wore pyjamas! Several became notorious for taking more than their fair share of the in-flight rest time; most of the others, at least, made a semblance of sharing the duties to enable the relief crew to attain a reasonable amount of rest. Having made a name for themselves among the more senior first officers, these sleep-loving captains each became the recipient of a set of silk pyjamas stuffed into their crew room mailboxes. The group were forever known after that as the 'Silk Pyjamas Brigade'.

As far as my body was concerned, it was about one or two in the morning, and sleep would come relatively easily. But, after an hour or two, I would begin to toss and turn in the heat and stuffiness of the crew rest compartment. The air from the upper atmosphere was very dry, and often, niggling turbulence seemed to deliberately shake me awake just as I was drifting off to sleep again. In a semi-stupor I would lie in the dark, curtained-off bunk knowing that sometime soon, we would be awakened by the other first officer: time for my shift! After dressing, gritty-eyed, I would take my place in the captain's seat, after a brief handover of the aircraft (fuel state, weather, any unserviceabilities, air traffic agency, or other traffic). On Europe flights, we would be over India and the aircraft always seemed to be approaching Delhi when my shift began. I saw the glowing orange sprawl of the teeming city ahead through the raked windscreens – if the night was clear – and the radio speakers crackled with continuous traffic and the rapid-fire, high-pitched accents of the Indian air traffic controllers. It would still be dark, because the sun was chasing us only slowly while we winged westwards, and it would barely rise by the time we arrived at our European or British airport.

Until the mid-1990s, air traffic control over India, Pakistan and Burma was 'procedural'. Although radar was available – and certainly to the military authorities – the civilian air traffic controllers, notably in India, would not, or could not, use the system. Airliners each carrying hundreds of passengers were separated from each other by controllers using paper strips and relying on the radio reports of position, altitude and estimated time over the next reporting point or radio beacon. Late every night a fleet of airliners, reminiscent of the nightly 'bomber streams' that lumbered out of England for Germany during World War II, set course out of Hong Kong and other Asian ports westbound for Europe. Along each airway, India, in those days, required fifteen minutes' separation between succeeding flights that cruised at the same altitude. An airliner's weight determines the best altitude to fly for the most efficient fuel consumption. Still heavy with fuel, we were relatively low, but as fuel burnt off, our flight management computers and graphs indicated that a climb was necessary in order to achieve a new, efficient cruising altitude. This would usually occur, along with the 'shift change', around Delhi, some four hours into the flight. But only certain altitudes were available, in order to maintain separation with aircraft coming the other way. Then more aircraft out of busy Singapore joined the Europe route over Delhi. On our charts, multiple air routes radiated from Delhi's radio beacon like spokes of a wagon wheel. We could not climb if aircraft were heading in the opposite direction above us. And we could not climb if the other altitudes for our direction were already taken, and the Indians required the fifteen minutes between successive flights. But if we could not 'get our level', we would burn too much fuel, resulting in an expensive and inconvenient diversion, probably to an unfamiliar airport, to take on more fuel. So while the captain and first officer slept, it was up to us – the relief crew – to get the Jumbo up to its optimum level. We ran a 'plot' in our heads and on hastily scribbled-on notepads. We listened to the position reports of the other aircraft at multiple altitudes above us, knowing that we had to have fifteen minutes between them and us; otherwise, the Indians would not grant clearance to climb. Sometimes we resorted to calling other aircraft on a separate radio – a 'chat' frequency – to determine intentions and if we could 'massage' our estimated time reports to our mutual benefit. Sometimes, grudgingly, Delhi Control granted permission to climb.

More often than not, they said, 'Negative, negative, Cathay, maintain present level,' and washed their hands of us as we recalculated fuel and pondered our next course of action. Sometimes, joining traffic on the airway would even require us to descend, further eating into our fuel reserves and reducing climb options even more.

It could go on for hours, fighting for a climb and in summer, picking our way through the lines of thunderstorms that winked on the horizon ahead, then grew into towers of flashing light and threatening red blotches on the weather radar as we neared them around the curvature of the earth. That resulted in more battles with the overloaded air traffic controllers as we negotiated diversions left or right of our assigned route with other aircraft calling for their own deviations, sometimes the storms getting worryingly close while we waited for our clearance to avoid them. We skirted one 'CB' past Delhi (a cumulonimbus: the classic thunderstorm cloud), which soared well above our altitude. It was so loaded with energy that a streak of lightning continuously fizzed and flickered down its centre like the filament of an old-fashioned light bulb. Manipulating the 'heading' knob on the autopilot panel to give it a wide berth, I looked down the side of the monster cloud to see globules of 'ball lightning' bouncing on the ground beneath from the massive strikes. I thought of the Indian villagers below – they must have been terrified.

Then, we would pass the India-Pakistan border, marked by a waypoint called 'TIGER', and because the two countries had fought each other during several wars, communication and reporting requirements were strict (more of those little 'ball flags' on the charts!). On most nights the border was visible from miles away. These aid-receiving nations had resources to illuminate their entire border from horizon to horizon: hundreds of miles of fences and lights. Thankfully, over Pakistan, traffic would ease slightly after some of it peeled off for the Middle East while we swung north-west towards Iran, and there was the faint chance of a climb – if not to the optimum level – then to, at least, a higher, more fuel efficient one. Aircraft above us – their twinkling beacons often visible overhead for hours – also climbed, allowing us to take their now-vacated level in turn. But there was a new threat, apart from weather and traffic. Mountainous terrain loomed, and our Escape Charts would be at hand. These detailed the routes to fly and heights to descend to if we depressurised or suffered engine failure. On moonlit nights, jagged white summits were visible sliding past below, sometimes almost half of our height above sea level, which in winter generated vicious 'mountain waves' as the jet stream curved over their peaks. Then, the Boeing juddered heavily with the 'fasten seat belt' signs turned on, and passengers and crew wishing the turbulence would stop. Pilots watched the speed readouts and the thrust setting like hawks, looking for sudden increases in speed as the airliner penetrated the waves that might over-speed the jet, or cause a sudden loss of airspeed and with the autopilot robotically trying to maintain level, the speed rolling towards a catastrophic stall. Immediate intervention would then be required by the crew.

Over Iran, their air traffic controllers were heavily-accented and shouted over radios that made them sound like they were talking into tin buckets, but they were generally helpful. They used radar, so separation was reduced and this enabled us to climb. Sometimes we audibly breathed sighs of relief after our clearance came through and I could set the new altitude and press Flight Level Change on the autopilot panel. After hours in the seat, it would be morning in Hong Kong, and with the fuel log looking healthier, tiredness set in after we checked weather for our destination and its alternate. We still needed to be aware of high ground, and escape charts were still at hand. At last, we would be over eastern Turkey, where it always seemed to be the same lady on Ankara Control. Approaching Istanbul, Europe lay ahead and, in an hour or two, we would wake the captain and first officer. We bantered with them about our night's battles with air traffic control and weather while they slept – 'The hard work's done, it's all yours!' – before I would try to snatch an hour or two of rest in the bunk, still warm from the captain's body, the compartment stifling. Now well into a Hong Kong morning, I wouldn't be able to sleep, particularly if I had used coffee to sustain myself through duty at the controls. Invariably I would just give up and sprawl in one of the cockpit jump seats, staring out at cold, blue early dawn light and the cloud deck below, sometimes groggily chatting with the fresh crew or thinking about planning sleep and activities for the layover at destination.

Due to the constant 'relief' flying, I often approached 'un-currency', where I would not have the required number of take-offs and landings over a certain period that were required by law. I was then rostered both as 'relief' and 'critical', meaning I not only had to carry out the relief duties, but I had to fly the take-off and landing as well. As much as I enjoyed the opportunity of a heavyweight take-off, at almost 400 tonnes from Hong Kong, and a landing (much lighter with the fuel burnt off) into a busy yet civilised and efficient European airport, I sometimes felt as if I had single-handedly flown 400 people from Hong Kong to Europe.

In the initial years of the -400 operation, most layovers were long, sometimes over several days, because many of the destinations were not served daily. However, once demand was sufficient for a daily service, crews would consider themselves fortunate if they had more than one full day 'clear of duty' to recover from the flight from Hong Kong and prepare their bodies for yet another overnight odyssey home. It was now 1993, and I was becoming familiar with the -400, and I had seen the tourist sights. After the ubiquitous early-morning arrival at the European destination, exhaustion had me falling into the hotel bed. Except, I had to set an alarm for just a couple of hours' time. Sleeping through an entire European day led to a boring, sleepless night. How many times could I watch the BBC or CNN news? If I did not get myself up, the cycle would repeat the next day. So the alarm hauled me up from unconsciousness and head spinning, and mouth dry, I would drag myself out for a meal, a walk, and possibly to meet the other pilots later for food and drinks. It was rare to meet up with any of the cabin crew.

Cathay Pacific, in those years, recruited its flight attendants from ten different Asian countries. The airline rightly promoted this in their advertising, positioning itself as *Asia's* airline, not just Hong Kong's. Cathay's mostly female cabin crew were overwhelmingly petite and feminine, but with many variations in culture, personality and language. Labour was still relatively cheap in Asia with correspondingly low wages for the flight attendants, so cabin crew relied on the 'allowances' (cash paid when we checked into the hotels intended to cover food, drink and laundry over the period of the layover) to bolster their income. These allowances were a significant proportion of their earnings, so they were reluctant to spend them. Also, their Asian culture generally remained prevalent: the majority of the cabin attendants, having 'seen the sights' as newly-joined crew, were usually content just to sleep, head to the nearest Chinatown for a cheap meal, return to the hotel, and then sleep some more! This was understandable because their work was physical: they had to traipse up and down the aisles, as tiny girls (with a few slightly-built male stewards) pushing heavy trollies against the tilt of the cabin's deck. They would have a few hours' sleep in their crew rest area: six or seven bunks squeezed into a roof cavity near the 747's tail. They rarely, if ever, drank alcohol, but some Japanese girls could drink pilots 'under the table'. English was not most crews' first language, which usually discouraged banter, jokes or serious conversation. The Chief Purser (the flight attendant in charge) set the tone of the whole crew both professionally and socially. Sometimes a Westernised or more outgoing 'Chief' would crack the whip, and the entire crew would come out with the pilots for a meal (usually Asian), where for a night it would almost feel like being with a Western airline.

Val, a personable Irish captain, recounted a night on a German layover. Cathay Pacific crews shared the hotel in Mainz with American Delta Airlines crews, who were everywhere. Next to the hotel was a medieval-style restaurant, where the patrons shared long, refectory-style tables. The restaurant served a German specialty called *Schweinshaxe* 'pork knuckle', a huge roasted joint described by one pilot as 'a heart attack on a plate'. The restaurant was boisterously full of American pilots and flight attendants and Val, a first officer, and a flight engineer shared a table with a Delta crew. As they tucked into their *Schweinshaxen*, a grizzled Delta captain leaned across the table.

'Hey, I bet you guys are Cathay,' he shouted above the din.

'Yes, we are,' replied Val. 'How did you pick us?'

'You've got no women with you,' the American said, 'and you're bitchin' about your management!'

His observation was appropriate. Apart from the developing tensions with management, cultural differences between the mainly-European flight crew and the Asian cabin attendants led to widely differing activities during extended layovers. No matter the city, unless the Chief was up for a night out with the cockpit crew, the cabin crew invariably gravitated towards the local Chinatown. Invitations to flight attendants to come out with pilots for a few quiet drinks and a meal were, in the majority of cases, met with, '*Wah!* You cockpit crew, you always go to pub!' Once again in Mainz, two flight engineers found a solution. The airline's lounges and check-in areas around the world were adorned with life-sized, coloured cardboard cut-outs of a pretty Cathay Pacific flight attendant with a welcoming smile. One of these was purloined by the engineers. There was hilarity in the usual Mainz watering hole when the two flight engineers walked in and set themselves up to drink from their foaming steins, the smiling cardboard flight attendant propped up against the bar between them.

Back at the hotel, falling asleep at the end of the European day was like dropping into an abyss. But soon the body clock would nag: two a.m. in Europe was nine a.m. in Hong Kong and, inexorably, I tossed and turned and finally surrendered to wakefulness, yet again to watch repeated news on whatever English television channel was available or even to walk the streets in grey dawn, desperate to get out of the stuffy room and exercise. The hours dragged on until around midday, and finally the room telephone would trill and it would be into the white shirt and dark blue trousers to mill about with the crew at Reception before the bus ride. We would drag our bags through the airport, undergo immigration and customs checks, then board the 747, which would have been on the ground for a few hours since its early-morning arrival.

In the late afternoon skies, the Jumbo's nose pointed eastwards for the flight home, on pretty much the reverse of the route of the flight over. After a few hours of fitful rest, perceptively a tiny bit 'adapted' to local time, even after a short layover, I was once again back in the seat as the 'relief' pilot, over Turkey this time, with the mountains, storms and traffic of Asia ahead. Racing towards the sun, it would soon set behind us, and now here we were again in the velvet darkness, the screens colourful against the lightly floodlit brown of the panels. Obtaining our desired cruising level was easier out of Europe, and we were usually sitting pretty at our 'optimum altitude' for our weight, but this happy situation would not last. Approaching Pakistan, we were required to call their air traffic agency early. More often than not we were 're-routed' (told to fly on a different airway due to traffic), which added miles to our flight plan. And because it eventually re-joined our planned route to Hong Kong, we would have to descend, sometimes around 6,000 feet – or 1,800 metres – lower, our fuel log hit by the double whammy of longer flight time and a non-optimum altitude. If the Hong Kong weather forecast was poor, a bit of fuel in hand became a critical necessity. Once again, as on the flight westbound, the battle would be on with Delhi Control to fight for a climb, their archaic air traffic control system completely unsuited to handle the hundreds of airliners crossing the subcontinent every day.

Hours later we would be over southern China, our red eyes squinting with the sun rising in our faces. In the 1990s, the poor quality Chinese radios squawked and squealed as the controllers 'shiied' and 'shurred' in Mandarin to their local aircraft, switching to broken English to assign us yet another radio frequency change, or to demand yet another position report. We knew their military were watching us on their own radars, and the Chinese used the Soviet system of multiple, small Flight Information Regions and convoluted air routes to avoid sensitive military areas. At last, time would come to wake the captain and to present him, we hoped, with a good trend on the fuel log, and once again I would flop and twiddle in a spare seat somewhere, just wanting to be home and asleep.

At Kai Tak, usually steamy even in the early morning, I would slide into one of the ubiquitous red taxis and almost exhaust my Cantonese vocabulary at the driver: '*Tsing Sui Wan Do, m'goi*' ('Clearwater Bay Road, please'). The taxis' vinyl bench seats were not fitted with seatbelts. The driver's foot continuously goosed the accelerator, jerking the car backwards and forwards. Out of Kowloon in lighter traffic, he would throw the cab around the tight curves and steep descent of Clearwater Bay Road. Willing the drive to be over, I would slide on the shiny vinyl until, at last, outside our villa, I could drag my suitcase up the steps and fall into bed. My wife and Ruth would be preparing the children for kindergarten and school, and despite the noise, I would once again fall into the abyss, but with yet another alarm set to drag myself up at lunch time in order to ensure a subsequently sleep-filled night.

After this routine established itself, punctuated by the occasional Asian regional flight or a precious and eagerly awaited Australia pattern, the newness of living overseas and flying long haul began to wear thin. In my early days with Cathay Pacific, the rosters gave reasonable time off between long flights, but I began to find Hong Kong stultifying, and even boring. There was no concept of just going out with the family for a drive somewhere: the roads were packed, and out of the car's air conditioning, the humidity was just as draining as before we got in. We joined a sports club for ex-military families in Kowloon. It was not of the same level of the exclusive ones on Hong Kong Island, but at least it was a facility where we could enjoy a Western meal and the children could swim in a pool. Social life could be busy, especially with Ruth as a full-time child minder. But one could eat and drink only so much. Yvonne readily took to life in Hong Kong, which, when compared with many other Cathay marriages, was a blessing. Our children spoke in cultured British accents, had friends and were settled. But I missed open space, clean air, and seasons. I missed cobalt-blue skies, having a workshop, open roads, the fresh and plentiful Aussie food, a beach not strewn with garbage, my own house in which everything worked, and even a lawn to mow with the smell of newly-cut grass. I forced myself to count my blessings and constantly reminded myself of the poor devils who were still unemployed after the Pilots' Dispute. There was Cathay's generous salary and conditions; wonderful holidays thanks to subsidised travel; and the prospect of a Command in a few years. But, week after week, month after month, I arrived home tired, peevish and jet-lagged. When my wife began unburdening herself of the domestic problems that had accumulated while I was away sometimes – just sometimes – I wished that I was not fighting sleep for half the month, and had other things to do on days off besides eating, drinking, and walking around the bloody shops.

The -400 had the capability to fly from Hong Kong to Los Angeles, California, all year round, with a good payload. L.A. flights began appearing regularly on our rosters with, correspondingly, more time over the Pacific Ocean. These flights were easier, but longer and often bumpy when eastbound, because the route was planned to ride the meandering jet stream across the Pacific and its associated turbulence. Departing Hong Kong in the late afternoon, the sun rapidly set behind us as we raced with the earth's rotation, and after a brief night, the sun was in our faces while, once again, we were suspended in a blue dome over an even-bluer Pacific. On most days, 'streets' of fair weather cumulus cloud were laid out far below, the same forms that floated above HMAS *Melbourne* fifteen years ago, just a little to the south in this same ocean … the panorama stretched from horizon to horizon, unchanging, hour after hour. While the captain rested, I was in charge of a 747 while it crossed the largest ocean on the planet, in my mid-thirties, also responsible for a family, living in Asia ... I had not foreseen *that* while living in an old warship that pitched and rolled on the Pacific swells, men and noise everywhere.

Los Angeles International was always busy, but the American air traffic controllers were equal to the calm British in competence. Americans, however, used slangy and fast instructions. From hundreds of miles out, they slowed us down to sequence us over a radio beacon north of the airport to make a calculated time that saved fuel-wasting 'holding patterns'. We soon found ourselves part of a never-ending string of airliners in the sequence to make a morning touchdown on one of LAX's four east-west parallel runways.

Cathay Pacific crews were accommodated in the L.A. suburb of Torrance – the hotel belonged to a well-known global chain. However, this particular establishment was rather average in quality. For morning arrivals there, I followed the same routine as in Europe: a couple of hours' sleep to take the edge off the exhaustion before getting myself up and moving for the afternoon. One morning, the buzz of the alarm hauled me out of the depths of unconsciousness. Dry mouthed and headachy from the stuffy room, with eyes half-closed, I fumbled about in the darkened room for the switch on the bedside lamp ... *it must be at the top near the bulb ... is that it*? *Zap! Crash!* A violent electric shock flung my finger out of the fitting, knocking the lamp to the floor. My arm tingling, I leapt out of bed and flung open the curtains. Someone had removed the light bulb, but left the switch on. I was now fully awake, angry at the hotel, but thankful that the Americans used 110 Volts, not the Australian 240.

There were the sights to see in Los Angeles, but a hired car was necessary to get to them. In the early nineties, the monstrous eight-engine Howard Hughes 'Spruce Goose' flying boat sat under a vast dome next to the moored British trans-Atlantic liner *Queen Mary*. Suitably awestruck, a British captain and I explored them both. As we left, the Briton remarked, 'Well, that was a British success next to an American failure.' When paired with any enthusiastic captain, I was always a 'starter' to share a car and drive to the various museums and

414   WRITTEN IN THE SKY

airports around Los Angeles. In the country that virtually invented aviation, we were never disappointed.

Homeward bound, the flights initially curved north-west to enter the now-familiar NOPAC system in order to avoid the worst of the headwinds. Winter's strong jet streams could not be avoided, but during the last third of the flight, there were plenty of airports in Korea, Japan and Taiwan that we could divert to if the fuel trend became a concern. Once again, arrival into Hong Kong was usually in the early morning, with Hong Kong's local time sixteen hours (and one day) ahead of Los Angeles. After the taxi ride to Clearwater Bay, the jet lag would kick in with a vengeance.

Frankfurt … L.A … Frankfurt … L.A … These flights, almost always as relief pilot, were predominant on my monthly rosters. Like most of the other relief-qualified first officers, I always seemed to be 'scratching' for a take-off or landing to maintain some semblance of currency and competence. Most regional flights were taken for training and checks. However, there were other regional patterns on which a pilot could still lose sleep: these were called 'split duties'. They comprised a late-night departure from Hong Kong to either Manila or Taipei, and after arrival, we would go straight to a hotel. But three to five hours later, the bedside telephone would drag the pilots and cabin crew out of deep sleep for a quick shower, then straight back to the airport in pre-dawn darkness to operate the first departure of the day for Hong Kong. This counted as one 'duty period' under the Flight Time Limitations rules, and saved the company money on hotel rates and meal allowances. But there was little time to spare for delays or the inevitable airport bus journey under these rules. In order to cut travelling time to and from the airports, the hotels had to be nearby, and the Chiang Kai Shek hotel was conveniently situated right at Taipei airport.

China and Taiwan – the 'breakaway province' – are still

technically at war. Chiang Kai Shek's Nationalist forces, that Farrell and de Kantzow had helped supply over the Burma 'hump' during the Japanese war, were later driven from the Chinese mainland by the Communists, and they regrouped on Taiwan. In the early nineties, 'air raid' procedures were still published on our charts for Taipei's Chiang Kai Shek International Airport, as it was then named.

At around midnight, our crew would file into the CKS Hotel's lobby, and be assigned rooms. The rooms smelled of mould, and were cold and damp. The banging of slamming doors echoed from the thinly-papered concrete walls. Every room had a smudged clear round patch on a corner of the large, chipped mirror, which conspiracy theorists among us theorised had been once used for spying. Knowing that the 'wake-up call' was coming in just a few hours, I climbed straight into the hard bed, which, on one occasion, was still warm: the sheets had not been changed from the previous occupant. Fingernail clippings and a used tissue between the sheets completed the ambience. But by the time I got changed, traipsed down stairs and arranged a new room, I would have lost my precious sleep time, so … there was nothing for it … I shimmied into the tepid sheets and tried to drift off.

Notwithstanding the relentless long-haul relief duties, an opportunity was in the wind for experienced first officers. Cathay Pacific, with its unrelenting expansion, was having problems training the numbers of new second officers who were flocking to join: there were not enough Training Captains to teach them. In addition, the airline was now offering young, talented Hong Kong Chinese men and women a valuable opportunity for free flying instruction in Australia under a cadet scheme prior to training them as Cathay Pacific Second Officers. I could become a 'Training First Officer': pass on my experience to newly-joining pilots in the aircraft, the classroom and the flight simulator, and be paid extra for it. A few days in the classroom or simulator would replace a long haul flight each month, its associated jet lag and overnight flights. Weary of the Frankfurt – L.A. routine, I jumped at the chance.

As a trainer, each month's roster would include two or three days in the classroom and on other duties, including running a simulator session or two. This would be an equivalent total duty to the time away on a long-haul pattern, but I could sleep in my own bed! There would, of course, still be flights as 'relief' assigned for the month, but now they would mainly be training flights, where I would sit with a newly-joined second officer in the cruise. On training sectors, I carried out the 'relief' duties to Europe, fighting for flight levels, avoiding the storms, being ready for emergencies over the mountains, and setting the aircraft up for the captain to take over after his rest, hopefully with lots of fuel in hand and the weather reports good. However, with a military instructional background, I enjoyed training the 'new joiners'. Quality of teaching had never really been Cathay Pacific's strong point; the airline was even now still notorious for 'checking' rather than training. Also, many of these new second officers were not so experienced after the airline cast its net wider for pilots, so a high standard and a considerate and patient manner were important for those of us given the responsibility of training them.

Through the dead of night, educating the new pilots helped to pass the time and their searching questions kept me 'in the books' and my brain alert and busy. As I had found during my own training, there were mysteries to be cleared up by practical experience: weather avoidance, dealing with ATC and minor aircraft 'glitches', in-flight fuel planning … And, with the long flight over, as a training first officer there would be something to look forward to: more often than not, I would operate a 'shuttle' flight on the morning following a night's rest. Economics dictated that Cathay Pacific Airways could not fly non-stop to every European airport on its network, so shuttle flights were 'tagged' onto the long-haul services from Hong Kong. For example, Manchester was served from Amsterdam; Zurich from Rome; Heathrow from Paris. On a shuttle flight, it felt like I was flying for a domestic airline because the flights were short and conducted in daylight, and I looked forward to each of these short flights that appeared on the monthly roster. The company had a policy of assigning the training first officers to these shuttles to keep us current with take-offs and landings. I had to wake up early, which was easy with my body still on Hong Kong time. Then a quick, busy flight, just the captain and me, in European or British airspace – which was still a novelty to an Australian with much to learn – followed by a rapid turnaround for the brief flight back. And, best of all, I could do a take-off and a landing! After the arrival back in Paris, Amsterdam or Frankfurt for the afternoon, I would go for a walk, meet the other pilots for a few drinks in the early evening and, pleasantly tired, have a reasonable night's sleep, with the following day free of duty to rest up for the long flight east back to Hong Kong.

The even longer flogs across the Pacific were also enlivened by the training duties, and meanwhile the years had rolled by: three years for us now in Hong Kong, and at last we felt financially secure. But, I looked with envy at the senior captains and first officers who were able to take part in a new scheme of 'basings' out of the Asian city-state. Management had finally worked out that it was cheaper for the company to offer senior crew the opportunity to live out of Hong Kong at ports on the Cathay network. It would therefore save the vast sums of money normally spent on Hong Kong housing, education and health care. And thanks to the continuing expansion of the airline, I now *just* had the seniority to live in Australia, but it would be as a first officer. Imagine! Living in Victoria as a Cathay Pacific pilot! But after promotion to captain, I would again be at the bottom of the captains' seniority ladder when I would have to return to Hong Kong for my 'command', because only the corresponding senior captains were able to take an overseas base. Additionally, Yvonne had taken to Hong Kong well and had a network of friends, loved travel and was getting employment as a piano accompanist. The children were settled in school and my own Command Course was now just three or four years away. It was galling, but I had no choice: I had to remain in Hong Kong and keep on with the 'hard yards'.

It was November in 1993. Most Hong Kong residents looked forward to November. The heat and humidity disappeared – seemingly overnight – after the prevailing monsoon winds swung from the warm, moisture-laden south-westerlies born in the tropics to the cool, drier north-east trade winds that blew from the temperate north Pacific. I looked forward to cool, clear days and even chilly nights, and about four months of relatively comfortable, if not occasionally cold, weather when vigorous winds from Siberia penetrated as far as southern China. Aside from the crowds in the streets, there was now a semblance of life in a more temperate clime and a pilot's workload became easier with the ebb of the thunderstorms, typhoons and heavy rains of the wet season. Some expatriates referred to November as 'Granny Season', when relatives would visit Hong Kong from their home countries, before the busy Christmas flights, to take advantage of the good weather. However, on this early-November evening, cartoon 'Freddie' appeared on the television weather report. He clip-clopped onto the screen, looked up, and grey clouds rolled in. With an 'Ohhhh!', his umbrella popped out, which was promptly blown inside-out by windblown rain. Freddie himself was then blown off-screen. A typhoon was approaching Hong Kong, and the common wisdom was when a typhoon appeared in November, it would be a strong one, as it would have accumulated enough energy to maintain itself despite the falling sea surface temperatures. Oh well. I was on the last couple of days off following a long trip away, and the tropical storm would have passed by the time I was back at work.

Our bedside telephone trilled very early the following morning. Rain lashed the window. The typhoon had not struck Hong Kong directly, but its outskirts were bringing gusty winds and squally showers. After I groggily answered, the usual Hong Kong Chinese-accented voice came over the line: 'Hello First Officer Carr, this is Josephine calling from Crew Control. There has been crash at the airport, causing lots of disruption. We know you are on day off, but can you help out? We'd like you to crew Taipei flight.' Without hesitation, I agreed. Years of military service and the inactivity on

Reserve duty from the Ansett days had maintained my motivation to fly when I could, and I had vowed to give one hundred per cent to my generous employer. On this rainy day, I would have been sitting bored at home anyway. Hong Kong to Taipei was one of the shortest flights on the network, and Taipei was a familiar port. The service was the Cathay Pacific equivalent of Ansett's Melbourne to Sydney: quick, familiar and frequent. The typhoon seemed to be moving away. Get to Kai Tak, a short sector to Taipei, turn around and return, including a take-off and landing I could do, and home in time for dinner … a grand day out would be had!

On that same morning, while I was sleeping, the captain of a China Airlines flight from Taipei to Hong Kong, a Boeing 747-400 call sign 'Dynasty 605', wrestled with the controls as the huge machine bucked and lurched down the IGS approach towards the checkerboard. Minutes before, the captain of a British Airways Jumbo had refused to make the approach, after he analysed the weather and wind shear warnings that he had received. The Briton had diverted to his alternate airport, but the captain of Dynasty 605 elected to continue into Kai Tak. He turned right, low past the checkerboard in crosswinds that flicked and curled around the buildings and terrain while the squalls came and went, drastically changing the air's speed and direction over the Boeing's massive wings and control surfaces. This was the infamous 'wind shear'. '*Windshear, windshear, windshear*,' a deep synthesized American voice would have shouted through the cockpit speakers, generated by a computer in the aircraft. The pilot tried to throw the Boeing onto Runway 13, but there was confusion in the cockpit as the aircraft, not slowing on the rain-slick runway, floated and kept floating. Belatedly, the captain had pulled back on the reverse thrust levers on the backs of the four throttles, and his feet pressed the tops of the big rudder pedals to apply maximum braking. Now, he had overridden the automatic brakes that he had set at too 'soft' a setting for the conditions. Too late. The far-end of the runway loomed. They would soon be over the rocky sea wall and into the choppy grey-green water as, despite their efforts, the

Boeing would just not slow down enough. In a desperate attempt to avoid running off the far-end of Runway 13, the captain kicked the left rudder pedal and the jet yawed left into a grinding 'ground loop'. It swerved off what remained of the runway and bucked and tore through the sodden grass. Then, with the momentum of well over two hundred tonnes of metal, fuel, cargo and humanity, it lurched over the rocks of the sea wall, the landing gear now ripped off and the airliner on its belly and finally slowing; but, still, the jet fell into Hong Kong harbour. It surfed along for a few metres, then came to rest floating alongside the rocks, ending up almost parallel to the runway but its nose incongruously pointing back in the direction from whence it had come.

396 passengers and crew were safely evacuated from the ditched airliner, with great credit to the Taiwanese cabin crew, For days, the 747 floated in Hong Kong harbour: a prominent symbol of its pilots' poor judgement and lack of cockpit coordination. Meanwhile, John, a personable Northern Irish captain, and I lifted off for Taipei during a lull in the storm, our jet full of disrupted passengers. We were able to steal quick glances down at the first Boeing 747-400 to be crashed, still afloat with the water at deck level, an almost brand new aircraft, its paint still glossy. John and I would fly on to Taipei, then wait to operate a flight back to Hong Kong. However, the typhoon had re-intensified and there was a delay in departing Taipei. In the dark of the late evening, we were established on the IGS approach to Kai Tak, with extra fuel we had loaded in hand. My mind drifted back to the morning's sight of the floating Jumbo. We had been monitoring the Hong Kong weather reports carefully. We descended into blackness with very heavy rain rattling against the windscreen and flight deck ceiling, loud even under all the insulation and thick glass. White and red from the Boeing's strobe lights and beacons flickered through tears of water on the windows. Streams of rain lashed through the

shafts of the landing light beams. Then – 'bing!' – a chime and the 'master caution' light directed us to look at a message on the EICAS: 'RUDDER TRAVEL FAULT.' The heavy rain had infiltrated a probe on the fuselage that controlled the available rudder deflection for varying airspeeds, and immediately we discontinued the approach and climbed away.

While John flew the aircraft, I flicked through the Quick Reference Handbook to find the appropriate actions. We could not land at Kai Tak. Due to the fault, we could not accept the blustery, squally crosswind that still prevailed, so we had to fly off to Taipei once more, where the weather was good. I assisted John with cleaning up the aircraft, and negotiated a clearance over the radio with the jet lurching and jolting until we were clear of the outer belt of the typhoon. Again on the ground in Taipei, followed by another wait, we were finally 'passengers' home, out of 'crew duty time' very late that night. I had worked eighteen hours for the airline on this rostered day off, but most other Cathay Pacific pilots would have gladly done the same.

However, the new management could not resist tinkering with the conditions of service of their pilots and flight engineers: highly skilled employees who were responsible for over 400 lives and 150 million U.S. dollars of company equipment each time they presented for work. The new second officers had already joined on a reduced salary scale, still generous but not up to the level of the established crews. For us, a new contract had appeared with some reductions, including increased flying hours and reduced leave, in exchange for a small salary increase. A list of motherhood statements called 'The Cathay Pacific Commitments' was published, and highly-qualified pilots and flight engineers were rostered for infantile 'commitment days' where they were taken off the flying roster and harangued by managers in the auditorium about how 'bad' things suddenly had become, and how expensive we flight crew were. The airline had reached a critical mass and was no longer reminiscent of a close-knit military unit. Now it was just another corporation. To us, its executives seemed intent on cost-cutting that would add to their bonuses before they moved on, increasing the company's share price, and the cunning use of industrial psychology consultants to extract concessions from their staff. Those in charge subtly made it known that those of us who did not sign the new contract would never be eligible for a basing in their home country later.

The airline was still expanding, but now other airlines were getting into the long haul business with their own new 747-400s. Competition was hotting up. Management's new obsession with cost cutting disturbed that delicate balance between motivated but well remunerated and managed employees, unique to Cathay Pacific Airways. With my military background and unpleasant memories of the Australian Pilots' Dispute, I tried to shut all this out and instead concentrate on my work. Despite having to live in Hong Kong and deal with the night flying and jet lag, I still loved my job. And now, two significant events loomed: first, my upgrade to Captain was on the horizon; and second, the airline had decided that it was going to buy revolutionary new passenger jets from Europe's Airbus Industrie.

BUS DRIVER

1 9 9 5 – 1 9 9 8

We hit turbulence, and I instinctively moved to lightly grasp the control yoke to steady myself and monitor the autopilot: a habit ingrained after nearly twenty years of flight. But there was no yoke. In fact, I felt a little exposed, because there was nothing in front of me except flat electronic screens in grey plastic frames. Compared with Boeing's 747, this aircraft felt light, even though it could still take off at well over 200 tonnes. Its long, slender wings rocked with the bumps and the nose nodded up and down with the wind changes. There was no upper deck behind us, because in this airliner the entire cabin crew and passenger complement sat directly behind the cockpit door on one deck, so this passenger jet was like thousands of others. However, it differed in another respect: there were no direct mechanical connections, the traditional cables or rods, between a small joystick protruding from a flat panel to the side near my right hand, and the hydraulic rams or 'jacks' that moved the aircraft's elevators, ailerons and spoilers in response to movements of the 'side stick'. I recalled Prime Minister Hawke's terminology regarding our profession during the Pilots' Dispute – I was now, ironically, a 'bus driver'. I was flying an Air-*bus* A330!

Airbus Industrie was a European and British consortium formed from an amalgamation of several aerospace companies in the 1970s. Airbus had produced the A300, the first 'wide-bodied' (twin-aisled) airliner with two engines. Boeing's 747 had its four engines and the only other wide bodies in existence, also American, the TriStar and the DC-10, had three. The A300 could carry over 250 passengers, and its twin-engine configuration made for compelling economics. With this 'clean sheet' aircraft, Airbus deliberately chose a fuselage width that would enable standard cargo and baggage containers to be efficiently accommodated in the under-floor holds. Otherwise, the A300's systems were similar to any other airliner of the time. Its flight controls were conventional. Its cockpit was festooned with the traditional 'round gauges' and included a flight engineer's position. But after the pioneering 'big twin' A300, Airbus produced a new smaller twin-engine jet, the A320, several of which Ansett had acquired just prior to the Pilots' Dispute. Although its fuselage was single-aisled and much smaller than that of the A300, the A320 was revolutionary. Its flight control system was known as 'fly by wire'.

The Orion, and the Boeings that I had flown were controlled from the cockpit by cables, pulleys, rods and levers connected to hydraulic jacks. The jacks provided the force required to move the rudder, elevators and ailerons. The Boeing 747 was over seventy metres long: imagine the lengths of the cables required to run from the cockpit out to the tail and wings to each control, and then back again, to complete the 'loop'! Because of the powerful hydraulic rams, separate complicated mechanisms 'fed back' forces to the control yokes and rudder pedals in order to imitate a natural 'feel' for the pilot. Then there were further mechanical interfaces between the controls and the electronics of the autopilots. More cables ran from the pilots' thrust levers out along the wings to the four engines. Similarly, wire cables and drums transmitted the crews' selections from the cockpit trim, flap and spoiler knobs, wheels and levers to those respective controls. Landing gear selectors were connected with yet more cables to hydraulically powered locks and rams in the undercarriage itself. With aircraft becoming larger and heavier, the complication, weight, maintenance requirements and likelihood of failure of these conventional controls became significant. Engineers at Airbus Industrie must have thought, 'We can't get rid of the hydraulic jacks, because we still need the power to move the big control surfaces on the wings and tail. But if we replace the mechanical cables between the pilots and the hydraulics operating the control surfaces with electrical wiring and computers, we can get rid of lots of weight, reduce maintenance, make the pilot's job easier and make the aircraft safer. No strong "feel" forces to fight. Importantly, there would be redundancy thanks to the multiple computers. No need for the pilots to "trim" the changing forces from the controls for varying speeds – the computers can do that. It is much easier for the autopilots to be integrated into the system. We can even program in "protections"! Let's make it so that the pilots cannot stall or over-speed the aircraft. And if a control surface fails or is damaged, the computers can compensate by adjusting the other surfaces.'

The Airbus engineers implemented all this and went further. The cockpit throttles – or thrust levers – could be electrically connected to the engines, because the engines were electronically controlled by their own FADEC systems anyway. Flaps and landing gear would also be signalled through electrical wires and dedicated, redundant computers. The fuel system would be automated. 'And let's make the handling of emergencies easier: we will get rid of the old emergency checklists written on paper,' the Airbus technicians decided. 'There will be so many sensors throughout the new jet, a Flight Warning Computer can present the problem to the pilots as a "message" on a screen and with the required actions as well, in the form of an electronic checklist. As each action is completed, the "action line" will disappear. Add advanced Flight Management Computers to simplify navigation, flight planning and performance calculations, and we will have a new generation short-haul airliner that will challenge the Boeing 737. And when the A320 is proven and sells successfully, we will produce a family of bigger "fly by wire" Airbus wide-bodies to challenge the Americans and take airlines into the twenty-first century.' With the A320 proven and selling well, these bigger designs were duly built, with their fuselage structure and width based on that of the 'big twin' A300. But everything else was new. These jets were the A330 powered by two engines, and a long-range four-engine sibling, the A340.

I was comfortable with this idea of 'fly by wire' in an airliner: the A320 had been in service for years. Cathay's new A330 had five 'flight control computers' where any one of which, even in its most degraded state, could safely control the aircraft. Three of them were designed and produced by one company, and the other two by a separate manufacturer. Therefore, the chance of a design, programming or manufacturing fault affecting all the computers was infinitesimal. Even if all the computers failed, there was a last resort back-up: conventional rudder controls, old-fashioned cables from the rudder pedals, and a backup mechanical pitch trim. These traditional systems would allow the pilots to manually fly the aircraft in the astronomically unlikely event that all five of the flight control computers failed completely. During simulator training, we were able to land the aircraft using this *in extremis* method.

Cathay Pacific's A330s were powered by a further development of the trusty Rolls Royce RB-211. After redesign, more advanced digital engine controls and upgraded metallurgy, the engine was given a name, and in the Rolls Royce tradition, the name was again that of a river, the Trent, which drains the English Midlands, then joins the River Ouse, (pronounced 'ooze'), and empties into the Humber estuary on England's east coast. Decades prior there had been an original but obscure Rolls Royce Trent, one of the first turboprop engines, fitted to a Gloster Meteor flying test bed, and the Trent name had been revived. I could understand Rolls Royce not wanting to call the engine the Ouse.

The A330's twin engines were fed from five fuel tanks – two located in each wing – and like the Boeing 747-400, another was located in the tailplane. But, unlike the old Boeing, the Airbus fuel system was automated: redundant computers ordered pumps to transfer fuel between the wing tanks and the tail, depending on the aircraft's weight, calculated centre of gravity and phase of flight. The weight change of the fuel in the tail adjusted the trim of the aircraft for cruise without requiring drag-producing settings of the tailplane.

The Airbus cockpit was unlike any other. With no bulky control yoke in front of the pilots, Airbus had provided a pull-out table, ostensibly for charts and paperwork, but also for making meal time very civilised; we no longer had to balance our inevitable 'beef, chicken or fish' on a pillow on our laps, with only one pilot eating at a time. At meal time for Airbus pilots, cabin crew would set a tablecloth on the tables with cloth serviette, cutlery, water glass, salt and pepper shakers, bread roll on a plate, then serve the meals, both together. We joked about a vase of flowers and a picture of the wife placed on the table to accompany dinner. On a long flight after dessert, pastries, and the tables cleared and stowed, stirrups could be extended down from below the instrument panel that enabled us to put our feet up, with no control yoke in the way. We could not do that in a Boeing!

Six cathode ray screens, later updated to liquid crystal displays, were laid out in front of the crew in a similar configuration to the -400. Neat little thrust levers sat in conventional form on the pedestal between the pilots that could be used to control the engines in the conventional sense, but were normally set in 'detents' to allow the advanced automatic thrust system to fly set speeds or 'rated' thrust settings. Grey panels with neat rows of pushbuttons comprised the systems controls, with radios and navigation aids controlled by multipurpose keyboards. The landing gear control, flap selector and speed brake levers were petite because, in effect, these were merely electrical switches wired to the appropriate computer. I can recall an engineer telling us to think of an A330 as '150 computers flying in close formation!' The cockpit ambience was completed with dark blue carpet, blue and grey seats and stylish trim. Large, flat windows gave a light, airy feel and provided wonderful visibility.

Six years earlier, I had only dreamt of getting my hands on

one of Ansett Airlines' then-new Airbus A320s. I had always liked technology and been interested in the new Airbus family of aircraft. Now I was an Airbus pilot, and I 'hand flew' the '330' with the side stick that fell naturally to my right hand, supported by an adjustable armrest. Thankfully, the actual aircraft felt more stable and solid than had the simulator, but still, the stick took some getting used to. The behaviour of the Airbus flight control system was governed by a set of programmed 'laws' that varied and blended into each other depending on the phase of flight or the status of the computers. In 'normal' law, a fore or aft movement of the side stick demanded an infinitesimal amount of g 'positive' (nose up) or 'negative' (nose down), which 'told' the elevators at the tail to provide this. The pilot could then release the stick, which then 'demanded' one g, meaning that the pitch attitude would stay where it was (within normal limits). A sideways movement of the stick demanded a roll *rate*, and again on release, any bank would remain, but also within certain limits. There was no need to trim the aircraft with changes of speed or thrust, because the computers adjusted the flight controls and tailplane angle to provide exactly what the pilot had demanded. Essentially, the pilot selected a flight *path* by gentle movements of the stick, which was quite sensitive. I felt as if I 'squeezed' my way about the sky.

Apart from the aircraft itself, for me the Airbus fleet was a new world. The A330 also represented a new era for Cathay Pacific. The airline was reinventing itself, and the makeover included a new colour scheme for its jets. With the arrival of the 330s, the dignified and traditional green and white livery with the 'cucumber sandwich' on the fin and 'Cathay Pacific' emblazoned in red letters on the forward fuselage had gone. The Airbus fuselages were still white on top, but were now a two-tone pale grey below. The greys would become dull and dirty very quickly after a few weeks in the filthy South China air. The airline's name was now in subdued dark green letters, but thick bands of the same colour on the nose and tail added some interest. On the tail fin, there was a new swooping, bird-like 'brushwing' motif, contrived by consultants. At the same time, management was also becoming ever more aggressive with cost-cutting, and relations between it and its pilots began to noticeably deteriorate. I still paid little heed to this – I was just grateful after the mediocre pay of the military and the turbulent Ansett days to be employed flying international heavy jets. I concentrated on just doing my job and getting to grips with the new airliner.

The A330 initially replaced the TriStar on regional Asian services, which meant more frequent but shorter flights, fewer night flights and, best of all, little, if any, jet lag. I could make regular take offs and landings because there was no need for a 'relief' crew: just myself and the captain. No more rustiness! Most Airbus pilots were new faces to me because they were ex-TriStar crew, and they were used to the slick routine and hurly-burly of multiple short sectors around Asia. They were intimately familiar with the airports. Old TriStar hands asked, 'What made you volunteer to come off the Boeing onto this thing?' I had my answer ready: first, I had been an Airbus 'fan boy' for some time. Second, an opportunity for my own 'command' would be coming up in two years, and it would most likely be on the Airbus. And I had had enough of courses and training. In less than eight years after leaving the Orion, itself a 'heavy turboprop', I had to learn the Friendship, Fokker Fifty, Boeing 737, the 747 'Classic', -400 and now the A330. The Airbus was of a completely different design philosophy. The training on it had been quite intense, and had taken months. Over the same period I had also gone from the air force, to Ansett, followed by an international move to join Cathay: three vastly different organisations, each with its own culture, procedures and operating areas of the world. The Cathay Pacific Command Course was legendary in its length and toughness. New Commands were offered in strict seniority irrespective of a first officers' current aircraft, and indications were that most of them would be on the expanding Airbus fleet. Having flown the A330 for a couple of years as a first officer meant that I would know the aircraft intimately, and I would just move from the first officer's seat across the cockpit to the captain's 'chair' to start training: go 'right to left'. Into the bargain, I would be familiar with all the Asian ports that I would operate into as a captain under training (and assessment!). I was determined to pass, aiming to eliminate as much uncertainty as possible. A few years of 'bouncing' around Asia in an A330 would achieve just that.

One port was already familiar: at Butterworth, with the RAAF Orion detachments, we had often flown practice instrument approaches into Penang Airport, on the west side of the island just off Malaysia's west coast, its peak over 2,700 feet – or 830 metres – high, a hazard when cloaked in tropical rain, mist or boiling thunderstorm clouds. After two sectors in our 330, the second one short and busy from Kuala Lumpur to Penang, John the British captain and I were bussed with our cabin crew to the Penang hotel. During the drive I recounted my air force days: the Orion flights, the 'traps runs', the trishaw races …

'Let's go to one of my old air force haunts,' I suggested to John, who had also never taken a trishaw. 'It's appropriately called the Hong Kong Bar.'

That became the plan. Our wiry driver pedalled the vehicle to the Hong Kong Bar, where Orion crews had inevitably met for a night of eating and drinking before the late ferry and bus back to Butterworth. Half-jokingly, as we travelled I described the constant refrain of either 'Khe Sanh' or 'I Was Only Nineteen' that had emanated from the bar's juke box, incessantly played by the young Australian Army soldiers, and the seemingly innocuous photographing and questioning of the Orion crews by the barmaids. We arrived at the bar, where our trishaw driver waited outside with the promise of a return fare and tip from our 'allowances'. The bar was still frequented by the army but these days only an occasional Orion crew. As we entered, 'I Was Only Nineteen' emanated mournfully from the jukebox. Straight away the barmaid recognized me, even after a decade.

'Hello, you back! What crew you on?' she asked.

'The Cathay Crew!' I replied. 'Two Tiger beer please!'

John was incredulous.

The A330 had its foibles. Its wings waffled and wobbled in turbulence. It flew higher, but cruised slower than the old Jumbo. And Cathay Pacific Airways had become one of the first operators of the aircraft. An old aviation adage is 'Never fly the "A" model of anything', but the new Airbus was desperately needed by the airline to replace the aged, inefficient TriStar. Thorough testing of new airliners by the manufacturer can never reveal or foreshadow all of the problems that can crop up during the constant usage of their products by their demanding new owners. Airliners operate around the clock, in all weather conditions, long flights, short hops, and quick 'turn arounds' on the ground between ... time is money! They are tended and operated by average 'line' engineers, mechanics and pilots: the cabin fittings and seats are abused and knocked about during the frenzied activity of getting the machine ready for its next flight, with so little time to spare ... and, accordingly, the relative ease of routine operations in the A330 became clouded by 'glitches' that sprang up. Computers had to be routinely reset. Performance information changed. A problem with engine ancillary gearbox lubrication led to some engine shutdowns; the fleet had to be grounded until a solution was hurriedly found. The weather radar was inadequate. A new Airbus crew, used to the basic but powerful radar of the old TriStar, inadvertently flew into a tropical cumulonimbus storm cloud over the South China Sea. Abruptly, ice rattled against the windscreen and roared on the cockpit roof (the insulation was inadequate but was later rectified). The aircraft bucked and jolted inside the towering, boiling 'cell'. The computers of 'fly by wire' aircraft are dependent on the external probes that gather speed, air pressure, angle of attack and temperature information – moisture had blocked one or all of them. For an instant, confusion reigned in the cockpit with a simultaneous and conflicting *'Stall!'* (a loud synthetic voice) and 'overspeed' warnings on top of the noise of the precipitation and the bucking of the turbulence: 'Stall, stall ... *ding ding ding ding ding* [the overspeed warning] … *stall, stall … ding ding ding ding ding … stall, stall,'* which led to a further problem. After the autopilot disconnected itself both pilots instinctively grasped their side sticks, one pushing, reacting to the stall, the other pulling, to prevent overspeed. The flight control computers, overwhelmed by the conflicting inputs from the probes and the pilots, lapsed into a degraded flight control law. Realising this, the captain positively took control and applied basic 'attitude' flying to hold the jet steady as it was thumped by the convective turbulence. Suddenly, it popped out of the weather and the shaken pilots hand-flew the 330 home, with its controls operating in degraded mode.

After that, Airbus urgently fitted a new design of outside probes, a slightly better radar was sourced and, above all, pilots were warned to ensure that one pilot flew and one pilot monitored, and further warning systems were fitted; without the old fashioned control wheels or yokes, pilot discipline was essential to ensure that these 'dual inputs' were avoided. In most respects, operating these new aircraft was easier, but more difficult in others, particularly in the new situations that they could throw at a pilot. But airline accountants loved the new machine. Although smaller than Boeing's Jumbo, it could still carry over 300 passengers. Importantly, the new Airbus could lift up to fifteen tonnes of baggage and freight in two huge underfloor holds, optimally sized for containers; far more than the big Boeing could. And it could do this with a vastly reduced thirst for fuel thanks to its more efficient engines, structure and aerodynamics. It was an excellent 'medium haul' jet for Cathay's Asian and Australian destinations. But many destinations lay in Europe and North America, still served by the 747. Some of them did not warrant such a large aircraft with its often excess and wasteful capacity, so while I was mastering the A330 and coping with all the changes and modifications, yet more training loomed. Cathay Pacific had ordered the 330's long-range sister: the four-engine A340, and it would be arriving soon. And, in a philosophy new to the airline industry, Cathay Pacific's Airbus pilots would routinely fly both types.

I pulled back on the side stick, about half-way to the perceptible increase in spring tension on the control, and held it there. For a few heartbeats, nothing happened as the aircraft accelerated painfully along the runway, the cockpit bouncing and shaking with then typical annoying Airbus squeaking rattle while the nose wheel pounded along the runway. It was even more pronounced with today's higher take-off speed. We were over 150 knots – or 280 km/hr – and still on the ground! At last, grudgingly the nose lifted, and rather than leaping into the air as an A330 would have done, the A340 I was flying gently rotated up, with its main wheels still on the runway. It painfully lifted into the tropical air and began to climb, so slowly – the far end of the runway disappearing low under the nose – the climb only slightly better after I called 'gear up', until we were at 1,500 feet – or 450 metres. Gently, I lowered the pitch attitude by a small amount and the 340 accelerated, but the stages of flap retraction came slowly until, at last, the aircraft was 'clean' and in a leisurely climb towards South China on our long aerial voyage to Europe.

The A340's twin-engine sibling, the A330, was 'over-powered'. It had to be because all airliners were required to be capable of suffering an engine failure after that 'decision speed', 'V1', on the runway, and still able to accelerate further to lift off and safely climb away. The 330 was a 'twin', so, in the unlikely event of one engine malfunctioning, where the aircraft would lose half of its total power, the other, running engine had to provide enough thrust to be able to meet this requirement. Therefore, with both engines operating normally, a 'twin' exhibits spirited performance, leaping into the air, climbing steeply away clear of the terrain, and rushing up to its cruising altitude. But if an engine failed in the four-engine A340, the aircraft would lose only one-quarter of its total power, so each engine could be smaller and less powerful, and the aircraft could lift far greater weights, even with one engine failed. An A340 could carry over fifty tonnes more than the 330, and if most of this mass was fuel, the aircraft could almost span the globe. However, there would be far less excess thrust available for a normal take-off at its maximum permitted weight, so its take-off and climb performance off the runway when full of fuel, passengers and freight, could be politely described as 'stately'. The old Jumbo – weighing over 400 tonnes – had to be flown carefully and more accurately as it lifted gently into the sky on long-haul flights, but the A340 had been designed to a knife edge of efficiency at its maximum take-off weight. Its four engines were only just powerful enough to do the job. It required extreme attention on 'heavy' take-offs, and the thought of an engine failure always was in the back of the pilot's mind, aware that the climb performance would be even worse with an engine 'out': just enough to get the heavy machine slowly climbing away, the remaining three engines at full thrust, their fans buzzing.

A major advantage of the Airbus 'fly by wire' design was the ability to make the flight decks of the two types, the 'twin' and the 'quad', almost identical. There would be no lengthy conversion courses for pilots to undergo if they switched Airbus types (my conversion training from the Boeing 747 to the Airbus had taken months). A short 'differences' course would suffice. The types could even be made so 'common' that pilots could operate both aircraft on the one 'rating'. That had been one of the many reasons that had driven me to volunteer to fly the A330 with the A340 also on the way – imagine! You could fly a short hop to an Asian destination and back in one day in a 330, then be off to Europe or North America in an A340 the next! And sure enough, training on the A340 comprised merely a couple of days in the classroom and flight simulator, then a few landings in the real thing. A month of flying the 340 exclusively followed to consolidate the training, and then the day arrived: once more, a regional A330 flight was rostered, and now I had joined a small band of airline pilots qualified for interesting and varied 'Mixed Fleet Flying'.

Airbus had put much thought into the design of the two stable-mates, the A330 'twin' and the A340 'quad'. The fuselages, wings and tail were essentially the same. The resemblance of the flight decks to each other was uncanny. A standing joke was, 'Go into the cockpit and count the number of thrust levers to tell whether you got into a 330 or a 340!' Operating procedures and checklists were almost identical between the types. The only major differences were the numbers and types of engines, and the fuel capacity. Airbus Industrie had selected a variant of the famous CFM56 for the A340, the same reliable and efficient turbofan that had powered the Boeing 737 that I flew during my last months with Ansett Airlines. Naturally, there were four, instead of two, thrust levers on the pedestal between the two pilots, but Airbus had even gone to the trouble of making their knobs narrower, which resulted in the same 'width' and 'feel' of the four levers under the palm of the pilot's hand to that of the two wider ones of the 330. The long range A340 needed to carry more fuel, so a capacious 'centre tank' was fitted into the fuselage between the wings. With the fuel distribution system on an Airbus managed by redundant computers, there were just a few more push buttons to select extra pumps and manual backup valves on the neat grey fuel panel above the pilots. A fuel jettison (dumping) system was added to the 340 in order to get the aircraft down to a suitable weight for landing in the event of a return to its airport of departure. Because of the extra weight that the A340 could lift, another set of wheels was fitted under the belly between the wings to support the heavier fuselage. The two-wheel unit protruded like a peg leg between the conventional four-wheeled 'bogies' on their long legs that reached down from the high underside of each wing.

However, operating the A340 also meant a return to long haul operations: night flights and jet lag. A windowless rest compartment was provided for the flight crew behind the cockpit, but unlike the 747, it was provided with screens connected to the passenger in-flight entertainment system. But we had to share the toilet outside the cockpit with the passengers. A larger box-like room was fitted under the rear cabin floor, accommodating seven bunks for the cabin crew, reachable by a hatch and a steep ladder. On long-haul flights, these compartments were essential to obtain the rest opportunities required by law, which would be even more critical than those on the Boeing 747: the A340 could fly further, and the aircraft was so *slow*.

Its comparatively slow cruising speed was a result of the compromises required for fuel efficiency and range. Both the A330 and the A340 flew twenty knots – or forty km/hr – slower than the 747 and Cathay Pacific's new Boeing 777. The reduced speed was not significant over shorter regional sectors, but it added to the flight time over the distance of a long haul service. Cathay's 'Bus Drivers' suffered ribbing from the Boeing pilots: 'We call your aeroplane "Babe" because it's a pig that thinks it's a dog!' or 'Why did Richard Branson take so long to fly around the world in his balloon? Because he got stuck behind an Airbus!' Even Airbus pilots derisively commented about a special bulletin put out by the manufacturer that extolled the A340's efficiency through four less powerful engines married to an efficient airframe; its leisurely climb and slow cruising speed, according to Airbus Industrie, was that of a 'well-tuned quad'! Air traffic controllers disliked the increasing numbers of Airbuses plying the airways, because their slower speed disrupted spacing of any faster Boeing that was catching up behind it at the same altitude. However, the 'well-tuned quad' could climb earlier than the Boeing, as its weight burned off, to get up out of the way. Then, the American jets would be stuck at lower levels, with the slower Airbus above blocking them from climbing for hours but leading to more ribbing about 'calendars on the flight deck,' and the Boeing pilots being well established in the bar long before the Airbus crew would arrive.

Regardless, together with the company's accountants, I really liked the 'Bus'. I was in my late thirties, enthusiastic, and I occasionally felt as if I was a voluntary publicity consultant for Airbus Industrie. The Mixed Fleet Flying suited me well, with regional flights on the 330 reducing the number of long-haul services I had to fly with a concurrent reduction in jet lag, but with the occasional 'heavyweight' long-haul flight to keep my hand in. The cockpit was far quieter than that of the old Boeing, and the pull-out table for meals and paperwork, the absence of a bulky control yoke and the ability to put my feet up made long flights more bearable. Even the Airbus's slowness, in comparison with the Boeing was, for pilots anyway, a weird advantage. Cathay Pacific crews were contracted to fly a certain number of hours for each month and year before overtime payments kicked in, which the company desperately tried to avoid. The slower the aircraft flew, the fewer trips away would be required in order to 'fly out one's hours', which resulted in more days at home! After gibes and criticism of the Airbus from a neighbour – an aggressive and abrasive management pilot of Cathay's Boeing fleet – I pointed this out to him, and he stalked off in a huff.

Gone were most of the European 'shuttle' flights, because the smaller A340 had the range and efficiency to move lighter loads non-stop from Hong Kong to destinations such as Zurich and on other 'thin' routes. But with 'cross qualification' on the A330, there was a reasonable amount of regional flying around Asia on the twin, which maintained our skills. The 340 could also add capacity to established, busy destinations such as London, Frankfurt and Los Angeles in a smaller increment than another big Boeing. Also, now reasonably comfortable with both varieties of 'Airbi', I had resumed my training duties because the A340 crews required a second officer on the long flights to Europe and North America. Now, apart from the disadvantages of life in a teeming Asian city – far from the space and sky of Australia – professionally, life was good. I flew to Zurich in an A340 with a couple of days free to see Switzerland, then flew through the night back to Hong Kong, tired and jet-lagged. Bored and restless, I spent the required days off at home. But, next, I had a busy multi-sector flight: Hong Kong to Taipei, then on to a Japanese port with an overnight stay there, before two sectors back the following day. Following that, I spent a day lecturing 'new joiners' in the classroom, or perhaps training a new second officer in the flight simulator. Then, the next evening, a gruelling overnight flight, just me and a captain, dodging the winking thunderstorms over Borneo and Bali due south towards Perth for a dawn landing. But after a few hours' sleep I could wander the gleaming, clean city under cloudless skies, the Swan River sparkling, while I pondered the two long journeys I had made: the literal one from Hong Kong to Perth, and the figurative one from a young flying instructor at Pearce, a few kilometres north, to the cockpit of a wide-body, fly-by-wire, international jet transport.

It was now mid-1997. The blue Hong Kong colonial ensign with the British Union Flag in its canton had been ceremonially lowered at midnight on the thirtieth of June, replaced by a new red flag with a white flower motif. The last British Governor would sail away in *Britannia*, the Royal Yacht, the following day. In steady tropical rain, ranks of drab-uniformed, white-gloved Communist Chinese soldiers posed woodenly in the backs of their trucks as one after another the Soviet style vehicles rolled south into the former colony to occupy the vacated military facilities of the British. Televised ceremonies depicted their grim-faced masters and the more relaxed British officials, the humourless Chinese entourage of China's Premier described, privately but appropriately, as 'appalling old waxworks' by Britain's Prince Charles. Most Hong Kong institutions had treated the long-awaited occasion as a celebration, a cynic would say in order to curry favour with their new totalitarian masters. While the rain poured all night, some Hong Kong citizens alluded to the heavens crying for Hong Kong's future. Others, unappreciative of British rule and how under it, Hong Kong had prospered, for decades a jewel of modernity and order on the south China coast, described the rain as washing away its evil colonial past. At what had been HMS *Tamar*, the naval dockyard located near bustling Central where HMAS *Melbourne* had docked sixteen years ago, our daughter danced and swung a lantern at the main ceremony as part of her school's contribution to the somewhat-forced gaiety.

In the months that followed, there was little apparent change to day-to-day life for 'expats' and locals alike, in what had become China's

'Special Administrative Region' of Hong Kong. The traditional British red post boxes were repainted green. The Royal Observatory, which produced Hong Kong's weather forecasts, became the Hong Kong Observatory. The Government Flying Service's American-made Beechcraft King Air search and rescue aircraft changed its radio call sign: it had been known as 'Kingair Zero One', simply based on the aircraft type. But there were rumours that a mainland Chinese airline pilot, on hearing the Hong Kong air traffic controllers calling Kingair Zero One, had interrupted indignantly: 'Hong Kong Control, why aircraft called *King* Air? Hong Kong now belong to China!' The Communist soldiers remained in their barracks, never to be seen on the streets. Those Cathay Pacific pilots who had had the intestinal fortitude to purchase real estate prior to the handover (I was not one of them) cleaned up handsomely when property prices soared with the handover incident-free and the prospect of cashed-up 'mainland' Chinese flooding into the market.

However, I had little time to ponder Hong Kong politics or real estate. I was busy with the flying roster as usual. And another course loomed, this one almost that of a lifetime: the Cathay Pacific Command Course. It was legendary in its length, toughness and opportunity for failure. There would be classroom work, then simulator training which would include several tough check sessions to assess how I handled multiple emergencies. Then I would fly sector after sector with a training or checking captain acting as first officer and, later on, looking over my shoulder from the jump seat. Every move I made would be documented, assessed and debriefed. Just one 'bad day' – coping badly with poor weather; a mishandled emergency; a personality clash; an 'unstable' approach or a silly mistake; meant back to the 'line' as a first officer. I would be offered, perhaps, one second and final attempt at the course a year later. Unlike most airlines where on the successful completion of a pilot's last 'command check' flight the assessor would present the new captain with his 'four bar' rank slides, Cathay Pacific was different. At the end of all the flying, a board of management pilots would pore over the records of the pilot's flying skills, leadership, interaction with the first officers and cabin crews, fuel loading decisions (it cost the company money to carry extra fuel), passenger comfort, the simulator check reports ... but, if after a few days' deliberation they were satisfied, the candidate's efforts would be rewarded: he or she would be given a significant rise in salary (and responsibility), and awarded the title of Captain. This was my lifetime chance after twenty-one years of military and airline aviation. To get through it, I would have to work, and work, and work.

I was approaching forty, and study did not come so easily now. With this in mind, I 'put myself' on the command course six months prior to its actual start date, reading every publication and studying every form that the airline produced – and there were many! I wrote copious summaries and workflows, memorised rule of thumb calculations and figures for weight and fuel and, of course, sections of the Airbus Flight Crew Operating Manual: four thick volumes which were constant companions at home and on layovers.

Now it was on. I signed on for a first training flight in the left seat – the captain's seat – in an A330. The Airbus had no passengers on board, just some other command trainees and a British Base Training Captain in charge. We would fly to Shenzhen, just north of Hong Kong. In the circuit there, a fluky, gusty crosswind blew, and the lightly-loaded Airbus wobbled and danced as it floated just above the runway while I tried to set it down nicely for each landing. Despite the simulator training in the left hand seat, I still found the Airbus a very 'handed' aeroplane: after almost three years in the right-hand seat manipulating the sensitive side stick with my right hand, I was still teaching my left hand how to fly! Also, in French style, the instrument panel coaming was curved, and from the left-hand seat, the picture through the windscreen looked different to the right. Damned by faint praise from the base Training Captain, I took comfort in the large number of sectors that I would fly as a captain under training: that should smooth everything out. Also, I hoped that my preparation prior to the course would leave brain space to cope with the tasks and responsibilities of command training.

Throughout the course came the demanding simulator assessments in which multiple emergencies and situations were presented. It was not sufficient just to immediately cope with the problems – they had to be taken to some form of logical conclusion: a return, a diversion to another suitable airport or, preferably, use of a captain's judgement and knowledge of the regulations in an attempt to get the 300 fictional passengers to where they had paid to go. I tried to 'go down fighting' but, above all, I had to remain safe and legal. Successfully completing the last of these assessments was a great relief.

I did not need to worry about the actual flying. From the first flights with passengers on board, I was treated as if I actually knew something! This was not the Cathay Pacific that I had come to know. I was fortunate to be allocated 'gentlemen' as Training and Check Captains who supervised my flights. As in most airlines, there were ogres in Cathay Pacific Airways: some difficult to deal with, some nit-picking, some insecure and some just 'different', with occasional unfortunate combinations of these traits. I was grateful that those trainers and checkers with whom I flew just let me get on with the job and run the show, with them there to offer advice and criticism where warranted. After a few sectors, I was assessed as suitable to have a 'line' first officer in the right-hand seat, with the training or checking captain now occupying the jump seat. This upped the ante, because how I interacted with the first officers was observed minutely. I had to be inclusive, friendly and courteous, but I had to cross a fine line when the first officer made a poor decision, a miscalculation, or a flying error. Knowing when and how to intervene when the FO was controlling the aircraft or to even to take over control in a developing situation was an art form. My experience instructing in the Orion had become invaluable. However, most FOs were very supportive of captains under training or assessment because they knew that, one day, it would be their turn.

'I'll see you in the debriefing room upstairs in ten minutes,' said the Check Captain at the end of my final command assessment flight.

I had had enough. I was 'over it'. The last few weeks of training had seemed interminable. For a year I had been studying, preparing, writing, thinking, 'what if … what if …' I could not cram any more numbers, facts or drills into my head. Almost beyond caring, I operated the first two busy sectors of my final check: Hong Kong to Taipei, then on to Kansai (Osaka) Airport. We rested for a brief overnight, then operated the two sectors back. Throughout each flight the Check Captain – a dour Scot – had mostly stared out the window from the jump seat, offering little comment, criticism or encouragement. He asked few technical questions, but in the quiet Airbus cockpit I would occasionally hear his pen click, then scratch on his note pad. At last, parked on the bustling tarmac at Kai Tak, the A330's Engine Master levers were moved to OFF and the rumble of the Trents died. We completed the Shut Down Checklist, the Scot waved the FO off home and even now, with the huge machine's engines ticking and cooling, its hundreds of passengers filing off into the aerobridges, he gave no indication as to whether I had passed. When I reported 'upstairs in ten minutes', he had little to say apart from that, as far as he was concerned, the check had been satisfactory. Drained, I slithered onto the vinyl bench seat of the ubiquitous red taxi. My brain was happily blank while the vehicle jerked and weaved through the stop-start traffic towards Clearwater Bay, home and family.

Several days later, I was called into the office of the senior pilot manager. He said that I had completed the training satisfactorily, and to my consternation added that I had impressed the taciturn Scot. A camera clicked for the staff magazine as he handed me a clear plastic packet that contained two black cloth slides, each adorned with the four gold stripes of a Cathay Pacific Captain.

18

NAIVETY'S END

1998 – 2006

I t was July 1998, and although it was monsoon season, the weather on descent into Hong Kong was clear this early morning, and the air was silky smooth. This was the return flight from the usual Taipei 'split duty' pattern after four hours' sleep on a hard bed in the mouldy Chiang Kai Shek Hotel. I wondered what our passengers would think if they knew how little rest their crew had had, just to save the airline a few bucks in accommodation and allowances. Eyes stinging and with a rising sun behind us, I was thankful for the benign weather. The Trents were at idle but, occasionally, their thrust motored up and down while the A330 adjusted to its optimum descent path, 'drawn' by the flight management computer in three dimensions, which we, of course, were monitoring closely. We were now south of the lush but mountainous terrain of Hong Kong's Lantau Island and when clear of that, we would bank to the right towards southern China, then make a final right turn east towards Hong Kong itself. But we would not be flying the familiar IGS to land at Kai Tak. Our destination was a vast new airport sitting on reclaimed land off the northern edge of Lantau, with one, soon to be two, long east-west parallel runways. Lantau's peaks soared just to the south of the airport, but the approach paths were clear enough to provide standard 'straight-in' Instrument Landing System (ILS) approaches: the famous IGS with its low right turn over the grimy buildings of Kowloon was no more. But in windy or stormy weather, the terrain, in close proximity to Chek Lap Kok, Hong Kong's new airport, provided interesting experiences for those who would land there. This would be my first landing at the new airport, on little sleep, but thankfully the winds remained light. There was even less to be concerned about, because with me was a capable and highly experienced first officer. Aviation can be a very small world. Again, that saying, 'Always be nice to people who you deal with while you are on the way up, because you may meet them on the way down' came to mind. My first officer this morning was Mal, my very first Training Captain on the old Friendship after I had joined Ansett Airlines as a raw first officer. Although superior in skill and experience, he had joined Cathay Pacific after I had done following the Pilots' Dispute, and under the implacable rule of seniority, he was still waiting for his own turn at once again becoming a captain.

After landing, the long journey home from the new airport would be even more tedious following a split duty with yet another 'Cathay Pacific sunrise'. Before the new airport opened had been an opportune time to move into Kowloon itself. We now lived in a relatively spacious, older style multi-storey apartment block. It was close to King George V School, which had retained its British name and heritage despite the handover to China, and the flat was convenient to Hong Kong's mass transit railway system and teeming Mong Kok and Tsim Tsa Tsui.

On a later flight, my eyes were gritty as usual and I felt, and no doubt looked, tired and drawn as our A340 descended towards Hong Kong. After nearly a year of operating only the A330 twin as a new captain, in 1999 I was now commanding long-haul flights on the A340. We had departed London the previous afternoon, and the airways lead us over Scandinavia, Russia, Siberia, Mongolia, into China, then a turn to the south approaching Beijing. As on most long-haul flights, sleep in the stuffy bunkroom had been fitful and, as usual, I gave up trying to sleep several hours before descent. I changed out of my track suit and into my uniform, and returned to the cockpit early to give one of the other pilots a break: there was no point in three of us sitting there.

China was a demanding place for Western airline crews to operate. In 'normal' countries, military aircraft are restricted to 'corridors' or designated areas, and civilian aircraft have the rest of the airspace to themselves. The reverse was true in China. Airliners were restricted to narrow corridors that zigged and zagged between a Soviet-style plethora of radio beacons and reporting points. The Chinese People's Liberation Army Air Force controlled the rest of the airspace over the vast country, using its own controllers: the heritage of a communist dictatorship founded on military revolution. A line of thunderstorms across a civilian air route meant much argy-bargy on the radio, because the civilian controllers had to approach their military counterparts to clear airliners into military airspace in order for them to avoid the hazardous weather. The Chinese were paranoid about over-flights of their air bases and sensitive border areas; we cynically wondered why, because smog and cloud almost always covered the ground. It was not unheard of for airline crews to threaten to – or actually – declare an emergency in order to obtain clearance to deviate around boiling anvil-headed storm clouds as their jets rushed towards them at eight nautical miles – or fifteen kilometres – every minute. But on this summer's early morning with the grey light of dawn to our left, we were now on the final stages of descent over southern China towards its border with Hong Kong. The Guangzhou controller was cooperative with clearing us to deviate around developing coastal thunderstorms as we descended south and homewards: soon, we would be Hong Kong's problem, not his. Head down and concentrating on the instruments and weather radar display, the British first officer deftly adjusted the 'heading' knob of the autopilot to send the Airbus banking left and right around blossoming yellow and red storm returns on the screen. A longer line of storms, a red sausage shape on the display, loomed across our path, but thankfully we were now descending through 25,000 feet – or 7,600 metres – and had been handed over to Hong Kong Radar. The controller's accent would be British, Australian or Hong Kong Chinese, 'the sound of home,' and signifying relative flexibility to manoeuvre over the South China Sea to the south and west of Hong Kong, especially in light early-morning traffic. Hong Kong granted us a substantial deviation as we were enveloped in grey cloud at the ragged edges of the storm line, the grey light of dawn now masked by the gloom. Icy rain rattled on the windscreen where fingers of Saint Elmo's Fire danced, and through the big flat side windows, other lights flickered: the reflections of the double flash of the bright white strobe lights on the wingtips and the regular beams of the red beacons on the fuselage. Yellow-white sheets of reflected lightning lit up the mist and now the cockpit shivered in turbulence. We manoeuvred the Airbus around the western side of the storms with the shaking increasing to a crescendo, and then with a final jolt we burst into clear sky, the walls of the line of clouds behind us lit by saffron light, the sun now on the horizon to our left, fingers of light climbing into a bright blue sky with the South China Sea glittering below. We doubled back under radar control, then turned directly to face the rising sun to land eastwards, the storms embedded in a towering orange-yellow wall of cloud to our left. These would move into Hong Kong later with bursts of rain and rumbles of thunder, but by then we would be beyond caring. For me, after the taxi ride through the morning traffic jams, I would get a couple of hours of sleep amid the clamour of the children being readied for school. Then would come a tedious afternoon of fighting sleep before I collapsed back into bed in the early evening, now able to sink into unconsciousness for as long as I needed.

I was a mixed-fleet Airbus captain enjoying a noteworthy variety of flying: taking a 330 to Japan one day; flying a 'procedural' (no air traffic control radar) approach into Hanoi, north Vietnam, flying an A340 the next; then the following day, a departure to take another 340 across the Pacific to Anchorage. From there it was onwards through the evening to Toronto, sometimes with the green, purple and mauve of aurorae flickering to the north. In the sometimes-draughty Airbus cockpits, I involuntarily shivered as I looked down on whiteness beneath. In daylight or moonlight, it looked flat from horizon to horizon and studded with innumerable frozen lakes after we crossed the saw-toothed peaks of Alaska. On later flights, we would fly from Hong Kong to Toronto non-stop, almost fourteen hours airborne, the jet stream pushing us along, but that same river of air necessitating the customary refuelling stop and crew layover in Anchorage on the return flight to Hong Kong. Toronto's weather could be spectacular due to its northerly inland location combined with proximity to the Great Lakes. Once, in wintry sunlight, I watched yellow lightning bolts forking down from a ragged line of purple clouds that were dumping thick clumps of snow.

On one clear winter's morning I landed an A340 at Anchorage from a completely 'visual' approach to the 'displaced threshold' of the only runway cleared of snow, without the guidance of any ILS or visual guide lights, just like the light aircraft flying from nearby Merrill Field. It was a refreshing change from the rigidly controlled and guided approaches at other airports. A shallow layer of blowing snow drifted across the ground below our cockpit while we taxied in – it was like how it is in the movies. On one late night descent into Anchorage, our Airbus would be abruptly hammered high at 20,000 feet – or 17,000 metres – on descent by a seeming 'wall' of turbulence caused by wind streaming over nearby mountain ranges. Forewarned, we had the cabin crew strapped in, and 160 tonnes of airliner lurched and danced all the way to touchdown.

In the new century I began to operate flights to Australia. Foreign accents of the radio calls from the domestic airliners grated on me, but ironically, as a result of the dispute, in my early forties I was in command of an international Airbus, rather than still awaiting captaincy of a lowly Fokker. But from early 2002, Ansett no longer existed. What would Sir Reg have thought, his airline asset-stripped by the group that had taken it over, then its aircraft grounded for months by a disastrous labour dispute exacerbated by a fool of a prime minister? Hawke had been replaced by Paul Keating in 1991, and Sir Peter Abeles died in 1999. Ansett had been acquired by a consortium from New Zealand, but in a few years, the pioneering Australian airline collapsed under a mountain of debt. After arrival at Japan's Kansai Airport one evening, I encountered an ex-Ansett pilot from my old intake course who had 'gone back' early in the dispute. Now he wore the uniform of a Japanese airline as a 'contract pilot'. Distantly polite, I pointed out that it was ironic that he had to move overseas, just as I had done thirteen years previously.

But all was not well with relations between Cathay Pacific's management and its pilots either. With a sense of *déjà vu*, we ex-Ansett and Australian Airlines pilots watched our new airline's industrial relations deteriorate. In 1999, management had issued an ultimatum for its original 'A Scale' pilots (since 1992, new joiners had signed up on inferior conditions known as the 'B Scale'). We were presented with three options: sign a new contract, which compensated a pay cut with the award of share options; take a voluntary redundancy scheme; or be dismissed from the company. With this heavy-handed approach, crew morale and work ethic deteriorated. To the airline's surprise, the redundancy offer was oversubscribed by disillusioned pilots, so seniority had to determine those who could take it. After tense negotiations with the pilots' Association, the share option offer was accepted, but the deterioration in many pilots' dedication to and respect for the company had begun.

I had come to realise that I could no longer subscribe to the loyalty I would have held if flying with a military squadron, a small family business, or a new-start company with a tightly-knit team of enthusiastic employees who would go that extra mile to make things work. Cathay Pacific pilots were now working for businessmen running a large company based in an Asian enclave that had very loose labour laws and a government unashamedly on the company's side. These executives were paid bonuses for cutting costs. The rapidly growing airline had reached a critical mass where highly skilled employees were just another cost to be cut. Management's relations with its pilots would never be the same. There would be no more working eighteen hours straight to help out on rostered days off, or volunteering my services during typhoons, or even answering the telephone to Crew Control, unless required to do so on a rostered standby duty. Following the redundancies, the rest of us were working harder. After completing routine flight simulator training one morning, I was told that instead of the normal rostered simulator check the next day, I would be 'operating to Taipei tonight', after the minimum legal rest, for a split duty. The next day, on three hours' sleep, it was back to Hong Kong in the early morning light, with 'minimum rest' at home, and then back to the simulator that evening for a proficiency check.

It was nostalgic to operate to Perth. Arrivals were in the early mornings and our A330 would be almost gliding in towards the airport from the north, engines idling, and there was usually a chance for me to snatch a glance down at Pearce, where its personnel were getting ready for work. The large white tarmac carports were still prominent, but propeller-driven PC-9s were ranged under them, the jets long gone.

One day I had been assigned late 'standby' duty with the children noisily home for the day. I couldn't sleep. That evening a duty assignment came from Crew Control: I had to operate to Perth that night. However, there was no return flight the next day for me to operate or to position on back to Hong Kong. Rather than pay for one or two days' accommodation in Perth, the company would 'passenger' me to Melbourne with a domestic airline on a cheap industry 'standby' fare for a one nights' stay in the crew hotel there. Then I was to be flown back to Hong Kong as a passenger on a Cathay Pacific flight the next day. I operated the overnight flight – there were just two of us, because Perth flights were short enough to not require a third 'relief' pilot. After hours of waiting in Perth Airport for the connecting Melbourne flight, I crossed the continent in a full, noisy cabin, with sleep impossible. On arrival at the Melbourne hotel, I had been awake for thirty-two hours straight. But the company had saved a few bucks.

2001 was not a good year for Cathay Pacific's pilots or in fact, the airline itself. It was still short of crew. In 'normal' airlines, flying rosters are published well in advance and there are very few changes to them. There are sufficient pilots on 'standby', as I had spent most of my days in Ansett, to cover crew sickness or flight disruption. But Cathay Pacific now teetered on the edge of what would be deemed insufficient crew to fly the task. The monthly flying roster was routinely published only two weeks ahead. And then flight duties chopped and changed: I would plan my activities (and rest) at home, arrive at the airport, and find that my flight had been altered. In the sweltering humidity of one Hong Kong summer's afternoon, I signed on for my rostered regional pattern of two and a half hours to Cebu (an island resort in the Philippines), then back to Hong Kong that same evening. However, there had been a late change. I landed in Anchorage, Alaska.

Because of the crew shortage, exacerbated by apathetic and even hostile pilots refusing to answer the telephone to Crew Control with their incessant changes, it was a requirement to call Crew Control after arrival in Hong Kong from every flight. On doing that, more often than not my next scheduled flight would have been changed – the published rosters were now not worth the paper they were written on. After making the call, a pilot would often have their next rostered duty cancelled and allocated standby duty instead, only for the phone to ring at home with a short-notice duty immediately after the standby period started; and so on for the next flight after checking with Crew Control after arrival from the last one …

Because of the crew shortage, Crew Control were increasingly ringing pilots on their days off, begging them to work. The annual Hong Kong Rugby Sevens was a famous international tournament, and sponsored by the airline. The Sevens was on for the year, and Hong Kong Stadium was filled to capacity with beer-swilling fans – expatriates and locals – who were noisily enjoying the fast-pitched games. The tournament was widely televised, and spectators could pay to have messages put up on the electronic scoreboard between games, such as a cheerio to a friend, a 'Hi Mum' or even a marriage proposal. During one lull in the play, a roar erupted from the spectators. Off-duty pilots had arranged for the scoreboard to flash up with 'WOULD ANY CATHAY PACIFIC PILOT PLEASE CALL CREW CONTROL.' At the end of the next match, the scoreboard flashed again to more mirth and cheers from the boozy crowd: 'WOULD ANY *SOBER* CATHAY PILOT PLEASE CALL CREW CONTROL.'

Crew Control always seemed to be on the line allocating changes to the pilots. Something had to give. In July 2001, a breakdown in negotiations with management led to the pilots' Association initiating a 'go slow': euphemistically called 'Maximum Safety Strategy', which, to a point, it was: many pilots were chronically fatigued by constantly working to the legal limits. The Association instructed us, *inter alia*, to take our time studying the flight documents, to taxi slowly, and to not go into 'discretion' where, after a delay or disruption, government regulations allowed us to extend our duty period for a few more hours with the individual pilot's approval. Most of us were continually tired and fed up with the constant roster changes, which made it difficult for us to plan rest or home life properly. The company reacted angrily to the campaign. Management decided that it would send a message to its pilots: forty-nine perceived troublemakers, and some who had had personality clashes with managers, were to be dismissed from the company. Flight operations managers – most of them also pilots themselves – reviewed the files of every pilot in the airline. We called this group the 'Star Chamber'. Most of those terminated by the Star

Chamber were advised of their fate by telephone. One pilot who was on leave in North America was fired by fax. Another reported for his assigned flight at company headquarters, but the turnstile would not click over as normal when he presented his company ID. A red-faced junior manager had to come down to tell him to his face that he no longer had a job. The number of sacked pilots had grown to fifty-three, but for decades to come, the terminated pilots would be known as the Cathay Pacific 'Forty-Niners'.

Under Hong Kong law we were essentially contract workers, and support for any escalation in industrial action or strike was by no means universal. However, Cathay Pacific had planned for a strike after the dismissal of the Forty-Niners. Some of us speculated that management wanted one, because then they could tear up the strikers' contracts and offer new ones to those they reemployed (on reduced terms, of course); that is, bring on a 'lock out' similar to the Australian dispute. There were other shades of the dispute when white-tailed foreign chartered aircraft flew in to Hong Kong, all set to fly Cathay's passengers. But to the airline's chagrin, no strike was called; there would be no lock out. Having been scheduled and paid for, the chartered foreign jets flew Cathay Pacific's bewildered passengers while most of the airline's own pilots sat at home on standby during the disruption, with the crew allocation system unable to cope. Instead of any strike, the Association resorted to legal action that dragged on for years until most of the Forty-Niners were compensated or reinstated, at a great cost to the company. John, the captain I had taken to the Hong Kong bar in Penang, was one of the Forty-Niners. A tough street fighter type, he led the legal action and would subsequently write a book about the affair, which sold well in Hong Kong.

Tragically, in the early stages of the dispute, one of the dismissed pilots fell to his death from a high-rise window. As someone who had excitedly joined Cathay Pacific Airways as a young man after a previous dreadful industrial dispute, I was now in no doubt that the airline industry could be brutal, unstable and unforgiving to those in the wrong place at the wrong time.

Later in 2001, my wife and I were celebrating our wedding anniversary in one of the most famous hotels in Hong Kong: The Peninsula. We had enjoyed a sumptuous meal in the hotel's restaurant and were about to leave. The Chinese waiter cleared our table and as he worked, he was saying something about aircraft and buildings. His English was not good and what he was trying to say did not register with us. It was late, and we went up to our room. In the morning, as was my usual hotel habit, I flicked on the television to catch the news. Muslim terrorists had killed thousands of people in the United States by flying airliners full of passengers into buildings after murdering the pilots with box cutters. I am still horrified today at the thought of what would have transpired in those cockpits after the terrorists burst through the flimsy flight deck doors.

Soon, our workplace was isolated by a heavy electrically-locked armoured door. Wide-eyed children or interested adult passengers were no longer allowed to visit the cockpit to gaze at the panorama of sky with the earth many kilometres below, marvel at the instruments, screens and switches, and to tentatively ask a few questions of their pilots. Airline Pilot was no longer the respected profession that moved millions of people and tonnes of goods around the planet day after day, night after night. Pilots had already become little more than an expense on a balance sheet; something to be dealt with by airline managements as necessary tools to operate their expensive machinery safely and efficiently.

Now they had also become targets for insane religious fanatics.

I had flown several patterns to Johannesburg. Back in 1999, I had been getting ready to leave home to operate the non-stop flight, through the night as usual, to arrive in South Africa in the early morning. Squalls of rain rattled against the windows of our flat, flung from a typhoon that lingered north-east of Hong Kong. I anticipated getting thumped by the outskirts of this weather when we would climb out towards the Indian Ocean. As my wife got ready to drive me to the taxi rank, the telephone rang. Hong Kong airport was closed. An MD-11, a development of the Douglas DC-10, which was of similar layout to the old TriStar with its wide body and three massive engines, had been on approach to Chek Lap Kok airport in heavy rain and gusty crosswinds. It belonged to a Taiwanese airline, and on board were 300 passengers and fifteen crew. As the pilot flared the big airliner to land, the right wing dropped suddenly and the weight of the aircraft crashed down heavily onto its right hand landing gear. Incredibly, the right hand wing snapped off like that of a child's toy aeroplane. With the left wing still producing lift, the jet flipped over and skidded along, then slewed off to the side of Runway 25 in flames. On its back and with its rear fuselage on fire, it came to rest on the sodden grass, the broken wing almost 300 metres ahead of the MD-11's inverted cockpit. Imagine the chaos in the cabin: 300 passengers in an upside-down wreck, many still dangling by their seat belts, the aircraft on fire. Three passengers died but, fortunately, the heavy rain suppressed the blaze and Hong Kong International Airport's brave fire and rescue crews were at the scene quickly and everybody else survived. With the airport closed, I was not flying to Africa that night. Any complacency that pilots had about the newly-opened airport's perceived better weather conditions than Kai Tak were comprehensively dispelled.

Whenever I flew to Johannesburg, during the long crew bus ride to the hotel I always reflected on how fortunate Australians were. Substantial fences around the houses and gated communities were noteworthy, with many not just topped with rolls of razor wire, but with insulators and signs warning of *electrified* razor wire. Also, it was on every take off from 'Joburg' where the major shortcoming of the A340 made itself manifest. Cathay Pacific's accountants had already begun to cast their eyes on the aircraft's relatively small capacity compared with Boeing's 777, which the airline now operated, and the weight and maintenance of its four small engines, rather than the more efficient, bigger units of the A330 and the Boeing twins. Jan Smuts International Airport, later renamed Oliver Tambo, sat on South Africa's high *veldt* at 5,500 feet – or 1,680 metres – above sea level, the air perceptively thinner. The traditional joke that the A340 relied on the curvature of the Earth to get airborne after its leisurely take-off run took on new significance at this airport. On a warm South African afternoon bound for Hong Kong, I pushed the four thrust levers forward to the take-off power detent. The jet leisurely began rolling, the nose wheel below running along the runway while I avoided the 'thump thump thump' of running it over the embedded centre line lights. Ever so slowly the Airbus gained speed, but it would not fly for a long time yet. The take-off roll seemed interminable. My scan flicked down to the central engine display. The engines were delivering the thrust that they were supposed to, but look at the exhaust temperatures! The numbers scrolled towards the upper limits on two of the engines. Still, the nose wheel remained firmly planted.

'Vee one!' called the first officer.

We were now past the point of not being able to stop on the runway – we were committed to fly. In Johannesburg's thin, warm air, the heavy Airbus had to gain a greater speed than normal along the runway before it would lift off. For an age, we remained in limbo, the end of the runway looming, until, finally the first officer called 'Rotate!' At this call I could almost painfully ease the sidestick back. The nose lifted slowly, and with the runway's end disappearing seemingly just under our feet, the jet reared up and grudgingly broke ground. Two exhaust temperature readouts were now red, which we ignored until after the landing gear had rumbled and groaned into the wells, and we were a few hundred feet up to deal with them. Judiciously, we adjusted the thrust levers of the offending engines as we bumped and clawed for altitude in the afternoon sky, brown fields and shanty-towns sliding by not far below. At last we were high enough to set what passed for 'climb thrust' and retract the slats and flaps, but we had to virtually level out to accelerate to a safe speed for the procedure, as one would in an overloaded light aeroplane. Cathay Pacific's performance engineers were among the best, but out of Joburg, I always hoped they had their figures correct: what would this evolution be like if an engine failed? Thankfully, all four of the CFM 56s kept buzzing away, but the slat and flap retraction took so long that it seemed that we had only just got the aircraft 'clean' and climbing away to cruise altitude when we entered another country, Mozambique.

From southern Africa, our flight crossed Madagascar, then on into the night over the Indian Ocean, passing not far from Diego Garcia with memories of Orion operations through there, then a few tantalising hours in Australian Indian Ocean airspace before swinging north-east towards the pre-dawn storms of Sumatra and the South China Sea. Then, the usual early morning arrival home, the air already greasy and humid. I was testy and sleep-deprived and not in any mood to hear about what domestic problems had appeared during my absence, or to put up with the noise from the Chinese family in the flat above, their heavy wooden furniture scaping along the bare parquet floor while their two Filipina maids carried out their interminable cleaning chores.

Even Airbus Industrie had realised the limitations of its A340, the 'well-tuned quad'. As a result they had developed a new version of it, far more powerful, larger and with an even longer range. It should really have been regarded as another Airbus type altogether, but the manufacturer had designated it the A340-600. As far as the pilots' ratings were concerned, this meant that the 'Six Hundred' was considered a 'common type' with the original A340 and its twin-engine sister, the wildly successful A330. And I would have to get in the books yet again, because Cathay Pacific Airways had leased three of them.

The A340-600 was what the original A340 should have been. Its extended fuselage, seventy-five metres of it, was twelve metres longer. Far longer than the Boeing 747-400 and over two metres longer than the massive Airbus A380 that would appear later, it was the longest airliner ever produced until Boeing, in turn, 'stretched' its Boeing 747 into the 747-8 version. And there would be no take-offs out of Johannesburg at the limits of performance for this machine. It had four de-rated versions of the A330's twin powerful Rolls Royce Trents. In fact, I found that it would even lift off from Joburg with its engines at the lower, 'flex' thrust rating used at most other airports – maximum power not required – to reduce wear and tear and noise. With its four Trent engines, I regarded the A340-600 as two A330's tied together! The -600's new wing was broader and with a span three metres wider than its A330 and 340 siblings. The larger size of the wing and fuselage enabled more fuel to be stored in extra tanks: over 150 tonnes of it. The weight of the fuel load alone was more than the empty weight of a complete A330, yet Airbus and Cathay Pacific regarded the aircraft as basically the same type! With the extra tanks, the fuel distribution system was more sophisticated, and with some design flaws of the older A340 corrected. The extra weight of the new 'stretched' A340's fuel and structure dictated replacement of the twin wheels of the 'peg leg' centre landing gear with a proper four-wheeled 'bogie'. The nose wheel strut was lengthened and strengthened, so the 'Six Hundred' did not have that head down, tail up 'sit' when on the ground – a characteristic of its smaller sisters. While it did not have the bulk of the Jumbo, the new jet still looked impressive.

But despite the significant differences from the A330 and the original A340, because of the Airbus design philosophy, its cockpit and controls were virtually identical; however, no flight control computer could compensate for the far greater mass of the big machine. It handled differently. The increased weight and momentum made it reminiscent of the old Boeing 747; descent and deceleration had to be judged carefully in order to slow it down to configure for landing. It seemed to levitate off the runway in a flatter attitude thanks to its big wing and flaps, and it landed in the same fashion. In turbulence, the wings did not waffle about in roll, but the cockpit shimmied from side to side, a phenomenon of the bending stresses in the long fuselage. With its impressive range, non-stop flights reaching over the Arctic from Hong Kong to New York were practical and, incredibly, the new Airbus could fly the return trip, also without a fuel stop, even against the prevailing jet stream winds.

Pilots of Cathay Pacific's Airbus fleet now had to stay on top of three different sub-types (I do not know of any other airline whose line pilots routinely flew such differing aircraft: the A330, the 340 and the A340-600). My bookshelves took on a distinct bow under the weight of the multiple volumes of three different operating manuals, in addition to the generic company 'light reading' I had to keep up with. However, the mixed fleet flying kept my brain active and it was always exhilarating to take a -600, up there in size and weight with the Jumbo, on a regional flight or, later, to Sydney, Los Angeles or New York.

I flew to New York for the first time in 2005. Our '-600' rode the jet stream east past Japan, then turned north east across the far north Pacific, the Aleutian Islands, and within 60 nautical miles – or 110 kilometres – of the North Pole. The A340-600's fuel transfer system, which fed fuel via the multitude of tanks to the engines, was complicated and, on this occasion, the fuel management computer was not transferring fuel as it should; one valve had failed. We attached sticky notes prominently on the instrument panel to remind us to operate other backup valves manually in order to use all the fuel available yet not to starve the engines. The Arctic was not an area in which to be frantically operating a complicated fuel system to restore an engine 'rundown', and busy New York was not the place to arrive at with unusable fuel in a tank. Interestingly, Airbus had also thoughtfully provided a button on the instrument panel that changed the aircraft's heading reference system from 'magnetic', useless in the polar regions, to true north. After fourteen hours of flying we landed in rainy gloom on a wet, comparatively short runway at JFK. Rapid-fire instructions in New York accents had burst through our headsets as the air traffic controllers directed our flight and many others through some of the most complicated airspace in the world. Eventually, we fell into our beds in the basic and noisy Manhattan hotel to the slamming of doors and the shouts of the cleaning staff in the corridors, but a few hours later we walked the vast city, block after block of vertical buildings before a few drinks and a meal, then made an attempt at a night's sleep, on the other side of the planet.

Professionally and financially, flying for Cathay Pacific from Hong Kong was extremely rewarding and I was fortunate to be in this enviable position. But the company's relations with its pilots never improved in the years (and decades) that followed the Sign or be Fired, then the Forty-Niner affairs, and still the flying rosters chopped and changed. The noise from the Chinese family who lived overhead our flat was never-ending; it was as if they randomly dropped ball bearings on their parquet floor, which was our ceiling, at all hours of the day and night. The pounding of children's feet running in the flat upstairs, the jet lag, the 'red-eye' flights, the heat and humidity … It all coalesced into poor sleep, stress, and frustration with living in the crowded city state.

The local culture was 'different'. Hard-working, and with little scope for any leisure activity that required open space, many Hong Kong Chinese were avid collectors. The McDonalds chain of fast food restaurants was well established in Hong Kong and popular among the Chinese, and the company had offered a sales promotion at its outlets: a plastic Snoopy figure came with each meal, attired in the national dress of one of a number of countries. Queues snaked outside the restaurants as locals bought meals in order to collect the full set of Snoopys, the food often just thrown into the street. Domestic helpers were detailed to stand in the queues in place of their employers. Fights broke out as frantic locals pushed and shoved, and I think of this as the time of the 'Snoopy Riots'. Hello Kitty was also extremely popular: many of Cathay Pacific's cabin crew sported soft toys depicting the mouthless cat hanging from their luggage and handbags. Row after row of stuffed toys adorned the desks in the airline's offices. Plastic figures of Snow White and the Seven Dwarfs were arrayed on the dashboards of the taxis, private cars and even large trucks, or there might have been a Garfield grinning amid a line of other unknown figures, their identities best known to the owner.

Notwithstanding the chronic roster instability, constant call outs and flying to the maximum legal hours, I was still bored and restless on the now fewer days off. And I developed a worrying health problem. Small muscle twitches in my face, arms and legs developed into uncomfortable spasms and cramps. The muscle spasms were called 'fasciculations', and they rippled around my body like ants crawling. Painful cramps wracked my legs. It felt as if I was wading through treacle while my skin crawled. I was referred to the best doctors. In the early 2000s, Cathay Pacific provided their pilots with excellent health care. Even after multitudes of scans and tests, none of the doctors I saw seemed to have any idea as to what was causing it. To my surprise, the company's aviation medicine doctors did not seem concerned about my condition, and I was not grounded. They possibly considered it imaginary. One said, 'Call it "Fred" and learn to live with it!' So between rounds of the doctors, I flew the busy rosters and tried to ignore what was going on physically. I was taking more and more sick days off because of it. The internet had arrived – I trawled it with my symptoms, and I wished that I had not. The information indicated that I could be developing the dreadful degenerative motor neurone disease. I was referred to a supposed top neurologist in Hong Kong, who ran a painful test of electric shocks through my extremities. At the end of the tests, the Chinese specialist said, unsubtly, 'I think you may have motor neurone disease,' and ushered me out.

Surely I was not going to end up in a wheelchair with this illness, that later claimed the physicist Stephen Hawking? I could not bring myself to accept that I was developing motor neurone disease. I forced myself to walk and walk the streets on days off, through odorous and thronging Kowloon south of our flat, trying to dispel the feeling that I was wading through treacle. In desperation, I returned to the internet, and eventually stumbled on a site that discussed excessive coffee drinking. Yes, I was drinking lots of it: several cups in the morning, and of course cup after cup on the increasing number of overnight flights. Unlike Kai Tak, the new airport did not have a night curfew, and as the daytime slots filled with air traffic, Cathay Pacific took advantage of being able to schedule flights that departed well after midnight. In addition to long haul in the A340, we were now flying all-night regional flights in A330s, carrying freight for a major parcel delivery corporation in the jets' ample belly holds, along with passengers travelling on cheap 'red-eye' fares. On long haul flights I was gulping coffee after my rest breaks in order to get myself alert for the arrival and landing.

So, on that next morning, there was no more coffee for me. Pounding headaches over the next day or two were the result but, thankfully, the fasciculations and cramps very, very gradually began to ease. I was in my late forties, and this had been a worry. It had gone on for a year, and along with the busy rosters, the noisy neighbours and the interminable heat and humidity, the uncertainty about what was wrong with me had contributed to a low point in my life.

Among other areas, the airline was cutting back on the quality of the hotels where its crews were accommodated, although it had to finally and reluctantly stop using the infamous Chiang Kai Shek Hotel at Taipei Airport. It had been condemned due to structural cracks following an earthquake. The establishment was not missed by pilots or cabin crew. Several other mediocre hotels were found further away that were assigned variously. For longer stays, crews were accommodated in Taipei city itself.

The first officer and I had been out for lunch in central Taipei, prior to an early night before three busy sectors the next day: up to Japan, back to Taipei, then on to Hong Kong. The high-rise hotel belonged to a famous worldwide chain. Upon entering my room, I heard a rumble. My first thought was 'Earthquake!', which was very possible in Taiwan. But the noise was emanating from the metal trunking of the air conditioning system that was attached to the ceiling. It had large circular vents that fed air into the room. The rumble became louder, and I heard squeals. Being Australian, my first thought was, 'That sounds like possums in the roof.' But there would not be any possums on the twelfth floor of a high-rise hotel in Taiwan.

Then, a small, dirty brown rat fell out of the ventilation grille and scuttled around on the carpet. It had been chased by its much larger cousins that I could still hear pounding up and down in the ventilation trunking. Desperately trying to to escape, the rat had pushed itself through the hole. Even following a room change, I did not sleep well that night.

Management's relations with its crews deteriorated further. For decades Cathay Pacific had run an incentive system where employees were paid a certain amount of 'profit share': this had been significant during the early days with the airline, but the amount had lessened over the years as the airline expanded its employee numbers. Also, there always seemed to be an excuse for management to cry 'poor' and reduce it, or occasionally not pay it at all, despite the concessions and hard work of their pilots, cabin crew, engineers and other staff. This profit share was proportionally a significant amount of cash for Cathay Pacific's cabin crew, who were employed on 'local' conditions. On one flight, a message ticked out from the cockpit printer. It was from management, announcing the amount of the year's profit share that would be paid to all employees. I handed the message to the Chief Purser who was in charge of the cabin (later, the traditional Chief was redesignated as the 'Inflight Service Manager'). On this day, our Chief was a feisty Chinese lady. Furious at the paltry amount of profit share that would be paid, she shouted in loud Hong Kong Chinese English, 'I am so angry at management! After arrival and while passengers getting off I am no' going to stand at door and smile – I will just tell them all to fuck off!'

However, for me at least, some things began improving after my health scare. A top floor flat had become available in our building, which meant there would be no more heavy furniture scraping on our ceiling at one o'clock in the morning. Our daughter was about to complete her education at King George V School, and was going to attend the University of Melbourne while living in a residential college, Queen's, very close to University College where I had lived as a medical student and met my future wife. Best of all, Cathay Pacific now had 'temporary bases', where for a few weeks, or even months, pilots could elect to live at selected destinations, as long as they provided their own accommodation. This saved the airline hotel costs, and made pilots available for useful standby duty at the 'outport'. For a precious few months, I lived in the small but convenient high-rise apartment in Melbourne that we had bought off the plan years ago, when our leaves were spent in Australia with two small children. Living out of suitcases and shuttling between relatives had been incentive to stringently set aside money to be able to purchase the little flat. I routinely operated from Melbourne to Hong Kong, then back the next night, or on to other destinations on the network. My mind was made up: although there would be a financial sacrifice in leaving Hong Kong early, as soon as our son Rohan, who was developing into an accomplished musician, finished his high school education, I would apply for a permanent basing in Melbourne. I was closing in on fifty years old and enough was enough.

There was another bright spot. Owning and flying a historic aircraft had only been a dream when I was a military pilot and then a very junior Ansett first officer. Ed, now a Boeing 777 captain who had long since departed on an Australian basing, owned a business that restored aircraft at an airfield north of Brisbane. An aviation museum also located on the airfield had decided to sell one of its exhibits. The aircraft had not flown for almost sixty years, was very rare, and it required a long and expensive restoration. But I was committed to

Hong Kong for several more years, anyway, and all I would have to do was to send money! Ed's company could restore it over that period. I *had* to buy it. The aeroplane was the de Havilland Moth 'Minor' that I had remarked on as a child, while it hung from the ceiling at Gilltrap's Auto Museum on that family holiday, a lifetime ago.

19

LEARNING TO FLY AGAIN

2006 - 2016

I tossed and turned in a passenger seat. As usual, the wax plugs rammed into my ear canals did little to block the noise of snores, conversation and the flight attendants at work. The cabin was dark under drawn window blinds. There it was – *'ding dong-ding dong'* – the chime initiated by the pilots to call a flight attendant, and I knew what the request would be: 'Please wake up the captain.'

I tore off my eye mask and I was already hauling myself out of the seat as the petite Asian girl walked down the aisle towards me. I gave her a thumbs up and staggered towards the toilet. I had had the usual rotten sleep, my eyes stung and my muscles cramped (the Business Class seat fully-reclined, but it was hard and narrow). But soon, tiredness was replaced by thoughts of home and a few days off. I was operating an A330 home – home to *Melbourne*!

I had done the hard yards. Sixteen years in Asia had resulted in financial security, our children educated, command of a wide-body airliner and now a base in Australia. We were suspended high in clear air a few hundred kilometres north of Darwin, before we would cross the Australian continent in clear dry season skies. I was admitted through the security door to the cockpit, and I squinted in the glare of the newly-risen sun. The dull green mangroves of the northern coast of Australia lay ahead. Australian voices came from the cockpit speakers with their clipped, formal radio phraseology, in contrast to the casual competence of the British or the rapid-fire slangy efficiency of the Americans. I spent a few minutes getting my bearings, and stretching muscles to work out the last vestiges of cramped rest. I was briefed on the fuel in hand, the aircraft status and the weather reports. The first officer would go back to try to rest for a couple of hours, leaving the second officer with me, who had been on duty from just over two hours out of Hong Kong. Approaching descent we would wake the FO, who I hoped would have had a reasonable chance to sleep through the clatter of the breakfast service.

Darwin glinted far below to our right and, as always, I thought back to the days of flying in and out of the frontier city with the navy, air force and those few layovers with Ansett Airlines. I made my stock-standard and predictable comment to the SO, 'Many a beer I've had down there …' After an hour or so the jungle and escarpments of Australia's 'Top End' gave way to grey-green scrub from horizon to horizon until beyond Tennant Creek, where Australia's red-brown desert began.

Habitable Australia is just the thin shell of a desert island-continent. The halfway point between Melbourne and Hong Kong lies only a few hundred kilometres north-west of Darwin. A large proportion of our flight was over the Australian land mass, and it is noteworthy how much of it is arid. The speckled green of spinifex and scrub petered out as we passed a few hundred kilometres east of Alice Springs, and far below us spread rust red desert broken up by the occasional road, dry river bed or survey track. Later, the surface would turn into a more sandy brown, further south towards Broken Hill.

Our Airbus, having burned off some of its fuel, was now at its maximum altitude of 41,000 feet – or well over twelve kilometres – above the Earth, so high that the blue of the sky directly above was tinged with the darkness of outer space. Had this been a night flight, the stars would have been hard points of light in the blackness. There would not be sufficient wavering atmosphere above us to produce any twinkle. Sometimes in the quiet of a long night flight, I joked to myself that this would be the closest I would get to space flight: suspended in utter blackness dotted with unblinking stars beyond large flat panes of thick glass, the Earth invisible beneath. In daylight, the horizon is noticeably lower at these altitudes, the curvature of the planet almost discernible. At night our world was the stars, and the colours of the display screens and panels: cyan, magenta, green lines and numbers, the blue and brown of our attitude references and row after row of illuminated labelled square pushbuttons on the panels. In smooth air there was no sensation or indication of movement except for the readouts of distances to run on the navigation displays.

As would travellers in deep space, long-haul airline crews can spend days in permanent night. On some westward flights, because of their speed the sun may never rise behind them. When operating flights from Hong Kong to Europe we left for work in the dark, flew all night in the dark, and, in winter, landed in the dark. After taking the edge off the tiredness that morning in the hotel, on short winter days it would soon be dark again.

Twelve kilometres up! Most people regard an airline pilot's job as desirable and cushy. I agree: when everything is working, you are not tired and the weather is good, it is the best job in the world. But I suggest, 'Get in your car and drive twelve kilometres along a straight stretch of road. That will give you an idea of how far off the planet we are. There, we are responsible for hundreds of lives in addition to our own, in 200 tonnes of machinery moving at eight tenths of the speed of sound. Now, imagine something going wrong.' I resist the urge to bore people about the hard work that an aspiring airline pilot must put in to get to that coveted flight deck. I hope that my own story provides the reader with some idea as to what is involved.

Past Broken Hill, the recently-awakened first officer and I planned the descent and landing at Melbourne, including assessing the weather, studying the 'standard arrival' and runway in use, entering data into the flight management computers and obtaining a clearance. At last, after most of the night in the air and the sun climbing in the left hand windows, we approached Swan Hill on the Murray River. If this had been a night-time arrival, from this altitude the glow of Melbourne would already be prominent on the horizon ahead. The A330's nose eased down, the engines ran back to idle with a rumble and we crossed almost the entire state of Victoria on our descent path. Desert finally gave way to a patchwork of paddocks, green or brown depending on the season, dotted with the towns and regional cities. The words of the poet A. B. Paterson were so appropriate then: 'And he sees the vision splendid of the sunlit plains extended.' Things got busy while we skimmed relatively high terrain near Mount Macedon, watching our descent profile and speed carefully with the engines still idling. We had to descend and decelerate at the same time, taking care to comply with Melbourne's speed and altitude requirements. There were checklists to complete and frequency changes. In the terminal area, there might be delays, a wet runway with a gusty crosswind or a landing on Melbourne's shorter runway, 27. But we would get there in the end.

Eventually, our crew, three pilots and ten or eleven cabin attendants, all on a little over two hours' sleep, made its way through Melbourne's crowded Immigration hall, negotiating queues and sometimes abrasive or downright rude staff – welcome to Melbourne! But, at last, we could stretch our legs outside the terminal while waiting for the bus that would take us to the city and to sleep. Job done. I inflated my lungs with the pristine air of the southern hemisphere. Not only was I home, but I would soon be learning to fly again.

During my final years in Hong Kong, Ed's company had made steady progress on the restoration of the Moth 'Minor' that I had acquired. But we found that its wooden wings were from a different aircraft and in very poor condition so, in essence, the project had become a complete re-build. I had made a very conservative estimate of the cost of the restoration and, knowing aviation, doubled it, and arrived at a possible total amount. Well, I should have tripled it. Fortunately, Cathay Pacific's share price had increased since the ultimatum given to the pilots by management in 1999, and thanks to my share options, I was able to cope with the payments. As soon as Rohan's schooling was complete in Hong Kong, I was off on that Melbourne basing; however, the Minor did not fly until two years after that.

Flying airliners was rewarding, both financially and professionally. Despite the computers and automation, there still were challenges. Landing 190 tonnes of heavy jet in a gusty crosswind on a wet runway called on a pilot's 'stick and rudder' skills, the evolution even more demanding of attention after an all-night flight. But now I was approaching fifty and I took less pleasure in it. The overwhelming feeling at the end of every flight became one of relief: another flight over, with the passengers where they wanted to go and, above all, no foul-ups. I was doing this for pay. Now it was time to fly for pleasure again, and I was well off enough to buy a second aircraft, one that would be more robust than the little Minor. An aircraft that could go places, and could be thrown around in joyous aerobatics in the blue skies of northern Victoria. I could also cover some of its costs by offering rides in it for the public. The machine would have to be ex-air force, so that pathetically I could relive my years as a young military pilot, but it would have to be relatively affordable, and reliable. While still living in Hong Kong, one morning I picked up the telephone and called Ed.

'I've found a Winjeel advertised for sale,' I said. 'It's still flying, but it needs some work. Can you have a look at it?'

'Good choice! Welcome to the "Little Eagle Club",' Ed replied.

During the 1950s and 1960s, Australia boasted a world-class aviation industry. The young nation had capitalised on the expertise it had gained during the desperate years of World War II. Under licence, it produced jet fighters (the Sabre and Mirage) and jet trainers (the Vampire and Macchi). One of the world's first practical pilotless 'drones', the Jindivik, had been designed and built in Australia, and it was sold to armed forces around the world for the towing of gunnery practice targets. During the '40s and '50s, the British designed and Australian built Tiger Moth biplane was the air force's basic trainer (much as the CT-4 would be decades later) to provide basic instruction and to weed out those unsuitable for further training. Student pilots who mastered the 'Tiger' would go on to advanced instruction in the Wirraway, a highly modified Australian version of an American training aircraft. However, by war's end both these types were obsolescent, so Australia's Commonwealth Aircraft Corporation stepped up to design and produce a basic trainer that would meet the requirements of the coming jet age and the Cold War. It would be of metal construction, seat the instructor and student side-by-side and it would eventually be powered by an American radial engine. The trainer was called the Winjeel, an Aboriginal word for 'young eagle'. Significantly, it would still be fitted with the traditional tail wheel undercarriage, a configuration that provided the unforgiving ground handling characteristics that sorted the men from the boys. Those students who tamed the beast would progress to the Vampire jet for advanced training, which would later be replaced by the Macchi.

One of my favourite aviation cartoons dates from World War II: a fighter with the traditional tail wheel undercarriage lands back at its base on a slippery, icy winter runway and as it slows down in a blistering crosswind, it spins around 180 degrees in a 'ground loop', slides backwards and ends up with its tail wedged in a snow bank.

'Red Two, are you having trouble?' the concerned tower controller transmits.

'Hell no, Tower, I always land this way!' the pilot retorts sarcastically.

Soon, I would be flying two tail wheel aircraft, the Winjeel and, later, the Moth Minor. After almost two decades flying nothing but heavy jets, I would have to dig deep to become competent to safely fly these machines. It was as if I would be learning to fly again.

The Winjeel is big, yet small. It is a large aircraft for a basic trainer, but for me it is tiny compared to what I have flown over the years The aircraft is solid in its feel, yet light to manoeuvre. In this military trainer constructed when defence budgets were generous, the pilots sit high in a slab-sided fuselage on square-cut wings. They look ahead through a flat windscreen over the black topped barrel nose that houses the Pratt and Whitney Wasp Junior radial engine. A square-cut tail fin still looks relatively modern, and it sits slightly forward of the rear-end of the fuselage because the air force considered the prototype too benign in handling: the service wanted it to readily spin, so the manufacturer moved the fin forward. The landing gear is fixed and the tail wheel, provided the control column is held fully back, locks the swivelling tail wheel into the rudder controls to aid steering on the ground. To make tight turns, the pilot moves the stick forward, which unlocks the tail wheel, and the toe brakes are used to lock the appropriate main wheel. Large electrically driven flaps assist with approach and landing. Somebody had thought it was a good idea to install a third seat behind the pilots, from which a second student would look on while the other was being trained. What actually happened was the second student would usually get air sick. However, present day Winjeel owners are grateful for this addition, because it enables a second passenger to enjoy the experience of flying in a famous Australian military trainer. If only the aircraft's designer could see his creation now, almost seventy years later, flying civilians for pleasure instead of being declared obsolete, scrapped and replaced after a decade or so, as was the wont of air forces during the serious business of the Cold War.

I began flying a Winjeel that was partly owned by Ed. It became apparent how little I knew about tail wheel aircraft, and even radial engines, despite my Auster and Tracker flying a lifetime ago. Under Ed's tutelage I was re-familiarised with the operation and foibles of radials. They are prone to 'hydraulic lock', where oil gathers by gravity in the lower cylinders. If the engine is forcibly rotated under these conditions, I learned, the oil forms a solid mass under the head of the piston and the connecting rod can bend, leading to a catastrophic failure afterward. The propeller is gently 'pulled through' before starting the engine, to feel for the dreaded 'lock' on every cylinder. Radial engines do not have much of a crankshaft to absorb torsional (twisting) forces – just a 'master' connecting rod to which all the other 'con rods' are attached, so power changes should be made slowly. My motto became, 'Look after a radial and it will look after you.'

We wheeled and looped in the little trainer near Bribie Island, to the north of Brisbane, with the Tasman Sea gleaming to the east and lush fields and pine forests below. After a decade of Airbus fly-by-wire I was kept busy. I had to stop squeezing my way around the sky: there were no flight control computers that would ensure a constant trajectory here! Once again I had to trim with every change of power and speed, but what a joy it was to throw the Winjeel about to the chatter of the little radial engine. Sky and earth gyrated in the flat windscreen as I wilted under g that I had not felt for two decades.

I re-learned about handling tail wheel aircraft on the ground the hard way. Becoming confident with the little beast, finally I pulled off an acceptable landing on the grass runway. With the turn-off area coming up, I disengaged the tail wheel lock too early. The physics of the 'tail dragger' aircraft's centre of gravity being well behind the main wheels came into play when the Winjeel wrapped up into a tight swing off the landing strip. Fortunately, the area was clear grass, no damage was done, and I reminded myself that flights in 'tail draggers' are not complete until the aircraft is parked. Learning to fly the Winjeel also begged a sobering question: had I had commenced training at Point Cook in the more demanding Winjeel, also in use at the time, rather than the CT-4, would I have even scraped through the course at all? I had been so lucky.

Victoria was now home, so my interest and enjoyment in flying airliners was somewhat rekindled with the troubles of life in Hong Kong gone. I would still get jet lag and tiredness from long, overnight flights, but waiting at home would be space, open roads, and our own home, all of which I could enjoy after sleeping it off. Work rosters began from Melbourne, generally with an early morning start for the daytime flight to Hong Kong, or a late 'sign on' for the 'red-eye' that departed after midnight. Occasionally, due to crew sickness or disruption, I was called from standby duty to position on a domestic airline to another Australian port in order to pick up a flight to Hong Kong the next day. For flights from Melbourne, about sixty tonnes of jet fuel would be loaded into our aircraft for the Hong Kong service. We would burn a little over fifty tonnes moving some 250 people and some freight to our destination, just one flight of thousands daily around the planet.

Almost half of the outbound flight north-west to Asia again crossed the continent to coast out near Darwin, then passed over the Indonesian archipelago and into the South China Sea west of the Philippines, bound for the China coast. On every flight there would be the Inter Tropic Convergence Zone (ITCZ) to cope with, the global belt of thunderstorms that tracks the sun's apparent movement with the seasonal tilt of the planet's axis. The ITCZ would lie in wait south of Darwin at the height of the southern summer, and just north of Hong Kong at the peak of the northern. Even at our cruising altitude that varied between ten and twelve kilometres in the sky, lines of anvil-shaped thunderheads towered well above us when we weaved through the zone. Thunderstorms are monstrous bubbles in our atmosphere, relatively warmer than the surrounding air because their moist air does not surrender its heat as much with altitude, and being warmer, they rise high in the atmosphere before the bubble cools to give up its moisture. The moisture becomes falling hailstones and raindrops, which increase in mass as they are caught in subsequent updrafts and downdrafts. They accumulate static electricity until … 'whoomph'! A lightning bolt relieves the electrical difference, whether or not there is an aircraft in its path. However, the metal skin of the aircraft acts as a 'Faraday Cage', the current flowing around and out of the aircraft helped by the 'static wicks', the little rubbery cables that a passenger can see hanging from the rear edges of the wings, tail and flight controls. The panels and structure of modern aircraft are well bonded to ensure that there is no chance for a spark to jump between them that could ignite fuel vapour or damage controls, electronics or engines.

Sometimes the pilots are blind to these storms when the airliner is mired in layers of cloud or masses of embedded thunderstorms. In those cases, the pilots are glued to the radar, adjusting 'tilt' and 'gain' controls to interpret the green, yellow and ominous red splotches on the display. Cabin crew and passengers are belted in while turbulence nibbles at the aircraft. Modern autopilots handle turbulence well, and the manipulating pilot's scan flicks between the attitude indicator and the radar display, his hand hanging from the lip of the cockpit coaming, fingers twisting the 'heading' knob of the autopilot panel as he weaves the jet around the 'returns'.

Lightning strikes that I experienced varied from a dull 'click' and an electrical 'transient' flicker of the cockpit displays to a full-on simultaneous 'bang' and blinding flash. Sometimes, we could sense a strike coming as white tongues of St Elmo's Fire licked up from the bottom of the windscreens, growing and growing, then dancing all over the panes, until – 'wham' – a flash, when the electrical potential between aircraft and cloud equalised. I could not help but think of the electronic flight control computers in the special bay below the cockpit; I trusted that the designers and engineers had hardened them sufficiently to cope with lightning. However, the overwhelming consideration for pilots in stormy conditions is the hazard of turbulence.

A thunderstorm cloud, the cumulonimbus, can be an awesome sight at altitude. An experienced airman can visualise the turbulence – 'vertical wind' – the boiling outsides of a 'CB': its head a visibly rising, roiling dome until it can rise no more. It is then whipped into an anvil-shaped plume by the winds of the upper atmosphere. A wispy 'pileus' cloud often sits like a feathery cap where stratospheric winds rise up and over the 'bubble', like rapids arcing over a submerged rock. When cruising at altitude the jet flashes quickly through the thin air of the stratosphere, its momentum high, so an encounter with one of these storms can be violent: the sudden onset of vertical currents jolts the aircraft like a hammer. Unrestrained objects and people are thrown about the cabin, and in extreme cases the aircraft can be damaged or even broken up. Blasts of hail can damage instrument probes, leading edges, noses and windscreens. Fortunately, cumulonimbus are usually relatively distinct both to radar and to the human eye, and can be readily avoided by alert flight crews (yes, even at three am while the passengers sleep; the lightning gives them away!). A deviation of between ten and forty nautical miles – or up to seventy-five kilometres – is usually sufficient to keep the flight safe and comfortable. However, the lines of boiling storm clouds in the ITCZ stretch for hundreds of miles, and it is not unusual for an airliner to be over 200 kilometres off-track in an effort to find that elusive gap between them.

In heavy rain at the lower altitudes of approach or departure procedures, almost the entire radar display is red with the amount of moisture in the surrounding air overwhelming the radar's beam, and things get busier with the constant radar adjustments and radio calls through the roar of rain on metal and glass. At busy airports, the radio is alive with chatter as other pilots also call air traffic control for clearances to deviate around 'weather'. Voices become strained after unsuccessful requests for weather avoidance because of the proximity of other aircraft or the difficulty of getting a word-in through the constant radio calls, the aircraft inexorably heading for hazardous storm clouds. At the lower altitudes the aircraft should be slower, but developing cumulonimbus clouds or those embedded in the murk still bring a rough ride that can seemingly last for ages during protracted 'vectoring' by air traffic control radar, or when holding and waiting for weather and traffic to clear. The pilots' minds race in these conditions: *Watch the fuel! What's the weather at the airport doing? What about alternate airports if our destination closes? How long before we would have to divert? What's the alternates' weather like?*

Even in benign conditions, Hong Kong International Airport was becoming known for delays to arriving traffic, and after well over eight hours of flight we would often still be airborne, the Airbus banking kilometres high over the South China Sea flying holding patterns while we were stepped down in the 'stack' of airliners waiting to land. At last, our turn would come for the radar controllers to guide us in a huge square circuit, either right turns around the bright green peaks of Lantau Island to land to the east, or to the left over teeming Kowloon and Sha Tin to land westwards, on the 'daylight' flight into the afternoon sun, high peaks only few hundred feet below and just a mile or two to the right of the Airbus as we idled down the ILS beam. After landing, we fortunate 'based' pilots would have just a short shuttle bus ride to Cathay Pacific City, which was the airline's complex of offices, simulators and training facilities. Attached to it was a hotel. This hotel was 'home' for based crew – we could be ensconced in a comfortable and quiet room within an hour of landing!

The Headland Hotel, as it was called, was unique to the airline industry. Hong Kong's astronomical cost of housing made it worthwhile for Cathay Pacific to offer senior crew the opportunity, as I now had, to live in their home countries. This saved the company a fortune in accommodation, medical costs, and other allowances. Balanced against that was the requirement to accommodate these pilots in Hong Kong for a night or two prior to them operating to other destinations on the network or back to their home ports. So the airline commissioned the Headland Hotel, regarded as a necessary evil by many based pilots because, located at the airport, it was quite a distance from it into town. With little interest in Hong Kong's night life, I had no problem with the concept: the rooms were quiet and clean, and provided ample opportunity for rest and study. The days of long, jerking taxi rides home, sweating in the exhaust fumes at bus queues or jostling onto the Mass Transit Railway with bags on barely four hours' sleep were over. Naturally the Headland, a flight crew hotel, included a pub-style bar. Officially called 'Dakota's', it was known as 'The Gay Bar', because the majority of its clientele were male pilots: based crew, and locals who dropped in for a beer or two after a pattern, along with the odd manager enjoying a few drinks after a day in the office. Ladies in Dakota's were a rare sight, especially when noisy sports channels featured on the televisions. So the Gay Bar was appropriately nicknamed. It just seemed to be always full of hairy, beer-swilling pilots. The name became universal among Cathay flight crew and even some family members, but not among the local staff. With my family accompanying me on one pattern, my son asked the Chinese and Filipino hotel reception staff where the Gay Bar was because he was meeting his father there. After seeing their reaction, it took a while for him to explain what he meant. He had never heard any other name for it.

I was an avid watcher of the *Thunderbirds* television series during my childhood, and as a based pilot staying in the Headland Hotel, I could sometimes identify with the puppet characters. On the morning of an early start, or very late at night, the bedside telephone trilled with the wake-up call and one hour later, having taken the hotel lift to a few floors below, I would be in uniform at the Dispatch area counter, wading through the paperwork prior to meeting the cabin crew and boarding the crew bus that would take us to the aircraft. It was reminiscent of the famous series, where the characters slid down chutes and were changed and deposited in their machines automatically, minutes after a call-out.

Although the hotel was sometimes a little wearisome, it served its purpose well. I was always happy to be operating back to Melbourne on the next day or night after arrival in Hong Kong. There were also the occasional regional turnaround flights that were enjoyable to operate and required no tedious travel to or from the airport. However, there were still the overnight 'split duties', India and Sri Lanka patterns (all flights through the night), other flights that arrived in Hong Kong very late at night and still the inevitable roster changes: 'Captain, we now require you to fly to Brisbane [also through the night], then to travel on a domestic positioning flight home to Melbourne.' With that, I would be in for a very long night (and day).

Meanwhile, days off at home and the occasional leave period were devoted to flying the Winjeel. Mine was now hangared at Benalla, in north-east Victoria. The Moth Minor was progressing in its restoration and at last came the time, following test flights by the restorer, for me to learn to fly that.

I had never experienced anything like the de Havilland DH-94 Moth 'Minor'. Designed as a 'club' aircraft, it was a sleek monoplane intended to replace the popular biplane Gipsy Moths and Tiger Moths of the late 1930s. However, my aircraft had been 'impressed' into the Royal Australian Air Force during the desperate times of early World War II, which added a pleasing historical connection. The Minor is of wooden construction: a timber framework covered with plywood and fabric. The narrow fuselage accommodates two open cockpits, one behind the other. Unlike the Tiger Moth biplane, the Minor is flown from the front seat, and to the pilot, it feels like sitting in a plywood bullet; there is no tracery of biplane wings, struts and wires all around. Its little engine is an inverted, four cylinder unit reminiscent of the famous Gipsy Major that powered the old Auster that I flew as a teenager, and the Tiger Moth. Designed especially for the Moth Minor by de Havilland (in those days it was common for manufacturers to produce both aircraft and the engines to power them), it was appropriately called the Gipsy 'Minor'. The restoration of the engine had been a significant part of the whole process of getting my aircraft back in the air after sixty years on the ground.

The Minor's monoplane wings are long and slender, almost glider-like. Large pivoting wing trailing edges and the 'tail feathers' are of the traditional wood framework and covered with fabric, which is stretched and 'doped' to a drumhead-like surface. But pivoting trailing edges on the wings are not flaps. They fold upwards in order to access a substantial handle, which unlocks the main supporting spars of each wing to enable it to be swung back for folding and storage. The wings hang off special hooks that unclip from the horizontal tailplanes. It is easy to picture a Moth Minor, wings folded back, being towed home behind a Morris car along an English laneway to be stored in the garage at home. Whenever I visited the restorers as they worked I wondered: what would this machine be like to fly?

After only four hours in an open cockpit, I admired the stamina of the aviation pioneers. We flew in the relative warmth and good weather of Australia, but I was cold despite being rugged up. The wind was relentless – I could only hunker down into the cockpit so far and still, air blasted through holes and gaps in the wooden structure, eddied around behind, and tore through the windings of scarf around my neck. Our tiny yellow monoplane was high over the Pilliga state forest of New South Wales. Olive green scrub stretched unbroken from horizon to horizon, and Bertie and I trusted that the little engine would keep running, as there would be no open area to glide to if it stopped. Bert, the craftsman who had carried out the majority of the restoration work, was also an accomplished pilot, including flying gliders. During one of the Minor's early test flights the engine had lost power: a rocker arm had broken and with the little Gipsy throttled back, banging and vibrating, Bertie had 'thermalled' the Moth Minor like a glider to maintain enough altitude to make a safe landing back at the airfield. Now Bert sat reassuringly in the rear cockpit on our delivery flight to join the Winjeel at Benalla. Thankfully, the Gipsy kept running like a sewing machine as it pulled us through the air at about ninety knots – or 170 km/hr.

The Minor's wide wingspan promised easy handling characteristics for a 52-year-old airline pilot. Compared with the Winjeel, the Minor was benign. Even with its tailwheel design, it ran straight and true for take-off and landing, and apart from the aileron controls being comparatively heavy, the machine proved a delight to fly under Bert's guidance. I found that the Minor required little use of rudder during turns, because its ailerons were very differential: they moved up or down at differing angles to minimise the phenomenon called 'adverse yaw'. A lever tensioned a spring to provide trim in pitch. It sat like a rock in the cruise.

The Moth Minor was an improvement on its de Havilland predecessors, having been fitted with wheel brakes instead of the infamous tail 'skid' of the brakeless, biplane Moths. The rudder pedals could be used to differentially brake either wheel, and a pull on a lever applied the brakes evenly. Therefore, ground handling was relatively simple, and the lever could be locked on as a parking brake. This also made for peace of mind for engine starting, because the Gipsy Minor, not being fitted with an electric starter, was started by the 'Armstrong Method'.

Landing the Minor was straightforward. I later commented that the two easiest aircraft I ever landed were Boeing's 747 and de Havilland's Moth Minor; in both cases, their long, low wings develop a cushion of air beneath them when close to the ground, making touchdowns smooth enough to flatter any pilot. The Minor's slender wings are so efficient that a plywood board, perforated with large holes, has to be extended from under the fuselage to act as an air brake to steepen the approach and reduce floating before touchdown. The Moth Minor's original handbook is reminiscent of that of a motor car (the aircraft even has a 'parcel shelf' under the pilot's instrument panel). In the 1930s-vintage manual, the variable settings of the air brake, operated by another lever, is futuristically described as 'adjustable glide control'.

At last, the little aeroplane was home. A group of us had established an air museum at Benalla airfield, which had been a training base for RAAF pilots through World War II. The Minor had been restored to the colour scheme it might have worn after its impressment into the air force: yellow all over, with British-style red, white and blue roundels and fin 'flash' prominent. It also wore, discreetly, its civilian registration of VH-CZB. 'Charlie Zulu Bravo' had been the registration and call sign of the Boeing 737 that I had flown on my first 'line training' flights with Bob, decades ago with Ansett. The registration became available after Ansett's demise, with its aircraft sold overseas. The Winjeel was registered as VH-CZE. Prior to the Boeing 737s, the 'CZ' registrations had belonged to Ansett's sleek DC-9s, those I had watched climbing out towards Tasmania, high over Mornington all those years ago.

Years of dedication, work and luck had culminated in owning two aircraft that were part of an active air museum. I could fly on my own terms, loop and roll in the Winjeel, or just putter about in an open-cockpit Moth. Solo flights after all those years on crewed aircraft were a refreshing experience. In addition, approval to carry out military-style 'Adventure Flights' for paying passengers would help to pay the bills.

It was early in 2014, the eve of a very special air display at Point Cook that would commemorate one hundred years of military aviation in Australia. I had been invited to display the Moth Minor at this air show. On the still, overcast morning, I joined the circuit at Point Cook at the end of a chilly flight in the Minor's open cockpit from Benalla. The control tower gave me permission to overfly the base. At just 500 feet – or 150 metres – from the ground, I carried out the Minor's minimal 'before landing' checklist: brakes off, undercarriage 'down and welded', fuel mixture 'rich', quantity checked and selectors on, harness secure, and tail wheel locked.

At barely sixty knots, I could take a good look down at the historic base from the open cockpit. The wooden accommodation blocks, now classified as historic buildings, were still there, as were many of the hangars that had once held all those CT-4s and Winjeels. The lines of trees were as I remembered them, and I made out the parade ground, the sports ovals and the Officers' Mess. Memories rushed in a torrent: water fights in Block 46, study in my little wooden room, the vinyl and fuel smells of the CT-4 while fields and trees gyrated under stubby green and yellow wings, the aggressive, brusque instructors, running to the sight board after various transgressions, marching to lectures in my green flying jacket with my briefcase banging against my leg under cold grey skies to the noise of snarling propellers … I relived the frustration and anguish of a Basic Handling Test with Rocky … I had come within a hair's breadth of being scrubbed here, but after work, motivation and luck, Sir Richard Williams eventually pinned the navy's gold wings to my jacket. Almost one hundred years ago to the day as a young army officer, Dicky Williams had been among that first small band of Australia's budding military aviators, he himself preparing to become a man of the sky. He would be instrumental in forming the nation's air force.

With the Minor's plywood air brake extended, the engine chugging near idle and the aeroplane sitting slightly nose-high, I carefully brought it in on final approach, speed easing back to about forty-five knots – or eighty five km/hr – as the runway bloomed. Gently, I raised the nose to the landing attitude and as the speed began to wash off, I held more back pressure on the control column. This time I had judged the moment correctly and all three of the Moth Minor's wheels touched the earth simultaneously in a 'three pointer', cushioned by the 'ground effect' of that long, low wing. We bumped across the grass to the display area and I shut down and sat in the silence for a while, chilled after nearly two hours in an open cockpit, but quietly satisfied. After almost thirty-eight years, I had once again landed at Point Cook. From the Auster at Moorooduc to the rigours of this place, to Pearce and Nowra, a carrier deck, back to Western Australia, then to the air force and the Orion, then Ansett and Cathay Pacific. It had been quite a journey.

The following day, a wonderful air show would take place. But in two days I would be back to work with the airline and also getting on with this book, much of it written in the sky.

20

FLY 'TIL YOU DIE!

2016 – 2019

I settled well into the routine of a 'based' Cathay Pacific pilot. During the Hong Kong years I had only dreamt of motoring along the freeway from a home in country Victoria to fly an Airbus to Hong Kong and destinations beyond. Now, in my fifties, it was a reality. The Melbourne-based patterns involved at least one overnight flight, either 'up' or 'back', if not onwards on other regional flights, often to India or Sri Lanka. I had flown my last North America trip, and one night we departed Hong Kong for Amsterdam on my last long haul pattern. It was also one of my final flights on the four-engine A340. Cathay Pacific's somewhat unloved A340s would soon be relegated to regional flying for a few years, then sold or handed back to the lessors. On a wider scale, the era of the four-engine airliner was coming to an end.

The 'big twins' – the Airbus A330 and Boeing's 777 – were ascendant, because their engines and systems were deemed sufficiently reliable by aviation authorities around the world to operate long flights that spanned oceans. Boeing was also developing the smaller but revolutionary 787. Airline managements salivated at the thought of the cost savings that would be delivered by new fuel-efficient, wide body, long-range twins. Cathay's A340-600s had long gone, their four big engines deemed inefficient for the payload that the -600s carried, despite their excellent performance and range. Their routes were now being flown by an advanced version of the Boeing 777 twin, which could easily fly an equivalent distance. Cathay's venerable four-engine Boeing 747s had been relegated to flying freight. But with the advanced 777s already in operation and the 787 being tested, Airbus had not sat idle to allow the Americans to dominate long-range commercial flight. They flew the monstrous new double-decker A380, but sales of that would prove disappointing: the huge jet was just too big, too heavy and inefficient for many airlines, including Cathay Pacific. It had those four engines. It had taken some time, but rather than modify an existing design, as the Americans had done with the 777, the Europeans, as Boeing did with its new 787, started with a clean slate. The new long-range twin was called the Airbus A350. And Cathay Pacific had ordered a lot of them.

Aside from the epic, all new A380, all the Airbus twin-aisle airliners had fuselages based on the pioneering twin-engine A300. Even the A340-600's body had been of the same basic design, its diameter was the same and it had merely been 'stretched' lengthways to the proportions of a 'flying pipeline'. The cockpit window layout and nose profile of the aircraft had not changed. However, the new A350 was marketed as the A350 'XWB' ('eXtra-Wide Body'). Its fuselage, along with the rest of the aircraft, was new in every area.

By the end of 2016, I had spent several months of study in preparation to fly the new Airbus type, which culminated in weeks of computer-based training in Hong Kong. Nevertheless, on walking into the A350 flight simulator for the first time, I was awestruck. The 350 cockpit would not have looked out of place in a science fiction movie. Six large rectangular screens were arrayed around the captain and first officer's positions under massive, curved windows. The cockpit was paperless: in place of the multitude of charts, books of approach and departure procedures and manuals, each outboard screen displayed to each pilot all that they would need. Checklists – normal and emergency – were presented on the middle screens. A 'trackball' and 'clicker' close at hand on the centre console for each pilot controlled a cursor that jumped from screen to screen. Data were entered by an associated keyboard. In addition, the usual Airbus pull-out table could be flipped open to reveal a second keyboard. The cockpit was sufficiently wide for pilots to stroll back and forth behind the seats and stretch their legs. The flight deck's blue-carpeted space, advanced lighting and the elegant curves of the seats, lights and overhead console placed this aircraft firmly in the twenty-first century. On taking my place in the captain's seat, the instrument consoles were so big and deep I had to stretch in order to touch the immense side windows. The view from them would prove superlative.

Despite the revolutionary design of the aircraft, Airbus had marketed the A350 as a 'common type' to the A330, and Cathay Pacific latched right on to this. The training requirement for crew converting to the 350 could then be regarded as a mere 'differences' course, and Airbus fleet pilots could fly both types interchangeably, as we had done with the A330, A340 and A340-600. This philosophy provided cost savings and flexibility for the airline. In reality, the differences of the 350 in systems, performance and operation were significant, although the designers had tried to keep the terminology of the cockpit functions common with the older Airbuses. The 'differences' course lasted ten days, in addition to the study at home and multiple sessions in the flight simulator. Despite this, I threw myself into the training with enthusiasm: the aircraft promised to be beautiful to fly, have the latest technology, would fly faster and go to existing and new long haul destinations. In my late fifties, the A350 could be the last airliner I would fly. Compulsory retirement was only some six years away, but what a fantastic machine on which it would be to finish!

It was interesting how Airbus worked around the differences between their 'classic' A330 and A340, and the A350 in an attempt to make the types 'common'. Cockpit functions had the same terminology. This meant that checklists could be similar and the new jet could be operated in a broadly similar way. But how these functions were arrived at was different. The old joke of '150 computers flying in close formation' of the old Airbuses did not really apply to the 350. The number of multiple computers, each a separate black box that controlled only one system had been greatly reduced, and replaced by 'functions' within sophisticated, identical and redundant processors. For example, the old A330 used two redundant dedicated computers to control the retraction and extension of the landing gear. On the A350, landing gear control was reduced to a function that was 'hosted' in a processor as a separate partitioned area of its memory. The same computer commanded and controlled other services as well: perhaps the fuel management system or the brakes. These processors were identical, interconnected, interchangeable and redundant in a duplicated 'neural network'. They could be separately programmed to host the applicable aircraft functions, generally in pairs to maintain redundancy should one processor fail. Yet, for the pilots, the cockpit controls, terminology and system layouts were reminiscent of the older jets. For critical systems, there were still backup, 'hard wired' controls for emergency use.

In the simulator and later in the actual aircraft, the A350 was gorgeous to fly. Its controls were even more precise than its predecessors, yet the aircraft's bulk gave it a more solid feel. The happiness at the absence of paper charts and documents was offset somewhat by the frustrations of using the trackball and 'clicker' that fell to my right hand on the centre console to find and open menus on the various screens. So many times my colleagues and I would say to our instructors, 'I know what I want, but how in hell do I find it!' With exposure and repetition, we became proficient with the system.

Another enhancement of the A350 was its cockpit Head Up

Display (HUD). Again, it took study and discipline to use it properly, but once mastered it was an invaluable aid to precision flying. As we looked ahead through the huge windscreens, the HUDs presented attitude, speed and altitude data, their trends, and information about the energy state of the aircraft, along with precision landing aid information, all superimposed on the outside world.

From the outside, the aircraft looked stunning. Its nose was bluff but futuristic, curving downwards – it reminded me of the nose of the old Nimrod, which in turn was reminiscent of an old art-deco style American Diesel locomotive. The massive windscreens and side windows were curved to fit smoothly into its profile. There was no step for the windscreens: from nose to tail the topside of the beautiful new Airbus's fuselage was one smooth, uninterrupted line. Not only pretty, the 350 was a much bigger machine, its body noticeably longer and wider. Walking beneath the jet, I could not reach up enough to touch the bottom of the fuselage. It took off at weights equivalent to the old four-engine, long haul A340 thanks to its two advanced versions of the original Rolls Royce Trent engine. The new Airbus carried a prodigious amount of fuel, 110 tonnes of it, in a simplified tank layout. For efficiency in the cruise, the old 'fuel-tank-in-the-tailplane' system had gone, which been used for 'trimming' the older jets by means of complicated computers, pumps and pipework. The A350 had a revolutionary new system that automatically made tiny adjustments to the retracted wing flaps that optimised the shape of the wing. The wing itself spanned nearly 65 metres, its tip blended up into a beautiful curved 'winglet'. And the A350 was fast. It got along at the same speed as the old but speedy Boeing 747, Mach 0.85. This time, Airbus had produced a world-beater.

Once trained on the new airliner, I was again operating two distinct types of Airbus. However, most of my flying was still assigned on the A330, which was becoming a little tedious. Both it and the A350 served Melbourne, and there was nothing like flying home in the 350 as opposed to the old A330, its smaller and now noticeably older sister. In 1995 the 330 had been a revolutionary machine, a new concept in airliners, but now it had been in service for more than twenty years, its technology dated, and no facilities for crew rest. Who would have thought back in 1995 that I would later call it a 'clunker'! And each time I was rostered to fly the older Airbus out of Hong Kong on regional flights, 330 flights seemed always to be overnight sectors: India and back, or Colombo and back. A split duty. The all-night service to Melbourne. Or the late flight out of Melbourne for Hong Kong that left after midnight, and arrived in the grey mist of a Hong Kong dawn. The occasional flights on the A350 were a breath of fresh air and I enjoyed the aircraft immensely, but now I was feeling my age, and jadedness was setting in. I had been in military and airline flying for forty years and I was growing weary of staring at unblinking stars during the night flights, dealing with the weather challenges, regurgitating numbers on the regulatory simulator checks and idling around the Headland Hotel while I counted the hours down to the usual night-time 'sign on'.

There was still ongoing tension between Cathay Pacific's pilots and management. New pilots were being recruited on further deteriorating conditions, the airline taking advantage of young South Africans, most of them highly experienced, who were leaving their country in droves. And the following year I was turning sixty. The night flights were wearing very thin now, and there was so much to do at home and at our aviation museum. I had acquired a restored Nanchang military trainer, ironically Chinese, which was sleek and of better performance than the chunky Winjeel, painted in an eye-pleasing blue of the Chinese Navy and a joy to fly. It was added to my Adventure Flight concern as a further option for passenger flights. However, the airline rosters crimped the business, limiting the days available to offer flights. After packing for work, it became harder and harder to leave home. I was also starting to experience occasional abdominal pains. I put them down to the airline and hotel food that I subsisted on when away, but the pains became worse.

I was opened up from pubis to rib cage. More than a third of my large intestine was cut out. Thanks to an extremely capable surgeon and wonderful medical staff, I recovered well, and two weeks later it only hurt when I laughed. To my relief, I did not need a colostomy bag. But the removed 'plumbing' was tested and it contained cancer cells. I would undergo six months of chemotherapy followed by three months for recovery. Grounded!

I may now have flown my last flight with Cathay Pacific. I had never envisaged this. I had always imagined that in September 2022 there would be a rostered final flight, and after being met by management on arrival, I would shout drinks for all in the Gay Bar that afternoon before flying out as a passenger to a well-earned retirement. Alternatively, one day I would walk into the office to resign, having had enough after one night flight too many. I had always planned to leave Cathay Pacific on my own terms, to fly military trainers, develop our museum, assemble those model aeroplanes that I had never had time for, and never have to fly in cloud or through the night again. But unexpectedly leaving the airline due to a medical problem was one thing – what about flying for pleasure in Australia? The Australian authority's Aviation Medicine department was notorious for being arbitrary and risk-averse. For me, not being able to fly again was as serious as the cancer diagnosis!

Any complacency I had about how well I recovered from the operation was quickly erased by the side effects of the chemotherapy. They hit me hard. The chemicals would, I trusted, kill the cancer cells, but being poisons, they would have adverse effects on the rest of me. The treatments came in three-week cycles: a morning in a Melbourne oncology ward for intravenous administration, followed by two weeks of pills and to allow the intravenous drugs to do their work, with the third week off to give the body a rest, ready to take the next cycle. The visits to the cancer ward were sobering. There were young people in beds and wheelchairs, pale and thin, heads under scarves or hats, and in a far worse state than myself.

In the still, grey depths of an inland Victorian winter, I dramatically lost weight and shivered with cold, despite wearing layers of clothing. The first two weeks of each cycle produced constant nausea: I had to force myself to eat tiny meals and my hands and feet tingled and turned red, and their skin peeled off. My throat involuntarily closed if I drank anything remotely cold, which was an awful sensation. I felt as weak as a kitten. There was a glimmer of my health and appetite returning during the final week of each cycle, but then came time for the next treatment. I felt dreadful huddling under a sheepskin in front of daytime television. I was in despair. My aircraft were sitting idle, and I might never fly an A350 again, with the panorama of the Australian outback in the sunshine laid out far below through those huge windows.

Through this dark time, an idea formed. Resident at Benalla was a small aero club that operated 'Light Sport' aircraft, a relatively new category of modern recreational aeroplanes. A pilot only needed a 'car' type medical standard in order to fly these little machines. After the chemotherapy finished, another three months had to elapse before I could even think of approaching the Australian and Hong Kong licensing authorities regarding my medical status. That was when I would have some idea whether the cancer had been beaten. Surely I would feel better towards the end of 2017, with the drugs being gradually leached from my body. As soon as I felt well enough I would get back in the air. Even if the cancer *was* still there, I would fly Light Sport until I was unable to drive. The plan kept me going mentally, but the physical effects of the chemotherapy became worse; so bad in fact, that the oncologist terminated the treatment early and we accepted the associated risk.

Although my feet were numbed, and tingled, I could still work the rudder pedals. I was 'bashing the circuit' at Benalla, solo, in a little white 'Tecnam'. It was a metal high-winged aeroplane reminiscent of the typical Cessna, but even smaller. Its tiny engine buzzed as it spun at over 4,000 revolutions per minute while it drove a light, composite propeller through a miniature gearbox. I almost worked up a sweat throwing the aircraft around 'military type', oval circuits, tighter and tighter as my feel for the machine improved. On this weekday, I had the airfield to myself. 'Normal' … 'flapless' … 'low level' … 'glide' … another 'normal' … I finally achieved some reasonable landings and taxied back to the aero club. I was a pilot again. The Light Sport flying played a large part in maintaining my morale, and I was impressed with the performance, technology and affordability of these little aeroplanes. I had just turned sixty, the tests indicated that the cancer was, for now, inactive, and in any event I could fly 'til I died!

My health returned slowly with the chemotherapy's end. Buoyed by the Tecnam flying, I approached CASA regarding my medical status and, after they received continuing clear test results, they reinstated my Private Pilot medical. I could even fly commercially, provided that I had a co-pilot. And what about Cathay Pacific? Would they accept my medical condition? If they did, I would have to undergo weeks of refresher training for both the A330 and A350; go back to the night flights, the storms and crowded airspace of Asia; hanging around the Headland Hotel waiting to fly all night; the rigmarole of the constant procedural changes, simulator checks and the frivolous on-line computer courses. But I would go back to the airline. Although I had been on half-pay during my treatment and salary was about to stop altogether, the overwhelming reason was: 'Damn it. I'll leave on my *own* terms. I won't be "medical-ed" out. I'll get back into it and see what transpires.' So, with a 'Co-pilot Required' endorsement on my Hong Kong medical certificate – not a problem in multi-crew airline operations – after Christmas, I returned to work.

I completed several weeks of refresher training on both the A330 and the A350. It was nice to fly the A350 again. I never tired of the daytime panorama through those huge windows. On flights from Melbourne to Hong Kong or back, compared with the A330, it arrived twenty minutes earlier carrying forty more passengers, all for the same fuel burn. It had proper crew rest facilities: bunks in the dolphin-like curve of the fuselage above and behind the cockpit. In those I slept my usual fitful sleep, but at least there was no noise from talking or snoring passengers, or the cabin crew going about their duties: just the deep background booming rumble of the Trents.

However, in May 2018 they *did* roster one too many night flights. It had not taken long for me to have had my fill of them. Along with the overnight operations to and from Australia, every month's roster contained overnight flights to and from Delhi. It was also frustrating to hear that other airlines offered part-time rosters. Had Cathay Pacific offered such a scheme, I would have taken it in a heartbeat, but my employer would not entertain the idea. If I resigned, I knew that I would miss the people, particularly the experienced Australia-based first officers with whom I had been flying over the last twelve years, and had got to know so well. For many of these men and women, family commitments would keep them on their Melbourne base, unable to move to Hong Kong to become captains.

I would miss the beautiful A350, and the now very rare regional daylight flight in good weather in the A330. On the other hand, when I joined Cathay Pacific in 1990, retirement at fifty-five had been compulsory. Only much later had the limit been raised to sixty-five, so I had had five years' bonus. I was over sixty, and had endured a health scare. There were military trainers to fly for pleasure, that waited at an aviation museum. Our daughter, Avalon, had given us a new grandson. I steeled myself after several false starts, walked into the fleet office, and handed a manager three months' notice of resignation.

It felt odd to be flying home that night, having 'pulled the pin'. Even stranger, we were in an A350, but tonight we wished that we had been flying an A330. Fog was forecast for our early morning arrival. Both the 330 and A350 were easily capable of carrying out 'blind' automatic landings in fog, but because of a pronounced 'dip' halfway along Melbourne's Runway 16, the relatively new A350 was not certified at that time for a near-blind automatic landing on this runway, the only one usable in the conditions. I called Yvonne after we eventually landed, both to tell her that I was in Sydney, having diverted there, and that I had resigned. Over the next three months I flew my rosters, trying to stay motivated to keep up with the ever-present procedural changes and yet another proficiency check in the simulator.

On one of my last flights home to Melbourne in an A350, fog and very low cloud were forecast again, although not quite as severe as the previous occasion when we had diverted. We were still unable to carry out an automatic landing on Runway 16, but this time the Head Up Display, the HUD, would come to the fore. Amid all the other data, the HUD presented a synthetic runway as a green outline, generated by signals from the Instrument Landing System and the computers.

We approached the non-autoland 'minimum' height of just 200 feet, sixty metres from the ground with the autopilot still 'coupled' to the ILS while I peered through the HUD, interpreting its data but also looking through it into blackness, preparing to become 'visual'. This time, the fog layer sat just above 'minimums'. The HUD runway symbol suddenly 'filled in', with the runway lights now strung along its edges, the real world superimposed on the synthetic. I clicked off the autopilot and, still intently looking through the HUD, I flared the aircraft for touchdown. What an aviation world we lived in! But the next day, after sleeping off the night flight, I headed north-east once more to fly the 1938-vintage Moth 'Minor', its only aids to navigation a map, a compass and a clock.

In July 2018, Yvonne came with me on my last flight from Melbourne to Hong Kong. It was also the last time that I would fly the A350. The following day I operated my final pattern as an airline pilot. It was an afternoon A330 flight to Shanghai for the usual 'minimum rest' overnight stay, then to return to Hong Kong early the following morning. For me this was fitting, because Shanghai was the birthplace of the original Cathay Pacific: that of Roy Farrell, Syd de Kantzow and a single DC-3.

I was at Flight Despatch for the last time and I could not bring myself to believe the weather forecasts. Although it was getting on for summer, the wet season, there were no clouds, no rain, no storms. Accompanying me to Shanghai was a young Australian first officer, himself disillusioned with Cathay Pacific's pay and conditions. He was soon leaving to join an airline in his home country. We lifted into 'gin-clear' skies eastwards, then northwards, following the requirements of the complex and absolute control of the Chinese air traffic controllers to Shanghai. I had rarely seen China in these conditions. The atmosphere was utterly clear. The lights of the vast city of Shanghai were laid out to our left as we drifted in a lazy descent under radar headings over the Yellow Sea. We turned left over the flat, muddy coast then lined up to land to the south on one of Shanghai's four parallel runways. We could have flown a 'visual' circuit and approach, but that procedure would have been alien to the rigid Chinese. We obediently flew the required speeds, metric altitudes and radar headings, along with rates of descent they assigned through the drawn-out arrival procedure. The first officer was 'pilot flying', and he flew a precise approach to a nice touchdown. As expected, it was late at night by the time our crew dragged our bags into the hotel. There would be an early morning call for the flight out to Hong Kong, which would follow the usual convoluted transport, security, immigration and customs procedures.

On the next morning, after more than thirty years in the industry, I flew my last airline flight, from Cathay Pacific's birthplace to Hong Kong, fittingly in the trusty A330. I had been associated with this aircraft for twenty-three years. With the air over South China still absolutely clear, during the descent we could look northwards, far into China, to an actual horizon beyond the mountains and immense buildings that crowded Hong Kong Island and Kowloon. Now over glittering sea to the south of Hong Kong, we were vectored westward. I picked out the old runway at Kai Tak, still discernible where it jutted out from the dense urban area, now covered in containers, vehicles and building machinery. I made another of my standard comments, 'If that runway could talk …' as we idled past decelerating, the flap drive motors whining intermittently far behind us as we configured the Airbus for the landing. We shut down at the gate, my last passengers began filing off, and for the final time I called for the Parking Checklist. I bade the first officer farewell and good luck, walked alone to Immigration and emerged into the public Arrivals area. No manager met me on my last flight after twenty-eight years of service with Cathay Pacific. But Yvonne was waiting, and we walked out of the terminal hand in hand.

EPILOGUE

Mornington High School was closed down and most of the classrooms were demolished. I found this sad and unsettling after generally happy school-day memories. My old school had been consolidated into a new Secondary College on the other side of town, set in what used to be rolling green fields on the northern outskirts of Mornington. However, the original school hall and the library where I had successfully studied are still there, as part of a community centre.

On the other side of the busy highway opposite the new Mornington Secondary College, there is a suburban shopping complex. On visiting my parents during a leave from the military, I found John Thornton's restaurant, where I had once worked so hard as a teenager, burnt to the ground. What remained of its massive roof rested neatly on top of the charred wreckage. Dick Thornton had passed away before the fire. The site is now occupied by a huge warehouse store associated with a well-known hardware chain.

The Auster Mark III in which I soloed, VH-BYJ, was later wrecked on the ground by a storm, and its registration was assigned to another aircraft. However, at the time of writing this story, I was pleasantly surprised to see it in pieces at an airport not far from Benalla, to be restored to its former military colours and 'observation' configuration. The 'car windows' and ghastly blue and maroon interior will be replaced by glorious expanses of clear Perspex. Scraps of tattered fabric had yellow paint on them, still there after forty-three years.

No. 1 Flying Training School at Point Cook no longer exists. During the early 1990s, its 'screening' role was taken up by a civilian contractor based in New South Wales. Point Cook is now home to the RAAF Museum, but what remains of it is hemmed in by suburbia. Its associated base, RAAF Laverton, still has an administrative function, but Laverton's runways are long gone. Much of the historic base's area has been given over to housing. However, many CT-4s can be seen flying in civilian hands, some presented in the sickly yellow and green pattern of my time on the machine, others in the later white and orange scheme, reminiscent of the Macchis of 2 FTS.

At time of writing, 2 FTS at Pearce, WA, still conducts advanced flight training.

The navy's fixed wing aircraft, grounded by the Hawke government, met with various fates. Its Macchis, handed over to the air force, are now long gone, even from RAAF service, and although there are many civilian jet 'warbirds' flying in Australia, not one Macchi currently flies in the country. The air force replaced the sleek little jet trainer with the turboprop Pilatus PC-9 then a later version, the PC-21. These propeller-driven aircraft are slower, but quieter and cheaper. Even when they are demonstrated by the 'Roulettes' aerobatic team, they have nowhere near the *éclat* of the jets that they replaced.

The navy's Trackers were left to corrode in Nowra's salt air for decades until they were purchased and ferried to an aerodrome in Victoria, where again they sat idle for years until most were exported to North America for conversion to fire bombers. One or two can be seen in museums. The two HS 748s were sold, one of them eventually broken up. At time of writing, the other languishes outside a New

South Wales aviation museum that is due to be closed, and the aircraft has an uncertain future.

Ironically, HMAS *Melbourne*, Australia's last 'fixed-wing' aircraft carrier, was purchased by the Communist Chinese government in 1985. Bound for Shanghai, the hull was under tow by a Chinese tug when towline problems forced the vessels into Moreton Bay, near Brisbane. The old girl did not go willingly, running aground until they eventually got her off. On arrival in China, she was studied by their military, then broken up.

In 1993, a Russian MiG fighter crashed in the Australian Capital Territory. The classic single-engine Cold War jet had been imported and refurbished, and was being flown as a civilian 'warbird'. Both occupants died. The pilot was Errol Kavanagh, who had recruited me into the Royal Australian Navy. Ray, from my pilots' course and my colleague during my naval Macchi training, eventually joined Cathay Pacific Airways and worked his way up to Boeing 777 captain. He died prematurely, and never got to retire.

Australia's Orions were scrapped or placed in museums, replaced by Boeing P-8 maritime patrol aircraft: jets based on the 737. Comparatively fewer numbers of P-8s were acquired with the balance, significantly, made up by unmanned aerial vehicles.

Not long after the Pilots' Dispute, Australian Airlines was absorbed into Qantas, and is now long gone, as is Ansett Airlines. Bob Hawke died in May 2019.

Cathay Pacific Airways is no longer the company that I joined, full of promise, the premium airline for all of Asia, a pioneer of long-haul commercial flight. While still of a high standard of service and with the latest aircraft in its fleet, competition in the industry is ferocious, and with cost cutting in order to remain viable, it is now just another airline.

Penang's notorious Hong Kong Bar burnt down soon after John and I visited.

The checkerboard on the cliff where we aimed our aircraft before the descending right turn to land on Kai Tak's Runway 13 can still be discerned from various points in Kowloon, but it is unloved and much faded. Unless local people take an interest, the red and white squares will completely erode from the cliff face under the assaults of rainstorms, sun and vegetation. But they will not fade from the memories of Kai Tak pilots.

Hong Kong's airspace became very crowded. During my final years with Cathay Pacific, delays were longer and longer, particularly when we were waiting to depart south for Australia in the evening. Flight after flight from the Chinese mainland would pass overhead, also Australia bound, on our route and occupying our planned flight levels – there seemed to be a virtual 'air bridge' between China and Eastern Australia.

At the time of writing, I am clear of cancer. I fly Adventure Flights for the public again, with the privilege of being able to introduce sometimes-nervous passengers, if they wish, to 'military style' manoeuvres in blue, free Australian skies. I fly some steep turns, then introduce some g, ease around a gentle barrel roll, maybe do a loop, then make a jet-style 'initial and pitch' to land. There are few other countries in the world that allow the freedom to do this. I have flown World War II RAAF veterans on flights arranged by their families. One had just turned 100-years-old. Another was an ex-Beaufighter pilot, aged in his nineties. An ex-Liberator bomber pilot took the controls of the Moth Minor and, once again he was flying in an open cockpit, albeit that of a monoplane instead of a biplane Tiger Moth, over the field where he had trained as a raw student: Benalla. I had let them all fly, and their hands fell naturally to the control column as if they had never been away from it. The red, white and blue air force 'roundels' were proud and prominent on the wings of the aircraft. Long ago they had seen conflict. I had not, but in lesser respects I had experienced quite a ride myself.

I have been very fortunate to have had the opportunity to fly the wonderful aeroplanes described in this book. My early childhood was spent in a fibro house beneath an iron roof, with an outside toilet. I attended government schools. However, the Cold War and its proxies raged, and during those years a seventeen or eighteen-year-old boy could leave school to train as a military pilot. No university degree was required, just some academic ability, and, most importantly, commitment. Opportunity was there for those with ambition and a work ethic.

With that said, I wish to stress – particularly to younger readers – first, the importance of hard work and learning, especially when your brain is young and absorbent. Second, dedication to whatever you choose as a career. And third, the idea of 'going down fighting' when things are against you. A recurring theme of my life has been: 'It can be funny how things turn out.' A crisis may become an opportunity that could take your breath away.